FLEET STREET, PRESS BARONS
AND POLITICS

FLEET STREET, PRESS BARONS AND POLITICS
THE JOURNALS OF COLLIN BROOKS, 1932–1940

edited by

N. J. CROWSON

CAMDEN FIFTH SERIES
Volume 11

FOR THE ROYAL HISTORICAL SOCIETY
University College London, Gower Street, London WC1E 6BT
1998

Published by the Press Syndicate of the University of Cambridge
The Edinburgh Building, Cambridge CB2 2RU, United Kingdom
40 West 20th Street, New York, NY 10011–4211, USA
10 Stamford Road, Oakleigh, Melbourne 3166, Australia

© Royal Historical Society 1998

First published 1998

A catalogue record for this book is available from the British Library

ISBN 0 521 66239 7 hardback

SUBSCRIPTIONS. The serial publications of the Royal Historical Society, *Royal Historical Society Transactions* (ISSN 0080–4401), Camden Fifth Series (ISSN 0960–1163) volumes and volumes of the Guides and Handbooks (ISSN 0080–4398) may be purchased together on annual subscription. The 1998 subscription price (which includes postage but not VAT) is £50 (US$80 in the USA, Canada and Mexico) and includes Camden Fifth Series, volumes 11 and 12 (published in July and December) and Transactions Sixth Series, volume 8 (published in December). Japanese prices are available from Kinokuniya Company Ltd, P.O. Box 55, Chitose, Tokyo 156, Japan. EU subscribers (outside the UK) who are not registered for VAT should add VAT at their country's rate. VAT registered subscribers should provide their VAT registration number. Prices include delivery by air.

Subscription orders, which must be accompanied by payment, may be sent to a bookseller, subscription agent or direct to the publisher: Cambridge University Press, The Edinburgh Building, Shaftesbury Road, Cambridge CB2 2RU, UK; or in the USA, Canada and Mexico: Cambridge University Press, 40 West 20th Street, New York, NY 10011–4211, USA.

SINGLE VOLUMES AND BACK VOLUMES. A list of Royal Historical Society volumes available from Cambridge University Press may be obtained from the Humanities Marketing Department at the address above.

Printed and bound in the United Kingdom by Butler & Tanner Ltd, Frome and London

CONTENTS

ACKNOWLEDGEMENTS

A number of debts have been incurred in producing this volume. Tony Kushner bears the responsibility for alerting me first to the existence of the journals and for pestering mc constantly to seek them out. John Ramsden provided invaluable advice at the initial stages when I was seeking a publisher. During the editorial stage, David Eastwood, Literary Director of the Royal Historical Society, has patiently responded to my queries. Yet again, my wife Charlotte has had to live with the trials and tribulations of me producing a manuscript, although for this project she bears some responsibility since it was her frequent retreats to bed with a volume of the journals which suggested to me the possibility of doing an edited edition. In the course of the editorial process I have been helped by archivists at the BBC Written Archive, Caversham Park; P.M. Rossiter, the *Daily Mail* librarian; the Staff of Birmingham University Special Collections; and A.W. Potter, research assistant, Royal Academy of Arts.

However my greatest debt is owed to Vivian Brooks, her brother Edward and his wife, Sheila. Between them they have cheerfully responded to my many queries, provided hospitality (being particularly generous with peanut butter!) and have encouraged the completion of this project. It is to them that I dedicate this volume.

N.J. Crowson
Bournville, October 1998

ABBREVIATIONS

In the text

ADC   aide-de-camp
A.H.M.   Arthur Mann
A.P.   A.P. Herbert
C.B.   Collin Brooks
DM   *Daily Mail*
DT   *Daily Telegraph*
D.W.   David Woodford
F.E.   F.E. Smith, 1st Earl of Birkenhead
FN   *Financial News*
Gvt.   government
H-B   Leslie Hore-Belisha
HQ   headquarters
J.B.   Joseph Ball
K.   Robert Kindersley
K.W.   Kingsley Wood
Ll.G.   Lloyd George
M.   Oswald Mosley
N.L.A.   National League of Airmen
P.F.   Philip Farrer
PR   proportional representation
Q.   Lord Queenborough
R.   Viscount Rothermere
SD   *Sunday Dispatch*
TBW   *The Business Week*
YP   *Yorkshire Post*

In the notes

Adm.   Admiral
Agric.   Agriculture
Amb.   Ambassador
Assist. Assistant
b.   born
Bd.   Board
BofT.   Board of Trade
Brig.   Brigadier
Bt.   Baronet
BUF   British Union of Fascists
CCO   Conservative Central Office
CID   Committee of Imperial Defence
C-in-C   Commander-in-Chief

cand.	candidate
Chanc.	Chancellor
Chm.	chairman
Co.	company
Comm.	Commissioner
Con.	Conservative
Corp.	Corporation
cr.	created
CRD	Conservative Research Department
Ctte.	Committee
ctted	committed
d.	daughter
d. year	died in ....
Dep.	Deputy
Dir.	Director
diss.	dissolved
Div.	Division
E.	east
Ed.	Editor
edu.	educated
Fed.	Federation
FO	Foreign Office
FS	Financial Secretary
FST	Financial Secretary to the Treasury
For.	Foreign
Gen.	General
Gov.	Governor
Govt.	Government
HofC	House of Commons
HofL.	House of Lords
Ind.	Independent
kt.	knighted
Lab.	Labour
Ld.	Lord
Lib.	Liberal
m.	married
Min.	Ministry
MOI	Ministry of Information
MP	Member of Parliament
N.	north
Nat.	National(ist)
nk	not known
Perm.	Permanent
PM	Prime Minister

PPS   Parliamentary Private Secretary
Pres. President
prop. proprietor
PUS   Permanent Under Secretary
rep.   representative
rtd.   retired
S.   south
s.   son
Sec.   Secretary
suc.   succeeded as
W.   west
WO   War Office

INTRODUCTION

The Devil's Decade is an analogy often drawn to describe the 1930s.[1] A decade that opened in the grip of world economic recession and closed with the democratic nations of Europe fighting a desperate struggle to resist the hegemonic ambitions of the dictators provides the backdrop to observations of one William Collin Brooks, variously financial journalist, editor, novelist and confidante of the 1st Viscount Rothermere.[2] Toiling over his typewriter, typing with two fingers, Brooks (or C.B.) would record for posterity his observations of the journalistic, political, literary and financial sets in which he circulated during the 1930s.

The name Collin Brooks is not instantly recognisable to the student of the 1930s, but this lack of 'status' does not diminish the historical value of his journals. They remain a testimony to the times in which he lived, written by an keen observer and interested chronicler. The social scene into which C.B. was elevated has all but disappeared, but the journals offer a fascinating perspective written by a man who saw himself as an outsider, lucky enough to have shinned up the greasy pole, but uncertain as to whether he should be there and inclined on occasion to be awe-struck, despite witnessing the great at their most indulgent. The journals provide a snapshot of the tribulations of working as a journalist and editor on Fleet Street at a time when the press was dominated by a small coterie of press barons and proprietors, principally Lord Beaverbrook, Viscount Rothermere and the Berry Brothers. This edition of the journal opens with C.B. working at the *Financial News*, witnessing at first hand the guerrilla warfare between proprietor, Brendan Bracken, and editor, Oscar Hobson, as both men fought each other and the third force of economic recession. C.B.'s move to the *Sunday Dispatch*, his rise to the editorial chair, and his closeness to Rothermere means that the journals offer a unique insight into the operations and mentality of a press baron. It has been a criticism of recent biographical studies of Rothermere and his son Esmond that

[1] C.B. used the phrase himself to title a biographical volume of 'key' figures from the 1930s. *Devil's Decade: Portraits of the Nineteen-Thirties* (MacDonald, 1948).
[2] Any reader wishing to derive an overview of the period see A.J.P. Taylor, *English History, 1914–1945* (Penguin, 1965); Martin Pugh, *The Making of Modern British Politics* (Blackwells, 2nd edn. 1993); P. Addison, *The Road to 1945: British Politics and the Second World War* (Jonathan Cape, 1975); R.A.C. Parker, *Chamberlain and Appeasement* (Macmillan, 1993).

little light has been cast upon their *modus operandi*;[3] this charge cannot be sustained against these journals. Yet given the intimacy between editor and proprietor over a five-year period, C.B.'s presence appears for some reason to have been obliterated from the biographical testimonies.[4] The value of the journals can also be assessed in terms of the perspective they cast upon dissident Conservatism during the 1930s. This is all the more significant given that it is dissent from the right of the party over India, (air) rearmament and foreign policy as well as the continued flirtations with Mosley and fascism. Given the plethora of archival material relating to the centre-left 'anti-appeasement' scission of the party this is welcome redress.

1. The Diarist[5]

William Collin Brooks was born on 22 December 1893, the second child of William Edward Brooks (1864–1914) and Isabella née Thomas (1863–1915).[6] Immediately, three observations regarding C.B.'s name should be made. The unusual spelling of Collin with the double 'l' came from his mother's Welsh family. Normally it was a name given to girls born into the family. However his mother Isabella (herself second-named Collin) broke tradition and christened the young boy William Collin. In giving the first name as William, C.B.'s parents followed a Brook family tradition that went back through his father, grandfather, great-grandfather and possibly even further. The surname also needs explanation since it had mutated from Brook to Brooks between the registrations of the marriage of C.B's grand-father in 1862 and the birth of his father two years later. Family legend suggests that the registrar was most likely a drinking partner of C.B.'s grandfather who felt it unnecessary to ask for the name, but inscribed Brooks from the frequent northern habit of speaking of people in the possessive.[7] Originally the Brook family hailed from Blackburn and were involved in the cotton trade. His grandfather, William Brook (1838–1882) worked for the family firm acting as a wool purchaser and it was in the course of his travels in 1862 around the north of England and the Scottish

---

[3] Anthony Howard's review, *The Sunday Times*, 22 March 1998.

[4] S.J. Taylor, *The Great Outsiders: Northcliffe, Rothermere and The Daily Mail* (Phoenix, 1996); Richard Bourne, *Lords of Fleet Street: The Harmsworth Dynasty* (Unwin Hyman, 1990)

[5] Information on the family history is derived from conversations with Edward and Shelia Brooks and Vivian Brooks, an unpublished manuscript of an autobiography that C.B. was preparing in the years before his death (hereafter referred to as 'Draft' *Memoirs*) as well as the journals.

[6] Daughter of Griffith Thomas and Isabella Harrison.

[7] 'Draft' *Memoirs*, pp. 13–14.

borders that he met and married Janet McMinn, the daughter of James McMinn, a Lochmaben farmer. The marriage was turbulent, with one separation occurring at least. The scandal of separation obliged C.B.'s great-grandfather, William Brook (?1810–1872)[8] to expel his son from the family business, forcing William Brook (the second) to take a job as a travelling salesman and, once reconciled with Janet, to move his family to Liverpool. However, the toll of excessive drinking took his life prematurely, leaving Janet a widow with three sons (including C.B.'s father) and a daughter. William Edward Brooks (the third), with an education at the Liverpool Institute in the 1870s and after an apprenticeship in the cotton trade, became a travelling salesman for Lever Brothers. He was married on 26 May 1890 just north of Carlisle at Tue Brook and honeymooned in the Isle of Man. The first daughter, Hilda,[9] was born in 1891. C.B. followed two years later. Shortly after the birth his father suffered a temporary six-month loss of eyesight. This was followed by the first of a series of moves for the family, initially to Preston, then Lytham, followed by Ansdell and finally settling in Southport in May 1901. C.B.'s father immersed himself quickly in local Unionist politics, first as a member of a ward committee then as chairman. He inducted his children in the ways of the political meeting by taking them to witness local Southport MP, Edward Marshall-Hall, an ardent Chamberlainite, on the platform.[10] The 1906 general election provided the young C.B. with his first taste of political activism when he acted as a messenger on polling day.

Following a seven-year spell in formal education, and an even shorter period as a trainee accountant with James Platt and Sons, C.B. followed in the footsteps of his father and grandfather and became a commercial traveller for various companies, an occupation that preoccupied his late teens from fifteen years of age to twenty. Already the genesis of his future career was evolving when he spotted an opening in the journalism market and founded in 1913 the Manchester Press Agency, which benefited from a reciprocal deal with a photo agency in Fleet Street and included the *Manchester Guardian* amongst its clients. The onset of war in 1914 was, as with many of his generation, to have a profound effect upon the young Brooks. It was marked also by considerable personal upheaval. His father died on 14 June 1914 just weeks before the outbreak of hostilities, and his mother died on Christmas Eve 1915. Two weeks later, on 8 January 1916, Collin took Lilian Susanna Marsden (1891–1981), as his wife at a registry office in Ormskirk, and

---

[8] Married Elizabeth Edmundson (1811–72) in 1831.

[9] In 1917 Hilda (1891–1964) married the brother of C.B.'s wife, Cyril Marsden.

[10] C.B. draws a character sketch of Marshall-Hall in *More Tavern Talk* (James Barrie, 1952), pp. 70–1. Marshall-Hall was MP for Southport from 1900 to 1906, East Toxteth from January 1910 to 1916.

they followed this by reading their wedding vows to each other in a local church. Unfortunately this happy event was marred by the estrangement between Lilian and her father, Ernest Marsden (d. 1931) and step-mother. It obliged the bride to be 'given away' by her cousin, Halstaff Coles. Ultimately the union led to the conception of five children: Barbara (1918–1920); Rosemary (1920–1971); Vivian (1922–); Austen (1924–1986) and Edward (1928–). Within a month the newlyweds were separated, as Collin was posted on 9 February to his new regiment The Kings (Liverpool).

Brooks had sought to join originally the navy, but his poor eyesight had disqualified him. Therefore on 20 November 1915, aged 21 years and 11 months, he joined the army, registering at Seaforth. His army record notes that on admission to his regiment he weighed 154 lbs and measured 5 ft $9\frac{1}{2}$ inches.[11] Once again Brooks' eyesight determined his future posting. Initially trained to drive a 'Daimler' tank, his need to wear spectacles meant that when the new 'Ricardo' tank was introduced with its horizontal periscopes necessary for driving he found the task impossible.[12] Consequently he was transferred on 26 July 1916 to the Machine Gun Corps (Infantry) 23rd Division with whom he would serve the remainder of the war.[13]

Brooks had a good war, not least because he survived. He saw action in Italy, engaged with the 23rd Division on the Asiago Plateau, although he considered himself fortunate to have had only two experiences of severe fighting: the Austrian break-through at Asiago (June 1918) and the final victory as the Allied forces crossed the Piave (October 1918).[14] In later years, Brooks was very reticent about his military experiences and when drafting his memoirs made no mention of having won the Military Cross. The citation records that the medal was awarded:

> For conspicuous gallantry and devotion to duty during the attack across the Piave on the 27 October 1918. This officer led his four guns forward under heavy shell and machine gun fire with the forward waves of the infantry. On arrival at the objective, by his

[11] Public Record Office (PRO), William Collin Brooks, war record, WO339/88414.

[12] 'Draft' Memoirs, p. 111; having consulted the definitive studies on World War One tanks and armoured cars: D. Fletcher, War Cars: British Armoured Cars in the First World War (HMSO, 1987), and D. Fletcher, Landships: British Tanks in the First World War (HMSO, 1984) it would appear most likely that in naming his tanks C.B. is referring to the type of engine powering the vehicle. Landships, pp. 48–9 lists the Daimler 6–cyclinder engine as powering the Marks I–IV heavy tanks, and the Ricardo 6–cylinder engines as powering the Mark V onwards.

[13] PRO, William Collin Brooks, war record, WO339/88414.

[14] 'Draft' Memoirs, pp. 105–19. For further details of the 23rd Battalion's Italian campaign see H.R. Sandiman, The 23rd Division 1914–1919 (Edinburgh, 1925); J. Wilks & E. Wilks, The British Army in Italy 1917–1918 (Barnsley: Leo Cooper, 1988).

skilful handling of his guns, he formed a defensive flank and in spite of heavy casualties he maintained his position.

The coolness and energy of this Officer was throughout the action a fine example to the men under him.[15]

The down-playing of his 'recognition' may have stemmed from a sense that it was a collective award for him and his men, and from a degree of 'guilt' at having survived when others had not. In later years Brooks took care to attend regimental reunions, to make donations to appeals for support from ex-comrades in distress, and had a considerable affection for the Machine Gunners' memorial 'David and Goliath', sculpted by Jagger, and situated at Hyde Park Corner. To his mind it was a statue that 'celebrates the warrior virtues of the dead, and not the grief merely of those who survived'.[16] Although upon demobilisation in March 1919 he had no employment and needed to support his wife and new daughter he observed retrospectively that 'it did not seem to matter very much. I was young. Save for a touch of shell-gas and a spent bullet in the ribs, the war had improved rather than impaired my health. I could write and I could speak without nerves.'[17] For the development of Brooks' personality it was this last observation that is most significant. His war service had heightened his political and intellectual awareness. Whilst at one training camp in England he had met and formed a friendship with fellow officer William Warman. This meeting of minds evolved and led to collaboration in producing a slim volume entitled *Soldier Colonists: A Plea for Group Organisation* (1918) in which the need to foster the Empire and provide the opportunity of migration for the military veteran was advocated. Brooks helped Warman with the two opening chapters, and a foreword by Lord Selborne ensured that the War Office purchased several hundred copies for circulation. At Christmas 1918 Brooks found his leave extended as he helped Warman draft clauses for an Empire Migration Bill which Prime Minister Lloyd-George was intent upon introducing. Ultimately this bill never saw parliamentary time because the first of the demobilisation mutinies obliged the hasty release of the conscripts in service. C.B. had now served his apprenticeship and saw before him a world filled with opportunity.

[15] Citation Telegram, Major H.C. Owen, A & O Branch of Staff, 23rd Division to 2nd Lieut. William Collin Brooks, 29 November 1918.
[16] Journal: C.B. to Norman Watson 10 June 1934; G.L. Jackson to and from C.B. 4 January–8 January 1933; diary 25 April 1946.
[17] 'Draft' *Memoirs*, p. 126.

2. The Journalist

Following demobilisation in 1919 C.B. held a variety of short-term posts in the world of newspapers, separated by a period as a professional area organiser for the League of Nations Union in Liverpool. His break came when he was engaged to write occasional pieces for the *Liverpool Courier* and then to act as a music critic for the rival *Liverpool Post*. In 1921 he resigned from his League of Nations Union job and secured a position as assistant editor, leader-writer and literary editor for the *Liverpool Courier* under the direction of George Peacock. His journalistic vocation was confirmed when he joined the staff of the *Yorkshire Post* in October 1923 under the editorship of Arthur Mann, obliging relocation to Leeds. It was a formative period in C.B.'s career: apart from the obvious invaluable experience, it introduced him to a number of individuals, journalistic and political, who would continue to feature in his exploits over the coming decades. For one young man the impact of meeting C.B. for the first time remained etched upon his memory:

> He burst into the room in which I was sitting and at once proffered his hand, a cigarette, a box of matches and a torrent of sound advice to a very young man on the threshold of a new career. While he talked he scanned one paper after another, and when there was a pause on the monologue, he tapped away at a typewriter. He was penning a leader; page after page of lucid English, and, as I struggled desperately to pen one word after another to give the right shape to a leading article, I marvelled at the industry and versatility of Collin Brooks.[18]

Relations between C.B. and his editor were not always cordial, and this encouraged the former to seek a London posting. Despite efforts to join *The Times*, Brooks actually found himself moving to the capital in January 1928 to bolster the *Yorkshire Post*'s London office. With the move C.B. became an accredited member of the Lobby, an experience that tarnished his vision of Parliamentary democracy. In September 1928 he found himself recruited to the *Financial News*, a city paper recently corralled into the stable of Brendan Bracken. The move was facilitated not by C.B.'s economic pedigree, but because of the technical skills of print production and paper management he had acquired. The experience on the *Financial News* 'made' C.B. a city journalist, but also provided stark experience in the economies necessary to run a paper. The 1929 Wall Street crash and the resulting economic depression

[18] Sybil and Glorney Bolton, *Two Lives Converge: The Dual Biography* (London: Blackie & Son, 1938), pp. 122–3.

impacted upon Fleet Street. The *Financial News* was hit heavily by lost advertising revenue which obliged the introduction of economies, including its staff taking a $17\frac{1}{2}$% salary cut in 1931.[19] The insecurity of this period took its toll. C.B.'s response was to improve his financial independence by increasing his individual writing output, but the journals clearly illustrate the concerns about financial survival and the demands of the Inland Revenue. He sought also to find more secure employment: negotiations were begun with *The Daily Telegraph* late in 1931 about the possibility of becoming City Editor, but nothing came of the discussion.[20] Ultimately Brooks' involvement with the *Financial News* ended with his sacking in 1933 yet, despite his reservations, he found himself taking another staff job, this time with the *Sunday Dispatch*. At the time little did C.B. suspect the impact this move would have upon his life.

At his new post, with its salary of £1000 per annum, C.B. quickly slipped into the routine of preparing a Sunday paper: into the office at Northcliffe House for 11.00 to catch up on correspondence before calling into the City Office. He would remain at work until 6.30 making it home for 8.30 and the opportunity to write up his journal and fulfil his private writing commitments.[21] All changed when he met Lord Rothermere in person and found himself being ushered into the inner coterie of the press baron. Within a matter of weeks C.B. was given a £500 pay rise as the two men window-shopped near the National Gallery.[22] His elevation to the editorship of the *Sunday Dispatch* was accepted with the recognition that it represented a potential poisoned chalice, but was a post taken out of personal loyalty to Rothermere. He held the position from 25 September 1935 until November 1937. C.B. admitted to an initial fear that the means of his promotion would hit staff morale and he was concerned that he may have to threaten individual staff to revive the paper's fortunes. However, the initial qualms were soothed after he sacked the fashion editoress who had been 'guilty of a sudden silly, feminine impertinence, which I could not

---

[19] See David Kynaston, *The Financial Times: A Centenary History* (London: Viking, 1988), pp. 102–29, for more on the troubles of this period and the main personalities on the paper. In addition, Paul Einzig, *At the Centre of Things* (Hutchinson, 1960), pp. 63–9, 98–110; C.E. Lysaght, *Brendan Bracken* (Allen Lane, 1979), pp. 98–102, 119–28; A. Boyle, *Poor, Dear Brendan: The Quest for Brendan Bracken* (Hutchinson, 1974), pp. 175–6. In neither of these last three volumes does C.B. feature.

[20] He was approached initially via R.J. Barret, a member of the Camrose board. The discussions continued with Lord Burnham before finally he met with Camrose. Ultimately the post was given to Leonard Reid, although he died shortly after. Reid actually made an approach to C.B. in 1933 to see if he was willing to become his assistant: Journal: 31 January, 17 February, 5 April 1932, 22 April 1933.

[21] Journal: C.B. to Norman Watson, 11 February 1934.

[22] Journal: 3 February 1935.

tolerate'. To his relief when she attended then a 'party' hosted by one of the young Irish reporters on the paper he found she bore no ill-will.[23] C.B. was battling constantly to halt the paper's declining circulation, but ultimately failed.[24] His editorship did witness some innovations, such as the introduction of a column, 'Your editor speaks'. However, for substantial periods of his editorship he was abroad accompanying Lord Rothermere, leaving the paper in the hands of his deputy Leslie Wilson. The additional problem that C.B. experienced as editor was Rothermere's tendency to favour the management over the journalists. Consequently a culture where the management sought to interfere in the editorial and journalistic process made matters difficult and frustrating for an individual editor who wished to make his mark. Overall, C.B.'s verdict was that the editorship was 'sometimes tedious, sometimes stimulating, always exciting to some degree and always absorbing.'[25]

After his period as editor, Brooks found the terms and conditions of his employment with the *Daily Mail* group revised with a reduction in salary and a nominal role as special features writer. By this time Rothermere had retired from active newspaper work and the Board of the Group felt no personal loyalty to C.B. His formal ties with the group were severed in 1938.

Brooks' journalistic skills had not gone unnoticed in other quarters of the political world. The eccentric right-wing owner of the *Saturday Review*, Lucy Houston, recruited C.B.'s services to write under the pen-name Historicus. In 1940 Lord Queenborough sought to utilise C.B. for the quarterly journal of 'The Royal Society of St. George'. His first article was 'Honour and the Home Front' which Queenborough then made C.B. follow up with a 'spoof' reply under the pen-name Ajax. From the summer of 1939 onwards, Queenborough, Brooks and a number of other right-wingers were involved in discussions about creating a new right-wing daily paper.[26] It was hoped that Rothermere might be persuaded to inject finance into the project, but his declining health and ultimate death ended the scheme. However, C.B. found himself presented with a new journalistic opportunity. In the autumn of 1940 he was offered the editorship of the weekly journal *Truth*. The journal had a certain notoriety for its robust defence of Chamberlain and attacks on Eden, Churchill and Hore-Belisha.[27] Although this

---

[23] Journal: 30 January 1936.

[24] In 1930 the *Sunday Dispatch* had a circulation of 1,197,000; by 1937 this had declined to 741,000. D. Butler and J. Freeman, *British Political Facts* (Macmillan, 1968), p. 285.

[25] Journal: 30 January 1936.

[26] Journal: 15 June 1939.

[27] For example, *Truth*, 27 July, 3 August, 28 September 1938, 27 October 1939, 12 January, 8 March 1940. For a historical perspective on *Truth* from 1936 to 1940, see R. Cockett, *Twilight of Truth: Chamberlain, Appeasement and the Manipulation of the Press* (London: Weidenfeld & Nicolson, 1989).

edition ends with Brooks taking over the editorship and chairmanship of *Truth*, the journals continue to reveal how C.B. struggled to maintain publishing schedules against the vagaries of chronic staff shortages, newsprint deficiencies, bombs and the general impact of war. His tenure at *Truth*, which ended only with his decision to sell his controlling interest to Staples Press in March 1952, was not without controversy. On his office desk C.B. kept two in-trays: one for letters; the other for libels. Late in 1941 C.B. found himself being named in Parliament by the Labour MP, Josiah Wedgewood. Wedgewood, assisted by Aneurin Bevan, used an adjournment debate to accuse C.B. and *Truth* of being quisling, fascist, and anti-semitic. These allegations (staunchly refuted by C.B.'s parliamentary friends) and the actual ownership of *Truth* (the paper had been effectively owned by the Conservative party since 1936 without anyone knowing) caused some embarrassment for the Conservative party, but were brushed aside by the Home Office.[28] However, *Truth*'s continued robust criticisms of the 18B regulation, the Americans and the Soviets, caused a certain degree of discomfort in government circles. Ironically the allegations against Brooks were made at a time when he had reconciled himself to mainstream Conservatism. From mid-1941 C.B. had begun associating with Sir Alec Erskine-Hill, chairman of the 1922 committee, and his new Tory group, and was helping to draft their speeches.[29] About this time Brooks also began writing for *The Statist*, a financial journal. His former boss at the National Savings Committee, Robert Kindersley, was instrumental in this arrangement. In time C.B. became chairman of *The Statist* and remained involved until his death.

3. The Writer

During his lifetime C.B. was a prolific writer.[30] His first publication was a collection of poems brought out on the eve of war in 1914 when he was aged only 21,[31] his last volume would have been an autobiography had not the debilitating illness of Parkinson's Disease rendered completion of the script impossible. As a writer he appeared prepared to cast his pen to almost any subject, whether it was economic non-fiction

---

[28] *Hansard*, 9 October 1941, vol. 374, col. 1108, when Wedgewood first raised the matter at ministerial question time; and the adjournment debate 15 October 1941, vol. 374, cols. 1454–64; Journal: 9–11 October, 17 October 1941; *Daily Express*, 17 October 1941; *Truth*, 17 October 1941.

[29] Journal: 15 October, 11 December, 19 December 1941, 11 January, 1 April 1942; J.A. Ramsden, *The Age of Churchill and Eden* (London: Longman, 1995), p. 30.

[30] See appendix E for C.B.'s bibliography.

[31] Published by David Nutt and Company with a print run of 500.

texts as William Collin Brooks, sensational thrillers ('shockers' to C.B.) as Collin Brooks or his serious novels under the pen-name Barnaby Brook. Despite a limited formal education, C.B. as a young man had developed a veracious appetite for reading, ranging across the complete spectrum from poetry to biography to philosophy to novels.[32] It was this interest in literature that enhanced his journalistic career when he became literary editor of the *Liverpool Courier*, a position he retained until October 1923.[33] During the 1930s, had C.B. felt able to sustain his family purely from writing he would have chosen to. However, whilst he enjoyed success with *Three Yards of Cord* (1931) which went to a second edition and his book on finance, *The Theory and Practice of Finance* (1st edn. 1928), went to a third imprint others did less well; *Something in the City* (1931) failed to move its first thousand print run. In later years C.B. felt 'proudest' of his edited volume of the 1931 Kyslant fraud trial *The Royal Mail Case* (1932). Apart from his interest in the case as a City journalist C.B. was an 'enthusiast' for legal trials, becoming a member of Our Society dining club which convened to re-live and discuss major trials with key figures from the case in question. C.B. obviously viewed 1932 as a good vintage, since he also rated *Mad-Doctor Merciful* (1932) as his best thriller. Something of C.B.'s attitude to his writing can be deduced from the prefaces to his books. The dedication in *Frame-up* (1935) warns his readers that 'this incredible story' involving murder, mystery and sudden death in the environs of Westminster and country retreats 'is dedicated to all those jolly people who read shockers for fun and not as a mental discipline'. Inspiration for his writing was derived from his own experiences, and quite often characters were based upon known acquaintances. With *They Ride Again* (1934), a re-working of the classic Dick Turpin, 'the heroes are heroes, the villains villains, the buffoons buffoons – and there's an end on it. It contains no taint of our own complicated times.' The novel had evolved during the course of a family holiday when C.B. had amused his children with nightly tales of the exploits of the highwayman. Brooks' writing productivity during the late 1920s and early 1930s owed much to his work regime and methodology. Until his departure from the daily paper *The Financial News* his day would be characterised by devoting the afternoons to his own literary output, before spending the evening at the Press, usually finishing duty at 2.30am. He deliberately operated with three manuscripts in simultaneous preparation. This enabled him to maintain his interest, and select a draft according to his desire and mood each day.

---

[32] To gain an impression of the breadth of C.B.'s reading, see *Tavern Talk*, pp. 52–81, and *More Tavern Talk*, pp. 24–49.

[33] Paid a salary of £500 he retained the position for 18 months.

Undoubtedly C.B.'s writing commitments in the early 1930s provided valuable extra income. He anticipated in 1932 that his writings would gross him £300 for that year, whilst his occasional reviews would generate a further £75. Similarly his commitment to the 'American Letter'[34] would bring a further remuneration of £200. Whilst working for *The Sunday Dispatch* C.B.'s book-writing suffered. Only when Rothermere decided to finance a series of 'right-wing' books, employing Lovat Dickson on a royalty to handle them and take whatever profit or loss there may be, did C.B. return to print again, first with *Can 1931 Come Again?* (1938) and then with a much re-drafted *Can Chamberlain Save Britain?* (1938). Rothermere sought also to utilise C.B.'s literary skills, getting him to 'ghost' his apologias *My Fight to Rearm Britain* (1939) and *Warnings and Predictions* (1939) and to help Ward Price with *My Campaign for Hungary* (1939).

4. The Broadcaster

Two features of C.B.'s career made him something of a 'personality'. First his tenure as editor of *The Sunday Dispatch* gained him a degree of public recognition because his face appeared on poster hoardings as part of a publicity sales drive for the paper. The second was C.B.'s involvement with radio broadcasting. He had first broadcast in 1925 for a ten-minute unscripted and unrehearsed talk on 'The Editorial'.[35] His next opportunity arose in late 1936 when he was recruited to give a twenty-minute book talk. Although the death of King George necessitated the broadcast's cancellation it was eventually given on 7 January 1937 from 6.20pm. In all C.B. secured a fee of 16 guineas. The broadcast even resulted in a small postbag of 'fan' mail.[36] His broadcasting services were called upon again in 1938 when C.B. gave a series of empire talks to Canada, and thereafter he became an occasional but regular fixture on the wireless. During the opening years of the war he would broadcast either under his own name or that of 'North-countryman'. The decision to use that particular pseudonym is less clear. Admittedly C.B. was a Lancashire man, but also historians of

[34] The American Letter or Survey was a weekly (occasionally bi-weekly) report that C.B. prepared in his capacity as London correspondent for *The Business Week* initially, and then the American *Journal of Commerce*, 1928–38. Initially it confined itself purely to economic and financial matters, but from mid-1932 C.B. also began including a 'survey' introduction which provided a discursive over-view of the British scene (in domestic and international affairs). C.B.'s carbons of these articles survive and are retained with the journals.

[35] *Tavern Talk* p. 120.

[36] BBC Written Archive, Caversham Park: Collin Brooks File 1A 1936–42.

the media have noted that the BBC was anxious during these years to promote 'northern' values.[37] Broadcasts during this time had to conform to the latest dictates from the Ministry of Information, something that evidently frustrated C.B.'s producers. Nevertheless his broadcasts during 1940, including his 'Once a Week' series and 'Taking Stock' round-table discussions, were expected to emphasise the toughness of Britons (as opposed to Englishmen), accentuate the benefits and strengths of the Empire and avoid the issue of post-war reconstruction.[38] His broadcasting career continued to blossom in the post-war era as he became a regular participant in 'Any Questions?' and the 'Brains Trust'.

5. Brooks and Friends

It is evident that C.B. enjoyed a wide and varied circle of friends and acquaintances. The journals reveal Brooks' rapid movements around Fleet Street: whom he met, anecdotes he wished to collect, gossip. But Brooks did not restrict himself to purely journalistic and political companionship; he could count amongst his friends and acquaintances many theatrical and literary figures. At a memorial service to com-memorate his life in 1959 the reading was performed by Sir Beverley Baxter MP and the address read by T.S. Eliot.[39] One of the earliest family photographs of C.B., dating from 1902, shows a young boy dressed in a 'Hornblower' naval uniform ready for his 'turn' in a local amateur dramatic performance. He had been raised on a diet of Gilbert and Sullivan having been taken frequently to the theatres of Blackpool by his father. This love of theatre remained into adult life and the journal was regularly apprised of the latest play seen or the tales of thespian woes from his acting friends.

One of the principle reasons C.B. drew upon such a variety of friends was his membership of numerous gentlemen's clubs and dining societies. Throughout his working life these played a significant part in his everyday activities, and 'if anybody is a West-End clubman, I am he' declared C.B. in *Tavern Talk* (1950).[40] They provided an opportunity for him to indulge himself in debate (intellectual and trivial), collect gossip

[37] Siân Nicholas, 'From John Bull to John Citizen: Images of National Identity and Citizenship on the Wartime BBC', in R. Weight and A. Beach (eds), *The Right to Belong: Citizenship and National Identity in Britain 1930–1960* (London, IB Tauris, 1998), pp. 36–58.

[38] BBC Written Archive: G.R. Barnes to C.B. 29 July 1940, C.B. to Barnes 8 August 1940, Barnes to C.B. 9 August 1940, 12 August 1940, Collin Brooks File IA 1936–42.

[39] *The Statist* obituary and tributes, 11 April 1959, vol. CLXIX; programme for memorial service, St Bride's Church, Fleet Street, 1 May 1959.

[40] C. Brooks, *Tavern Talk* (Barrie, 1950), p. 12.

and consume both good food and fine drink. In the earliest Liverpool days, the Press Club was his chosen venue. Here in this male bastion friendships were formed that lasted over many subsequent decades. The move to London provided fresh opportunities. He was elected in 1928 to the Compatriots Club, having been proposed by Haden-Guest, although he only began attending with any frequency after 1934.[41] This date carries significance since it was shortly after the move from a daily to a Sunday paper working regime with the associated evening freedom. It was in May 1934 that he was elected to the Savage. This club was held in particular esteem by C.B., something he illustrated by the elevation of the Savage tie to the status of 'favourite'. The increased financial security that came with working for the Rothermere press afforded C.B. the opportunity to join other London clubs, including the Reform, Carlton and Royal Thames Yacht Club. Imagine Brooks' distress when at the height of the Blitz a series of bomb blasts rendered Clubland inaccessible and obliged the Reform and Savage, among others, to seek temporary accommodation elsewhere for the duration of the war.[42] Club membership also carried an additional attraction. C.B. never learnt to drive, relying upon taxis: these were always easier to hail late at night from a club. C.B.'s thirst for intellectual stimulation and companionship encouraged his involvement with a number of dining clubs. This was especially the case with the Whitefriars, where to be eligible the diners would have a connection with journalism, writing, publishing or the law. C.B. also founded his own dining club in 1932 with Clarence Sadd, Brian Manning and R.V. Rodwell. Calling themselves the Fore Club they would convene with their guests on a monthly basis at the Reform. The club's title was designed to convey a warning to guests to look out for themselves, since 'the club's intention was that table talk should be uninhibited and provocative.'[43] With the death of Rodwell the vacant chair was offered to John Senter.[44] As were his father and grandfather, Brooks was also a Freemason. C.B. derived a sense of fulfilment at having risen high enough upon the social ladder to be admitted to a Lodge.[45]

---

[41] J. Barnes and N. Nicholson (eds), *Empire at Bay: The Leo Amery Diaires, 1929–1945* (Hutchinson, 1988), p. 415; 30 April 1936, Amery's entry for his date regarding the Compatriots, refers to Collin's presence and this is one of the very few occasions his name appears in another archival collection or published diary.

[42] Journal: 15 October 1940.

[43] In its earliest days the Fore Club met at Kettner's. 'Draft' *Memoirs*, pp. 305–6.

[44] Journal: 18 December 1941.

[45] Journal: 21 January 1932.

6. Politics

Politically Brooks' stable was on the right of the Conservative Party. From his earliest years he had been raised on a diet of politics. In January 1910 he abandoned a fledgling career in accountancy when he secured a position as a committee room clerk for the forthcoming general election, earning the princely salary of £3 per week for the three-week duration of the post. A few years later he helped to establish a Junior Unionist Association branch in Southport and supplemented its street-corner and village-green meetings with the Southport Parliamentary Debating Society in the winter months.[46] During these formative years his political heroes were F.E. Smith and Arthur Balfour. His family background and own 'life' experiences taught him to distrust bureaucracy, the moves towards egalitarianism, and the domination of the Jews he encountered in the world of finance. C.B. aspired to an idealised vision of leadership, hierarchical and aristocratic and based upon deferential values.[47] However during the 1930s Brooks' political vision was faltering. This was due to a number of correlated factors. The creation in 1931 of a coalition National Government, headed first by the former Labour leader Ramsay MacDonald, and then Conservatives Stanley Baldwin and Neville Chamberlain, blunted (to Brooks' mind) the ability of the Conservative party to fulfil its natural ideological desires. The disillusionment with official Conservatism was boosted by his association from 1935 with Rothermere, which facilitated Brooks' fraternisation with other disaffected right-wingers. The Fascism of Oswald Mosley held appeal briefly, but the fiasco of the Olympia meeting in 1934 and the growing menace of continental European Fascism highlighted its dangers and shortcomings.[48] At the same time the rise of European Fascism contributed to Brooks' political speculation. The National Governments, despite their huge Conservative majorities, appeared unable to deal with the problems in economy, defence and foreign policy; problems that personally involved Brooks as an economist, chairman of the National League of Airmen, and as a confidante of Rothermere. Furthermore these were problems which the Fascist dictatorships appeared to overcome so readily. It raised questions concerning the effectiveness of British institutions and asked questions about their sustainability.

[46] 'Draft' *Memoirs*, pp. 64, 69, 84–6.
[47] Paul Addison, 'Patriotism under Pressure: Lord Rothermere and British Foreign Policy', in G. Peele and C. Cook (eds.), *The Politics of Reappraisal 1918–1939* (Macmillan, 1975), p. 199; regarding C.B.'s anti-Semitism, his views were not uncommon for the period: see N.J. Crowson 'The British Conservative Party and the Jews during the Late 1930s', *Patterns of Prejudice*, vol. 29, nos. 2–3 (1995), pp. 15–32.
[48] Journal: C.B. to Norman Watson 10 June 1934.

7. C.B. and R.[49]

Brooks' friendship with Rothermere transformed his political activities from peripheral bystander to active intriguer – a role he clearly revelled in. As a consequence the political names who flow across the pages of the later 1930s read like a volume of *Dod's Parliamentary Companion*. The disillusionment, shared by both men, with official Conservatism (and later with the Edenite anti-appeasement faction of the party) meant that they assisted the candidature of Randolph Churchill in the February 1935 Wavertree by-election and on other occasions sought to promote 'suitable' candidates in by-elections. Brooks was even persuaded (for a short period) to allow his name to stand as an Independent Conservative candidate in the Norwood by-election of 1935.[50] The behaviour of the press baron and his editor was enough to concern David Margesson, the chief whip, who summoned C.B. to meet with him to see if their differences could be resolved.[51]

C.B.'s growing friendship with Rothermere was one of mixed blessings. It brought increased financial security. At the end of 1936 he was given a further pay rise, bringing his salary to £2000 with a £800 expenses account.[52] This enabled Brooks to adopt a life style of high living, to join the right gentlemen's clubs, and even to commission a portrait of his daughters from Dick Nevinson, the acclaimed war artist.[53] From 1937 Rothermere loaned the family a cottage, The Mount, near his Stody estate.[54] At the time the cottage had no electricity, but the children, especially Edward, enjoyed the Norfolk countryside.[55] C.B. also had the opportunity to travel the world extensively: Europe, North

[49] Rothermere was frequently abbreviated to R. in both general conversation and the text of the journals.

[50] Journal: 12 February 1935.

[51] Journal: 6 March 1935.

[52] Journal: 31 December 1936. In addition, C.B.'s writing commitments to the *Joseph's Review* created £8 per month; *Business Week* £12 per month; and *Saturday Review* £25 per week. And since the death of Lil's father in March 1931, she could rely upon a private income of £800 per annum.

[53] Journal: 5 August, 19 October 1936.

[54] Rothermere had suggested in 1935 that C.B. find a cottage in Norfolk because 'I can't bear the thought of your children being bombed in London.' He first proposed the idea of The Mount in March 1937, but nothing was accepted until 9 September whilst both men were in Quebec. The Mount was actually quite a large house. It had two live-in servants, one daily maid and a gardener, as well as a chapel (excellent for ping-pong!) attached.

[55] With Rothermere's death The Mount proved a point of conflict between C.B. and Esmond Rothermere. Before R had left England he apparently signed the cottage over to C.B., and when his will was published the Mount was left to C.B.: *Daily Mail,* 28 April 1941. However, Esmond sought Brooks' eviction from the property. Privately C.B. admitted that aside from 'sentimental attachment, its going will be a blessing, for my diminished income cannot go on paying for its upkeep'. Journal: 22 June 1941.

America and Africa. During one such trip to Canada in 1937 he was
taken seriously ill, which necessitated five operations, but he emerged
from the Toronto hospital 'eased for ever of that twisted gut which had
been my perpetual pain-giver since the end of the war. After eighteen
years of perpetual discomfort I find myself at ease again.'[56] When both
men were in London a routine emerged whereby C.B. would join
Rothermere first thing for breakfast and exercise. As Brooks increasingly
became a confidante and sounding-board for Rothermere a private
telephone line was installed at C.B.'s home to enable the press baron
easy and frequent access to his new lieutenant. Perhaps unsurprisingly
this placed strains upon C.B.'s family life. The embrace of the Harmsworths was all enveloping. Rothermere persuaded Brooks to move to
Regent's Park, to his wife's considerable annoyance. The rationale
behind the relocation was the close proximity of C.B. to his master,
making the early morning visitations all the easier. Despite the gen-
erational and social gaps considerable affection grew between both
men. Gifts were frequently exchanged: for example, Rothermere gave
C.B. a gold cigarette case with a sapphire clasp embossed with the
motto 'Collin Brooks: a mark of esteem and affection from Viscount
Rothermere.'[57] The social difference meant of course that they could
never be equals, but the impression arises that Rothermere looked
upon Brooks as a surrogate son in his last years. Given that relations
between Rothermere and his own son, Esmond, were often fraught
gives added plausibility.[58] Furthermore, the family legend suggests that
Esmond's eviction of the Brooks' from The Mount after he inherited
the Stody estate was motivated by jealousy of C.B.'s relationship with
his father.[59] For his part C.B. became increasingly concerned that he
was being too closely associated with Rothermere. He recognised that
Rothermere did not wield the same influence on the board of *The Daily
Mail* from 1938 despite acting to the contrary; and he failed repeatedly
to provide C.B. with the directorships that he craved for financial
security and which Rothermere so often referred to.[60] Nevertheless a
sense of loyalty made C.B. stick with Rothermere virtually to the very
end.

One cause which Rothermere espoused during the mid-1930s was

[56] Journal: 20 December 1937.
[57] Journal: 18 December 1936.
[58] S. Taylor, *The Great Outsiders*, p. 313.
[59] It perhaps should be pointed out that when Rothermere died he left his finances in
a considerable mess, and as executor it took Esmond several years to resolve matters
(clearly C.B. had a lucky escape in 1939 when Rothermere changed his mind about
appointing C.B. as his executor). Esmond is supposed to have claimed that he was
obliged to find £36m to cover the losses on his father's estate. Bourne, *Lords of Fleet Street*,
p. 155.
[60] Journal: 20 June 1939.

rearmament, and especially air defence. Articles published in the *Daily Mail* did much to propagate the populist myth that at the outset of any war with Germany, Britain would be subjected to an immediate and deadly aerial knock-out blow.[61] C.B. was quickly drawn into this cause in 1935, when Rothermere asked him to help found an air propaganda organisation, the National League of Airmen (N.L.A.). After seeking financial support from Lucy Houston, C.B. and Rothermere inaugurated the N.L.A with a lunch at the Savoy, at which Mosley was amongst the guests. It is evident from the journals that the idea that Rothermere had severed all links with Mosley after the 1934 Olympia meeting is not the whole picture. The N.L.A. kept C.B. busy recruiting and addressing meetings but also trying to provide the League with an organisation and sound financial base.[62] Rothermere entrusted Brooks with more than with just creating the N.L.A.. His advice was sought on matters regarding finance and investment. In 1937 C.B. was dispatched to Canada to defend Rothermere's interests in the reorganisation of the Abitibi Power and Paper Company which had gone into receivership. Furthermore, C.B. was entrusted with the delicate task of securing a peerage for Rothermere's brother, Cecil; a task which earned Brooks a £1000 bonus. What is evident from the journals is that in the five years he knew Rothermere, C.B. became intimate with the press baron's closest affairs.

With the outbreak of war in September 1939 Brooks was eager to assist the war effort. Ultimately it was his journalistic skills that were utilised when he was recruited to the National Savings Committee as honorary press secretary, with Rothermere paying his salary. Nevertheless C.B. was clearly frustrated by the bureaucracy associated with the Committee, and when it appeared that Rothermere was offering him some tangible war work by assisting in a rearmament mission to the USA in May 1940 he seized the opportunity. Unfortunately, the 'mission' was not as 'official' as C.B. had hoped; a view frustratingly communicated once the ship had departed from Liverpool. As London became subjected to the German blitz Brooks looked for an opportunity to return to Britain and his family. When he broke the news to Rothermere the ageing press baron sought (unsuccessfully) to persuade C.B. to accompany him to the Bahamas. It was the last time he would see his 'beloved' R.

---

[61] See S. Taylor, *The Great Outsiders*, pp. 302–10; Addison, 'Patriotism under Pressure', pp. 195–7, 207.
[62] *Sunday Dispatch*, 17 February 1935; *Daily Mail*, 19 February 1935.

8. The Journals

The journals represent a substantial document, running, as they do, from 1925 through to 1956. They fall into two categories. The main document is Brooks' personal diary, but also from mid-1935 to 1937 (at the behest of Rothermere) Brooks began keeping a journal that highlighted the deteriorating international situation and the reaction of British public opinion.[63] Known as the Rothermere-Brooks diary (or Rother-Brooks diary) the authors claimed it was 'written with no thought of publication in the ordinary sense of the word, but in the belief that it may, at some time, be a valuable historical document'.[64] From Rothermere's perspective it was clearly designed as a useful aide-memoir that would serve notice in later years to the foresight of a press magnate in predicting Armageddon and would leave any future biographer in little doubt as to his patriotic concerns about rearmament and air defence.[65] The entries, normally daily of a few hundred words, become less frequent during 1937, in part due to Brooks' illness and world travels but also with Rothermere's declining interest in the issue of rearmament, and contain only a few sporadic notes for 1938. Included amongst the journal entries are a number of memorandums prepared for the National League of Airmen and translations of several letters from Hitler to Rothermere dating from 1935.[66]

The personal journal was usually written daily (although there are substantial gaps) with the entries covering more that 12,000 quarto sheets of paper and surely running into many millions of words. Consequently the version condensed in this edition is seriously truncated and restricted to the years from 1932 to 1940. The attraction of these diaries is their very readable, witty and fluent style: the bitchiness of 'Chips' Channon; the Fleet Street and society gossip of Robert Lockhart; and the insider political perspectives of Headlam, Amery and Alan

---

[63] Journal: 7 May 1935. Parts of the journals have been utilised by three historians prior to this editor. The late Stephen Koss for his magisterial study of the *Rise and Fall of the British Political Press: vol. 2* (Hamish Hamilton, 1984); David Kaynaston, *The Financial Times: A Centenary History* (Viking, 1988); and Paul Addison's seminal *Road to 1945* (Cape, 1975). Addison followed this up with the chapter 'Patriotism under Pressure' in Peele and Cook, *Politics of Reappraisal*

[64] Rother-Brooks journal: p. 1 n.d. [June 1935].

[65] Some years after Collin's death a decision was taken by the family to return to Rothermere's heirs correspondence and other miscellaneous papers relating to the two men. A statue of the 1st Viscount Rothermere sculpted by K. Troll in 1931 was also returned. Vere Harmsworth promised that these documents would be 'carefully looked after for the use of future historians' (Vere Harmsworth to Lilian Brooks, 17 November 1971). The failure of Sally Taylor to mention Collin in her recent biography of Rothermere might suggest an alternative answer.

[66] The Hitler–Rothermere transcriptions are included in the appendices.

Clark, all combine into one.[67] They make compulsive reading, being peppered with piquant gossip about the theatre, poetry and literature as well as flourishes of social history, as much as politics.

Keeping a journal is a strangely personal exercise. For Brooks it was a love–hate relationship. Clearly at times he felt frustrated at his need to record his activities and with equal measure angry that the written testimony failed to deliver more that the smallest of glimpses of reality:

> my daily jottings diary is only possible by strict discipline and the exclusion of everything but a mere record of how the day has been spent. The old hope of recording thought and emotion, of picturing people met, cannot possibly be fulfilled.[68]

Late in 1935 while maintaining his personal journal and the Rothermere-Brooks diary he declared 'what a waste of time and effort – and how drug-like it becomes'.[69] For many a diary-keeper this is a problem. Equally Brooks considered it a hobby, believing its 'secret' to be in 'the amount of fussy things it provides for one to [do], the pagination and storage and the like'.[70] His purpose behind maintaining the diary is less clear. The journal's opening entry records

> during the past ten years I have often wished that I had disciplined myself into the habit of keeping a diary. To have recorded for the amusement of my children the people I have met and the incidents in which I have been a participator, as Locker-Lampson did, would have taken so little time, and the record would have pleased me no less than them.[71]

His desire that his family should one day read the diary and as a consequence understand their father is a reoccurring theme, but the suspicion lingers that Brooks retained a wider motivation. Although in his future published and unpublished memoirs the journals are never quoted specifically, passages and descriptions read uncannily closely. Care is taken to introduce characters while specific actions or items are

---

[67] R.R. James (ed), *Chips: The Diaries of Sir Henry Channon* (Weidenfeld and Nicolson, 1968); K. Young (ed), *The Diaries of Sir Robert Bruce Lockhart* (Macmillan, 1973); S. Ball, *The Age of Baldwin and MacDonald: The Diaries of Sir Cuthbert Headlam, 1924–35* (Historians' Press, 1992); J. Barnes and D. Nicholson (eds), *The Empire at Bay: The Leo Amery Diaries* (Hutchinson, 1988); A. Clark, *Diaries* (Weidenfeld and Nicolson, 1993).

[68] Journal: 26 July 1931.

[69] Journal: 4 November 1935.

[70] Journal: 25 December 1938.

[71] Journal: 1 July 1925.

recorded with asides like 'for social historians of the future'. Some of this rests with Brooks' belief that he was an outsider, 'the little boy from the Bastille', who had come good and now moved in the best of circles; the journals would provide the proof of this transformation.

The style of the journal changes over time. When it was first begun the tendency was towards long retrospective passages; however, substantial gaps exist between entries: usually coinciding with periods of considerable work-load, as for example, when Brooks became a lobby correspondent for the *Yorkshire Post* in 1928. By the early 1930s he had abandoned as hopeless an attempt to keep a specific journal and was instead making typed entries onto loose-leaf quarto sheets of paper whenever possible. On occasion these would be interspersed with carbons of a letter he might have written, although 'to make deliberate copies of letters is altogether too priggish. It transforms the letter from a letter to a designed record, with the result that neither as a record or as a letter is the final product tolerable'.[72] The length of entries varies throughout; sometimes it might be restricted to 50 words, but more often the record runs for several pages. This was particularly the case during 1935 when pressure of time tended to find Brooks making weekly entries based on the jottings of his note book. The inevitable problem existed that the more C.B. did then the greater the number of interesting episodes he wished to record, yet which left him in reality with less real time to 'jot' his impressions. Examples of the material he recorded in these jotting books can be seen on occasion when he felt obliged to quote verbatim from these entries.[73] The retrospective entry was not a habit Brooks approved of: 'I am not certain,' he wrote in January 1938,

> that the best journal could not be devised from letters and newspaper cuttings and odd bits of memoranda. The method of jotting reminders into a pocket diary and then writing them up at the first possible moment does not work with me. Either I don't jot, or I don't write-up. And if I do both, it is almost impossible to catch the atmosphere that makes any event memorable.[74]

Nevertheless for the most part, Brooks found time to make the entries on the day in question.

9. Editorial Policy

In editing these journals the criteria throughout has been to provide a faithful selected reproduction in the spirit of the diarist. Selection of

[72] Journal: 24 January 1938.
[73] Journal: 11 February 1940.
[74] Journal: 24 January 1938.

the material was based upon three criteria: Brooks' interest in politics
from the perspective of a right-wing (disillusioned) Conservative sym-
pathiser; his career as a journalist and editor; and his interest in theatre
and literature.[75] Matters of a personal nature or relating to the family
have been included only if they have a direct relevance to understanding
the edited entries. Brooks' capitalisation, punctuation and grammar has
been retained. Fortunately spelling mistakes are few, and more usually
exist because of mis-hitting a typing key. In these cases the error has
been corrected. Any mis-spelling of a name has been corrected too.
One particular example was that of Oswald Mosley whose name, in
an extreme case, was spelt three different ways in the course of one
short entry. The fullness of most entries has meant that editorial cuts
have been made. In keeping with the convention laid down by the
Modern Humanities Research Association '[...]' is used where an entry
excludes some words in the original. Where ellipses are in the original
journal entry, these are represented '...' without square brackets. In
addition it has been necessary to distinguish between entries from the
personal journal and the 1935–7 Rother-Brooks diary entries. The
mechanism employed has been to reproduce the Rother-Brooks entries
in italics. The characters that crop up in the pages of the text are many
and varied, ranging from the well-known national players to less-
recognisable individuals. When a person appears for the first time in
the edited transcript a bibliographical footnote has been provided. Alas,
this has not been feasible with every name that appears, but every
effort has been made to trace individuals via bibliographical sources,
secondary literature and discussions with the Brooks family.[76]

---

[75] In deciding my approach I benefited from discussions with Stuart Ball (editor of *The
Age of MacDonald and Baldwin: The Headlam Diaries* (Historians' Press, 1992)), and Robert
Self (editor of *The Diary Letters of Austen Chamberlain* (RHS, Camden Series, 1995)), and
from attending a seminar at the Institute of Historical Research on diary-editing held in
December 1991. The transcript of this seminar 'Editing political diaries' was subsequently
published in *Contemporary Record* vol. 7, 1 (1993), pp. 103–31. Needless to say any
shortcomings in the editorial policy rest with myself.

[76] The key bibliographical sources are *Who's Who* (A & C Black): *Who Was Who* (A &
C Black): *Dictionary of National Biography* (Oxford University Press): D. Griffiths (ed.),
Encyclopaedia of the British Press (Macmillan, 1992): M. Stenton and S. Lees (eds.), *Who's
Who of British Members of Parliament*, vol. III (Harvester, 1979); J. Wearing (ed), *The London
Stage, 1930–39* vols. I–III (Metuchen, 1990); *Who Was Who in the Theatre, 1912–76* (Pitman,
1978); *Dod's Parliamentary Companion* (1932–40); D. Linton (ed.), *20th Century Newspaper Press
in Britain* (Mansell, 1994); *The Times*; *The Directory of Directors* (1935, 1938, 1940); D.J. Jeremy
(ed.), *Dictionary of Business Biography*, vols. 1–5 (Butterworths, 1984–6); F.W.S. Craig, *British
Parliamentary Election Results, 1918–49* (Parliamentary Research Services, 1983). Additionally,
a considerable debt of gratitude is owed to those individuals who have previously edited
diaries and in their own notes provided biographical details for characters who appear
in this journal.

1932

Friday 1 January I propose to continue last year's habit of jotting down an outline of each day – nothing more than some record of movement in case it may prove useful later. The attempt I made some few years ago to keep a full journal could not be sustained. The resultant record seemed almost bare as does the present outline ... one missed one's reading, one could not commit to paper one's emotion, one felt a prig, and the thing was at once tantalisingly enjoyable and strangely uncongenial ... Last year's small loose-leafed sheets were not easy to work on, after so much typing on these quarto sheets. I return to the fuller sheet, but not to the fuller intention. [...] At the office, Hobson[1] and I keep on the very best terms. Chaloner[2] is rather subdued. The work at the Argus[3] gets very tedious in such surroundings, but it might be much worse. Poor old Baxter, of the *Mercury*, with whom I have taken my ale and cold meat these three years, has been axed from his job, which will end in March. Fleet Street is full of such victims of slump. I continue to make little planks for a freelance raft in case disaster overtakes me, also.

Saturday 2 January Rose latish. In the afternoon with Lil,[4] Ida[5] and the three older children[6] to a revival of 'Robin Hood' at the Q Theatre – quite good. It must be nearly twenty five years since I first saw it in Lewis Waller's[7] day. The Q stage was painfully small for such a play, but the producer had done wonders in a simple modern manner. The

[1] Oscar (Rudolf) Hobson (1886–1961): financial journalist, City Ed. *Guardian*, 1920–9, Ed. *Financial News* 1929–34, Ed. *News Chronicle* 1935–9; kt. 1955. Referred to as ORH.

[2] Sammy R. Chaloner: Ass. Ed. *Financial News* until 1934.

[3] The Argus Press was where the *Financial News* was typeset and printed.

[4] Lilian (Dilly) Brooks (1891–1981): wife of diarist m. 8 Jan. 1916.

[5] Ida 'Pida' Coventry: family friend from Liverpool; spinster; died aged 108. Regular visitor to family home during holidays and even into her nineties can be remembered playing on the floor with C.B.'s grandchildren.

[6] Rosemary Brooks (1920–71): eldest d. of diarist; MI5; later worked for Beaverbrook Library; Vivian Brooks (1922–): second d. of diarist; WAAF 1940–5; journalist *Isle of Wight County Press, Yorkshire Evening Press*; novelist, pen-name Osmington Mills; Austen Brooks (1924–1986): eldest s.; RNR; journalist *Candour, Yorkshire Post, Bournmouth Echo*; later second-in-command of Empire Loyalists League, under A.K. Chesterton.

[7] Lewis Waller (1860–1915): actor-manager.

cast was excellent, with Basil Gill[8] as John, Margaret Halstan[9] as Eleanor, the Queen Mother, and Jack Livesey[10] as a dashing Robin Hood, looking extraordinarily like Forbes Robertson[11] at times. Bruce Winston[12] was Friar Tuck. The children were mad with delight.

Monday 4 January   Things very quiet and normal at the office. Bracken[13] told Hobson and me that he had spent the weekend with Beaverbrook,[14] with Rothermere[15] as a fellow-guest. Rothermere is now out to smash the Berrys,[16] and has gone into his most warlike mood, hoping to beat everybody down by sheer money weight with bigger and better insurance schemes and cornering celebrities for *The Mail* and the *Evening News*. Bracken says Rothermere cleared nearly £3,000,000 by bearing Wall Street at the end of December and that he (literally) neither knows how much he is worth or where his investments are. B.B.'s own opinion is that the *Manchester Guardian*, *The Yorkshire Post*, and *The Liverpool Post* can stand the strain as only those properties are really vulnerable which have been over-financed by the banks. He was not surprised that the Berry negotiations with me were held up.

Wednesday 6 January   Up at 8.30 for breakfast but went back for more sleep. Down at 11.30 and did about eight slips of *Merciful*.[17] I enjoy shocker writing when I am actually at it, but many mornings it is a hard job to drive myself out of bed to the typewriter. [...] Am reading

[8] Basil Gill (1877–1955): actor.
[9] Margaret Halstan (b. 1879): actress.
[10] Jack Livesey (1901–1961): actor.
[11] Johnston Forbes Robertson (1853–1937): actor; Kt. 1913.
[12] Bruce Winston (1879–1946): actor, singer, costumier & designer, producer.
[13] Brendan Rendall Bracken (1901–1958): Con. MP Paddington N. 1929–45, Bournemouth 1945–50, Bournemouth E. 1950–1; PPS to W. Churchill 1940–1; MOI 1941–5; 1st Ld. of Admiralty 1945; Chm. of *Financial News* 1926–45, of *The Financial Times* 1945–58; cr. Viscount Bracken 1952: known as B.B.
[14] (William) Maxwell Atkin (1879–1964): Con. MP Ashton 1910–16; prop. of *Daily Express* 1916–64, of *Sunday Express* 1918–64, of *Evening Standard* 1923–64; MOI 1918–19; Min. of Aircraft Production 1940–1; Min. of Supply 1941–2; Ld. Privy Seal 1942–5; kt. 1916, cr. Baron Beaverbrook 1917.
[15] Harold Sydney Harmsworth (1868–1940): prop. of *Daily Mirror* 1914–31, of *Daily Mail*, *Evening News* & Associated Newspapers Ltd. 1922–40; Sec. for Air 1917–18; cr. Baron Rothermere 1914, 1st Viscount 1919.
[16] James Gomer Berry (1883–1968): Chm. of Kemsley Newspapers, Ed.-in-Chief *The Sunday Times*; cr. Baron Kemsley 1936, cr. Viscount 1945; William Ewert Berry, Viscount Camrose (1879–1954): newspaper prop., with brother Lord Kemsley controlled the *Daily Telegraph*, *The Sunday Times*, & a chain of provincial papers; Kt. 1921, cr. 1st Baron 1929, cr. 1st Viscount 1941.
[17] *Mad-Doctor Merciful* (London: Hutchinson, 1932).

Keynes' *Essays in Persuasion*[18] and was struck by his anxiety to relegate economics to the back seat where it belongs [*sic*] leaving us free to discuss the things that really matter, such as human relationships and religion.

Thursday 7 January   The office day was quite normal – with the bank results coming in and surprising everyone by their good showing, but raising all kinds of doubts as to the exact honesty of their treatment of such items as bad and doubtful debts. I say 'exact honesty' because there is a broad honesty which all bankers must embrace – an honesty of the letter. There is the narrower honesty, that of the spirit, which I doubt if, as cautious men, they ever embrace. If, for example, the banks had this year shown net profit after making all allocations – instead of making an allocation to contingencies and from that averring themselves to have made provision for bad and doubtful debts – and if they had stated with definition exactly how they had written down depreciated holdings of gilt-edged, their apparent showing would have been less good but the tonic to public opinion at home and abroad would have been all the stronger.

Sunday 10 January   I did not, I think, record the fact of Willie Graham's[19] death late on Friday. He was only 44. His was a remarkable career. The last time I talked with him was on the telephone, when he looked forward to becoming our Labour correspondent again after leaving office. He was reluctant to go to the Board of Trade, as his heart was at the Treasury, and would have preferred the Financial Secretaryship to the Presidency. However a man does not lightly refuse promotion for a preference. He was more intellectually honest than most of his Labour colleagues, but at the break-up of the second Labour Government it seemed that even he had lost his head in the sense of having compromised his principles. It was with something of a shock, too, that one heard he had gone to Swab and Snelling – as if he had again compromised a principle by allying himself with a part of the capitalist system to which he most ardently objected. He, of course, would not see it that way. Arthur Greenwood,[20] I see, repeats my diagnosis, that

[18] J.M. Keynes, *Essays in Persuasion* (1931): John Maynard Keynes (1883–1946): economist; member Macmillan Ctte. on Finance & Industry 1929–31 & Economic Advisory Council; cr. 1st Baron of Tilton 1942.

[19] William Graham (1887–1932): Lab. MP Edinburgh Central 1918–31; FST 1924; Pres. BofT., 1929–31.

[20] Arthur Greenwood (1880–1954): Lab. MP Nelson & Colne 1922–31, Wakefield 1932–54; Min. of Health 1929–31; Min. without Portfolio 1940–2; Member of War Cabinet 1940–2; Dep. Leader of Lab. Party 1935–54.

the pneumonia was but the secondary cause of his death – overwork being the first. I feel, and have always felt, that overwork kills no man until he relaxes. Had Willie Graham gone on overworking all would have been well with him. It is the reaction that tells so heavily. As if a gramophone spring were to run down suddenly with no check after long tension ... He will be hard to replace in the Labour ranks.

Reading the Doyle[21] and Jerome[22] books last night I was again struck with the greater ease with which writers in the 80's and 90's were able to make fiction their sole means of livelihood. There was not, of course, the immense competition then – the *Strand* and the *Idler* with the *Windsor* and *Pearsons* held the field, and a magazine reputation made therein was wider than any of this time. To-day with circulating libraries as they are and memories as short as they have become, few men can reach the livelihood level that Doyle and Jerome, Jacobs[23] and their peers so easily seemed to reach. Doyle's admiration for Wilde[24] was interesting, and his opinion that the later Wilde was definitely a pathological case even more interesting.

Monday 11 January   Home by the 12.3 from B'friars, travelling with the Gilliland brothers,[25] who discussed Parliamentary personalities most of the way. We discussed the chances of Jimmy Cassells[26] being made Solicitor General if Jowitt[27] resigns the Attorneyship in favour of Inskip.[28] The elder Gilliland avers that Jimmy has never touched more than between £5,000 and £6,000 a year at the Bar, as his cases while prone to excessive publicity are not high feed briefs. He said that the beginning of Jimmy's legal career was a wet night when he was still on the *Morning Post* Parliamentary staff. He and Bryant[29] were waiting in Downing

[21] Arthur Conan Doyle (1859–1930): author, incl. Sherlock Holmes novels.

[22] Jerome K. Jerome (1859–1927): novelist, humorous writer & playwright.

[23] William Wymark Jacobs (1863–1943): short-story writer.

[24] Oscar Fingal O'Flahertie Wills Wilde (1854–1900): novelist & playwright.

[25] Gilliland brothers: Salmon & William E.G. (1878–1937): the latter was war reporter, special correspondent *Daily Telegraph* 1914–18; joined Reuters 1920s.

[26] Jimmy Cassells (1877–1972): barrister; Con. MP W. Leyton 1922–9, N.W. Camberwell 1931–5.

[27] William Jowitt (1885–1957): Lib. MP The Hartlepools 1922–4; Preston 1929–31 (Lab. from 1929, Nat. Lab. 1931), Lab. Ashton-under-Lyne 1939–45; Attorney Gen. 1929–32; Solicitor Gen. 1940–2; Paymaster Gen. 1942; Min. without Portfolio 1942–4 & for Nat. Insurance 1944–5; Ld. Chancellor 1945–51; cr. 1st Earl 1945.

[28] Thomas Walker Hobart Inskip (1876–1947): Con. MP Bristol Central 1918–29, Fareham 1931–9; Solicitor-Gen. 1922–4, 1924–8, 1931–2; Attorney-Gen. 1928–9, 1932–6; Min. for Co-ordination of Defence 1936–9; Dominions Sec. 1939, 1940; Ld. Chanc. 1939–40; Ld. Chief Justice 1940–6; kt. 1922, cr. Viscount Caldecote 1939.

[29] Arthur Wynee Morgan Bryant (1899–1985): freelance writer, lecturer, political commentator & popular historian.

Street to pick up a story – wet and cold and miserable. 'This isn't good enough' said the youthful Jimmy Cassells, 'I'm going to the bar.' And to the Bar he went.

Friday 15 January   At 11–15 p.m. Baldwin[30] rang up, and at 11–45 I took Brocklebank[31] in a taxi to Berkeley Square, shed him there and joined Baldwin, who was bubbling over with a formula for the reparations muddle and anxious to get it to Ramsay MacDonald.[32] It was a Kiplingesque situation, but I told B I'd pass him on to Walter Layton[33] to be vetted and Layton if influenced could get to MacDonald. We descended to the lounge, where, it being then after midnight, the cabaret was in full swing. I was aware of a darkened room seen through an archway, and in the centre of the room, spotlights, and in the centre of the spotlights half a dozen queenly girls with naked bellies dancing for the edification of some fine specimens of plutocrats. As Baldwin and I were in morning dress we were politely informed by a flunky in a blue livery that we might not gaze on the dancing girls even from afar, so we retired to a neighbouring room and discussed the crisis over whisky and sodas – and my impending severance from TBW.

Thursday 21 January   Up at ten, after tea at 8–30. Did American letter[34] and then to committee of Gallery Lodge which lasted from 12–30 till 2–30. [...] It was odd to find myself bunged on to a sub-committee of the Gallery Lodge. When I recall how great a personage my Father seemed when he went down – perhaps Babbit-like – to a committee of his lodge at Southport, that I should now be doing the same kind of thing for a much more famous lodge gives a touch of traditionalism to my days which pleases me. Masonry is a queer window on life – within two minutes to-day we were wrangling about some petty matter of routine and voting funds to relieve a brother's distress.

[30] Arthur Elbert Baldwin: Prop. & Ed. *Business Week*, McGraw-Hill publishing, Paris; Company Dir. of various European & US companies.

[31] Thomas Brocklebank: journalist on *Financial News* early 1930s; later housemaster at Eton College.

[32] (James) Ramsay MacDonald (1866–1937): Lab. MP Leicester 1906–18, Aberavon 1922–9, Nat. Lab. MP Seaham 1929–35, Scottish Universities, 1936–7; Lab. Party Sec. 1900–12, Chm. 1912–14; Lab. Leader 1922–31; PM & For. Sec. 1924, PM 1929–35; Ld. Pres. 1935–7.

[33] Walter Layton (1884–1966): Ed. of *The Economist* 1922–38, Chm. 1943–66; Chm. Exec. Ctte., Min. of Supply 1941–2; Head of Joint War Production Staff, Min. of Production 1942–3; cr. 1st Baron 1947.

[34] Covered the topics of Britain's balanced budget; 'Buying British'; Stock Exchange reform.

Friday 22 January At the office today we were bombshelled by the Cabinet announcement that on tariffs the Cabinet is to speak and vote by sections. Hobson said 'the only title for a leader is "The Gutless Buggers"' but when I wrote a hot leader he spent quite a long time toning it down.

> At the end he said 'There, I don't think there is anything offensive in it now.'
> I said: 'I'm sorry about that.'
> He said: 'Oh, it was alright.'
> I said: 'I don't mean I'm sorry you've had to cut it down, I mean I'm sorry there's nothing offensive left in it.'

It is terribly hard to find an editor with courage, I find. The 'gutless buggers' must hedge [...] We agreed a final form still very strong in tone. My own view is that it is the end of Cabinet government without a replacement system which can command confidence, and that the objections to the method adopted are equally objectionable whether one is for or against tariffs.

Thursday 28 January The spate of bills at this time of year becomes amusing in its intensity. While one awaits a thunder bolt from the Income Tax authorities, the rates and the gas and the water and school and domestic bills fall like hail stones on one's poor plate. Breakfasted at 10–15 and did the midweek American letter.[35] General news this last day or two has been very strong – the Dartmoor revolt, a girl murdered in the middle of a city crowd in the morning rush hour, a submarine lost with all hands – It is queer how good news stories come in waves, like luck at poker – good news stories, of course, being really 'bad news' stories. Things normal at office. [...] Tonight Bracken came wandering in at about 10. I thought he had come to tell me of the Rothermere-Berry concordat, but he couldn't release it. We talked about newspapers generally – he seemed to be sounding me as to my feeling towards *The Sunday Dispatch* , but from what motive I know not. He said 'It's difficult to know what to do with Arthur Mann,[36] unless we put him at *The Sunday Times*', as if he (Bracken) were the arbiter of all destinies.

[35] Covered the topics: Empire conference; bankers and crisis; marine insurance development.
[36] Arthur Henry Mann (1875–1972): Ed. *Evening Standard,* 1915–19, *Yorkshire Post,* 1919–39; trustee *The Observer,* 1945–56.

Saturday 30 January   see 'Julius Caesar' at the Q. Theatre. [...] I went with very doubtful anticipations – but the production was most excellent. Basil Gill as Brutus, and a very wonderful man, St. Barbe West[37] as Cassius, with Lewisohn[38] as Antony. The production, qua production, on that small stage was quite masterly, and the cuts had been skilfully made. We were lucky enough to bag three good seats and altogether had a fine time of it.

Sunday 31 January   I am a little baffled by the shaping of my fate, if Camrose and I come to agreement on Tuesday. My incursion into the *Financial News* was a queer turn, really, and was mostly justified by my knowledge of newspaper production. As city editor of *The Daily Telegraph* I shall be a 'bluff-artist' in imminent danger of daily exposure – and I shall have all my tactical work cut out, assuming I survive at all, to extricate myself from the specialisation of the city for a big chair, for which, after all, is what I want in journalism. I would like either the *DT* itself or *The Sunday Times* to emerge from the change over, if there is to be a change over. The position is not now so much in my favour when we bargain, for if Camrose has been behind the proposed merger of the *FN* and the *FT* I shall have little claim for tenure on the *DT*. A month ago I had a strong claim. In any event, it is an odd and a pleasing thing in an impish way to have been invited to negotiate for the job at all.

Saturday 13 February   On duty. Reached the office at 10.30. There was a prize blunder in the paper. Neville Chamberlain[39] at Brum having said 'Let me remind you that a year ago I forecast a deficiency in the Budget' we reported him 'Budget Deficit' 'Mr Chamberlain at Birmingham last night forecast a budget deficiency....' ORH on the phone was angry enough, and I, too. I had not seen it in the first edition, so my conscience but not my repute was clear.

Wednesday 17 February   Wilkinson[40] of the *DT* city staff rang me up to ask [if] it were true that I was to be his new chief. I told him I didn't know and admitted the negotiations. He was in a funk in case I was

---

[37] Henry St. Barbe West (1880–1935): actor.

[38] Victor Max Lewisohn (1897–1934): actor.

[39] (Arthur) Neville Chamberlain (1869–1940): Con. MP for Ladywood 1918–29, Edgbaston 1929–40; Postmaster-Gen. 1922–3; Min. of Health 1923, 1924–9, 1931; Chanc. of Exchequer 1923, 1931–7; PM 1937–40; Ld. Pres. 1940. Con. Leader 1937–40.

[40] Clennell Wilkinson: financial journalist; City staff *Daily Telegraph*.

going to heave out all the staff and bring in *FN* men. [...] On the way up [to bed] I childlike played with the hope that the post might have brought two letters, one from C[amrose] making an offer and one from Higham[41] saying Barnaby's[42] novel was placed. The post had brought two letters – a stern demand for the gas bill and bill from the plumber ...

Saturday 20 February   In the evening to give a lecture at the Caxton Hall on 'The shocker as a fine art'. Hugh Williamson[43] in the chair. A queer audience, very like an ordinary literary society in the provinces. One or two interesting people, and a jolly discussion, of no great depth, afterwards.

Monday 29 February   The office is still astir with the impending dissolution of the paper and Bracken's rat-like rushings from one expedient to another. He has quite lost his nerve, Hobson says, and last night summoned Hills[44] to his house for an emergency consultation, drank himself asleep and snored the bout off on a sofa.

Tuesday 1 March   I had just done the cable when Chaloner rang to see if I could lunch with ORH and him at the Reform. I did — and we were a conspiratorial three discussing how to rid the paper of Bracken. I was all for a brutal frontal attack by ORH, but Bracken is such a loveable boy as well as such a dangerous bloody fool that we went to the office still without having our resolutions screwed up. I told Chaloner that in future I should sign all official letters 'Cassius Brooks, Assistant Editor'. It seems that when ORH and C were deciding to refuse any further salary cuts under the present management and to take a stand against B.B. the question had arisen between them 'will Brooks agree' and ORH had said 'Oh, Brooks will agree to anything that has any "fun" in it.' Later when C suggested that Brady, an Irishman, might be a desirable manager for the paper ORH said 'Yes, he can come and share all the jokes with Brooks.' But I noticed that he laughed

---

[41] David Higham: C.B.'s agent at Curtis Brown; publisher, David Higham Assoc. Ltd. (formerly Pearn Pollinger & Higham).

[42] Barnaby Brook: pseudonym under which C.B. published his serious novels.

[43] Hugh Ross-Williamson (1901–78): writer; Ass. Ed., *Yorkshire Post*, 1925–30; Ed. *Bookman*, 1930–4; Acting Ed., *Strand Magazine*, 1934–5; Dir. London General Press 1936–42, 1968– ; Anglican Priest 1943–55; reconciled to Roman Catholicism 1955.

[44] Major John Waller Hills (1867–1935): Bd. member & Chm. *Financial News*; Con. MP Durham 1906–22, Ripon 1925–38; FS Treasury 1922–3.

freely when I jollied them and made my apt quotations and quips, and seemed the better for a little jesting. Later he saw BB and delivered a negative ultimatum and came down and said that we would probably get a year's notice to-morrow. Later still BB came down to him apologetic and very civil, so that we were back to the opening position. The worry is the fate of all the subordinate ranks – for them to be flung into the street by the death of the paper would mean a terrible weight of tragedy on ORH and us. We have simply to humour B.B. and try to save the sheet – its jubilee is in two years time incidentally.

Wednesday 2 March   In the city there was tremendous optimism, built round several things – the announcement that a large part of the Franco-American Treasury credit is to be repaid, the removal of foreign exchange restrictions, the success of two recent new issues, the booming markets and the hope of a further reduction of bank rate tomorrow.

Tuesday 5 April   It is a month since I tapped an entry into this diary – for on the Monday morning after my last entry I was quite definitely conquered by the sciatica which has been gnawing at me for so long. [...] I cannot make a real entry even now, as I have to tap the machine one-handedly as I rest on my left elbow on my bed, but it has been a strange and disturbing experience. The first day I was allowed up and found I couldn't walk, I actually blubbered like a child, feeling that I was 'done'. (I must have been weak from incessant pain and a low diet.) Hobson has been very decent to Lil on the phone, but I naturally worried about the office, not wanting to see my main income cut off suddenly. At the beginning of the affair Camrose wrote asking me to leave the *DT* in abeyance.

Friday 15 April   in gathering income tax return materials I was surprised to find that my books had made for me last year a net £307. It isn't good, for there were four new ones,[45] but it was more than I thought.

Tuesday 26 April   Hobson left in the afternoon for the funeral of Ted Scott[46], editor of the *Manchester Guardian* who was drowned in

---

[45] *This Tarriff Question* (London: Arnold, 1931); *Three Yards of Cord* (London: Hutchinson, 1931); *Mock Turtle* (London: Humphrey Toulmin, 1931); *Something in the City* (London: Country Life, 1931).

[46] Edward Taylor 'Ted' Scott (1904–32): journalist with *Manchester Guardian*, 1911–32, Ed. 1929–32; POW 1918; s. of C.P. Scott.

Windermere on Friday. The row at the Argus – the refusal to alter headlines according to Hobson's instructions on the plea of economy, raising the vital principle of who is to edit the paper – has reached a dull compromise.

Thursday 28 April   I took the first parts of this journal from their original file bindings to put them into a couple of spring-backed files. I didn't dare read 'em, but I looked at a page or two and was staggered to find how the tone of the thing has changed. Now it is always a jotted record of the day with no indication of what has happened to my mind or heart or soul – if any of any of these excellent things. That change is partly due to slackness and partly to the discovery – or re-discovery – that the vital things cannot be recorded.

Tuesday 3 May   At the Club [Whitefriars] we had a goodly gathering, sitting till three o'c. The talk turned on the leadership or lack of it in Campbell-Bannerman,[47] the character of Hicks-Beach,[48] of Balfour,[49] whether Hamlet was dilatory of purpose – I hold that he was not – emendations of Shakespeare's text, the inevitability of each generation of intelligent persons being against the religion of its elders and several other equally interesting and futile topics. Hield[50] of the *Morning Post*, Hamilton Fyfe[51] and I were the chief protagonists with Hugh Williamson egging us on.

Thursday 5 May   In the afternoon to the Thursday Club. It was very

---

[47] Henry Campbell-Bannerman (1836–1908): Lib. MP Stirling Burghs 1868–1908; FS, WO 1871–4, 1880–2; P.S., Admiralty 1882–4; Chief Sec. for Ireland 1884–5; Sec. of State, WO 1886, 1892–5; PM 1905–8.

[48] Michael Edward Hicks-Beach (1873–1916): Con. MP Gloucester E. 1864–85, Bristol N. 1885–1906; PS, Poor Law Bd. 1868; PUS Home Office 1868; Chief Sec. for Ireland 1874–8, 1886–7; Sec. of State Colonies 1878–80; Chanc. of Exchequer 1885–6, 1895–1902; Pres. of BofT. 1888–92; cr. 1st Earl St. Aldwyn 1915.

[49] Arthur James Balfour (1848–1930): Con. MP Hertford 1874–5, Manchester E, 1885–1906, City of London 1906–22; Chief Sec. for Ireland 1887–91; 1st Ld. of Treasury 1891–2, 1895–1905; PM 1902–5; 1st Ld. of Admiralty 1915–16; For. Sec. 1916–19; Ld. Pres. 1919–22, 1925–29; Con. Leader in the HofC., 1891–1902, Con. Leader 1902–11; KG 1922, cr. Earl of Balfour 1922; author of the 'Balfour Declaration' on Palestine 1917.

[50] Robert Hield (1866–1948); Dep. Ed. *Morning Post*; on merger with *Daily Telegraph* remained until 1943.

[51] Henry Hamilton Fyfe (1886–1951): journalist; Ed. *Morning Advertiser* 1902, *Daily Mirror* 1903–9, *Daily Herald* 1922–6; special correspondent *Daily Mail* 1909–13; reporter *The Times* 1913–22; *Daily Chronicle* 1926–30; thereafter freelance; author *Sixty Years of Fleet Street* (1949).

unexciting. The chief 'star' was a Mrs Hewitt[52] who had done a good first novel called *Mardi*, which I haven't read. She sat, rather like a young Hollywood queen smoking cigarettes and holding a little court. Ralph Straus[53] was there, and Colin Still,[54] Louis McQuilland, the dramatic and film critic, and the usual others. I talked with Mrs De Crespigny[55] about the recent medium case. She had had to advise counsel on the technicalities of spiritualism and was vastly annoyed with MaCardie's[56] summing up.

Saturday 7 May   Then to the Gallery Lodge at 4. At the social board we had no musical programme but a free discussion inaugurated by Ritchie[57] in which I flung myself. It turned mainly on the origins of the Craft, with a long digression inaugurated by Commander Daniel, on when and where to give grips and signs. It has always seemed to me that those historians of the Masonry who deride the legendary history confuse Free Masonry with Grand Lodge Free Masonry. The beginning of the Grand Lodge era did two things – it began the preservation of records and it imported publicity into what had been a secret society. Last night we had the paradox of a mock grumble that *The Times* had omitted some news about one of the institutions and also an elderly P.M. insisted on the preservation of the utmost caution in revealing oneself as a Mason. Since Grand Lodge era we have begun to bring women and strangers to the social board at guest nights, which means that the original secrecy – when brotherly love was a very vital thing – has gone and only a small part of the ritual now remains secret. But in the pre-Grand Lodge era there must have been a long history of masonry without written record – Lodges without minute books. The most striking thing, it seems to me, is the amount of Mithraic symbolism in both Masonry and Christianity. However – it was a good discussion, and the night passed much more quickly than with the normal musical programme.

---

[52] Katheleen Douglas Hewitt: author, incl. *Mardi* (London: Noel Douglas, 1932).

[53] Ralph Straus (1882–1952): novelist, biographer & book reviewer.

[54] Colin Still: author; *Shakespeare's Mystery Play* (London: Palmer,1921); *Timeless Themes* (London: Nicholson & Watson, 1936).

[55] Mrs de Crespigny: wife of Air Vice-Marshall H.V. Champion de Crespigny (1897–1969): Lab. cand. Newark-on-Trent 1945; Fighter pilot; Regional Comm. for Schleswig Holstein Control Commission 1946–7.

[56] Henry Alfred MaCardie (1869–1933): judge & lawyer; ctted suicide.

[57] Charles Ritchie (1866–1948): Vice-Chm. Port of London Authority 1913–25, Chm. 1925–47; suc. 2nd Baron.

Sunday 8 May   finished Benson's[58] book on Charlotte Brontë. It is a most satisfactory life and marches with my own feeling about her. Benson, in the politest way in the world, talking of her marriage, says that what she needed was a man. Her early homosexual passion of [*sic*] Ellen and her unrequited passion for Herger [*sic*] have always seemed to me to reflect two things in her psychology. [...] Benson, without going as far as Alice Law,[59] pleads strongly for the collaboration of Branwell in *Wuthering Heights* and makes an excellent case for Branwell's having written the first two chapters and helped with some of the detail of the rest. The most interesting thing in the book is the hay [*sic*] he makes of Mrs Gaskell[60] as a biographer.

Monday 9 May   Hobson, home from Berlin, very impressed with the new buildings there and the cult of athleticism, which has replaced the old militarism and its concomitant bourgeois relaxation. He says that before the war one never saw a pretty German woman but now one sees many. At the opera the audience was well dressed but there was no rush of taxis or private cars at the end and street traffic generally is palpably declined. He remarked, oddly for him, that the Berliners are sexually more gross than our people, by which he meant, it appeared, that they conduct a kind of rustic wooing and harlotry in the popular cafes. He gave me the impression of a distinct German renaissance. At the office things were quiet.

Friday 13 May   I am drinking my third pot of tea. My head begins to busy itself with plans. I am almost ready to start the banking book, and I propose to write a history of modern America, beginning with the death of Lincoln. The shocker will finish itself, and until *Val Verity*[61] finds a publisher I can't write another Barnaby Brook novel. *The Times Lit. Supplement* was quite nice to *Dr Merciful* yesterday – not glowing but approving and condescending to say that it was clever and convincing. By the skill of the précis I deduce an understanding reviewer. But the *T.L.S.* has always been nice to me, starring both Barnaby novels and always approving with C.B. and W.C.B.. In the meantime the executive

[58] Edward Frederic Benson (1867–1940): author, including *Charlotte Brontë* (London: Longman, 1932); British Archaeological School, Athens 1892–5; Mayor of Rye 1934–7.

[59] Alice Law: poet & author, including *Patrick Branwell Brontë* (London: A.M. Philpot, 1924) & *Emily Jane Brontë and the Authorship of Wuthering Heights* (Altham: Old Parsonage Press, 1928).

[60] Elizabeth Cleghorn Gaskell (1810–65): author of *The Life of Charlotte Brontë* (London: Smith, Elder & Co, 1857).

[61] Re-titled *Gay Go Up* (London: Gerald Howe, 1933) on recommendation of referee.

work on Kylsant[62] lags behind, although Hodge[63] has the introduction
in final draft. Incidentally, the news this morning is that the Lindbergh
baby[64] has been found dead. The impact on Lil and the maid, Ethel,
was that of a personal tragedy, and even I found myself roused to quite
a flame of indignation. [...] At the office I learned that C.J. Hamilton[65]
was sacked, his engagement to end on August 31st. This is purely an
economy move, and not really unexpected, but unsettling. Hamilton
for all his funniosities is a good man to work with. Hobson thinks he
(Hamilton) will never get another Professorial chair, but believes that
he will not be down and out by the loss of his job with us. He is the
husband, or *was* the husband, of Mary Hamilton,[66] the politician
novelist essayist and biographer of Ramsay MacDonald.

Wednesday 25 May   The news this morning is the riot of alarm caused
by a few words in *The Times* leader of yesterday that Britain is preparing
to pay off the American war debt irrespective of the action of our own
debtors, and to the prejudice of the Lausanne conference. The story
caused us some trouble at the press, and I don't doubt Hobson will
want my head on a charger for mishandling it.

Thursday 26 May   Things normal at the office. Hobson still beating up
his policy for Lausanne. Reginald McKenna[67] and others favourable
but cannot speak over their own names. Sprague[68] of the Bank of
England had rung up very enthusiastically. J.A. Hobson[69] is sending a

---

[62] Owen Cosby Philips Kylsant (1863–1937): shipowner & financier; Lib. MP Pembroke
1906–10; Con. MP Chester 1916–22; Pres. London Chamber of Commerce; cr. Baron
1923. Jailed for twelve months after the Royal Mail trial. C.B. edited a volume on the
trial, *The Royal Mail Case* (London: Hodge, 1933).

[63] William Hodge: publisher for Royal Mail trial book.

[64] Kidnapped baby, son of Col. Charles Lindbergh (1902–74): American aviation
pioneer & technical adviser to the US Air Force who established close links with Nazi
Germany.

[65] Prof. C.J. Hamilton: ex-don of an Indian University; leader writer, *Financial News*.

[66] Mary Agnes (Molly) Hamilton (1882–1966): Lab. MP Blackburn 1929–31; journalist &
writer, biographer of Ramsay MacDonald & Arthur Henderson; Gov. of BBC 1933–7;
Temp. civil servant 1940–52.

[67] Reginald McKenna (1863–1943): Lib. MP Monmouthshire N. 1895–1918; FS, Treasury 1905–7; Pres. Bd. of Educ. 1907–8; 1st Ld. of Admiralty 1908–11; Sec. of State,
Home Office, 1911–15; Chanc. of Exchequer 1915–16; Chm. of Midland Bank 1919–43.

[68] Oliver Mitchell Wentworth Sprague (1873–1953): Prof. of Economics, Imperial
University, Tokyo 1905–8; Prof. of Banking & Finance, Harvard University 1908–31;
Econ. & Statistical Adviser, Bank of England 1930–3.

[69] J.A. Hobson (1858–1940): liberal economist, writer, occasional lecturer London
School of Economics, founder-member Rainbow Society.

copy of the article to Ramsay MacDonald for an opinion. Most commentators want a second article on disarmament to catch the American interest – but I fear that once disarmament is dragged in a huge wave of prejudice will be created on grounds far removed from the original need of saving civilisation from an economic deluge through fiscal defaults. The two are really one, but emphasis becomes a matter of crucial importance in discussing the disarmament side of the problem in a public print.

Thursday 16 June   At the office all things normal, with conflicting reports from Lausanne as to the stand MacDonald is taking against the French proposal for a six month moratorium.

Thursday 23 June   Up at 10–15 and did the American Letter,[70] not touching either progress at Lausanne or the Hoover disarmament plan. My own view of Hoover[71] is that the offer coming now is very cunning Presidential campaign propaganda, but that it cannot go through in its present form – the abolition of bombers, for example, means that our North-west frontier and middle-east 'police component' is hurt. Also, I have great sympathy with the French view that security is the condition precedent for any proportional disarming, and as long as France doesn't trust the Covenant and Article 10 some other means must be found for giving her the assurance she needs. I have no patience with the deriding of France for the possession of an 'inferiority complex'. A land twice invaded in living memory doesn't display an inferiority complex but a healthy realism when she demands security against renewed attack.

Tuesday 28 June   Grig[72] was full of woe at the foolish selection of new type made for the *YP* by Arthur Mann. The paper has had protests from all the Yorkshire M.P.s, the college of ophthalmic surgeons and many others. The odd thing is that the same face in *The Herald*, lavishly broken up by bold headlines and many blocks, is very successful: it is the *YP* habit of setting solid columns that makes it astigmatic.

---

[70] Covering topics: survey, independent adaptability in Britain; tariff applications.
[71] Herbert Hoover (1874–1964): US Pres. 1929–32.
[72] Geoffrey Edward Harvey Grigson (1905–85): journalist & poet; Ed. *New Verse* 1933–9; staff *Yorkshire Post*; Literary Ed. *Morning Post*; BBC; m. Jane Grigson (1928–90): cookery writer.

Friday 1 July   Yesterday I was lunched at the St. James's Club by George Buchanan.[73] I always like going to that fane of diplomats, with its pleasant pictures and its general air of aristocratic security. They have touched modernity by installing a small cocktail bar – because they hope to make sordid money thereby, particularly when they house White's in the autumn – White's being a hard drinking crowd by repute in the St. James's. They still show the casual guest the very corner where old Clanricarde,[74] the rack-renter, decided to leave all his money to a poor subaltern in the Guards – Harry Lascelles,[75] whose sudden millions made possible his marriage to the Princess. Last night was very strenuous at the Press. The fall in the bank rate to two per cent following a little gilt edged boom and Neville Chamberlain's return from Lausanne caused us all to expect a conversion of sorts, but most people thought it would be Treasuries. At nine thirty I had a call from Shaw to say it was the big thing – war loan. Our stuff didn't reach us till twenty-past ten, and last copy down first edition is nominally 10-30. However Shaw's tip had given us time to prepare, and I raked Hobson from a dinner to bear an expert hand, I in the meantime contriving to alter a leader to fit the new event – having, also, to alter the Lausanne leader.

Monday 4 July   At the office things were normal but for the technical mess caused by the Stock Exchange lists being nearly two hours late, as the gilt edged boom following the conversion offer had flowed into industrials, where there was a small quantity on offer and a growing demand. A tight market always makes for sudden jumps, but this was out of all reason. Many 'duds' appreciated and there will be some burnt fingers. Bear covering in a panic was partly to blame. Ostensibly the conversion offer goes well, but in the city itself the alternatives to the new $3\frac{1}{2}$ are being more and more openly canvassed.

Friday 8 July   At four ten I jumped into a taxi for the Treasury to

[73] George (Cunningham) Buchanan (1865–1940): civil engineer; served Mesopotamian Expeditionary Force 1915–17; member Indian Munitions Board 1917–19; 1924 visited Australia at request of Federal govt. to report on transportation facilities; kt. 1915.

[74] Hubert George de Burgh Canning, 2nd Marquess Clanricarde (1832–1916): absentee Irish land prop. & rack-renter.

[75] Henry George Charles Lascelles (1882–1947): Grenadier Guard; 1905–7 Hon. attaché, Rome; aide-de-camp Gov.-Gen. of Canada 1907–11; Freemason & man of the turf; m. Princess Mary 1922.

confer with Elliot[76] and other city journalists on the progress of the conversion scheme. There were about thirty of us there, and we had tea and plumcake in the Chancellor's room, talking very informally over pipes and cigarettes. Mill, of *The Times*, Williams,[77] of *The Herald*, and I were the main talkers. Major Elliot has grown less and less 'Major' since the present government put him in office. With his rimless spectacles and his quiet almost-Irish sense of humour he is far from being the conventional Scot. Sir Richard Hopkins[78] was in support for the Treasury, a narrow eyed, narrow headed Celt whom I have never regarded as being either a good type or a good Controller of the Treasury. I came into contact with his ineptitude over the conversion of a few years ago and still think him inept. It was an interesting confidential pow-wow, and a beautiful example of the Kiplingesque informality of British government.

Tuesday 12 July   The paper was a bit difficult at the press, and when I was in the tube I happened to look at a late *Star* and found that our first edition had missed 'the news of the night for us' – Chamberlain's reassurance about returning to a gold standard. This meant agitated 'phoning when I got home – but it was all right for the City edition.

Monday 25 July   Grave trouble at the office. The 'splash' should have carried a large table inside – and it was not given! There was no defence for anybody, although I had asked the chief-sub if a table was not necessary. It was due to a combination of faults – Thompson[79] who did the story and table did not mark the table for Sunday night and did not indicate on copy that the table was attached. Hobson in charge on Satdy did not note it on the menu. The sub who handled the story saw the par. saying 'elsewhere we give a table' but did not check the cross reference. I read down the splash in galley and assumed that the table mentioned was given, but was some small table ... Altogether a bad business from the technical viewpoint. A factor inviting such a

[76] Walter Elliot (1888–1958): Con. MP Lanark 1918–23, Glasgow Kelvingrove 1924–45, 1950–8, Scottish Univ. 1946–50; PS Health for Scotland 1923–4, 1924–6; Under-Secretary, Scotland 1926–9; FST 1931–2; Min. of Agric, 1932–6; Scottish Sec. 1936–8; Min. of Health 1938–40.
[77] Francis Williams (1903–70): author & journalist; staff *Daily Herald*, Ed. 1936–40; MOI 1941–5; Adviser on Public Relations to PM 1945–7.
[78] Richard Valentine Nind Hopkins (1880–1955): Chm., Inland Revenue 1922–7; 2nd Sec. 1932, Perm. Sec. of the Treasury 1942–5; kt. 1920.
[79] Lucius Perroriet Thompson-McCausland (1904–84): Herbert Wragg & Co. 1928; *Financial News* 1929–34; Moody's Economist Service 1929–39; Bank of England 1939–65, advisor to Gov. 1949–65.

disaster was the arrival of the Ottawa cable at 11, just when the page was in proof, which distracted Lyon[80] and Renolds and me from the splash. This is the second blunder in a week by the Press, and I actually offered Hobson my resignation.

He said 'For God's sake don't talk about resignations or they'll be asking for mine!'

Just to cheer us up tonight as the page was being made up in forme the third section of the page one stock indicator (most important thing on the page from some viewpoints) was hopelessly pied, and we had to fill with misc and get away. Altogether, a bad day.

Friday 5 August   At the office. Nothing very exciting. Bracken back from a short holiday bounced in and tried to be Northcliffian – but I countered him by a vicious attack on his cheeseparing economy methods which stultified all our effort etc etc etc. I fear that before the month is over Hobson will hear either of a colossal row or a complete capitulation of BB.

Wednesday 17 August   A blazing hot day again, with affairs at the office very slack, save for a suggestion that the present embargo on new issues, imposed for the sake of Conversion might be partly removed. The thought that a bureaucrat in Whitehall should discriminate between free borrowers and free lenders for the sake of a dubious bargain at Washington drove me into a fine frenzy.

Tuesday 13 September   I left the family in a taxi cab at Victoria Station, after a picnic luncheon from railway baskets in the train, washed and took tea and so to the office. The inevitable post-holiday bombshell had greeted Oscar on his return. On the economy plea and the fact that Chaloner's agreement ends this year the Board – which means Bracken – demand that he select one of the two, Chaloner or I, for the plank.

I offered to hand in my resignation if that would ease his position, but he said 'It would gravely embarrass me, as on the grounds that the best defence is attack, I am replying thus ...' and produced several sheets of vehement attack on the management.

Chaloner and I fed together at the Falstaff to talk it over, but laughed too much to approach the thing seriously. In my case, I fancy my side

[80] [?] A. Neil Lyon (1880–1940); journalist, author; worked *The Critic, Topical Times, Sunday Chronicle, English Review*; wrote plays & *Robert Blatchford* (1910).

lines would support my family, even if I couldn't find another staff job.

Wednesday 21 September At the office today all was quiet. B.B. came in with all kinds of stories, direct from Walter Elliot about Herbert Samuel's[81] failure to implement the agreed police cuts at the Home Office, direct from Rothermere about his (Rothermere's) refusal to continue the chairmanship of the *Daily Mail* group because with the new cut-throat competition war if he looks after his net sales he must imperil his dividend drawers and if he tends to his dividend drawers he must imperil his net sales, and therefore son Esmond[82] is left with the job. He said no word about Hobson's memorandum which he had this morning, nor did he imply that he had poised a sword of Damocles over the twin heads of Chaloner and me. Nor did I imply that I knew.

Thursday 29 September Things at the office were quiet. The news, of course, this last two days has been the resignation of the Free Traders and the re-shuffle of the Ministry. [...] Young Hore-Belisha,[83] who looks like being *le* Disraeli[84] *de nos jours*, has the Financial Secretaryship to the Treasury. He is able and energetic, but greatly disliked in the City, as a pushing Jew.

Sunday 16 October I began to review the *Life of Asquith*[85] for us and for the *Yorkshire Post* – interrupted first by Whitman and next by the sudden thought of taking Vivian to a matinee of *Macbeth*. The production, done in a small Q. Theatre was really excellent. Esmé Beringer[86] as Lady Macbeth more than satisfying. Basil Gill as Macduff was good,

---

[81] Herbert Louis Samuel (1870–1963): Lib. MP Cleveland 1902–18, Darwen 1929–35; Chanc. Duchy of Lancaster 1909–10, 1915–16; Postmaster-Gen. 1914–15, 1915–16; Pres. Local Govt. Bd. 1914–15; Home Sec. 1916, 1931–2; High Comm. Palestine 1920–5; kt. 1920, cr. Viscount Samuel 1937.

[82] Esmond Cecil Harmsworth (1898–1978): Con. MP, Thanet 1919–29; Chm. of Associated Newspapers from 1935; Prop. of *Daily Mail* from 1938; suc. 2nd Viscount Rothermere 1940.

[83] (Isaac) Leslie Hore-Belisha (1893–1957): MP Plymouth Devonport 1923–45 (Lib. to 1931, Nat. Lib. 1931–42, Nat. Ind. 1942–5); PS Trade 1931–2; FST 1932–4; Min. of Transport 1934–7; Sec. for War 1937–40; Min. of Nat. Insurance 1945; cr. Baron Hore-Belisha 1954.

[84] Benjamin Disraeli (1804–81): Con. MP & leader; PM 1868, 1874–80; cr. Earl Beaconsfield 1880.

[85] John A. Spender & C. Asquith, *Life of Herbert Asquith, Lord Oxford & Asquith* (London: Hutchinson, 1932), 2 vols.

[86] Esmé Beringer (1875–1936): actress.

as always, and a man called George (?) [*sic*] was as good as one expected, since no man's reading of Macbeth can avoid making him *too* weak. This fellow made him far too much of a philosophical gentleman.

Thursday 20 October   I should really have entered under yesterday's date a line or so about the unemployment riots – not as serious as they sounded, with only 13 citizens and 37 police injured, and none very seriously. The significant things at the moment are, I think, the gradual realisation everywhere that we are in for a bad and troubled winter and the sudden fall in the £ after Ramsay MacDonald's Tuesday's speech. By common consent, Ramsay is a complete muff at the game of being National Prime Minister – and talks his usual platitudes about even keels and ships of State when he should be offering the electorate, and particularly the unemployed electorate, something to bite on.

Friday 28 October   At the office to-day ORH was very perturbed, and rightly so, at certain slips in the paper – subeditorial carelessness. I defended the Argus on the old grounds, that economies have left everybody with too much to do and too many inevitable interruptions to single jobs. He suggests that I go down early to the Argus to read news proofs. I said nothing, but decided that this wasn't good enough. At midnight Lil and I talked the matter over, and weighing up the several factors agreed it would be better for me to 'throw in my hand'. The paper is in a precarious state, so that the drama of being without a staff job could be no more worrying than the constant anticipation of a bust-up, I have certain sources of income which may be worked up, I have chances of alternative staff jobs – and to spend many weary hours doing a proof reader's job would be a waste of my peculiar faculties and of life itself, to say nothing of a peril to eyes already none too kindly treated by proof reading.

Monday 31 October   At the office I was held up first by the accountant and then by Bittles but wandered into Hobson's room eventually, where he sat with Chaloner.

'Why did you do it?' he said, 'Damn it, you don't want to leave a sinking ship. Your letter is before me, in two seconds it will be behind me.'

He refused to accept my resignation – asked me to put the letter in my pocket – said I could do it any day if I really insisted – and that was that! I couldn't, in the face of his tone insist, nor was I dying to insist. For the rest, the day normal and busy.

Wednesday 2 November   This afternoon the famous memorandum to ORH from Bracken was delivered. It was a slashing, cruel attack on every feature of ORH's editorship – from 'dull political leaders which nobody reads' to 'a paper like an uninteresting scrap book'. ORH cut up, but determined not to resign but to fight Bracken. On my advice he had a copy taken and sent to Major Hills with a request for an interview. He now agrees with me that the only hope for the paper is to get it out of Bracken's hands.

Wednesday 9 November   ORH stays put, and we are in a lull, waiting for the next shot in the war. It is absurd – a paper dying of inanition with the Managing Director, the manager and the editor in chief conducting a triple feud while it dies.

Thursday 1 December   Yesterday was eventful in a quiet way. Sir George Buchanan and I had a pleasant bachelor lunch at his flat and talked until 3–30, chiefly about Burma and the mess into which a half-baked attempt at self-government has driven the Burmans. [...] Later in the afternoon Hobson had a letter from Bracken saying that the Board still feels that one assistant editorship must go, and terminating Chaloner's agreement, but suggesting his retention on the present supplements at a month's notice either side. I like Hobson and I like Chaloner – but there is irony in this turn of events, for C. came in like a roaring lion, contemptuous of all the rest of us and ready to lick creation – and alas, when my resignation is newly refused, he is subject to this indignity.

Friday 2 December   When I returned to Bishopsgate Oscar was still with B.B.. He (Oscar) came on after dinner to the Press to deal with the second British note to Hoover, and there told me what had passed. The situation is quite hopeless. What is needed, as I have for a year maintained, is for Hobson to get a price for the group and find a syndicate to buy it. Both sides are right in the quarrel. Hobson has killed the paper by preaching bitter Cobdenism when the country was protectionist but Bracken and Hills by ineptitude have failed to get business. After all, the job of the salesman is to sell the product as he has it, not, because he finds the work hard, to damn the product to the very people to whom he is trying to sell it.

Wednesday 7 December   When I reached the office Oscar told me that the Board had met and that Major Hills had come down to him and said that he (Hills) had told the Board that Hobson couldn't see his way to going on after the expiry of his contract and the Board thought there was no more to be said. This has rather taken the wind from ORH's sails – but it seemed to me to be obvious. On Monday we had had the extraordinary spectacle of an Editor-in-Chief confronted at the hands of the overseer with an entirely new dummy make-up of his paper on which he hadn't been so much as consulted. The position now is awkward. Hobson stays on until May 1934, openly at war with his directors who feel (and with justice) that he has ruined the paper by his stiff-necked policy on free trade and his highbrowism.

Saturday 10 December   On Wednesday I had lunch with Will Warman[87] at his place in Chelsea and saw the baby – Ann Verity, a charming little eight-weeks old creature. [...] Will told me that he was responsible for the Meat Quota report on which the Ottawa agreements are based. He thinks well of Walter Elliot. He also said that Ann Verity's godmother is the Princess Victoria,[88] and the old lady descends upon them to his embarrassment – since they have recently been maidless and the little house is by no means equipped for the maintenance of formal relationships.

Saturday 17 December   Last night Arthur Grey,[89] of the *YP*, died after an operation. He was a very good friend at the London office of the *YP* and was a good, honest English yeoman. In the Lobby of the House he looked far more like a German professor from fiction than an astute newspaper man. He was far from the conventional idea of a Doctor of Laws and a barrister. His taste in drink was for good sherry. His mind moved slowly but accurately and he was always filled with a nostalgia from the countryside which bred him.

---

[87] William H. Warman: civil servant, Ministry of Agriculture, later Ministry of Food; During European War reached rank of Major; Brooks provided two chapters for Warman's *The Soldier Colonists: A Plea for Group Organisation* (London: Chattos and Windus, 1918) with foreword by Lord Selborne; also author *Agricultural Co-operation in England & Wales* (London: Williams & Norgate, 1922).

[88] Princess Victoria Alexandra Olga Mary (1868–1935): sister of King; Princess of Great Britain.

[89] Arthur Grey (d. 1932): journalist, Lobby correspondent *Yorkshire Post*.

1933

Tuesday 3 January   To the Whitefriars for luncheon; a good muster. Cecil Harmsworth,[1] owner of Johnson's house where we meet, was there, and I thus found myself in the odd situation of standing a sherry to Northcliffe's[2] brother. Cecil is rather a charming man, built on the Rhodes[3] model, with hogged moustache and a general savour of tweeds about him, very quiet in a solid way, and extremely courteous. He says that his son Desmond,[4] the publisher, is 'too highbrow'. 'Desmond seems to have a flair for this modern high-brow poetry, but I simply don't understand it.' We sat at one end of the table, with Jones and me at Harmsworth's left and Fyfe on his right. When Harmsworth had gone Fyfe told us that Northcliffe always said that Cecil was the only gentleman in the family. [...] At the office all was normal, but Hobson's nerves a bit on edge, due to the return to offensiveness of Brendan Bracken, I surmised.

Tuesday 10 January   arrived for lunch at 1–15 with Oliver Baldwin[5] with whom I sat and talked. We wondered that all reasonable people were not bilingual – their own cultured language and dialect of their native districts. He said that if Ramsay goes out of the Gvt for any cause his father[6] will go too.

---

[1] Cecil Bisshopp Harmsworth (1899–1948); Lib. MP Droitwich 1906–10, Luton 1911–22; PUS Home Office 1915; PM's Secretariat 1917–19; Acting Min. of Blockade 1919; PUS, FO 1919–22; cr. Baron Harmsworth 1939.

[2] Alfred Harmsworth (1865–1922): Newspaper Prop. inclu. *The Times*; cr.1st Viscount Northcliffe.

[3] Cecil John Rhodes (1853–1902): diamond miner; Head of Consolidated Goldfields, Witwatersrand; Cape House of Assembly 1881; Treasurer 1884; cr. British South Africa Company to establish British colony in Rhodesia 1889; Cape PM 1890–6.

[4] Desmond Bernard Harmsworth (1903–90): newspaper manager & artist; est. publishing company; painter 1930s living Paris & Tahiti, New York from 1940; suc. 2nd Lord Harmsworth 1948.

[5] Oliver Risdale Baldwin (1899–1958): s. of Stanley Baldwin; Lab MP Dudley 1929–31, Paisley 1945–7; Gov. & C in C. Leeward Islands, 1948–50; suc. 2nd Earl of Bewdley 1947.

[6] Stanley Baldwin (1897–1947): Con. MP Bewdley 1908–37; FST 1917–21; Pres. BofT. 1921–2; Chanc. of the Exchequer 1922–3; PM 1923, 1924–29; Ld. Pres. 1931–5; PM 1935–37; Con. Leader 1923–7; cr. Earl Baldwin of Bewdley 1937.

'Even if (said I) there is a camouflage National Gvt arranged under Simon?'[7]
'No – not then. I hadn't thought of that. But it's what Simon is working towards.'

I asked him how his autobiography *The Questing Beast*[8] had been received in the home circle. He said with neither praise nor blame – praise would have tended to make one grow self-important, and blame would have implied that the book was important as to deserve a judgement ... He said that as far as they know Stanley Baldwin is the only fair one (in colouring) of their stock. They are Salop people who went into Worcestershire in the 18th century, but they intermarried with Northumbrian stock some generations ago and acquired a touch of gypsy, which came out most markedly in Oliver's grandfather, who was dark, swarthy, and patriarchal.

Friday 13 January   What an ominous fall of date! Up and down by 9–30, and did some 2,250 words of economica[9] before lunch. At the office all as usual save that my dinner break was bedevilled by the Boots affair. Neville Chamberlain has issued the fiat against the transfer of so large a sum, but the Treasury has had to confess publicly to a change of mind during the negotiations. Montagu Norman[10] and Ernest Harvey[11] have outweighed the Treasury.

Friday 20 January   The office was much as usual, with ORH a bit on edge and Chaloner very busy with our new make-up for Feb. 5th. The news was the unexpected engagement of Montagu Norman, which was the cue for all kinds of bawdry. The collection of names aided the jests. His bride's first husband was called Wynandkoch Worsthorne and Norman himself lives at Much Haddam, Herts. The stock exchange opined that as he was 61 nothing would go up except the Bank Rate, and Jonk had a cartoon showing Norman glancing at a pretty leg just

[7] John Allsebrook Simon (1873–1954): Lib. MP Walthamstow 1906–18, Spen Valley 1922–40 (Lib. Nat. from 1931); Solicitor-Gen. 1910–13; Attorney-Gen. 1913–15; Home Sec. 1915–16, 1935–7; For. Sec. 1931–5; Chanc. of Exchequer 1937–40; Ld. Chanc. 1940–5; kt. 1910, cr. Viscount Simon 1940.
[8] Oliver Baldwin, *The Questing Beast: An Autobiography* (London: Grayson and Grayson, 1932).
[9] Manuscript for *The Economics of Human Happiness* (London: Routledge, 1933).
[10] Montagu Collet Norman (1871–1950): merchant banker 1894–1915; entered service of Bank of England 1915, Dep. Gov. 1918–20, Gov. 1920–44; cr. Baron 1944.
[11] Ernest Musgrave Harvey (1867–1955): joined Bank of England 1885, Comptroller 1925–8, Dep. Gov. 1929–36.

disappearing off the edge of the drawing with the legend 'Worship of the Golden Calf – Ban on new Issues Raised.'

Bracken, as usual, was witty to the point. 'Ah,' said he, 'in future he'll call himself Professor Foreskinner.' (A reminiscence of the voyage when Montagu Norman set two continents gossiping by his nom-de-voyage of Professor Skinner.[12])

I jot down these squibs as they seem to me to reflect the lack of respect with which the city treats its demigods.

Monday 23 January The country is in the grip of a 'flu epidemic and London is smitten by an unauthorised strike of busmen. The weather has turned wintry cold – not unpleasant. The morning was filled by economica. At the office things were very flat – no news of importance except the 'ballyhoo' surrounding Roosevelt's[13] offer to talk debts in March. America, incidentally, has at last changed her obsolete system of waiting until the following March after a November election for the inauguration of her new Congress. The long delay was due to the time it took in the days of Washington for the furthest flung congressman to make his way to the Capital. So strong has been tradition that this lag has been maintained all through the railway and motor eras. It played havoc with Lincoln in the sixties and has played havoc with all the economic world in 1932–33.

Friday 27 January I should be content with the variegation of life. Today *Mr Daddy-Detective*[14] was published. All morning I worked on the economics and psychology book. In the afternoon I took over the *Financial News* which kept me busy in quite a romantic and pleasant way till midnight. By the afternoon post came a letter suggesting that I should become London correspondent of *The Journal of Commerce of New York* and at home a letter awaited me from Howe[15] saying that they would like to 'do' Valentine[16] if I would consent to certain revisions suggested by their reader, whose report they enclosed. His suggestions were sound and penetrating and the general compliments in his report

[12] Prof. Clarence Skinner: American academic; famous for having had his cabin on board ship invaded by journalists wrongly assuming him to be Montagu Norman. Norman would travel in the name of his Private Secretary Ernest Skinner. As a consequence Norman nicknamed Clarence Skinner by 'Treasury' & City.

[13] Franklin Delano Roosevelt (1882–1945): Ass. Sec., US Navy 1913–20; Gov. of New York State 1929–33; Pres. of USA 1933–45.

[14] *Mr Daddy-Detective* (London: Hutchinson, 1933).

[15] Gerald Howe: publisher; produced early Barnaby Brook novels.

[16] Lead character in *Gay-Go-Up* (London: Gerald Howe, 1933).

quite pleased me. The maze of activity almost made me forget that I was in bodily pain all day – not serious but bad enough – through my wretched interior reminding me that there had once been a war and that enteritis was mine old familiar enemy.

Sunday 5 February At the Press the change-over worked relatively smoothly, although it was a worrying night. ORH – looked a drôle in a suit of stale-dung coloured 'plus fours' that was too big for him and grey stockings that concertinaed about his short legs – came in at about nine, rather ill tempered. We fretted about a sentence in Einzig[17] which ORH declared was not English and which I defended, but later achieved a reasonable harmony. The poor devil's nerves are on edge after 'flu and after the recent harassment by Bracken.

Monday 6 February The office was one long harassment – with post-mortems and adjustments on and to the new make-up, conferences, and the churning out of a long review of a book on Kreuger[18] in the middle of the chronic interruptions of the ordinary routines. ORH looked in at the Press after dinner and his presence, though pleasant, was a nuisance. A man should either take command for the whole of an action, or keep out of the way.

Saturday 18 February There was no time for a meal so I swallowed two eggs in milk and she and I ate sausage rolls in the taxi, and washed them down at the Theatre Bar. It was 'The Sherlock Holmes of Baker Street'[19] – Sherlock twenty-five years after his retirement with a daughter Shirley anxious to follow in his steps, against his bitter wishes. Sherlock is a saddened widower; his science of observation and deduction made the necessary small deceptions of married life impossible. The bees have taught him that the ideal civilisation does not compel its units to mix work and love – a woman should be either a queen and a mother or a neuter. From this gambit a very amusing play developed, with Nigel Playfair[20] superb as Doctor Watson. The critics haven't been too

[17] Paul Einzig (1897–1973): financial journalist; For. Ed. *Financial News* 1922–45.
[18] Ivar Kreuger (1880–1932): financier & 'match king'; Managing Dir. AB Kreuger & Toll 1908–13, Chm. 1930–2; ctted. suicide when Swedish Match Trust dropped value £180m to £45m. The book was Trevor Allen, *Ivar Kreuger, Match King, Croesus and Crook* (London: John Long, 1932).
[19] 'The Holmeses of Baker Street' by Basil Mitchell. Lyric Theatre from 15 February 1933 to 25 February 1933. Ran for 13 performances.
[20] Nigel Playfair (1874–1934): actor, manager & producer; kt. 1928.

kind to it, but we enjoyed every minute, and so, too, did Stanley Bruce,[21] who sat next to Lil, looking more like a common law K.C. than an ex-Premier of Australia.

Friday 3 March   At the office I found ORH angered by our treatment of the Transport Bill in the Lords – and after some talk I received my quietus.

> 'But why?' said I 'didn't you let me resign in October when I wished to?'
> 'Yes – you have that against me.'
> 'I don't hold it "against" you – but it makes me damned angry. I resign in protest against the conditions at the press and you won't accept the resignation and now those conditions are used to terminate my engagement ...'

He was full of personal explanations – It was Bracken – I said that I should want my full twelve months' notice or I would fight, and he said there would be no monkey business about this ... In my heart I was greatly relieved. The Argus has always been a strain and with the new make-up has been a nightly inferno. I should be able to find a new job between now and then, so to speak, and in any event I can make enough with a typewriter to keep the house in food.

Saturday 4 March   At the office by 10–45, a tangled morning. America declared two days general bank holiday and there were no dealings in foreign currency in London. At 2–30 Lil and Edward[22] picked me up at the office and I forgot world crises and my own crisis at the waxworks reaching home just in time to hear Roosevelt's inaugural over the broadcast. He came over very clearly and made a strong speech with a promise of dictatorship in it. Lil and I wound up the evening at the King's Theatre, where finding no stalls we had good seats in the Pit. The play was 'Springtime for Henry'[23] a poor play and the most

---

[21] Stanley Melbourne Bruce (1883–1967): Australian MP for Flindes 1918–29, 1931–3; PM & Min. for External Affairs 1923–9; Min. for Health 1927–8; Min. for Trade 1928; Min. for Territories 1928–9; Australian Min. in London 1932–3; High Comm. 1933–45; Commonwealth Rep., UK War Cabinet 1942–5; Chm. World Food Council 1947–51; Chanc., Australian National University, Canberra 1951–66; cr. 1st Viscount Bruce 1947.

[22] Edward 'Tich' Brooks (1928–): youngest s. of diarist; RAF; actor.

[23] *Springtime for Henry* by Benn W. Levy. Apollo Theatre, 8 November 1932–4 February 1933. Ran for 104 performances. Reviewed *The Times* 9 November 1932.

immoral thing I have ever seen but not unamusing, and Ronald Squire[24] and Isabel Jeans[25] quite good.

Sunday 9 April   When I was talking to Bracken [on Friday] at 4–30 about the *World's Press News*, on which Eyre and Spottiswode have a lien and which Martell's principal want to buy, he said that Leonard Reid[26] of *The Telegraph* wanted to talk to me with a view to my becoming his coadjutor on the *Telegraph*. I said that I wasn't keen on taking another staff job, certainly not as a subordinate, but would talk to Reid. Bracken then said he wanted to suggest me to Harmsworth as a city page man for *The Sunday Dispatch* and said he would give me a letter to Garvin[27] if I wished ... quite 'smarmy' – I thanked him and we parted.

Saturday 22 April   Yesterday I lunched at the Reform Club with Leonard Reid of the *Daily Telegraph*. With charming diffidence, almost apology, he offered me a job ... It seems that his second in command is hopeless in many directions – but cannot be sacked or demoted. Reid wants a good man to be a kind of ADC without claiming a title. He suggested that if I took on the job it would leave me time for my own work and that he and I might explore some other avenues together. But screw could not be more than £700. [...] When we were taxiing back to the City R. was describing his meeting with Roosevelt last autumn. Roosevelt had impressed him. In singing Roosevelt's praises he said:

> 'I hardly know how to give you an impression of him – very English – well, you sat there and wondered why the devil isn't this man wearing a 'Free Foresters' tie or something.'

I left Reid to talk with old Leopold Joseph[28] at his office for their next review. He was more flattering than I had expected about the last one. He and I despite his stone deafness are somehow 'friends' already. It is amazing to hear his intent commentary on world affairs – on

[24] Ronald Squire (1886–1958): actor.
[25] Isabel Jeans (1891–1985): actress.
[26] Leonard Reid (d. 1933): city editor, *Daily Telegraph* until death.
[27] James Louis Garvin (1868–1947): Ed. *The Observer*, 1908–42, Ed. *Pall Mall Gazette* 1912–5; official biographer of Joseph Chamberlain.
[28] Leopold Joseph: founder of small family bank established in 1920s, Leopold Joseph & Sons; produced in-house financial journal, *Joseph Review*. Family retained control of bank until 1960s.

Germany particularly – the Jewish persecutions – 'No one has smitten Israel and prospered!'

Hobson was back at the office, more affected than he showed by his father's death.

Monday 8 May   Michael[29] on Thursday [at Cafe Royal] was delightful and quite captivated Lil. It was his 77th birthday. He told us many stories in his quiet Irish way. One remains – Lloyd George[30] being introduced to an American audience by a flamboyant chairman was described in eulogistic terms. 'He has done for his great Empire what Joan of Arc did for France ...' said the chairman, when an Irish voice from the back of the hall cried with anticipatory relish 'When are we going to burn him?' Michael wanted help in placing book, and I passed him to Higham. In the middle of the evening Bracken burst into the press with a tribute to St. John Harmsworth[31] scrawled on a menu card. I mentioned to him that I had been approached by a Beaverbrook paper and he said 'Why, I recommended you to Beaverbrook himself this afternoon for the *Sunday Express*.'

'That is the paper,' said I.
'What figure did you name?'
'Two thousand.'
'I said fifteen hundred.'
'I can make fifteen hundred without turning a hair without any staff job – I'd need two thousand.'
'I'll tell him that.'

An odd business!

Friday 14 July   I am lunching at the Chinese Restaurant as the guest of some Chinese trade people. In the interstices of all this I have spoken to Admiral Usborne[32] about becoming Press secretary to the India

[29] Michael O'Mahony (b. 1863): journalist friend from Liverpool days; 'Father' of Liverpool Press Club in 1920s; author of *St Columba: A Biography* (Liverpool: Publishers & Advertisers, 1926).

[30] David Lloyd George (1863–1945): Lib. MP Caernarvon Boroughs 1890–1945; Pres. BofT. 1906–8; Chanc. of Exchequer 1908–15; Min. of Munitions 1915–16; Sec. for War 1916; Coalition PM 1916–22; cr. Earl Lloyd-George of Dwyfor 1945.

[31] William Albert St John Harmsworth (1876–1933).

[32] Rear Adm. Usborne (1880–1951): navy officer 1903 rtd. 1933; cr. Rear Adm. 1928; Dir. Naval Intelligence Div. 1930–2; Dir. of Censorship Div. of Press 1939–40; rejoined navy 1941–5; Special Service, Admiralty 1941–5; Chief Org. India Defence League.

Defence League, which I didn't want to do, so slipped from under on the plea that I couldn't join 'em immediately, and have today recommended Tower,[33] who seems keen. [...] (Later.). While I was hurrying with my work to get down to a lunch Bracken rang me up to say that he had told Harmsworth that I was the man wanted as financial editor of *The Sunday Dispatch* and would I get into touch with McWhirter[34] ... In the afternoon I rang McWhirter and am to see him at noon on Tuesday.

During the afternoon I said to Hobson, 'What is wrong with Bracken? This is the third job he has tried to put into my way?'

Hobson said, 'Well, I'm responsible – not for this specific job – but I told Bracken that he had damn well got to find something good.'

I thanked him, and said, 'With these three things of Bracken, and although I have taken no active steps, I have had six jobs offered to me in the last month or so. And the trouble is – ' (Hobson's face fell in sympathy) ' – the trouble is that it will end by my having to take one.'

'What, don't you want one?'

'What I really want is a good excuse for not taking one. My capacity, if I could do all the odd jobs that come my way, is about £1500 a year. American publishers ring me up to ask why I haven't sold my book to them instead of to others. I lack courage – I should tell people with staff jobs to go to hell. Of course the work won't be there when I really need it – but none the less ...'

It was a queer piece of Gasconading – and ORH looked quite crestfallen after his kind heartedness. Both he and Bracken, I gather, feel that they haven't given me a square deal – though I have no complaint.

Monday 17 July   Life would be very pleasant if it were not for the wretched staff job and the Press. To spend the days writing at my own typewriter things that interest me – it will never be possible, I suppose. My poor *Val Verity* hasn't suggested yet that she will make my fortune for me as a serious novelist. Most reviewers seem to have missed completely the 'figure in the carpet'. The notices are very mixed – but as much appreciation as condemnation. When I mentioned to Sam Goldie, apropos *The Star* notice, that opinion was so divided, he said, 'I must read it – that's the sign of a good and significant book.' Very flattering of him.

[33] John Tower: journalist, *Yorkshire Post*.
[34] William Allen McWhirter (1889–1955): Ed. *Daily Mail* 1930–1; Dir. Associated Newspapers 1930; associated with Rothermere from 1907; often referred to as Mac. by Brooks.

Wednesday 19 July   Yesterday was an interesting day. Having done the cable I went down and at noon met McWhirter and Lane,[35] the editor of the *Sunday Dispatch*. After a talk, in which – being in the fortunate position of having been sent for and not having sought them – I did most of the condition framing, we reached a draft agreement – the financial editorship not to rule me out of other work, the salary to be £1000 a year for this admittedly part-time job, a month's holiday a year on pay, an agreement for 3 years etc etc. This was to be submitted to Esmond Harmsworth, but McWhirter thought it would go through. My alternative was a whole time job at £2000. I launched the bombshell that *The Sunday Express* had approached me at the opening of the talk, which helped a lot ... But I don't believe the thing will go through. It is too good to be true. [...] This morning I rang up McWhirter to ask him if the agreement was going through. He said he'd phone me later today. This I did because I had promised LPT to let him know so that he and I can boost Einzig for the *Express* job. Beyond this – no news.

Thursday 10 August   On Tuesday evening Grigson rang me up saying he would like to talk with me. I met him at the club at midnight. He had had a terribly vicious row with Arthur Mann. Having 'landed' the job of acting-literary editor of *The Morning Post* he had asked Arthur to release him on September 1st instead of October 2nd. A.H.M. had been rather 'snotty' about it and when Grigson pressed for an immediate yes or no turned on him and abused him roundly. Grigson then lost his own boyish temper and gave home-truth for home-truth. Arthur's dignified epithets included 'you bloody little shit – what school were you at to behave like this!' which naturally made Grigson splutter. At the end of the row A.H.M. lost all control and shouted 'I'll do my best to spoil your career' and rang up Gwynne[36] of *The Morning Post* apparently to stop the job. And Gwynne was away for many days! The whole thing was primitive and nauseating – Mann's vindictiveness being a revelation of some internal rottenness. Grigson has been with the paper five years and in charge of the letter for nearly two of them – and was A.H.M.'s pet for half a year. I suppose no editor of a paper in the whole of political journalism ever made so many enemies of younger men who began by worshipping him – Grigson, Hugh Williamson, Holt[37] (of the BBC), Francis Watson, Tower, Davy, Jobson,

[35] Harry George Lane (1881–1957): Ed., *Daily Sketch* 1919–28, Ed. *Sunday Dispatch* , 1933–4; Ed.-in-chief Northcliffe Newspapers Ltd 1928–32; Dir. Hull & Grimsby Newspapers Ltd 1930–46.

[36] Howell Arthur Gwynne (1865–1950): Ed. *Morning Post* 1911–37.

[37] Edgar C. Holt: journalist *Yorkshire Post* 1920s; Head of BBC News 1933; Dep. Ed. BBC World Radio 1934; Dep. Ed. *Listener* 1936.

Buller – a long list of 'em. It is just five years ago since I had my breach with him – but mine was a gentlemanly affair compared with Grigson's out-and-out slanging match.

Friday 25 August   On Wednesday at noon I presented myself at Carmelite House and saw both McWhirter and Lane – we hammered out an agreement – short term only – £1000 a year – permission to write books, to write for America, and to write anything in England not on finance and not for a competing paper with the group. We crossed to see Sir George Sutton,[38] for what was apparently a formal vetting. He and I talked for about five or ten minutes – I very much at home with him [...] So I join them on the 1st Oct. – although, incidentally, the letter of appointment hasn't yet reached me.

Friday 15 September   On Tuesday I managed to reach the [White]Friars a little late. Grigson had as his guests Stephen Spender[39] and another poet, whose name I did not catch. Spender is a charming personality – tousled hair, big of nose, with eager but shy eyes. I was so busy talking to Jones[40] that I had little speech with Spender. J told me that one of the rules of his office is that on no account must papers be left out of desks at night. Hankey[41] is in the habit of taking an occasional prowl round the place to see that all is orderly. They are housed in Whitehall Gardens and the rooms have old fashioned grates. Recently Maurice Hankey strolling round saw that a char had used a piece of paper as a grate screen and that the paper was not blank. He extracted it from the fire bars and found it to be a sheet from THE most secret of documents which had just been issued to THE most secret of committees. J says that all the tributes to Hankey's brilliance leave much to be said. Not only is he able, but he maintains his power. At Cabinet committees it is the habit for the Chairman to canvas Hankey's view in a whisper and then to re-enunciate it as a Chairman's fiat.

---

[38] George Augustus Sutton (1869–1947): Man. Dir Associated Newspapers, Vice-Chm. 1934–7; nicknamed by staff 'Satan'; kt. 1920.

[39] Stephen Spender (1909–95): poet & critic.

[40] Capt. Henry Albert Jones (d. 1945): served RAF & Army; Historical Section, CID 1918; Dir. Air Branch CID; official air historian 1922; seconded to Cabinet Office from Ministry of Labour 1930s; Air Staff Secretariat 1939; Dir. Public Relations Air Min. 1944–5.

[41] Maurice Pascal Alers Hankey (1877–1963): Sec. to the Cabinet 1916–38; Sec. CID 1912–38; Min. without Portfolio in the War Cabinet 1939–40; Chanc. of Duchy of Lancaster 1940–1; Paymaster Gen. 1941–2; cr. 1st Baron Hankey 1939.

Tuesday 19 September   Did the American cable[42] and went down to lunch with the White Friars at the Cafe Royal – a good muster – Hugh Williamson, Geoffrey Grigson, Hamilton Fyfe, Jones, young Lane[43] of the Bodley Head, and two or three others including Oliver Baldwin. We spotted at a neighbouring table Kerensky,[44] lunching a woman. After some talk on the 'nicety' of the matter, we sent Oliver Baldwin over to greet him, and invite him to dine some Thursday in Dr Johnson's garret, to which he responded graciously. We met him again in the hall, and to our salutes he responded as with gratification. It was like casually meeting Robespierre – not that the futile, legal Kerensky is by any means a Robespierre – this encounter with a man whose name once shook the world, is still potent. I had only met him once before, at a Benn lunch.[45]

Thursday 21 September   I had an early lunch and went down to see my new chief, Lane of *The Dispatch*. Apparently my appointment was made by Harmsworth over Meredith's[46] head, and Meredith was naturally sore. However, he has since seen Rothermere and secured a new contract as City Editor for the Group – and Lane and he and I will lunch together on Tuesday at the Savoy to ease all possible friction ... I talked over the general scope of my new job – which is obviously to be much wider than the city page, and met young Brittain,[47] the assistant-editor.

Sunday 8 October   I never remember feeling so professionally depressed as yesterday. *The Dispatch* page was a series of wrangles about space and make-up fiascos   and the result a mere absurdity. After taking on a man at a high figure and allowing him to run round all week, to confine him to about a net column and a half and that filled by big

[42] Covered topics: survey, oil from coal, 'hands wanted', tea and towels.

[43] Allen Lane (1902–1970): publisher; born Allen Lane Williams, changed name by deed poll; joined Bodley Head 1919, Dir. 1925–30, Chm. 1930–6; 1935 launched Penguin Books.

[44] Alexander Kerensky (1881–1970): Menshevik Leader of Russian Provisional Govt. 1917.

[45] This is a reference to C.B.'s first post-war employer, Benn Brothers, when he was employed on a commision-only basis selling advertising space before being offered a slot by Ernest Benn on the *Hardware Trade Journal*.

[46] Hubert A. Meredith (1884–1965): Anglo-International Bank 1924–9; City Ed. *Saturday Review*, 1924–31; City Ed. *Daily Mail* Group, 1931– ; Wing-Cmd. World War Two.

[47] William James Brittain (1905–77): journalist, Ass. Ed. *Sunday Express;* Ass.-Ed. & Ed. of *Sunday Dispatch*, 1934–6, Ed. of *Cavalcade*; Dir. *Time & Tide*; Chm. Brittain Publishing Co.

heads and leaded type is really the height of folly. Either, I imagine, Rothermere will turf me out or I will walk out.

Tuesday 31 October   It is ten days or so since I touched this diary. The effect of my new job is to break my time – and to tempt me to shake a loose leg as a social figure ... I know of nothing very exciting since I last wrote here. Saturday night was a jolly affair. As chairman of the dinner I had a kind of little triumph, but the real joy was meeting Helen Waddell.[48] She is a little, dancing-eyed Irish woman, with a taste in wines that probably comes from her friendship with George Saintsbury,[49] with whom she corresponded intimately for years. 'I met him first when I was young, and positively vamped him', she told me in her brogue – a funny brogue for an Ulster woman.

Sunday 5 November   At the end of the Friday conference, Lane, the editor, leaned back in chair and told us that he had been with the paper a year and that this was his last day – that he was parting with the company with no ill will – meant to cultivate philosophy as the directors had made that possible – and generally staggered everybody. Falk[50] had the paper for fifteen years – Bill Taylor had it for about two years – the next man for three weeks – and Lane for a year. Young Brittain takes the job under the supervision of McWhirter, who came in on Satdy and was very decent to me, saying that everybody had been pleased with my stuff. I groused at the farce of not having enough space and arranged to talk with him on Tuesday.

Saturday 11 November   On Tuesday at 2–30 Ivor Nicholson,[51] Watson[52] and I saw little Mr Barratt[53] the shoe king. Pathetic and likeable man.

---

[48] Helen Jane Waddell (1889–1965): medieval scholar, translator, and literary critic – MA dissertation on Milton examined by Prof. Saintsbury, Edinburgh University.

[49] Prof. George Edward Bateman Saintsbury (1845–1933): literary critic, academic & historian. The Saintsbury Dining Club founded in memory.

[50] Bernard Falk (1882–1960): News Ed., *Evening News*; Ed. *Sunday Dispatch* 1918–31; special *Daily Mail* correspondent & writer 1931–2; author N.B. D. Butler & G. Butler *British Political Facts 1900–1994* (London: Macmillan, 1996) p. 494 incorrectly list the editors since 1919 as 1919 B. Falk, 1930 W. McWhirter, 1933 H. Lane, 1934 W. Brittain, 1936 C.B.

[51] Ivor (Percy) Nicholson (d. 1937): Chm. Ivor Nicholson & Watson publishers 1931–7.

[52] Robert Norman Watson: Brooks' 'oldest friend' known from school days & 'Uncle' to children; resident of Southport, and shopkeeper with store in Lord Street, Southport.

[53] Arthur William Barratt (1877–1939): Shoe manufacturer & retailer; Lab. cand. Bethnal Green NE 1931.

In 1918 he had one little bootshop. Now he has eighteen. Says he misses the education he didn't get – he left school at 12 years of age – and so doesn't like writing a letter or making a speech. He is still a Socialist, and at the last general election fought a seat. Ramsay and Philip Snowden[54] got hold of him and persuaded him into the desperate deed –

'It cost me a thousand pounds – on the day of the poll I said "Mother, we're going to poll every possible vote, but I hope we don't win." And I was relieved when we didn't,' said he.

He is making desperate efforts not to let his money cut him adrift from his old pals – lives relatively simply – but finds the gulf naturally widens. [...]

Today I emerged from Mansion House station just in time to take part in the Great Silence at the Royal Exchange – an impressive sight – the packed mass of people thronging the Threadneedle Street and the plateau and up Cornhill – with the heart stirring bugles trailing the Last Post off into the silence that was a real silence but for the noise of the wheeling pigeons. Attempting to escape along the Bank Station subway I found myself with some others looking through a grille at the troops by the war memorial as the Lord's Prayer was said and *Oh, God, our help in ages past* was sung.

Sunday 31 December   I am in *Who's Who*, which would have sounded magnificent to the little boy who used to read that tome in a free library and envy the great therein.

[54] Philip Snowden (1864–1937). Lab. M.P. Blackburn, 1906–18, Colne Valley, 1922–31. Chan. of Exch., 1924, 1929–31. Ld. Privy Seal, 1931–2. cr. Viscount Snowdon 1931.

1934

Monday 15 January   I was amazed today on opening *The Mail* to find that Rothermere has gone Fascist. I hope this doesn't mean trouble, for I shan't truckle to the devil, and I am too much of a democrat to be a Fascist, though too much of a disciplinarian to be a democrat in any but the vague Walt Whitman[1] sense.

Thursday 25 January   On the 16th Jan the children were at John Simon's house for a party. I collected them on a dank wet night and J.S. was himself on his doorstep, looking dangerously like his own butler. We exchanged words and I took my bairns home. On the way I said to a sleepy Edward

> 'Well, how did you like the Foreign Secretary?'
> 'Which was the foreign secretary?'
> 'The bald headed gentleman.'
> 'Oh, I didn't notice the bald headed gentleman, but I liked Felix the cat that the conjuror brought.'

Tuesday 6 February   How tired one is and how little inclined to enter anything into a diary .... on Friday I actually took possession of a room of my own at Northcliffe House – On Saturday I thought I should have to vacate Northcliffe House altogether. Having done my city page, I found I could not get the big 'story' that Brittain wanted – 'who has made fortunes over gold shares?' But I did *a* story. By 6–45 I was at the *Financial News* Jubilee dinner. It was an odd gathering – 140 of us from all departments, with Bracken in the chair and a most devilishly strained atmosphere, because most knew that Hobson and Chaloner and Thompson were all leaving the ship. Bracken asked me to join him and Maurice Green[2] at Quaglino's at 10–30, and I promised I would do so – and at 10–20 a messenger came post-haste for me to say that *The Sunday Express*[3] had the very story I hadn't been able to

---

[1] Walt Whitman (1819–92): American poet.
[2] Maurice Green (1906–87): Ed. *Financial News* 1934–8; City Ed. *The Times* 1938–40, 1944–53, Ass. Ed. 1953–61, Dep. Ed. 1961–4; Ed. *Daily Telegraph* 1964–74.
[3] The journalist who scooped Brooks was C.W. Alexander, city editor, *The Express*.

get – a damned good scoop. I phoned Brittain – chased Bracken to Quaglino's to pick up some facts from him, and he hadn't arrived. I waited – and he came, and I had barely told him I couldn't drink his stoup of liquor but wanted him to tell me if it were true that John Bailey[4] and Latilla[5] had mopped up £5,000,000 in three days when Lord Portarlington[6] and a woman came along – which meant introductions and wasted time. But I shot away – taxied furiously to the Press and turned out a front page article that saved our faces ...

Tuesday 13 February   through the post to-night came, all uninvited, an envelope of catalogues for somebody's contraceptives, in a brochure called *The Shadow of the Stork*. Oddly enough, as I went upstairs to consult an encyclopaedia the broadcast news coming over was of the debate in the Lords on a Bill[7] introduced by Dawson of Penn[8] to control the advertising and sale of contraceptives. His motive was sound, that birth control has come to stay and should be conducted decently and not as a murky under-ground kind of trade. Banbury[9] – stout fellow – objected to the Bill as an interference with the liberty of the subject, saying that anyone who wishes has a right to have information about contraceptives, whether under eighteen or not. Dawson incidentally made the point that nobody today can advocate the big families of the Victorian era and yet nobody – on grounds of health and social policy – could preach celibacy within the married state. [...] Today has been an odd kind of wasted run of hours, but not unpleasant. I was down by about 9–30, having been astir since eight, and did the cable before leaving for the office which I reached at noon. After doing some letters, Brittain burst in to my room, and we discussed news ideas for next Sunday's issue. (Riots in Austria, with the guns out, and riots in France dominate everything this week.)

[4] John Milner Bailey (1900–46): Churchill's son-in-law, s. of Sir Abe Bailey.

[5] Herbert George Latilla: Company Dir. & Chm. of various gold & mining companies, including Henderson Transvaal Estates & Rhodesia Chrome & Asbesto Co. both of which had John Bailey as a Dir.

[6] Lionel Arthur Henry Seymour Dawson-Damer (1883–1939): suc. 6th Earl Portarlington 1900.

[7] *Parliamentary Debates: 5th Series: House of Lords* vol. 90 cols. 804–818 13 February 1934.

[8] Bertrand Dawson (1864–1945): Physician in Extraordinary to Edward VII 1907–10, to George V from 1907–36, Edward, Prince of Wales 1923–37; Also served successive Prime Ministers; Pres., Royal College of Physicians 1931; cr. Baron Dawson of Penn 1920.

[9] Frederick George Banbury (1850–1936): Con. M.P. Peckham 1892–1906, City of London 1906–24; Chm. Great Northern Railways; kt. 1902, cr. 1st Baron 1924.

Sunday 22 April   In the afternoon [of Tuesday 17th] Meredith had a Budget teaparty in the city office – a collection of representative jobbers and others from the various markets. The whole concentration of mind was on the possibility of 6d off the income tax, which duly came. My cold, dispassionate view is that men who make their livings by share-shuffling and money spinning are the most unlikeable of all human types except, perhaps, the ponce who lives on the harlotry of women for whom he has no affection.

Sunday 6 May   [Thursday] evening I attended the annual meeting of the Compatriots, in Committee Room 13 at the House, and at the dinner found myself next to Sir Michael O'Dwyer,[10] with whom I struck up a friendship. He is tall and has close cropped white hair and the long upper-lip of the Irishman. His charm is his modesty and his wisdom. We talked first about Germany (he has a son in the Berlin consulate) and Poland. Speaking as a Catholic he foresees trouble between the Lutherans and the Faith in Germany and thinks Hitler[11] may not be able to conciliate both. We spoke about Curzon[12] and Montagu.[13] Montagu was a pure oriental – feminine and brittle, vain and a little treacherous, but with a good mind. He virtually tricked Chelmsford[14] over the Chelmsford reforms. Curzon was without doubt one of the greatest administrators who ever ruled India, said Sir Michael, which compensated for his many faults. Apart from this dinner table talk, Henry Page Croft[15] was there making an oration about the distribution of white population in the Empire. He said nothing that was new, and afterwards was politely attacked as a hot-air merchant

[10] Michael Francis O'Dwyer (1864–1940): Indian civil servant from 1885; Revenue Comm. NW Frontier 1901–8; Acting Pres. Hyderabad 1908–9; Viceroy's Agent, Central India 1910–12; Lieut.-Gov. Punjab 1913–19; author *India as I Knew It* (1925); kt. 1913; assassinated by Indian Nationalist.

[11] Adolf Hitler (1889–1945): Leader of the National Socialist Workers Party 1921–45; Chanc. of Germany 1933–45; Head of State 1934–45.

[12] George Nathaniel Curzon (1859–1925): Con. MP Southport 1886–98; Viceroy of India 1898–1905; Ld. Privy Seal 1915–16; Ld. Pres. 1916–19, 1924–5; For. Sec. 1919–24; Con. Leader in the HofL. 1916–24; cr. Baron Curzon 1898, Earl 1911, Marquess 1921.

[13] Edwin Montague (1879–1924): Sec. of State for India 1917–22; responsible for the Govt. of India Act 1919.

[14] Frederick John Napier Thesiger (1868–1933): Viceroy of India 1916–21; 1st Ld. of Admiralty 1924; cr. 1st Viscount Chelmsford 1921.

[15] Henry Page Croft (1881–1947): Con. MP Christchurch 1910–18, Bournemouth 1918–40; US WO 1940–5; a leading protectionist, Chm., Organisation Ctte., Tariff Reform League 1913–7, Chm., E.I.A. Exec. Ctte. 1928–45; a leading 'Die-Hard' & Principal Organiser of the National Party, a breakaway right-wing faction, 1917–22; kt. 1924, cr. Baron Croft 1940.

by a very striking man, Sir Hal Colebatch,[16] Agent General for Western Australia. He looked strikingly like Disraeli's Lord Stanley[17] – big, round faced, beetling but lightly-marked brows, tight mouth in a heavy round jowl. His ears were like an elephant's ears, so that one suspected that a remote ancestor has been a transported bruiser. But he spoke pleasantly and with a blast of good sense. His main point was that organised migration was doubly wrong. If you so arranged general policy that any portion of the Empire had promise of prosperity, people would go there without being sent. If you carried people by State action they learnt to lean on the State. Difficulties that were taken with a shrug and a laugh by normal migrants became charges of ill faith against the authorities in the minds of organised migrants. Young Lindsay[18] followed with the remark that a viable media was needed – that group settlement was now a vital need, but within the framework of organisation there should be the maximum of individualism. This squared with the gospel that Warman and I preached to the desert air in 1918 in *Soldier Colonists* and thus pleased me. Amery[19] was good, and much more reasonable than one would have anticipated.

Sunday 10 June   C.B. to Norman Watson
After a busy day [on Thursday] – I made one of a party for the Mosley[20] meeting. Brittain and I were held up at the office so we had to send to the canteen for poached eggs which we bolted quickly before dashing to meet the others of our contingent. We set off merrily enough from Blackfriars station – 'the Hon.' (office name for Honourable J. Bingham,[21] our tame humourist and reporter), Tompkins and Mrs Tompkins, Brittain and Mrs Brittain and me. Average age of party excluding me about twenty-eight. Seeing a mob on Earls Court station we took a taxi to Olympia – amazing – only one door of Olympia being used instead of the usual dozen and everybody massed into a

[16] Hal Patershall Colebatch (1872–1953): Agent-Gen. W. Australia 1923–7, 1933–9; kt. 1927.
[17] Edward Henry Stanley (1826–93): Tory politician.
[18] Kenneth Lindsay (1897–1991): MP Kilmarnock Burghs 1933–45 (Nat. Lab. 1933–43, Ind. Nat. 1943–5); Ind. MP Combined Universities 1945–50; Pres. Oxford Union 1922–3; Civil Ld. of Admiralty 1935–7; PS Bd of Educ. 1937–40.
[19] Leopold Charles Maurice Stennett Amery (1873–1955): Con. MP Birmingham S. (later Sparkbrook), 1911–45; US Colonies 1919–21; FS Admiralty 1921–2; 1st Ld. of Admiralty 1922–4; Colonial Sec. 1924–9 (& Dominions 1925–9); India Sec. 1940–5.
[20] Oswald Ernald 'Tom' Mosley (1896–1980): MP Harrow 1918–24 (Con. to 1920, Ind. 1920–4, Lab. from 1924), Smethwick 1926–31 (Lab. to 1931, then New Party); Chanc. Duchy of Lancaster, 1929–30; Leader of New Party 1931–2, of British Union of Fascists 1932–40, of Union Movement 1948–66; interned 1940–4; suc. 6th Bart. 1928.
[21] Hon. John Michael Ward Bingham, 7th Baron (Ireland) Clanmorris (1908–88): novelist, reporter, & columnist *Sunday Dispatch*.

narrow street – a veritable scrum – no breathing room – women being squashed – and in the centre some mounted police – and at the other side of the mounted police a Communist demonstration – thus making the narrow street still narrower. Rate of progress – an inch in an quarter of an hour. (Item – while slowly surging with the dense mob past the corner of the Communist catcallers I heard a very black nigger unexpectedly equipped with a bowler hat turn suddenly to his nearest pal and snarl

'Yass – but done you say nathing 'gainst religion – I can look after myself – I'm a Commune-ist ... but done you say nathing 'gainst religion.')

At last, one bath of sweat, we got in – and then the stewards couldn't tell us where our seats were. Organisation! said we, all bitter-like. At last we found 'em, and by the grace of God were in a box-like place where we could cool down. After some forty minutes delay the place had filled up. The advertised time of the great oration was 8 o'c. At 8–45 the search lights were directed to the far end, the Blackshirts lined the centre corridor – and trumpets brayed as a great mass of Union Jacks surmounted by Roman plates passed towards the platform. Everybody thought this was Mosley and stood and cheered and saluted. Only it wasn't Mosley. He came some few minutes later at the head of his chiefs of staff. In consequence the second greeting was an anti-climax. He mounted to the high platform and gave the salute – a figure so high and so remote in that huge place that he looked like a doll from Marks and Spencers penny bazaar. He then began – and alas the loud speakers hadn't been properly tuned in and every word was mangled. Not that it mattered – for then began the Roman circus. The first interrupter raised his voice to shout some interjection. The mob of storm troops hurled itself at him. He was battered and biffed and bashed and dragged out – while the tentative sympathisers all about him, many of whom were rolled down and trodden on, grew sick and began to think of escape. From that moment it was a shambles. Free fights all over the show. The Fascists technique is really the most brutal thing I have ever seen, which is saying something. There is no pause to hear what the interrupter is saying: there is no tap on the shoulder and a request to leave quietly: there is only the mass assault. Once a man's arms are pinioned his face is common property to all adjacent punchers. As you know, the culmination was the cinema episode of a man in the high beams chased by six fascists.

Tompkins, an ex-airman, who sat next to me said quietly, 'If he falls, it will take him four and a half seconds to reach the ground from that height ....'

The audience below were cleared from their seats and the scrabblers in the roof – looking like performing monkeys – disappeared in the side shadows. Breaking of glass off-stage added to the trepidation of the old ladies and parsons in the audience who had come to support the patriots. More free fights – more bashing and lashing and kickings – and a steady withdrawal of the ordinary audience. We left at about 10–30, with Mosley still speaking and the loud speakers still preventing our hearing a word he said, and by that time the place was half empty. Outside, of course, were the 1,000 police expecting more trouble, but I didn't wait to see the aftermath. One of our party had gone there very sympathetic to the fascists and very anti-Red. As we parted he said 'My god, if it's to be a choice between the Reds and these toughs, I'm all for the Reds.'

Personally, I was rather interested because I have never believed a big meeting can be controlled without a chairman and I have never believed that you can hold a meeting unless you give your hecklers some rope before you resort to force ejectment. Olympia seemed to me to confirm these things. It was also interesting to find Mosley beginning cock-a-whoop when an interrupter was battered out (thrown out is a misnomer) and growing apologetic as the psychological tone of the audience changed into disgust and personal fear, no man or woman knowing when he or she might not either be borne down in a wild mêlée or be mistaken for an interrupter. Whatever the Press may say (incidentally *The News Chronicle* and *The Telegraph* were exceedingly good in their descriptives) the whole thing was a fiasco and has probably done more to rally opinion to the National Government than anything since 1931. As far as the 6,000 or 10,000 eye witnesses were concerned the personal appeal of Fascism has been drowned by such a display of un-English (sic) methods – thirty to one, perhaps, but even so one to hold and twenty-nine to bash is a bit thick, particularly if the bashee is already on the floor. However ... it was quite a memorable experience.

Monday 11 June The brutality of the Fascist stewards after filling the press has been the occasion of some pretty serious question and answer in Parliament today. Rothermere (who is quite certainly a maniac of a mild brand) filled *The Sunday Dispatch* with justifications for the Fascists – justifications which missed the whole point. The point of the matter surely is that to answer Communist brutality by Fascist brutality in the middle of an orderly audience of peaceful citizens is to undermine the whole theory of the modern state – and this the Government seems to have realised. While I am talking of the State, I noticed with interest that Snowden now announces his return to politics.

Sunday 24 June   I am still in a rather depressed mood. Journalism in the Rothermere group is farcical – a purposeless buffooning.

Sunday 1 July [Last Wednesday]   We were all three [Axel Kopp[22] and Lil] bound for Prince George's[23] garden party[24] at St. James's Palace – and in the midst of the drought had come a sinister cloudy day. Before our taxi had landed us at the Palace the heavens had opened. Imagine it – the narrow but pretty garden of the Palace flanked by a long marquee in which wet and miserable people huddled while the lawn and its round tables and the bandsmen grew more and more soaked. Hawkey took us over to a room in the Palace where there was a buffet and an awning – but this, too, gradually filled up. (To make matters worse my treacherous gut was giving me hell.) The Prince eventually came, moved about, smiled, and went. And we went too. [...] As the rain had washed us out, Lil and I took taxi home, where I had some tea and to change from my morning coat and topper into a more easy dark grey lounge suit and dash back to the House of Commons for a Compatriots' dinner. The First Lord (Sir Bolton Eyres-Monsoll[25]) was the guest, and having cleared the waiters out of the room he let go very frankly about Japan. He said that whatever their opponents might say, battleships were essential to the Empire. To replace battleships by cruisers would mean an enormous number of cruisers, and whereas our cruiser strength would of necessity be dissipated along our line of communication, the enemy could move his in mass. The one nation against which no plans are ever prepared is the USA – and if it was only a question of what USA and Gt. Britain should build, there would be no need for pacts. But America cannot build without affecting Japan, and Japan is in a very truculent mood against us. The Singapore base, we might depend upon it, was being hurried on. These were the main points of a very impressive unburdening to a confidential gathering of perhaps thirty or forty of us. He was followed, as usual, by asses who couldn't keep up to his level of seriousness – including General Byron[26] who went off at a tangent, but interestingly enough, about

[22] Axel Kopp: Dir. of Amalgamated Dental Co. Ltd.

[23] Prince George (1895–1952): Duke of York 1920–36; King George VI 1936–52.

[24] University College Hospital Centenary Garden Party; Prince George was president of the hospital.

[25] Bolton Meredith Eyres-Monsoll (1881–1969): Con. MP for Evesham 1910–35; Whip 1911–21; Civil Ld. Admiralty 1921–2; F.S. Admiralty 1922–3; Chief Whip 1923–31; 1st Ld. of Admiralty 1931–6; kt. 1929, cr. Viscount Monsell 1935.

[26] Gen. John Byron (1872–1944): Royal Artillery from 1892, service South Africa & European War, Lieut.-Col. 1915; Ass. Supervisor Royal Arsenal 1914–15; Min. of Munitions 1915–16; Dep. Dir. of Artillery, WO 1916–18; Commanded RA, Palestine, 1920–4; rtd. Brig.-Gen. 1925.

South Africa and the change of tone there – the new Imperial loyalty being attributable to Smuts[27] and the Status Bill and the realisation that if, as the First Lord had said, Japan were triumphant she would uncover South Africa no less than Australia and the Indies. By some mishap I found myself next but one to the chairman with Morrison,[28] member for the Tewkesbury division, between us and Geoffrey Peto[29] opposite. The House was excited, said M, over the betting bill. Peto said he had been trying to catch the Speaker's eye and had failed but someone else had made all his points but one.

'I don't believe,' he said 'that if a man or a woman goes to the dogs or the races they are necessarily going to ruin themselves ...'

'Did anyone make the elementary point,' I asked 'that a man has the right to ruin himself if he feels like it?'

'Good heavens, we never admit that nowadays!' cried Peto in mock horror.

Morrison says that despite cinemas, broadcasting and slick transport, there are still two distinct races in England – the rural and the urban – and that statesmen fail in not realising this. The dinner was very pleasant and stimulating, with its flattering effect of making one feel very much behind the scenes and in the know.

[...] Saturday was full of excitement – there was revolt in Germany – a strong attack by Hitler on his Steel Helmet malcontents. Such a day is interesting in a newspaper office even to a jaded old hand. I like the business of men being suddenly sent off in planes across half a continent – the telephone talks with Berlin and Rome – the attempt to keep pace with a running news story ... I left 'em hard at it at about 6–30 and went on to the Savage Club where the Australian Test team was being entertained at the Midsummer revel. The queerly assorted crush in the North West Room – a medley of men, with A.P. Herbert[30] and Mark Hambourg[31] in the thick of the mêlée – the jovial dinner – the concert afterwards with its retained bohemianism ... at one stage

[27] Jan Christian Smuts (1870–1950): Min. of Defence, Union of S. Africa 1910–19, PM 1919–24, 1939–48, Dep. PM 1933–9; S. African delegate to Imperial Conference 1917, member of Imperial War Cabinet 1917–19.

[28] William Shepherd ('Shakes' or 'Shakespeare') Morrison (1893–1961): Con. MP Cirencester & Tewkesbury 1929–59; Chm., '1922' Ctte. 1932–5; FST 1935–6; Min. of Agric, 1936–9; Chanc. Duchy of Lancaster 1939–40; Min. of Food 1939–40; Postmaster-Gen. 1940–2; Min. of Town & Country Planning 1942–5; Speaker 1951–9; Governor-Gen. of Australia 1960–2; cr. Viscount Dunrossil 1959.

[29] Geoffrey Kelsall Peto (1878–1956): Con. MP Frome 1924–9, Wolverhampton Bilston 1931–5; PPS to G. Lane-Fox 1926–8, to Earl Winterton 1928–9, to W. Runciman 1931; Regional Controller for S. England, Min. of Supply 1941–5.

[30] Alan Patrick Herbert (1890–1971): journalist with *Punch* from 1924; MP (Ind) Oxford University, 1935–50; kt. 1945.

[31] Mark Hambourg (1879–1960): Russian-born concert pianist.

there was a match between some of the Australians and some of the English sporting journalists – the pitch the centre table, laboriously 'rolled' with a wine bottle – the implements of a small boy's cricket set with stumps and a bat about a foot long and a ball of cotton wool – quite ridiculously puerile and ridiculously funny.

Sunday 22 July   On Thursday [19 July] [...] I was lunched as a guest by Holdsworth[32] at a Lobby dinner (held at the Victoria) to George Lansbury.[33] It was, I think, the most remarkable gathering I have ever attended. Some of the guests 'star scattered on the grass' – that is, not even honoured with a place at the high table – were Walter Elliot, Hore-Belisha, Ernest Brown, the Minister for Mines,[34] Arthur Greenwood, the Lord Chancellor, Sankey[35] and a round dozen others of their calibre. At the high table were Stanley Baldwin, Herbert Samuel and a score of others. The journalistic turn-up was, of course, strong. I sat between young Greenwood[36] (Arthur's son, who is going to the Bar, a pleasant lad) and Pritt,[37] K.C., with whom I had some talk on the Kylsant case. The big hall was laid out in small round tables, and was full. The chairman (Robertson,[38] I think was his name – the current President of the Lobby) read his speech but it was witty and good. Lansbury was his simple, sincere, delightful self. He made great play with the fact that we met at a function where everybody was under pledge not to report anything said, not even after the lapse of what might be considered 'a discrete [*sic*] interval'. He derided the superstition of Cabinet secrets – had, he felt sure, told many simply because he hadn't realised that they were secrets. He recalled one day when Ramsay in

[32] Jack Holdsworth: journalist, London letter editor, *Yorkshire Post.*

[33] George Lansbury (1854–1940): Lab. MP Bow & Bromley 1910–12, Poplar 1922–40; 1st Comm. Works 1929–31; Lab. Leader 1931–5.

[34] (Alfred) Ernest Brown (1881–1962): Lib. MP Rugby 1923–4, Leith 1927–45 (Lib. Nat. from 1931); PS Health 1931–2; Sec. for Mines 1932–5; Min. of Lab. 1935–40; Scottish Sec. 1940–1; Min. of Health 1941–3; Chanc. Duchy of Lancaster 1943–5; Min. of Aircraft Production 1945.

[35] John Sankey (1886–1948): judge of King's Bench Div. 1914–28; Ld. Justice of Appeal 1928–9; Ld. Chanc. 1929–35; Chm., Royal Commission on the Coal Industry 1919; kt. 1914, cr. Baron Sankey 1929, Viscount 1932.

[36] Arthur William James (Anthony) Greenwood (1911–): son of Arthur Greenwood; Lab. MP Heywood & Radcliffe 1946–50, Rossendale 1950–70; Sec. of State for Colonies 1964–5; Min. of Overseas Development 1965–6; Min. of Housing 1966–70; cr. Baron Greenwood of Rossendale 1970.

[37] Denis Noel Pritt (1888–1972): lawyer; prosecution in 1931 Royal Mail Steam Packet (Kylsant) case; Lab MP Hammersmith North 1935–50 (Ind. Lab. from 1945); expelled Lab. Party 1940.

[38] J.H. Robertson (pseud. John Connell) (1905–65): journalist, biographer & military historian; staff *Evening News* from 1932, leader writer 1945–9; Pres. of Lobby 1934.

his heavy way had enjoined on the Cabinet about some matter that they were not to say anything or even think anything, and that when he, Lansbury, left No 10, he saw a newspaper bill revealing the whole thing. This was exactly my own experience when Ernest Harvey told me in confidence the story of the bank credits, at the August bank holiday weekend 1931, and I wondered if it was the same 'secret'. Towards the end the old boy made a great plea for the preservation of liberty and democracy – and I nearly rose and cheered him, so exactly did he fill my own desires. He is the most human and certainly the most Christian man in public life – and must have been an odd man with whom to work either in politics or journalism. He is just recovered from an accident and he and the Chairman were right, I suppose, in saying that in no other capital in the world would such a luncheon be possible – the leaders of all parties as guests of lobby journalists gathered to honour the leader of the Labour party and the creator of 'Poplarism' in local politics.

Sunday 26 August I find that work goes down ill with me in the sense of *Sunday Dispatch* work. The utter irresponsibility and ignorance of the paper's treatment of every topic, Brittain's boyish zest to make all the 'stories' sensational and to omit any story, however vital, that cannot be made sensational is amusing but rather terrifying. And Rothermere telephoning leader instructions from North Scotland like a half-wit who has not comprehended the first thing about international commitments is equally terrifying but not so amusing. Even Meredith, being genial, irked me. And yet, it is infinitely better from most viewpoints than the FN – not so worrying, not so trying.

Monday 10 September One of the amusing episodes of the week has been Meredith's kindness in his papers to my dictionary. He suggested to Brittain that he should review it in the S.D. and did – and I wrote the review for him, except for two interlarded compliments. I mistrust him, somehow, and feel that his influence will bring my association with the Rothermere group to an end shortly. Meredith actually says he told R. that I should be made editor of the S.D., which I do not for one moment believe. '*Et donna ferentes ...*' is my present feeling.

Monday 1 October [Wednesday] afternoon Gibson Jarvie[39] asked me to

---

[39] John Gibson Jarvie (1883–1964): founder & Chm. United Dominions Trust Ltd & Group 1919–63, Pres. 1963–4; Regional Port Dir., Min. of War Transport 1941–2; High Sheriff of Suffolk 1951–2.

go up to see him. I did so and after talking about Ramsay MacDonald for a few minutes he thrust a pad at me and said, 'Write him a letter.' This I did, and G.J. promised to father and despatch it, with a few amendments. The point of the story was that he and certain other industrialists had been discussing whether to force Ramsay to action by withdrawing their support of this particular National Government. The idea of an alternative National Government was one under John Simon. Although I was among the first to foresee such a possibility, two or three years ago, there were so many tactical objections to it now that I persuaded G.J. that the great hope of action was to make Ramsay his own rebel. As G.J.'s mind and mine marched together it was not difficult to devise a letter. What will come of it, I cannot guess – but probably nothing.

Sunday 7 October   On Tuesday I lunched Brittain at the Savage, where we had talk with Hamilton Fyfe chiefly about the old days of Northcliffe. He is of opinion that Rothermere is a much kinder-hearted man than his brother, but says that Northcliffe was without doubt the most magnetic figure of his generation. The fault with both, he thinks, has been the readiness to gather and depend upon surrounding sycophants.

Sunday 21 October   On Wednesday Jarvie asked me to call. We sat in his big room. He had sent my letter to the Prime Minister and they are to meet to-morrow. We talked things out and he asked me to draft a free memorandum which he could leave with Ramsay MacDonald after their talk. Whether anything will come of it, I know not – and think not – but it may. In any event, it is something to have got as close as this to seizing the machine.

'Don't forget, that you will have to be very much in the picture. If we persuade him to make a machine it won't be run by a few people of social importance, but by men with brains like Gibson Jarvie and Collin Brooks,' said G.J. amusingly.

He said that at their staff dinner, of about seventy people, last week Montagu Norman came and made a very pleasant little speech. Norman is, apparently, cognisant of our gingering campaign and will back G.J.

Sunday 28 October   The week has been interesting enough. On Monday Gibson Jarvie saw the Premier and had a long talk with him on the lines of my memorandum. He asked me to see him again on Wednesday, which I did, when he said that Ramsay would make – he thought – almost any pronouncement we drew up. I prepared half a speech, embodying an outline five year programme for a National Government, which G.J. and I discussed again on Saturday morning. We also drafted provisional lunches with the editors of leading papers.

Thursday 1 November   Looked into the Bank at 3 o'clock to talk with Henry Clay.[40] He is much less pessimistic than I had anticipated. He thinks 're-recovery' is genuine enough. The gold bloc he says will make a longer fight than many people think. There is not a firm unity between them. If Belgium falls off the standard the others will not worry. France would bring them all off. Clay's room is in the new wing, which preserves that dignified quiet which I described in *Something in the City*.[41] Clay himself is more like a tired Sherlock Holmes than ever.

Monday 26 November   I have been for many days the victim of that malaise which the Mystics call the dryness of the soul. I have hated my work and have been wearied by the world about me. That I have moved in considerable physical pain these three weeks has aided the mood. But most it has been augmented, if not induced, by Brittain with his perpetual insistence upon 'jazzing the city page into tabloid' – which means outraging English still further as I have had to outrage sound economics by reducing thought to a tipster's aid. It is appalling when one thinks in cold blood what shallowpates and vulgarians produce our great daily papers – I not least, I admit. The greatest fault is a lack of continuity of knowledge. These eager sensation mongers can relate no contemporary happening to its causes or to its historic past.

Friday 7 December   At 3 o'c I reached the Ministry of Health. At 3–5 'the Minister'[42] would see me. I entered a big, gloomy room and found H.Y. there looking rather older than when we were together but not changed. For him he was effusive – sat me in his chair while he alternately sat on a settee or paced the quarter deck, looking, as Churchill said of him, more Nelsonic than Nelson. He talked first of the old brigade of the *Financial News* and said some pleasant things of

[40] Henry Clay (1883–1954): economic adviser, Bank of England 1930–44; kt. 1946.

[41] *Something in the City* (London: Country Life, 1931).

[42] Edward Hilton Young (1879–1960): MP Norwich 1915–23, 1924–9 (Lib. to 1926, then Con.) Con. MP Sevenoaks 1929–35; FST 1921–2; Lib. Nat. Chief Whip 1922–3; Sec. Overseas Trade 1931; Min. of Health 1931–5; editor-in-chief *Financial News* 1925–29 (responsible for recruiting C.B. to the paper); cr. Baron Kennet 1935.

my own work and even of the poems ... I had come to collect from him an article for the *Dispatch* on the Water Grid – and by luck and cunning he had just left the House after making a preliminary statement which had made it news. We discussed the article – the only dynamite in it being a vague forecast of new and stronger Government powers.

'Ah,' said I 'this is the Oil in Britain Bill all over again ...' and he concurred.

After a long talk about water supplies I dropped again into generalities and was going when he again asked me if I was happy and said how interested he had been in my activity in a field to which he had taken me originally. I said that even if I went back to general journalism the fact of having been a figure in financial journalism would be an asset.

'Don't go back to general journalism,' he said and renewed his praise of financial journalism as a career.

'A man must govern his life by expediency,' I said, 'and security of tenure with a Rothermere paper is not strong ...'

He said he agreed but that I should take some opportunity of sliding to a safer craft – 'I don't know how that may be ...' he ended. Then he said 'But, Matey! Your's is one of these papers with a mammoth circulation. Water is all right, but what about my Housing Bill!! You might help me there.' (Throughout our talk he had followed his old habit of calling me punctiliously 'Collin Brooks' – even when Lady Young came through on the 'phone he said as I made gestures of escape – 'don't go Collin Brooks' – but the Navy-style 'Matey' was a departure.)

I sat down again in his chair and he with his left hand filled a calabash pipe and lighted it skilfully-clumsily, as I remembered how. Then he quarter-decked about the room and explained his housing bill, postponed from this week to January. Here, indeed, was dynamite. I need not log all the details here – they will become history. Briefly the bill turns from the abolition of slums to overcrowding. The remedy is to be twofold – a limited number of persons per cubic feet of air space, graded by rooms of special size, and the segregation of sexes after ten years of age. He is under no illusion as to what opposition he invites, quoting himself cases of obvious injustice. [...] He is also quite clear that this Bill ends the pretence that an Englishman's house is his castle – for a hour or so we discussed it freely and frankly – not clause by clause through its eighty clauses but almost so. 'When can I use this?' I said and he answered, 'not until January when you get the Bill ...' We parted more than ever amicably, by which time he had returned to a still older form of address, 'Well, good-bye, my dear ....'

When I got back to the office McWhirter and Brittain were discussing Tory-Socialism, as they called it, and I found that Mac. had already had some outlines of the Scottish housing bill and was dead against it.

The English press is a funny institution. Between controlled private enterprise and socialism there is an enormous gulf – the one is the protector from the other – but anything other than laissez faire is to the average press-man socialism. Like the pulpit and the stage, the Press is half a generation at least behind the times.

1935

Wednesday 2 January   On New Year's Eve I saw Gielgud's 'Hamlet'[1] at the New Theatre. (Lilian, Ida and Rosemary, in all the glory of her first long evening dress, and I taxied down to Kettners for dinner, on to the theatre – R's first Hamlet – and taxied home through streets pleasantly riotous with New Year's Eve revellers.) Gielgud,[2] I thought, was better than when I saw his first Hamlet some four years ago, but is not wholly satisfactory. The cuts were few – a good deal of the political explanation went from Scene 1 but Fortinbras was retained and given his proper value in the last scene: there was an odd inexplicable cut in the play scene, Hamlet's renaissance mouthing of his quatrain being omitted – and the play was taken straight through with but one short interval. The Ophelia of Jessica Tandy[3] was disappointing. She conveyed excellently the toppled brain in the mad scene, but with her slight physique and thin voice she did not convince one that Hamlet had ever had any amorous feeling for her, and there was no contrast between Ophelia sane and Ophelia mad. She used no flowers – this was no innovation, but in view of the description of her death it still seems to me that Shakespeare meant actual flowers to be borne. Hamlet followed the tradition of no portraits in the closet scene. The real weakness of Gielgud was that he never conveyed the bantering side of Hamlet's character – in the recorder speech he worked himself into a great and ranting rage, but to my mind Hamlet is quiet throughout, and his sudden turn on the two who would pluck the heart from his mystery was surely quiet – banteringly – whimsically – contemptuously. Frank Vosper[4] as Claudius was excellent. [...] The setting was a series of Tudor pictures which were so good that they distracted the mind too much. One felt that Ophelia had been cast for her part as a decoration. The lack of noticeable breaks in the action for changes of scene was achieved by the use of round elevated towers with steps – giving the stage a Craigian[5] look. 'Something too much of this!' I thought several times – an apron stage would have been better.

[1] *Hamlet* by William Shakespeare. Performed at New Theatre from 14 November 1934 to 30 March 1935. Ran for 155 performances. Reviewed *The Times* 15 November 1934.

[2] (Arthur) John Gielgud (1904–): actor; kt. 1953.

[3] Jessica Tandy (1909–94): actress & film star.

[4] Frank Vosper (1899–1937): actor & dramatic author.

[5] Reference to (Edward Henry) Gordon Craig (1872–1966): actor, theatre designer, dir. & author. Founder theatrical journal: *The Mask*.

The Gielgud method robbed the quieter scenes of intimacy. But it was a good Hamlet, despite my quirks.

Sunday 6 January   At 4 p.m. on Friday [4th] I saw Sir Patrick Gower[6] at Conservative Head Office, to talk over my projected trip to the distressed areas. He was brutally frank about the stupidity of the Front Bench.

'All these fellows have been brought up in the old, staid tradition. They have no idea of publicity. Even when they demolish a slum, they just demolish and leave nothing behind but some ill feeling. Now if they'd allow a celebrity to touch a button and make a big bang with some dynamite ... I have urged 'em to make their borrowing spectacular – a big housing loan – but these old fashioned buggers at the Treasury say that the local authorities are already borrowing at 3 per cent through the Housing Loan Board – but who the Hell has ever heard of the Housing Loan Board! The only two with any sense of the theatre about 'em are Kingsley Wood[7] and young Belisha ... Kingsley Wood boosts his department and is content with the reflected glory – young Belisha boosts himself – that's a mistake – people will get tired of him – and they don't trust him ...'

That was the vein of his talk. He strongly urged me to drop in and see him after my tour to tell him how I found the electoral mind working, and I promised to do this. He is a round, rosy faced, genial man – very commonsensical and unlike the usual party bureaucrat.

Sunday 13 January   Monday 7th: [...] Brittain and I met McWhirter in his room at Carmelite House and discussed proposed reforms on *The Sunday Dispatch*. Brittain and I then took taxi to Stratton House. We waited there until Sir George Sutton, Morison[8] and McWhirter arrived and were then taken up the lift to Rothermere's flat and ushered in. We stood for a moment or two taking in a big room, pleasantly and richly furnished, with just a touch of litter about its atmosphere. The most striking thing in it was its window looking out over London in the twilight. 'Ah, ah – a Whistler nocturne !' I cried, to the pleasure of Sutton and Morison – it was exactly that. The next moment a bustling

---

[6] (Robert) Patrick Gower (1887–1964): PPS to Bonar Law, MacDonald & Baldwin 1922–8; Chief Publicity Officer, CCO, 1929–39; Chm. Charles F. Higham Ltd 1935–56, Pres. 1956–.

[7] (Howard) Kingsley Wood (1881–1943): Con. MP Woolwich W. 1918–43; PS Health 1924–9; PS Educ. 1931; Postmaster-Gen. 1931–5; Min. of Health 1935–8; Sec. for Air 1938–40; Ld. Privy Seal 1940; Chanc. of the Exchequer 1940–3; kt. 1918.

[8] Harry Morison: Personal Ass. to Rothermere until his death in 1940.

voice was heard, as it were, 'off' – and in came the Great Man. My preconceived notion of him was of a heavy, dour, fat man with a porcine face. It belied the actuality. He is a heavy man, with a face that seems almost brutal in his rugged pugnacity, but his aura is young and he is very forceful and direct in both speech and movement.

'Sit down, sit down,' said he, and opened the conference by tearing the paper to rags – by praising its rival. At one point he said 'the finance is not as snappily done as in *The Express*' at which I (having nothing to lose that worried me) prepared for fireworks, but he said hastily 'I don't say it isn't as good ...' As he talked I found myself liking him against my will. One or two of his quips made me laugh – and particularly a mental picture he gave me ... he was talking of Margot Asquith,[9] who has ceased to write for us.

'They told me a year ago that if you stand opposite to her windows over there you can see the lady every night stark naked – I didn't accept the invitation. ...'

The image of Rothermere like an adolescent voyeur peering at Margot's hag-like frame brought a great guffaw from me. As he went on I became a little embroiled with him about economics, and found him ready to listen and argue.

'But you agree, don't you, that we may have another crisis – Schacht[10] says that we are only enjoying an Indian summer – he told me so. I think Schacht the best financier in Europe, and so does Norman – did you know that? ...'

Eventually he asked me to write an article for the next issue 'Can There be Another Crisis' and later the conference adjourned rather unsatisfactorily with the five of us pledged to another lunch on Wednesday. [...] Tuesday 8th [...] When I reached the office at 11–45 I found a message asking me to ring McWhirter. I did so, and received word to go up to Rothermere at 12–30. This I did. I was again conscious that of all the men in his organisation I was best placed – for I had taken down that very morning my provisional resignation, which Brittain asked me to tear up. I therefore entered the flat in a fairly 'you-be-damned' mood. I was kept waiting for a while in a panelled dining room – wondering why the clock was kept twenty minutes fast and why it stood some inches from the true centre of the mantle shelf ... When I was taken into the presence Rothermere was on his hearthrug.

'Good morning,' said he, shaking hands, 'sit down. I want to talk

---

[9] Margot Asquith (1864–1945): Widow of the Lib. PM, Herbert Henry Asquith; styled Countess of Oxford.

[10] Dr Hjalmar Schacht (1877–1970): German Reich Min., Pres. of Reichsbank until 20 Jan. 1939.

about this article you are going to write ...' and launched into trade
figures and budgeting.

After a while I said, 'Hold hard, sir – it's no use discussing that until
I know how you feel on currency stabilisation ...' and inaugurated a
talk on the gold standard. He was again ready to listen and argue like
a sane man, and was not by any means the Rothermere of legend.
Something took him from the room for a minute or two. When he
came back I was determined to swing him round to the main thing
that interested me – Brittain and the *S. Dispatch*.

'Those were staggering figures you quoted yesterday about *The Express*
profits, sir.'

'Eh! What? They were right. I had 'em from Beaverbrook – I thought
they were blah but Stanley Bell[11] checked 'em up ...'

This gave me an opening. 'I don't believe they are right, unless they
are getting a much higher rate than we suppose –'

This led us on to newspaper talk – 'You'd better stay and have some
lunch with me, can you?' (I had sent a message to the White Friars to
tell Brophy that I would be hellishly delayed.)

'I'd love to,' I said.

'Rose,' he cried through the open door. Rose appeared. 'What have
we for lunch Rose? – eh, – veal? – what sort of veal? – and what
else? – boiled apple? Can you eat veal and boiled apple? – all right,
Rose we'll have lunch for two here ...'

As we resumed our talk some other caller was announced.

'Do you mind waiting in here?' he said, and shot me into his
secretary's room. When I emerged lunch was being set – very simply
on the big desk-like table.

'Don't sit on that thing – bring up an arm chair. Well, Rose, is that
the veal? – doesn't look very nice – did you cook it, Rose? – no? –
well then, tell me, do *you* think it looks nice? – if it isn't nice, I'll have
a boiled egg – have we any boiled eggs – I mean eggs to boil? What
would you like to drink? Wine, beer –'

I said: 'I'd like beer, if I may drink beer.'

'We've got some beer – drink anything you like. Now, what is the
trouble with *The Sunday Dispatch*?'

By this time our talk had flown so freely that I felt as if he and I
were two partners in a joint concern. He had responded vigorously
when I called the Treasury a crowd of old-fashioned bloody fools and
had tolerated my strongest epithets.

'I'll tell you what is one of the things wrong with *The Sunday Dispatch* –
too many bloody critics!'

'Eh, what! what do you mean ...'

[11] Stanley J. Bell: *Daily Mail* Bd., Managing Dir. to 1944; Dir. miscellaneous companies.

I enlarged. 'Nobody goes through that building without giving a kick at the poor old *Sunday Dispatch* – '

'What do you think of Brittain?'

I gave Britt a glowing certificate of excellence. 'He has one fault – he's apt to jump ahead of his news and to overcolour his stories – but it's a good fault in popular journalism. You've got the makings of one of the best editors in Fleet Street in that boy properly handled. But how would you stand up at his age to heavy-weights like Sir George Sutton and Lord Rothermere?'

'What about McWhirter?'

'There's a marshal that no Napoleon can afford to be without, sage, wise, and a skilled craftsman – he handles his editorial conferences like a man conducting an orchestra . . .. What is needed with that paper is a man putting in charge, being told, if you like, that he will get his bottom kicked twice a week but assured that it won't be kicked out of place – and young Brittain is your man . . . Then, if you were prepared to back him –'

Ten minutes of violent rhetoric on what a great Sunday newspaper might be – an outburst of whirling words and shaking fists – and he growing, I believe, as enthused as I.

At the end 'Come back at five and bring Brittain with you – you two can say what you like – I won't repeat it –' The battle seemed won. [. . .] After a few minutes talk I stood up to go and we straddled the hearth rug.

'Well, what do you think of me?' he asked abruptly. 'You think I'm a gloomy pessimist, don't you?'

'I'll tell you what I think of you – I think you're the biggest surprise of the last twenty years – I thought I was coming to meet a dour, heavy-sterned old man . . ..'

'What!'

'And when you ebulliated through that door it was like the entry of a streak of lightening. Another thing, I was staggered by your treatment of your subordinate officers – you talked and discussed things with me like one sane man to another – that isn't the legend that has been built round you . . ..'

He was frankly delighted at this. 'Oh, oh . . . you thought I was an old dud, did you? Well, I'm not am I?'

'I didn't think you were an old dud – but I think you were an older and dourer man. I thought I was coming to visit the late Lord Salisbury[12] . . .'

---

[12] Robert Arthur Talbot Gascoyne-Cecil (1830–1903): Con. MP Stamford 1953–68; Sec. of State, India 1866–7, 1874–8; Sec. of State, For. Affairs 1878–80, 1885–6, 1887–92, 1895–1900; PM 1885–6, 1886–92, 1895–1902; suc. 3rd Marquess Salisbury.

'Ah, that was what you thought. You thought I was just an old dud
...' He walked with me to the hall, put on his coat and hat and walked
with me half way down Piccadilly – which I took to be the great man
showing honour ... And so we parted. The whole of the conversation
of nearly three hours was heavily tinged with his gloom about an attack
from the air that is to bring Britain to barbarism – and was enlivened
with his anecdotes of his visit to Hitler and other matters – I cannot
hope to journalise it all. At five Brittain and I returned to his flat – he
was a tired man, then, but still in good mood. After some manoeuvring
I dragged the talk away from the incessant discussion of foreign affairs –
and gave Britt his cue to launch on to the paper itself. At the very last
moment, after he told us that he would put the thing into our hands
and that the 'old men' were not to worry us, Brittain said 'If you'd
give me some definition, sir ...'

'Well, what do you want – I know. I make you editor. Come back
on Thursday at three, both of you. You must both see me twice a week
or so in future ....'

[...] Wednesday 9th: When I got to the office, Brittain was agog to
talk with me, but no sooner had I entered the room that Mac telephoned
for us to go to Carmelite House.

'Something has gone wrong,' said Britt, 'he was most gloomy ....'

When we arrived at little Mac's room he solemnly handed an
envelope to me and one to Brittain. Mine read[13] – but I will file it here.
Brittain's was very similar. Mac also had one, reasserting his position
as director in charge of the paper. I looked at mine and pulled a wry
face – which caused Mac to raise his eyebrows.

[...] Thursday 10th: After a busy day of dashing about and doing
none of my own work, Britt and I went up at 3 to see R. again. This
time the talk was more pedestrian, with Morison there, but again I
found R. far more likeable and sane than ever I had anticipated. But
the fact remains that with a dictator of this kind, on whose whim
thousands of men depend for their livelihoods, a great business is
conducted like a Byzantium Court and not an enterprise nominally for
the honest dissemination of news and views. There are too many
sycophants, the tendency is to staff the place with ignorant men who
will not challenge a line of policy by their knowledge or their principle –
the whole community degenerates into a funk-ridden collection of time-
servers. I told Britt that one fatal effect on me of a contract was that I
no longer felt free to say just what I liked how I liked – it made me

---

[13] 'It is my desire that you should have an agreement for two years from 1 January,
terminable at the end of two years, at your present salary. You will be doing much more
work for *The Sunday Dispatch*, but, if the paper makes the progress I am hoping, you can
come to me in June next for a reconsideration of your remuneration.' R. to C.B. 9 Jan
1935.

feel more of an employee. Britt has devised an explanation for my new apparent power by calling me Political Adviser. . . .

Saturday 19 January   Off I went, took coffee and a waffle in the Strand and reached the office to find them in a turmoil. R. wanted me on the 'phone. Britt had time to whisper that all leaders might have to be changed as Randolph Churchill[14] had decided to fight Wavertree as an independent Tory. They phoned R. – and he repeated this and asked me to a do a leader backing Randolph. 'What do you think of it? Do you agree with it?' he asked, very differently from the bullying dictator of legend. Then – in the big general room – within ten minutes I had five calls from him and Morison. I began the Randolph leader and was half way through when Randolph himself came in. He and Brittain and I discussed his campaign. He had been covering the by-election for *The Daily Mail* and at four that morning had decided to fight the seat. Borrowing two chauffeurs and a car he had driven post-haste to London to ask R. to permit this, R. being, of course, his employer. He had not consulted Winston. His sole resources as he stood there were £200 which he had borrowed from young Watts, but he hoped to raise £200 as an overdraft. Off he shot, back to Liverpool, and we turned our attention to the paper. Brittain and I did the splash together, I finished the Churchill leader and wrote a new one on the Saar – R. ringing me to say 'Brooks – how did we leave the leader position?'

'We give a long to Randolph, and I propose to scrap the air one and do a new one on the Saar . . .'

'Right.' A few minutes after he rang again, 'Brooks – Morison says he was talking to you about a coincidence competition yesterday.'

'Yes – I've put that up to Brittain.'

'You can start it today – offer £5.5. each week.'

'Very good, sir, thank you.'

Within three minutes Morison came through. 'Oh, Brooks, about that competition –'

'Yes – we're starting today. R. has just been on the phone.'

'When?'

'Oh, a few minutes ago.'

'But I've only just left him in the street . . . .'

'Well, he's been on . . . what's bitten him?'

'As a matter of fact I was saying that I had told you that I was putting the idea up to the *[Evening] News* and you had as usual jumped to it and asked me to let the *Dispatch* have it, and R. said "If Collin

[14] Randolph Churchill (1911–68): journalist & author; Con. MP Preston 1940–5; s. of Winston.

Brooks wants it, he can have it." Your stock's rising rapidly, my boy.'
'Yes,' said I, 'It's a bit dangerous.'
'Why?'
'Ever heard of the proverb about riding a tiger ....'
'Don't worry – it's very flattering. I congratulate you ....'

Sunday 20 January   At nine-thirty my phone went. 'Oh, Brooks, I wonder if you can look in to-morrow about ten?' It was Rothermere.
    'Certainly, sir. Ten o'clock. At the Savoy, I suppose.'
    'Yes. I say! I'm going to project you into some big things. You're the man I've been looking for for a very long time.'
    'Right-oh, sir, I'm ready for anything you need,' said I, wondering if this was a directorship or merely one of his stunts or a joke.

Monday 21 January   What a farcical day! I went to R's flat in the Savoy and he said he wanted me to be the great man on his new air league as far as Associated Newspapers was concerned. Towards the end of the talk he said, half-jocularly, 'Go and get £10,000 from Lucy Houston.'[15] We were interrupted by the entrance of Morison and the talk turned to India. R. was as pleased as Punch about his wire to the Indian Princes. He denied any knowledge of their failure to arrive for the Princes Conference and said it was fortuitous. I suggested that *The Times* cable should be supplemented by a special *Daily Mail* Delhi message – and he was on to it like a pointer. (He has a private phone from all his rooms to Northcliffe House.) Leaving him, I sought Warner Allen.[16] Warner said Lady Houston was ill, bad tempered, and would see nobody. I said that I must see her. He said he would be phoning her later and we arranged to meet at the Club for sherry and news at noon. I dashed off to Northcliffe House and told the telephone man to get a call through to the Duke of Westminster,[17] 'I don't know where he is, but find him ....' said I, and they found him at Chester. A faint voice told me that His Grace was in the grounds but that they would fetch him ... the voice changed.
    'Hello!' said I 'I am waiting to speak to the Duke of Westminster.'
    'Westminster speaking ...'

[15] Dame Fanny Lucy Houston (1857–1936): philanthropist & eccentric; prop., *Saturday Review*.
    [16] (Herbert) Warner Allen (1881–1968): journalist & author; authority on wine; For. Ed. *Morning Post* 1925–8, London Ed. *Yorkshire Post* 1928–30 & contributor *Saturday Review*; For. Div., MOI 1940–1.
    [17] Hugh Richard Arthur Grosvenor (Bend'or) (1879–1953): served South Africa 1899–1900, European war 1914–18; suc. Duke of Westminster 1899.

In three minutes I had told him about the air league and had
borrowed a house in Grosvenor Square from him – which house to be
decided later. I rang R. up to tell him this. When I had left him there
had been the inevitable bawdy jokes about my virtue not being safe
with Lady Houston so his first remark was 'Honeymoon successful?'

'The bride won't see me – but I'll fix that later – what I want to tell
you was ...'

'All right. But listen Brooks when you go out to Hampstead to see
your girl friend call in at a good chemist and buy the necessary
medicaments – charge 'em to the office.' Such was his humour.

'For her, I suppose you mean?'

'What! Is that the kind of form you're in?

'I'm always in good form when I'm asking for money ....'

'Well, do what you like. I don't care what happens to you. You can
become the Lord High Gigolo if you like.'

'I can't do that – I don't wear the right sort of whiskers.'

At noon I joined Allen and we drank sherry. He had fixed an
appointment for me at 5 o'clock. 'You'll find her very difficult – use
tact – she's mad on Randolph and his candidature ....'

I again rang R. to tell him I couldn't come to him at 4 o'clock, and
he bade me to take a good meal of stout and oysters and return safely
when I could. [...] At 4–30 I took taxi to Hampstead. Bryon Cottage
is a white house at the end of a lane. You ring an old bell at its gates
and a maid comes cautiously down the patch and shoots back two
bolts. You are shown into a pleasant old English hall with a wood fire
burning and crackling. I made love to a friendly dog and waited. Back
came the maid to ask me to come upstairs as Lady Houston was in
bed.... I entered the room and found her lying on a divan covered
with rugs. She wore a red gown, had a red white and blue neckerchief
tied like a stock, and a red bandanna about her head from beneath
which a little blonde curl was allowed to peep – a plastered little curl.
Her puffy old face and her peepy little eyes were like a caricature of
her caricatures. This, then, was the famous millionaire harlot – the
child who at sixteen had married from a chorus after running the
streets as a gamin – who had had three official husbands and had
taken for the last of them Robert Houston[18] of Liverpool, who made
his fortune out of coffin ships. Remembering all that Allen had said I
was as greasily diplomatic as I could be – stooped over her hand and
touched it with my lips like Talleyrand.[19] She proved to be a good

[18] Sir Robert Paterson Houston (d. 1926): Con. MP W. Toxteth, Liverpool 1892–1924;
owner Houston Shipping Line.

[19] Charles Maurice de Talleyrand-Périgord, Prince of Benevento (1754–1838): French
statesman & political survivor.

sort – but mad – obsessed with the idea that Ramsay MacDonald is a traitor under the heel of Russia – that all people deny her publicity because they are frightened of the Traitor .... she is vain – vain of being a fighter – her mind leaps constantly back to her one obsession ... But she said that she would give £10,000. Rothermere had told me to tell her that she could be the Founder of the New League which pleased her. I could not, however, drive it into her that we were about to found a great propaganda body to ensure adequate air defences – she babbled about lending a forest in Scotland and a house for training airmen .... I spent an hour and a quarter with her and then went. A taxi from the Hare and Hounds to Stratton House – R. had left – a taxi to the Savoy – My guests, Lil and the Harry Shaws would be waiting at 7–15 – Rothermere was in bed, resting before dinner.

'Well?' he said.

'Well, I've got your ten thousand.'

'You haven't!'

'I mean the promise.'

'You haven't got it, Brooks!'

'I certainly have.'

'Well, I congratulate you – you're a marvel.'

'But you'd better write and thank her before she changes her mind.'

'Yes – dictate a letter for me on *Daily Mail* paper and I'll sign it.'

'Where can I get you?'

'Here. I'm dining here.'

'Well, I must first find some guests of mine and tell them I shall be late – I'll get off.'

It was five minutes to seven. Just time. A taxi to Northcliffe House – a burst into Warden's[20] secretary's room – a word of explanation – a letter dictated straight on to the machine – back to the Savoy – into the bedroom with no ceremony – and the letter signed. Five past seven.

'Are you in a hurry – sit down – I want to tell you something ...'

'Well, I must go in five minutes – guests waiting.'

'Listen – this is in confidence. I've had a very important Cabinet Minister here today.'

'I know who it was.'

'Do you – who?'

'Kingsley Wood.'

'Quite right. They want to compromise on the India Bill. Would they get in next time if my papers supported 'em? I told Kingsley Wood they'd no chance as things are – and even if I supported 'em they'd be licked.'

---

[20] William Luch Warden (d. 1942): Ed. *Daily Mail* 1931–5, Dir. Associated Newspapers until 1939.

'I don't agree. If you and Lord Beaverbrook swung behind them, they'd pull it off. That's an approach you must consider, sir. Of course, it all depends on what they offer. They'll have to be right on India and the air ....'

'Um – we must talk tomorrow. Look in tomorrow.'

I shot off and reached the Cafe Royal ten minutes late, but Shaw and his Ida were patient.

Wednesday 23 January   Rothermere had me down at Stratton House at about ten. As we talked his secretary flung open the door and ushered in Lloyd George. I shot out, and sat in Clark's[21] room. They talked, in loud voices, for about forty-five minutes. It was, I guessed, Lloyd George's hope to get support for his new deal and Rothermere's insistence to get Lloyd George's support for a strong air force. When Ll.G. went I strolled in again.

'We'd better get over – Clark, take everything to the Savoy – I won't come back here'

[...] We strolled down into Piccadilly and took a taxi. *Obiter dictum* on the way that the trouble with the English is that they eat too much white bread. R. announced that not only is he now a non-drinker and a non-smoker, but he doesn't eat meat. (This is new since a fortnight ago, when we took our maiden meal off veal.) I said nothing was so good as beer for keeping a man's stomach in tune. I also said that French women were a constipated race. He agreed eagerly and said the German's weren't.

'No,' said I. 'Why – because they drink beer.'

At the Savoy he said, 'You'll pay the taxi, my boy – charge it to the office.'

We wandered into the Pinafore Room. One young airman was there. Then in came Brittain – to whom R. was extremely gracious.

'You're having a leader on Randolph again. I've told Brooks to write it. He's to say Randolph Churchill has plenty of guts – understand that? – guts. You know – I'll frighten Brooks before I've finished.'

'I'll take a lot of frightening,' said I.

In came Sir George Sutton, McWhirter, some other young airmen. We waited for Mosley – but waited pleasantly over cocktails and cigarettes. In came Morison. But no Mosley. We began lunch – fourteen of us – and as excellent a lunch as I remember to have eaten. My own choice was oysters, a gorgeously treated sole, a bit of fowl, and a good ice sweet, with hock and old brandy to wash it down. Mosley came half way through. I had never met him before. He is more pleasant

[21] Francis 'Jimmy' Clark: Rothermere's confidential secretary.

and less aggressive than one imagined – much more stalwart in build. He dominates a table, but not unpleasantly and not wholly. R. and I were about the only two who talked to and at him – the others listened. I was amused by R. at one stage. He was telling Mosley that we hoped to do something or other.

'You hope that, too, don't you Brooks.'

'I *hope* so, but I don't count on it.'

He turned to Mosley. 'He's a very good fella, this' he said nodding at me. (Praise from Sir Hubert – but the comedy was that he should be thus dowering me in the presence of old George Sutton and little Mac. How often in his and Northcliffe's career it must have happened – the new favourite and the old gang.)

However, the lunch dragged on and we did nothing formal but at the end there was a vague idea that the League was practically formed. He asked Macmillan[22] and me to go up to see him at 6–30. Sutton lifted Brittain and McWhirter back to Tudor Street for an afternoon's work. At 6 I met Macmillan. We drank a sherry and then mounted. In his room R. was lying in dressing gown and pyjamas on a couch.

'Well, are you prepared to take this job on?'

'Yes, sir,' said Macmillan.

'Now what figure would you want?

'What do you suggest, sir?'

'Would eight hundred a year suit you?'

'I'm afraid I've been thinking in much bigger figures than that – I'm in the habit of earning £3,000 a year.'

'Ummm – what do we do now Brooks!'

'Well, we can't pay that.'

'I'd like to have a talk to Brooks before we decide anything.'[23]

But we explored avenues, as the politicians say – Morison drifted in and turned the talk to foreign politics – and so, after a while we left him.

Friday 25 January Lucy Houston drove down to see me – and in the snow she and I sat in her car in Temple Avenue while she complained that R. was not keeping his word – was not giving her publicity – that we were deceiving her – I did my best to smooth her down – but she is right – R. promised to give co-operation to her patriotic efforts but won't let her attack Ramsay in his papers, and that is all she cares for.

[22] Capt. Norman Macmillan (1892–1976): RFC, RAF 1916–19; test pilot 1919–30; Pres. NLA 1935–8; FRSA 1936–57; air correspondent *Daily Mail* 1936–9; RAFVR (Sqdn Ldr) 1939–45; author.

[23] Evenutally agreed £1000 per annum, £300 expenses, £500 for articles for the press, and a secretary.

The end of the talk was funny. She was advising me to treat Rothermere with sugar 'be diplomatic, my dear, I know that kind of man ...' as I left her I said, 'I'll do my best, but I'm not Lady Houston', and she beamed with pleasure. What a mountebank they make of me!!

Sunday 3 February   It's a mad world, my masters. On Monday (Jan 28th) I met Macmillan at Euston and we travelled to Liverpool together, talking Air most of the way. We reached the Adelphi Hotel about half-past two and found Randolph having a belated light lunch in his suite. A conference between bites with him and Cannall[24] and Monty Smith,[25] of *The Mail*, gave us the atmosphere of the election. Macmillan went off to look at the docks for his article on 'If Liverpool Were Bombed' and I, after visiting the barber, went over to the Press Club. [...] Caleb,[26] shrewdest and most sage of electioneers, said he would come with me to Randolph's Committee Rooms. [...] found what was called a taxi – and went off to the headquarters of the battle, down miles of drab, grey, Liverpool streets. The committee rooms was a disused pub, full of ardent workers. I was sent upstairs to see a Captain Hassall, like a man from a burlesque, round faced, with a rimless monocle. Lounging by the fire was a tall youngish man in rough tweeds.

'It's like old times to be in a committee rooms, again,' said I.

'It's like old times to hear fella's talking sense,' said he.

It was Eric Long,[27] Walter Long's son – more like a caricature of a young Tory even than Hassall. We stayed for a while and then with Monty Smith, big, comfortable, imperturbable, we borrowed Randolph's car and went back to the Adelphi. [...] we chartered a taxi – already late for our first meeting – and the damned fool lost his way ... When we found the Woolton Baths we found them crammed with an old fashioned audience – and before we had been there five minutes Randolph came in, all rosetted and cheery – and made an immediate ten minute speech which went down well. Macmillan followed and I followed him – getting 'em well warmed up. Off to the

[24] Robert Cannall (1908–1965): journalist; *Daily Mail* staff (Manchester from 1929; London from 1938); acting night Ed. 1940–50; *Daily Express* radio & TV correspondent 1950–65.

[25] Montague 'Monty' Smith (1889–1969): journalist; *Daily Mail* 1911–64; youngest-ever Lobby correspondent, later News Ed.

[26] Caleb Rhys: political journalist *Liverpool Daily Post*.

[27] Richard Eric Onslow Long (1892–1967): Con. MP Westbury 1927–31; 3rd Viscount Long; s. of Walter Hume Long (1854–1924): Con. MP Wilts. 1880–5, Devizes 1885–92, Liverpool W. Derby 1893–1900, Bristol S. 1900–6, County Dublin S. 1906–10, Strand 1910–18; St George's Westminster 1918–21. PS Local Govt. Bd. 1886–92; Pres., Bd. of Agric. 1895–1900; Pres., Local Govt. Bd. 1900–5, 1915–16; Chief Sec. for Ireland 1905; Colonial Sec. 1916–19; 1st Ld. of Admiralty 1919–21; cr. Viscount 1921.

next meeting – a much bigger show, where Dixey,[28] member for Penrith was in full swing – Macmillan followed and then I – and was half way through an oration when in came Randy. I carried on for a while in great style. Back at the Adelphi Mac and I had a sandwich and a lager and were then collected by George Thomson[29] who had prepared a supper for us over the way at a small haunt of his. We said adieu to Randolph, did justice to George's thin sandwiches and caught the midnight mail to Town – I slept like a top. Impressions of the election – people very much behind Randolph in his attacks on the Caucus, interested about India, and genuinely angry about the air defence-lessness. In my own speeches it was air and the Caucus that brought 'em up in cheers. On Tuesday (29th) I awoke at Euston and drank a cup of tea and dressed and left the train about 7–45. Took a taxi to the Savoy and had some coffee while I read the paper. At nine went up to Rothermere's suite. He was dressing. [...] R. was very interested in my account of Wavertree and asked me to tell Winston.[30] We got a call through to Winston to whom I gave my frank impressions.

'He's a very good speaker, isn't he?' asked Papa.

'Very good – and very versatile – I think you've every reason to be proud of him', I said.

'Thank you very much', said Winston, with a strange drop into frank gratification. He surveyed the campaign in a few words and decided that Randolph's cry for the last three days of the fight must be 'Plat[31] is beaten – Don't put the Socialist in – Vote for Churchill.' [...] I spent much of that day talking on the telephone to Lady Houston, trying to compose the differences between her and R., and to secure the £10,000 for our fund. It was hopeless. She was far more right than he. He had originally led her to believe that she could be in the forefront of the League – could in fact be its founder – and promised her publicity in his papers for her patriotic objects and activities. Now he realises that her only obsession is slinging clods at Ramsay and rightly feels that we can't have that kind of thing in connection with great National movement concerned with air defences. He should, of course, have

---

[28] Arthur Carlyne Niven Dixey (1889–1954): Con. MP for Penrith & Cocklemouth 1923–35.

[29] [?] George Malcolm Thomson (b. 1899): Beaverbrook's personal sec.; leader writer *Daily Express*, author & book critic *Evening Standard*.

[30] Winston Leonard Spencer Churchill (1874–1965): MP for Oldham (Con. to 1904 then Lib.), Lib. MP Manchester NW 1906–8, Dundee 1908–22, Con. MP Epping (later Woodford) 1924–64; Pres. BofT. 1908–10; Home Sec. 1910–11; 1st Ld. of Admiralty 1911–15, 1939–40; Chanc. Duchy of Lancaster 1915; Min. of Munitions 1917–19; Sec. for War & Air 1919–21; Colonial Sec. 1921–2; Chanc. of the Exchequer 1924–9; P.M. 1940–5, 1951–5; Con. Leader 1940–55; KG 1953.

[31] J. Plat: Official Con. cand. for Wavertree by-election; secured 13,771 votes but pushed into 2nd place behind Lab. owing to R. Churchill's intervention.

thought of that first – but he retains an Irish impulsiveness.

Sunday 10 February   This week has gone past even more quickly than
most weeks. On Monday we got the National League of Airmen
launched. As I expected the first day at 39 Grosvenor Square was semi-
chaos. Neither Macmillan nor Billham seemed alive to what was
needed. I went down on the Sunday morning expecting to find
Macmillan drilling his staff but he had vanished for the day into the
country. [...] Lil and Marjorie Coles[32] have been down at Grosvenor
Square each day working as volunteers – my room is the bedroom of
the Earl of Durham and they have a desk there, which interests them.
Paul Bewsher,[33] poet and reporter and ex-wartime pilot remarked to
Lil one afternoon as he stood at my window, 'I suppose we are looking
over the most aristocratic chimney-pots in the world ...' – which was
a point of view. [...] On Thursday I reached the Savoy by taxi at
9–10. [...] In a little while Sir George Sutton came in, and seemed
surprised to find me there. We talked politics until Esmond Harmsworth
arrived. R. moved to an easy chair, I took the sofa, Sutton and Esmond
sat at the table – Esmond having a scrappy breakfast and Sutton some
tea, while I had more coffee. To my amazement they plunged into a
very confidential talk about a big merger – Price Brothers.[34] I rose with
a remark that I must be in the way, but R. would have none of it, so
I listened in like one of the family, until the talk turned on to politics.
Esmond Harmsworth is a much stronger man than I have been led to
believe – very definite in his opinion, very emphatic in his talk – and
very like his father, save that his eyes are a very vivid blue. He must
stand about six feet four, and is broadly built.

Tuesday 12 February   A taxi took me from there [Connaught rooms] to
Liverpool Street and I began my journey – with F.E.'s *Historic Trials*[35]
to keep me interested. At Norwich a new Ford (which is more like a
Rolls) awaited me, and took me a fairy drive through miles of twisted
and green hedged lanes, showing strangely in the light of the headlamps.
It swung me into the drive of a pleasant white façaded house. The
butler told me that 'His Lordship' was resting but that Mr Shersham

[32] 'Auntie' Marjorie Coles: cousin of Lilian Brooks and sister to Halstaff Coles, who
gave Lilian away on her wedding day in 1916.
[33] Paul Bewsher (1894–1966): author, poet, journalist. Port of London Authority 1912–
14; *Advertisers' Weekly* 1914; RNAS 1915–18; RAF 1918–19; Sub-Ed *Modern Transport* 1919;
joined *Daily Mail* staff 1920.
[34] Price Brothers: printing & paper company.
[35] F.E. Smith, *Famous Trials of History* (London: Hutchinson, 1926).

was in the hall. One end of the hall was a lounge with a big open fire and a pleasant quiet man came forward and introduced himself to me. He joined the business in 1899 and had been on the pulp and paper side in Canada for many years. Barely had we talked each other into acquaintance when R. asked me to go upstairs. I followed the footman and came to his bedroom. He was lying on a large bed which was like a pallet bed from a studio. On the wall by its side was a big portrait of the wonderful old Mother of the Harmsworth family, very like her son. The mantle shelf carried a row of little family photographs, including one of the Father in wig and gown. On the nearby wall were two enlargements of his dead soldier sons.[36] For the rest, the room held a chest of drawers with books piled on to it, a dressing table and a desk and a couple of easy chairs. R. welcomed me warmly, and we talked for an hour. He had a touch of muscular rheumatism in the back he said, but was otherwise well. The talk was wide ranging, but included the one piece of news that Walter Greaves Lord[37] might be made a judge. I asked if Macmillan would be put up to fight the seat – Norwood – but R. said he thought it was too early, that the pilots might think we had merely organised them for political ramp. With this I agreed. [. . .] Weds. Feb. 13th [. . .] after lunch he grew again very melancholy about the twilight into which Britain is entering. To my own amazement I found myself striding up and down chiding and out-arguing him – a hey-ding-dong dialectical battle – I refusing to believe that Britain was yet in the twilight – declaring that there were yet resolute men to be found – that my generation would not take to obscurity among nations unprotestingly.

He said at last, 'My dear fellow, we've often agreed that you can't even raise money from these inert people for any patriotic purpose.'

C.B.: 'You can for the right purpose.'

R.: 'Do you think you could raise even a thousand pounds to combat this decadence.'

C.B.: 'With ease.'

R.: 'If you feel so sure, why don't you fight Norwood.'

C.B.: 'Hold hard, sir, I'm not sure the moment is ripe for me to fight, Norwood or anywhere else.'

R.: 'Of course it is. You stand and I'll support you. I can't finance you, but I'll give you £250 – you can raise the rest.'

C.B.: 'Yes. If I want it.'

R.: 'Do it, my dear fellow, do it.'

---

[36] Harmsworth Brothers: Vere (1895–1916): & Harold Alfred Vyvyan St George (1894–1918). Both killed in action during European War, 1914–18.

[37] Walter Greaves-Lord (1878–1942): lawyer & judge; King's Bench 1935–40, rtd. 1940; contested parliamentary seat, Ince, Lancs. Jan. & Dec. 1910; Con. MP Norwood 1922–35.

C.B.: (after a few minutes thought) Alright, I'll fight.'
R.: 'Good.'
On the word he took up the 'phone and dictated an announcement
to the *Evening News* saying that a powerful independent Tory candidate
was ready ...[38]

Thursday 14 February   A busy day. I rang Lucy Houston on the telephone
and asked her to back me to the tune of £1,000 if I wanted it. She
readily agreed and was glad that I meant to fight. R. had been on the
phone about 8–15 urging me to action. During the day I talked
with George Sutton. On Tuesday a sudden market slump had been
precipitated by a scare in the Paris *Daily Mail*. George was apprehensive
that it would ruin the business – had been on to R. yesterday and R.
had changed Meredith from a bear to a bull in the city pages, which
I had seen from the other end of the wire. George was not easy about
fighting Norwood. My company law lecture in the evening was much
of an anti-climax.

Friday 15 February   R. rang up early and said he thought I had better
issue a preliminary election address in Saturday's *Daily Mail*. The official
selection committee was to meet on Saturday and my announcement
might frighten them. I prepared an address (in the midst of doing my
city page matter) and read it over to him. He said that he had one or
two ideas and would dictate them to Morison and phone them back.
At noon I went to Coster's to be photographed and then lunched [...].
At the office at about three R. rang and in a glum voice said,
   'Brooks, Morison has been talking to me and has convinced me that
certain people in the city are right – if we split the vote at Norwood
the Socialist will get in and that will precipitate a crisis. I am disappointed, but it is quite true. I can't ruin the business. We'll have to
stand down.'
   'What! I wish I'd been at you elbow instead of Morison ...'
   'I know, my dear fellow, but I can't take the responsibility for losing
millions of money on the businesses, can I.'
   'Well, I'm damned sorry.'

[38] *The Evening News* 15 February 1935 under headline 'The Norwood By-election': 'An
independent Conservative candidate is ready to step in at Norwood. He is a young man
who has taken a life-long interest in Conservative politics. He served with distinction in
the war. Among his leisure activities are novel writing and the encouragement of civil
aviation. He is opposed to the Government policy on India. His participation in the
election will depend on the attitude of the official Conservative candidate on India.'

'So am I – never mind, my dear fellow, I'll see that you get your eighteen hundred a year –'

'That doesn't weigh with me two seconds or console me ....'

'No. I know it doesn't. But it can't be helped. We must withdraw ...'

And that was the end of our three-day abortive campaign. I went down and told Brittain and McWhirter. Britt and I agreed, talking it over later, that Sutton and McWhirter had probably used all their force. But when I talked with George he said no, and that it wasn't Morison but some powerful quarter in the city which had changed R's mind. Britt was foaming with wrath – and he and Broadbent,[39] our lobby man, and I had a very strange and curious talk. Broadbent says that Jimmy Thomas[40] accuses R. of bearing and bullying Britain just to make money, and Ramsay MacDonald had said to him (Broadbent) 'Do you get a bonus for devising picturesque lies for your master?' which had drawn a hot retort from B and caused a minor scene in the lobby. What I hated most was having got financial support from Claude de Bernales[41] and Erekson and others having to return their cheques with such an explanation – when the whole point of any candidature was to threaten the Central Office with the crisis we might have precipitated to make them revise their policy and climb down on India and build up on air.

Saturday 16 February I went down for a morning conference at the N.L.A., and had about ten calls from Norfolk. One was from Morison to say that R. wanted me to say in my Dictatorship article that the National Gvt is not a chatterbox Gvt – having turned round with a vengeance after Tuesday's panic. I flatly refused to do it and said that he was to tell R. that what I suggested was the insertion of a box dissociating the paper's views from mine. To this he agreed.

Sunday 17 February After a hurried morning on the Survey,[42] I had an early lunch and took the whole family, plus 'Auntie Marjorie' to Brooklands for the N.L.A. rally. It was a good fresh day – and while I wandered about doing the polite things expected of the chairman the

[39] Wilson 'Jack' Broadbent: Lobby journalist; *Daily Mail* & *Sunday Dispatch*.

[40] James 'Jimmy' Henry Thomas (1874–1949): MP Derby 1910–36 (Lab. to 1931, then Nat. Lab.); Gen. Sec. National Union of Railwaymen 1918–31; Colonial Sec. 1924, 1935–6; Ld. Privy Seal 1929–30; Dominions Sec. 1930–5.

[41] Claude de Bernales: Company Dir. various mining companies including Anglo-Australian Gold Development & Niluna Gold Corp.

[42] Covering topics: unemployment and government critics; air rearmament.

family amused itself by making its maiden flight .... which they all enjoyed enormously. I had to orate to a hundred or two people, and on the whole enjoyed the day immensely.

Thursday 21 February   A busy day at Northcliffe House, where I wrote my Conscription article[43] and quarrelled violently with Brittain about it. He said it was dull – I said I knew that but it had to make familiar points. (Later we agreed that it needed a new opening, so I did three sentences which pleased us both.) This bad temper coloured the mood of the day. After lunch at my desk I shot off to the N.L.A., where also I found a load of minor troubles. My phone went and Randolph's voice asked me to dash off to the Mayfair on urgent business. I finished my work there and took a taxi over, recalling that at breakfast Lucy Houston had rung me up to say that Eric Long would fight Norwood. When I arrived at Randolph's room he greeted me well, but when I said, 'Is Eric Long to stand?' he said, merely, 'How are you?'

C.B.: 'Very fit, but full of disgruntlement and disappointment about R's change of front.'

R. Churchill: 'That's why I wanted you to come round. I have a panacea for you. You *are* going to stand.'

For half an hour we argued, I trying to convince him that after refusing to stand and returning my friends' money it wasn't possible for me to re-enter the field. Either splitting the vote would imperil the funds or it wouldn't. He saw that and then said that he was determined to find a candidate. His sister, Diana Bailey,[44] came in as we talked and curled up on the sofa with a champagne cocktail as we drank our whiskys and soda – very pale and much more sophisticated than the rather pop-eyed girl I met at Londonderry House in 1928. She obviously worships the Grandolph, as she calls him, and as his grandfather[45] was called. Randolph said that his father, Winston, and Lord Lloyd[46] had both wanted the seat to be fought but that the India Defence League had turned down the project.

'I've quarrelled with "papa" about it, and I'm ready to quarrel with Rothermere, if necessary, but I'm going to fling somebody into the

[43] At Rothermere's instruction.

[44] Diana Bailey (1906–1963): eldest child & d. of Winston Churchill; m. John Milner Bailey 12 Dec. 1932, diss. 1935; m. Edwyn Duncan-Sandys.

[45] Randolph Henry Spencer Churchill (1849–95): Con. MP Woodstock 1874–5, Paddington S. 1885–95; India Sec. 1885–6; Chanc. of the Exchequer 1886–7; styled Lord Randolph Churchill, father of Winston Churchill.

[46] George Ambrose Lloyd (1879–1941): Con. MP Staffs. W. 1910–18, Eastbourne 1924–5; Gov. of Bombay 1918–23; High Comm. for Egypt & Sudan 1925–9; Colonial Sec. 1940–1; Con. Leader in HofL. 1941; Chm., British Council 1937–40; kt. 1918, cr. Baron Lloyd 1925.

seat. . .' He was full of vim and fire, and denounced Ramsay with as much vigour as Lucy Houston. He and Diana were both chagrined at the sad fate that had befallen him. He was to have had the reversion of Eastbourne, but thinking Slater[47] good for many years had tied himself (against my advice) to Wavertree a few weeks before Slater fell dead. I left them both, very excited and full of fight.

Sunday 24 February   R. rang me for a talk at 8–15. It began as a discussion of Findlay's[48] chances [in Norwood].

I said, ' I still think Randolph is on bad batting ground. Sandy's[49] is strong on air, he says he will vote against 'em on India – and he's a young Tory. What ground has Findlay for his intervention?'

R.: 'He's a fine upstanding young pilot – he'll get the women's vote.'

C.B.: 'But Sandys is that, too.'

R.: 'But Findlay is the right age, they like 'em over thirty. With hair on their chests. Have you seen the film 'Bengal Lancer'? See it, my dear fellow. The two heroes wash in one scene. Great hairy chested fellows. Now those film men are very cunning. They don't obtrude hairy chests on their audience unless they've made sure the modern gals like 'em. In my time we believed women hated hairy chests. P'raps they did. But these modern women are different . . .'

C.B.: 'None the less, Findlay may be a bad candidate. He only resigned the Blackshirts on Friday.'

R.: 'They don't care what sort of shirt he wore – blackshirt, greenshirt, blueshirt. They'd prefer him without a shirt – a fine upstanding young pilot.'

We passed into an exchange of bawdy jokes, Lil besides me in bed convulsed with laughter.

Wednesday 6 March   I shall make a special memo of to-day.

One day last week Steward,[50] of No. 10 Downing Street, rang me up to say that he wished to continue a snatch of talk begun in the

---

[47] John A. Slater (1889–1935): Con. MP Eastbourne 1932–5.

[48] R. Findlay: Ind. Con. cand. in March 1935 Norwood by-election. Polled 2,698 votes (8.5%) but lost deposit. Stood on a platform opposed to the government's India policy. Seat was won for Con. by Duncan Sandys.

[49] Lt. Col. Edwyn Duncan Sandys (1908–87): diplomatic corps, FO 1930–5; Con. MP Norwood 1935–45, Streatham 1950–74; disabled active service 1941; FS, WO 1941–3; PS, Min. of Supply 1943–4; Chm. of War Cabinet Ctte on V Weapons 1943–5; Min. of Works 1944–5; held ministerial office 1951–64; Chm. of International Exec. of the European Movement, 1947–50; cr. Baron Duncan-Sandys 1974.

[50] George Frederick Steward (1884–1952): appointed Private Secretary (Intelligence) by MacDonald 1931; Chief Press Officer, HMG 1937–44.

Reform Club on Wednesday February 27th. I suggested tea at the Savage, and after some talk there he asked me if I would meet the Chief Whip, David Margesson,[51] privately. I said that there was no reason why I shouldn't, and today was fixed for the appointment. At 11–30 I entered the Treasury, a very reasonable place for a financial journalist to visit. Steward was waiting for me in the hall, and hurried me through into a room in No. Ten. He then rang Margesson and after some talk asked if I would mind going through with him to the Chief Whip's room in No. 11. I said, no, and we passed through No. 10 into No. 11. After introducing me, and after Margesson and I saying we had met, Steward left us. I took off my coat and drew up a chair to the fire, with a glance at the familiar print of Pitt hanging over the desk. Margesson took out his pipe and we settled down to talk. It was understood between us that no one was to know of my visit and that any ideas I gave him for the reconstruction of the Party and the taming of the 'rebels' were to be his own, and not mine ... I began by telling him bluntly that the revolt was not, as Steward had thought, merely the peevishness of two megalomaniacs, but was something that went much deeper. I said that Lucy Houston would finance Randolph, or any other young leader, to any extent to fight every Ramsay MacDonald seat at the next election. I assured him that R. was very sincere and very much in earnest about India.

'We must go through with the Bill,' said Margesson.

'You must not be allowed to,' said I. 'Our opinion is that the Princes will not permit its passage.' (I did not tell him that Colebatch had told me that the Princes' legal advisers had said that they saw no hope of drafting amendments that would satisfy the Indian party and White-hall ...)

We discussed the grievances of people like myself with the conduct of the Party.

'What can we do?' he asked. 'We can't interfere with the autonomy of the local committees. Take Samuel[52] ... the local people want £1,000 a year spending there – that ruled out everybody but two possibles, of whom Samuel was the least impossible – from our point of view it is heart-rending – the safe Conservative seats held by those hopeless duds – if there is a landslide we shall be left with a minority composed of men who can't think and can't speak ...'

'Surely,' said I 'it is a question of organisation: if you had a fund and let it be known that for the right younger men the £1,000 would

[51] (Henry) David Reginald Margesson (1890–1965): Con. MP Upton 1922–3, Rugby 1924–42; Ass. Whip 1924–6; Whip 1926–9; Chief Whip 1931–40; Sec. for War 1940–2; cr. Viscount Margesson 1942.

[52] Marcus Reginald Anthony Samuel (1873–1942): Con. cand. unsuccessful N. South-wark 1929; Con. MP Putney 1934–42.

be supplied ... I know that means a hell of a fighting fund ...'

'It means a return to the Lloyd George method of selling honours – Ll.G. was kicked out because of the stink about honours, not because of his policy. I tell you, Brooks, that your city men will give us money for the National Government but they won't give a penny for the Tory Party alone ... We know that Ramsay is a liability, but what can we do ...'

We talked of 1931. He said Baldwin then had to accept the Ramsay leadership because of Buckingham Palace, and that the same influence is potent in keeping Ramsay in office still. We talked on, both of us very frankly, for an hour and a half. At the end of the time he said that I had been very useful and that when the big change was ripe, after the Jubilee celebrations, he would like to have another confidential talk with me. I donned my coat and suggested that I would find my way back to Steward's room, but he insisted on guiding me, in case anybody saw me ... and with that we stepped out and ... RAN STRAIGHT INTO THE WHOLE CABINET LEAVING THE CABINET ROOM. I dodged Hilton Young, who was the most likely to accost me by name, and as Neville Chamberlain turned to speak to Margesson, I slipped away. (The Cabinet, incidentally, had been discussing Ramsay's mad White Paper on Defence ...) Steward, looking perturbed, gathered me up – he had come part way to warn us that if we left the Chief Whip's room we should meet the Cabinet *en masse* – and shot me along to the Treasury again. There I talked with him for a while, and went on to lunch with Hobson and Vibart Dickson[53] at the Reform. There, in the briefest outline, was the David-Maine-like adventure. (David Maine? A character in my last 'shocker' *Frame-up*.[54]) The bulk of the talk was on how to reconcile R. to official Conservatism. I said from the first that I was very fond of R. and would not in any way betray his confidence, but if I could help to re-cement the Party, I would like that. I was brutally frank, and so was Margesson, and our exchanged opinions about Ramsay, Jimmy Thomas and Kingsley-Wood and others were scarifying. It was an odd episode.

Saturday 16 March Phone call from R. at 8–15 asking me to bring Macmillan to lunch at 1–15. I was up betimes and did some more copy, to the office, worked like a nigger, shot across town in a taxi to N.L.A. headquarters, picked up Macmillan and we went to Stratton House for

[53] Vibart R. Dickson: Dir. & member London Ctte. Witwatersrand Deep Ltd.
[54] *Frame-up* (London: Hutchinson, 1935).

lunch. R. was there in good form, with Morison and Ward Price.[55] The whole of the talk was about German preparedness. Ward Price made the good point that in Germany Britain's prestige as an unconquered nation was far more formidable than we thought and that in any event she had her Eastern frontiers to obsess her. R. had thought my Frederick the Great article not direct enough and asked me to see him to-morrow morning to talk it over. I suggested that evening instead. [...] At the office all was agog. Broadbent had come down and was busy ringing up all kinds of people. In the intervals he and I talked of Randolph. Broadbent says he will drink himself to death before he is thirty. He sits up till about four each morning, steadily swigging. B. has told him that he should be following his father's example at his age – storing his mind by omnivorous reading, but Randolph has such confidence in his own acquisitive brain that he won't read. Rothermere pays him £2,500 a year which is virtually a young man's pension. Broadbent also said that J.H. Thomas had told him on Wednesday, on Horder's word, that Ramsay MacDonald would be out of the Premiership in ten days, but because he (Broadbent) said something to that effect in *The Mail* Ramsay stiffened up, and has twice come up from Chequers to attend a Cabinet or a Cabinet Committee and has made certain that the press were informed of it. Eventually Broadbent and I took a taxi home and I dropped him at Turnham Green.

Thursday 21 March   dashed off to do my lecture at the City of London College and then by taxi to the Albert Hall, where a seat was being kept for me in the Royal Box for the India Defence meeting. I missed Lloyd and entered soon after Winston had got into his stride. He made a good fighting speech – but he has never conquered those weak 's's' of his. I had no chance to do more than hear Page Croft, because Warner Allen came in and took me out into the Corridor to ask whether he should advise Lady H. to finance the India Defence League as a new Tory organisation. I said, no. Let her finance Randolph's new organisation, said I, and the derelicts of the India Defence League will come to it. The move to transform the League into a new Tory body is really a job-savers' move. During the rest of the evening I was tackled by two young men, each like an imitation of Anthony Eden,[56] each

---

[55] George Ward Price (1895–1961): Journalist & author; European correspondent for *Daily Mail* for more than thirty years; Dir. Associated Newspapers; author *Extra-Special Correspondent* (1957).

[56] (Robert) Anthony Eden (1897–1977): Con. MP Warwick & Leamington 1923–57; PPS to G. Locker-Lampson 1924–6, to Austen Chamberlain 1926–9; US FO 1931–4; Ld. Privy Seal 1934–5 & Min. for League of Nations 1935; For. Sec. 1935–8, 1940–5, 1951–5; Dominions Sec. 1939–40; Sec. for War 1940; PM & Con. Leader 1955–7; KG 1954, cr. Earl of Avon 1961.

impressed with my power, each intent upon soliciting my support for a new club they are trying to form out of a medley of other clubs to bring Toryism back to its senses.

Wednesday 27 March   Spent the morning at the National League of Airmen. Young Findlay (Randolph's candidate at Norwood) came in to see me and I passed him to Macmillan. I lunched at the reform with Oscar Hobson and Lex.[57] In the evening took a meeting at Streatham with Macmillan. These N.L.A. meetings are surprisingly successful. Numbers are smallish – but one expects that with broad-casting and cinemas in competition. The people are very much alive to the German menace and very angry at the lack of an adequate air force here. The only questions we get as a rule that are antagonistic are from the no-resistant pacifist or from the cynic who has to be assured that we are not backed by aircraft makers. Great care has to be taken not to attack Germany solely, though when any incautious speaker does so it is only a few Fascists who object.

Sunday 31 March   After a busy morning on the Survey[58] Dilly and Edward and Austen came down to Waterloo with me where I met Brittain, and he and I journeyed to Leatherhead to visit Lord Beaver-brook. The drive from Leatherhead station is pleasant and the house pleasant, not very charming, as Stody is, and not really so friendly a house, qua house, but pleasant. Max (as all call him) welcomed us. There was a lout of a fellow, like a dull witted plough boy, with him (whom I learnt afterwards to my amaze was the brilliant Aneurin Bevan[59] – but obviously gone to seed with too much Cafe Royal and being taken up by the rich) and a pleasant German Baron, whose name I already forget. He was Chancellor of the Embassy when war broke in 1914. [...] Max is as informal as Rothermere – he opened the tea interval by seizing and buttering a piece of toast and munching it as he wandered about the rug, leaving us to forage. When he moves he is like some genial spider, his legs thin and long, his body short and round at the shoulders, and his face round and impish. He is small in

---

[57] Hargreaves Parkinson (1896–1950): financial journalist, used pseudonym 'Lex'; wrote column 'Notes for Investors', *Financial News*; Ed. *Financial Times* 1938–45; *The Economist* from 1945.

[58] Covering the topics: survey; jubilee story; to make skilled workers; Liverpool a free port; telemetring.

[59] Aneurin Bevan (1894–1960): Lab. MP Ebbw Vale 1929–60; Min. of Health 1945–51; Min. of Lab. & National Service 1951; Treasurer of Lab. Party 1956–60; Dep. Leader 1959–60.

stature and in limb. He speaks with a breezy Canadian accent, very frankly, and has an infectious laugh. Very soon he took Brittain and me into another room and lighted a log fire – it is noticeable that he has the temperament that would rather put logs on the fire than ring for a man to do it – and we sat with a copy of the *Sunday Dispatch* and the *Sunday Express* in front of us on the rug while he 'post-mortemed' them. I was greatly struck by his professional shrewdness and by his perfectly frank assessment of all factors. He laughs at the antics of proprietors, including his own. He spoke sometimes like an inspired chief sub-editor, sometimes like a statesman, and sometimes like a mischievous small boy. He invited perfect openness from us and promised perfect confidence.

'I want to see you two fellows make a go of it, I hear you've formed an effective coalition. Rothermere is a fine man. I'm his oldest and closest friend in some ways – we've known each other since 1910, never quarrelled. If we drift apart we come back in perfect accord. There is no competition between our two Sunday papers: they should be complementary. Our job is to create a bigger public for our kind of journal and eat into the six million circulation of the *People* and the *News of the World.*'

When, in his detailed examination of the various pages he came to my city pages he leaned back. I waited for some incisive criticism.

'Brooks, I think your finance is FINE. You should occupy a high position in finance,' he said.

'Do you mean that!' said I.

'I certainly do.'

'I take it you'd be brutal if you didn't. . .'

'I certainly should – mark you, by implication I infer what I've already said, I don't approve your choice of topics as a special writer, but that is because you and Rothermere chose them and he wants policy pressing . . .'

Later on I said to him, 'Will you now give us a quick resume of your attitude to the paper. Suppose for a moment I've met you casually at a dinner table and have said, "What's your opinion of the *Sunday Dispatch?*" '

He did so and then returned to compliment my finance – 'You've got ahead of my fellow – he's trying to be a highbrow and hasn't got one. You keep on treating those pages as they are – they're fine . . .'

We drifted out of that room. 'Have a drink?' said he.

Brittain drinks nothing. 'Thanks, I'd like a sherry to warm me for the road,' said I.

In the big room we found the other two and Castlerosse,[60] just back

[60] Valentine Castlerosse (1891–1943): Beaverbrook journalist, columnist 'Londoner's Log', *Sunday Express*; Viscount Castlerosse; suc. Earl of Kenmare (Irish Peer).

from Aintree with lively tales of the Adelphi dinner and some Regency scandals of the adulteries of the great and near-great. Max fired question after question at him, talked to me and asked me about foreign exchange dealings – making little notes all the time in a pocket book, which was on a table at his side by an enviable bust of Voltaire.[61] Once or twice he moved to where a private phone stood on a grand piano, and phoned to the *Express* much as R. phones to the *Mail*. We talked of Reginald Berkeley,[62] of whom I had written a memoir in the *S.D.*, and later Max relayed what I had said and what Beverley Baxter[63] told him on the telephone as the bones of the *Daily Express* orbit. [...] Brittain and I left about eight, were motored down to Leatherhead station, talked in the train, talked again over coffee at Waterloo – and so to our homes. I rang up R. and told him of the talk, including Beaverbrook's remark that ours was a better production than his.

Wednesday 3 April   left the [Air Force] Club as Macmillan and I had an appointment with R. at 3. When we reached Stratton House we found Ward Price with him. Our visit had a purpose. R's business colleagues have persuaded him (as Beaverbrook has also persuaded him) that too much insistence upon the imminence of war and the need for defence is harming the papers. He gave an order to slow down the N.L.A. space, and the fools in charge cut out all mention, including notice of meetings. On my protest to R. he explained that such was not his intention, and asked Macmillan and me to tea. Ward Price left at 4. (He is going to Stresa to meet Mussolini.[64] He said that Grandi[65] had told him that this is the last of the post-war and the first of the pre-war years.) R. and Macmillan and I stayed together talking about modern aircraft and air strategy until Macmillan left for the Lords at 4–45, where he was to meet somebody or another. R. kept me talking, chiefly about Beaverbrook's ideas on the paper but inevitably about Germany.

[61] François Marie Arouet de Voltaire (1694–1778): French Enlightenment writer & intellectual.
[62] Reginald Berkeley (1890–1935): Lib. MP Nottingham Central 1922–4; playwright.
[63] (Arthur) Beverley Baxter (1891–1964): Con. MP Wood Green 1935–50, Southgate 1950–64; journalist, Ed.-in-Chief *Daily Express*, 1929–33; public relations counsel Gaumont British Picture Corp. 1933–5; Ed. Adviser Allied Newspapers 1938; kt. 1954.
[64] Benito Mussolini (1883–1945): founder & Duce of Italian Fascist Party; Pres. Council of Ministers 1922–6; PM 1926–43; For. Min. 1924–9, 1932–6; Head of German puppet regime in N. Italy 1943–5.
[65] Count Dino Grandi (1895–1988): Italian Amb. to London 1932–9; Min. of Justice & Chm. of the Fascist Grand Council, 1939–43.

Thursday 4 April   At five I took taxi across a rain swept London to visit Beaverbrook at Stornoway House, in response to a telephone request this morning. Stornoway House lies just behind St. James' Palace. A butler admits you and you are passed into a long narrow room, where two young men secretaries work in great comfort at a round table. When I arrived the Little Man was on the telephone, but in three minutes he had me called in, shook hands, waved me to a settee, and for another three minutes finished dictating a letter to a third secretary. 'Well, Brooks, how are you getting on? Come to this end of the settee, where I shall see you better –' and that launched us on to the real purpose of the visit. He wanted to tell me that he was going to see Brittain alone to tell him that he must cultivate a better judgement, must not be sensational and must be guided by me, and that he was going to tell Rothermere the same thing. He drank half a cup of hot water and I a cup of thin China, but we did not eat. We talked of R's belief in an imminent war, and Beaverbrook was insistent that we kept it out of the papers.

'I agree,' I said, 'But I feel that Rothermere is right.'

'Does it matter, Brooks?'

'From the angle of selling ink and paper at a profit, no. But from the angle of a man with a mission, yes. But what I meant was that my own agreement weakens my advocacy when I am advising a cessation of the policy of telling the truth ...'

He grinned, impishly. 'A paper can't afford to prophesy disaster, can it?' he said.

'God knows, I've done it myself, but you're quite sound,' I said.

We talked a good deal about the *Financial News* and of Bracken. On Sunday just as I was leaving him Beaverbrook had said, 'Never go back to financial journalism, Brooks. You can't keep straight for life on those kinds of paper.' Today he was more insistent than ever that I should abide by general journalism. My training, he thought, was a marvellous grounding. One of his laughing remarks was, 'Journalism's a game for young fellows with old boys riding 'em.' He seems genuinely fond of Brittain and entreated me (there is no other word) to keep him subdued.

Friday 5 April   R. came on the private phone about 8–40. After some talk on affairs I told him about Beaverbrook and his view that Brittain goes off at half cock and that I should be the governor on the engine.

'That's what I think – have thought – I'm going to make you a super-editor – come and have breakfast with me.'

'Where are you.'

'Avenue Road.'

'It'll take forty five minutes to reach you.'

'All right, my dear fellow, have your breakfast then get out your car and come over.'

I had had my breakfast – my toast and tea – so I dressed and got out my taxi and went over. He and the Wilsons[66] and Warden and another (one of the young Harmsworths, I fancy) were just finishing the meal. After greetings he and I went into a smaller room and talked very frankly and fully of Brittain and his critics. I told R. of Brittain's career and found him much impressed with B's energy and experience in America and in the possession of his old local paper.

R. had begun by saying to me, 'You have your agreement with the company haven't you?'

C.B.: 'It's actually in my pocket, signed last week.'

R.: 'Now how can I put you in a position to take control without doing harm to the paper by killing Brittain's enthusiasm – can I find a new title for you.'

I drew him off this line. He then suggested Associate Editor.

C.B.: 'No. That is always fatal. It means a dual monarchy and factionalism.'

By the time we had finished threshing the matter out he said 'Well, can we achieve it without my writing a letter?'

C.B.: 'Easily. If you think I'm the man – '

R.: (interrupting) 'I certainly do. I have designed you for a seat on the Board of Associated Newspapers as soon as there's a chance.'

C.B.: 'That's a startling thought.'

R.: 'We want young men of great energy, like you.'

So after more talk, and talk on other business sides of the organisation, I left him.

Saturday 6 April   A crowded day. I began to type some copy at 9–30 and I left the office at 1–30 the following morning, technically Sunday. We changed the leader because R. was enraged by a remark on Lenin[67] in the *New Statesman*, suggesting that as the King[68] had been toasted in Moscow the time was coming when Lenin would be toasted in Britain. Later in the day he rang me to say that he had had a violent argument with Winston. After telling me of Winston's points he said, 'What do *you* think about that?' He was genuinely angry with Churchill. Later in

[66] Mrs Adelaide Wilson & Miss Judith Wilson: from Dublin, acted as companions to Rothermere. According to Brooks, R. proposed to his cousin Judith in 1938 following the death of his estranged wife, but the proposal was never taken further.

[67] Vladimir Illich Lenin (1870–1924): revolutionary; Bolshevik leader & premier of Soviet Govt. 1917–24.

[68] King George V(1865–1936): Prince of Wales 1901–10; King 1910–36.

the day I rang him with news of Mussolini's memorandum about applying Article XVI to Germany and we had another long talk on foreign affairs. After I had gone over the old familiar ground he said, in a kind of heavy grunt, 'You are perfectly right – perfectly right . . .' It was to-night that Goebbels[69] made the most provocative speech yet delivered – at Danzig.

Wednesday, 10 April   took taxi to 37 Avenue Road to dine with Lord Rothermere. He was sitting in an easy chair in his slippers when I arrived (we had had three phone talks during the day) and was glad to see me. 'Have a whisky and soda or something?' he asked, forgetting that he now thinks that Great Men (*a la* Mussolini and Hitler) live like Spartans. We were discussing Germany when Harry Morison came in and shortly after Mrs and Miss Wilson. We dined simply but well, R. and I arguing about something to the amusement of the others. After dinner the ladies retired to another room with a wireless set, and R. asked me what I would do with £200,000 in the belief that Germany means war, and will be successful. It was quite a serious query, and we discussed it in all aspects, but with several jests to lighten the topic.

At one stage, R.: 'I know that your suggestion will be – divide it equally between you and Morison.'

C.B. (pained): 'You are quite wrong – quite wrong – my suggestion is divide it unequally between ME – and Morison.'

And again:

R.: 'But you insist that war means a complete economic breakdown. You're a nice fellow to invite to dinner. What'll happen to newspapers?'

C.B. (cheerfully): 'Oh, they'll be gone.'

R.: 'What, dead?'

C.B.: 'Quite dead.'

R.: 'Then what'll happen to Morison?'

C.B.: 'Oh, he'll be over that very convenient lamp-post at the corner of Tudor Street.'

R.: 'And we hauling on the rope.'

C.B. (confidently): 'We'll be running like Hell.'

R. (glumly): 'Umn, my run isn't much of an imitation of Hell.'

I gave him several suggestions about investment for safety on his basic assumption, and promised to get certain information for him. He thinks that to buy gold and store it in Switzerland would be good (I suggested one of the Scandinavian centres) or to buy Reichsmarks and store them would be good. He admitted my thesis that after such a war personal ownership is most likely to vanish, and that the difficulty

[69] Dr Joseph Goebbels (1897–1945): German Min. of Propaganda, 1933–45.

of either obtaining remittances or of transporting oneself will be extreme.

At 11–15 he looked at his watch and said, 'I ought to have been in bed an hour ago – good night, you fellows....'.

Morison and I shared a taxi and wended our way homeward. On the whole, it was one of the pleasantest quiet evenings I have ever spent, to which this entry does no sort of justice.

Thursday, 11 April In the evening Brittain took Lil, and I accompanied them, to the Press Fund Dinner, George Sutton in the chair and Esmond Harmsworth replying as President. It was as brilliant and distinguished a gathering as ever the Mayfair has housed and we enjoyed it. Britt said the anteroom was like a piece of American film, but it was really like a chapter from a Disraeli novel. A mass of bejewelled women and decorated men do make a goodly show to the eye, whatever they make to the emotion.

Saturday, 13 April A busy and congested day, beginning with the usual morning talk, an N.L.A. committee and three city pages ... R. rang me up in the afternoon to ask what I thought of a remarkable article in the *Investors' Chronicle* on Germany's fitness for war ... After dinner I had a forty minutes talk with Lady Houston on the 'phone, chiefly to acknowledge her autographed portrait and to talk about her affairs. She and I flirt vigorously – one forgets the old lady and thinks of the young girl that was once all-conquering. 'You *are* a Dear!' she said as I prepared to ring-off.

Wednesday, 17 April Up early and did some city page pars on the Budget. I meant to go down early to the office but had a message asking me to see Rothermere at noon. Arrived punctually but was kept waiting for twenty minutes by some earlier caller. When I joined him and told him that I had been abed with a queer tummy, he said 'Let's have a walk.' So we walked through the sunny streets, talking of this and that. By one of the great Hotels he stopped and looked boyishly into a fruiterer's window. 'Look at those strawberries ...' He dived into his pocket and produced a handful of letters and two pound notes, like a boy with pocket money. 'Go in and buy them for me,' he said.

I went in. They were 20s. I told the man they were too dear, but he said yesterday they were 25s. So I bought 'em.

R. said 'Did you get them – how much were they?' and seemed quite pleased. He tucked them under his arm and said, 'If you're doing nothing special come and have a chat about five ...' [...] I went back to Stratton House. R. was in his bath, having developed a neuralgic headache. After talking for a while with Clark and Miss Ravon[70] I went into his bedroom. There was some talk between us of the course of markets and of the Geneva Resolution of Censure against Germany. He and I are still convinced of the imminence of war, and we decided to have a leader on it for Sunday. Then I made him have a hot-water bottle under his head and sent his man out for some solidified eau de Cologne. He said after a while that my remedy was doing him good and was making him sleepy. 'Come to breakfast to-morrow, my dear fellow ...' I left him, he looked very old to-night. Usually he looks like a man of forty-five or so. To-night he was every year of his sixty seven. At home I dined with Lil and Mercy,[71] wrote a special on Britain for holidays and the leader. And now it is nearly 10–45 and I am ending my day. I shall read *Bleak House* for an hour.

Thursday, 18 April   My taxi deposited me at 37 Avenue Road at 9–10. Lord Rothermere was not down, so I strolled into the lounge and found there a very caricature of a bald-headed Jew in a check suit. He said he had read many of my articles and then, in very broken English, began to talk a kind of Germanic mysticism. 'Now, who,' I thought, 'can this queer bird be? Is he one of R's secret service men?' In bustled R. – his neuralgic headache gone – and he and I and the Jew, Saloman, sat down to breakfast. [...] The little Jew turned out to be the inventor of a patent bread [...]. He talked incessantly, until R. got rid of him, asking me to stay for a few minutes.

'You're not in a great hurry, are you? my dear fellow?'

Eventually R. and I rolled down to Stratton House in the Rolls, where I had another two or three minutes talk.

'Come back at one for lunch,' was his dismissal.

I taxied over to Northcliffe House, did three paragraphs, looked at some letters, talked with Brittain, and went back to Stratton House [...] where Sir Edward Grigg[72] was already in talk with R. A few minutes latter Freddie Guest[73] came in, and our party was complete. R. really wanted to sound their minds about the menace of air war

[70] Miss Ravon: Rothermere's secretary.

[71] Mercy Clarke, Lil's cousin.

[72] Edward 'Ned' William Grigg (1879–1955): Lib. MP Oldham 1922–25, Con. MP Altrincham 1933–45. Private Sec. to Lloyd-George 1921–2; Gov. of Kenya 1925–30; PS MOI 1939–40; FS WO 1940, US 1940–2; Min. Res. in Middle East 1944–5; kt. 1920, cr. Baron Altrincham 1945.

[73] Frederick Edward Guest (1875–1937): Lib. MP East Dorset 1910–22, Bristol North 1924–9, Con. MP Plymouth Drake 1931–7; Junior Ld. to Treasury 1911–12; Treasurer to the Household 1912–15; Coalition govt. chief whip May 1917–Nov. 1921; Sec. for Air 1921–2.

from Germany. F.E. Guest was fully alive to it, but Ned Grigg was still maundering about the Empire coming to the rescue, and Dominion troops crossing the deep blue sea – oblivious, obviously, to the elimination of the time factor in modern war. We all agreed that the Air Ministry should actually put to the test the effect of modern bombers on a floating battle ship· ... Grigg was sound on one point, that the League of Nations feeling in the country should not be antagonised. Our blunder, he said, was that we had never used the Empire delegation properly ... R. and I insisted that *The Times* leader of this morning, which is 'pro-German' in its denunciation of the Treaty of Versailles had enormous significance. Grigg said Halifax[74] (Edward Wood as he still calls him) was the big influence on Geoffrey Dawson,[75] and that he leads the party in the Cabinet – which is woefully divided – in favour of concessions and justice to Germany. Ramsay no longer trusts himself, both Grigg and Guest said, to read a statement in the House. 'But he went to Stresa!' said three voices, simultaneously. Both Grigg and Guest agree that Baldwin is now fully alive to the realities of the situation. They say that Ll. George will be taken in, and by that means the semblance of a National Government will be preserved. Ll.G. insists upon his Cabinet of Action – would like the Ministry of Agriculture but would prefer to be one of a Junta of four Ministers with no Portfolio. Neville Chamberlain is now reconciled to the idea of George's entry, but Simon would probably have to go to the Woolsack ... After a pleasant, simple lunch, Grigg and Guest went, and Macmillan and I stayed to talk with R. – but we were interrupted by the entry of Francis Day,[76] the actress. (She has been to see Esmond at the office once or twice lately.) She came in, all platinum hair and dash and yellow face – gave R. a camellia, teethed at Macmillan and I and generally very like Francis Day.

R. said to me in a hurried whisper, 'come back in a quarter of an hour for a talk'.

[...] I returned. Shersham was with R., but R. bellowed to me to come in. [...] We talked finance for a few minutes until I was called to the phone, where Brittain told me that Granville[77] had told

---

[74] Edward Frederick Lindley Wood (1881–1959): Con MP for Ripon 1910–25; Pres. of Bd. of Educ. 1922–4, 1932–5; Min. of Agric 1924–5; Viceroy of India 1925–31; Sec. for War 1935; Ld. Privy Seal 1935–7; Ld. Pres. 1937–8; For. Sec. 1938–40; Amb. to Washington 1941–6; cr. Baron Irwin 1925, suc. 3rd Viscount Halifax 1934, cr. Earl Halifax 1944.

[75] (George) Geoffrey Dawson (1874–1944): Ed. *The Times* 1912–19, 1923–41; edu. Magdalen College, Oxford. Known as Robineson until 1917, when he assumed the surname Dawson.

[76] Francis Day (b. 1908): actress, singer, director.

[77] Either Granville George Leveson Gower (1872–1939): diplomatic service 1893–1933; suc. 3rd Earl of Granville 1891; or Edgar Louis Granville (1899–): Lib. MP Eye 1929–51; PPS to H. Samuel 1931, to J. Simon 1931–6; cr. Baron Granville of Eye 1967.

Donegall[78] that after the recess a question was to be asked in the Lords, arising from Baldwin's recent speech as to the actual German air strength, and that the figures would come out. Granville had said, 'People who have laughed at Lord Rothermere's talk of 10,000 to 20,000 will be staggered by the real figure.' I repeated this to R., went into Clark's room for a *Who's Who* and when I came back found R. hustling Shersham off. He rang for tea and then said, after we had checked Granville's identity (it was doubtful whether it was old Lord Granville or Granville, who is Simon's Parliamentary secretary) –

'Brooks, this is our death warrant: you need think of nothing else now. What do *you* make of it?

My deduction was that the real figures had been given by Germany herself. I said that after the fatuous Geneva resolution of censure there had no doubt been a verbal protest to our Ambassador, and that he had probably been told quietly what was the real strength of the censured Nation.

R.: 'I believe you're right. And *The Times* knew! That's why that leader appeared. And that's why it began as one leader and ended as another – it had been hastily altered ...'

We talked all round the situation and R. talked on the phone to Winston, who agreed with our view, and in a few minutes the evening paper came in, with a headline 'Berlin Makes Verbal Protest to British Ambassador'. I stayed until 5 o'clock discussing possibilities, and looking at Hitler's letters to R. – an amazing collection of letters from the head of a State to a foreign national. After I had commented on their historic value, R. told Clark to have the originals and one translation sent to Dornoch to be placed in the safe for preservation. [...] No sooner did I reach the office than I was given a message to dine with R. at 8 o'clock and to ring McWhirter, who had also been invited. [...] We dined alone, the three of us, with no women – and again plunged into foreign affairs. R. is convinced that war is really imminent – and I agree. We both make much of the point that after Simon went to Berlin and secured a full list of the German claims and grievances he actually moved the resolution of censure at Geneva. The talk was, naturally, gloomy, but we managed to enliven it with some jests and jesting analogies.

I said to R. over my glass of port (he doesn't drink these days and little Mac pretends not to in that house) 'In some ways I envy Hitler – it must be like sitting with five aces in your hand and five complete bloody fools round the table with you.'

---

[78] Edward Arthur Donald St George Hamilton Chirchester Donegall (1903–75): journalist, gossip columnist, *Sunday Dispatch*; war correspondent 1939–45; suc. 6th Marquess Donegall 1904.

R.: 'Yes and every one of 'em saying "the fella's got nothing, he's bluffing".'

I refused to assent to R's view that Britain will be the first target and he agreed that the odds were really only three to one on that being so. He repeated his analogy of Hitler, Goering[79] and Hess[80] being three young men making a success out of an old decrepit business.

Good Friday 19 April   R. was on the private phone about half-past eight for the morning talk. He agreed that our leader on Geneva and after was a bit gloomy for Easter Sunday and said that if I would do a lay-sermon we could replace it so [*sic*]. He said 'What does little McWhirter really think about the situation?' After I had diagnosed Mac's reactions he said, 'He's got a little mind, anyhow, he has what I call a *busy* little mind' which was singularly apt. Mac believes that war is imminent, but hates to hear it talked about ... In his own sphere he is decidedly good.

Saturday 27 April   A very heavy day – R. rang me about 8 and again about 8–15. He was interested in currency and that meant some inquiries. Also – I discovered that it was his birthday. In our first talk I quoted to him Whitman's 'How beggarly appear arguments in the face of a defiant deed' and he asked me to send him the reference. I went to Southerans and bought a leather bound *Leaves of Grass* and sent that with my birthday wishes – an odd present for a Press Baron ... At the Press I worked hard – dined Britt at Simpsons and got home about 1 o'clock a.m.

Tuesday 30 April   I dined Oscar Joseph at the Blue Train Grill, where, they knowing me for one of the Rothermere entourage, they were exceedingly servile, except for one waiter who tried to persuade me that I imagined an horrific draught [...] During the evening there was a cabaret which consisted of two niggers at a piano – one a full-blooded fellow and the other a chocolate coloured coon. It was again odd how my old Tory blood revolted at these self-satisfied niggers ogling our women, and at our women mooning over them with adulation.

---

[79] Field-Marshal Hermann Goering (1893–1946): C. in C. German Air Force 1933–45; Comm. for the Four-Year Plan 1936; Pres. of Gen. Council for the War Economy.

[80] Rudolph Hess (1894–1987): Dep. Führer; 10 May 1941 flew to Britain on unofficial peace mission, captured & treated as POW. Jailed for war crimes 1946 for life.

Friday 3 May   After the usual editorial conference at the office, Brittain
and Emrys-Jones[81] and I had another very lengthy one drafting some
ill omened letters. Britt with my concurrence has decided to pension
off Brebner[82] and Foulkard from their posts as Sports Editor and Art
Editor, to sack Gugan and to make other changes. He is attempting a
kind of Hitler purge. I have staved it off for some time, but it is
inevitable, but none the less unpleasant. [...] Lil and the children and
little Jille[83] [...] were out seeing the [Jubilee] decorations, and there
was no point in hurrying home, but I was so struck by the great mobs
of sight-seers even in Fleet Street, which has blossomed into flags and
gay colours, that I took a taxi and made the man lower the 'lid' and
drive me along the embankment, past the Houses of Parliament, up
Constitution Hill and so home to Chiswick. The flood-lighting was
itself lovely – revealing new pieces of London, as when the Middlesex
Town Hall, tucked behind the hospital and over against the Lincoln
statue, suddenly leapt out in beauty – but the crowds were the
stimulation. Around the Palace they were wedged, silently gazing, so
that the sentries had difficulty in keeping their beats clear. There were
many good humoured mounted police keeping the people circulating.
There can be no question of the spontaneous loyalty of these crowds –
and a very, very large number seem to be country folk seeing London
for the first time.

Saturday 4 May   I had better begin to-day's entry by harking back to
Thursday's telephone talk with Lucy Houston. She said she thought of
repeating her offer of £200,000 for the defence of London but wanted
my advice first. I saw that if she did the Government would again
refuse it, and she might then fall in with Macmillan's scheme and equip
a fighting squadron. I advised her how to repeat it and dictated a form
of words. This form she slightly altered and dispatched to Londonderry[84]
and Neville Chamberlain. On Friday she was annoyed that no answer
had reached her. (She lives at Hampstead, but with characteristic
inefficiency the Department had sent a reply to Jersey.) I told her of
Macmillan's scheme and this time she was attracted. I rang Macmillan

[81] J. Emrys-Jones: journalist *Sunday Dispatch*, Ass. Ed. until 1935 when obliged to resign;
then joined *Daily Express*.
[82] J.H. Brebner: Sports Ed. *Sunday Dispatch* until 1935; later Dir. News Div. MOI.
[83] Lesley Marsden, C.B.'s niece.
[84] Charles Stewart Henry Vane-Tempest-Stewart (1878–1949): Con. MP Maidstone
1906–15; US Air 1920–1; Leader of the Senate & Min. of Educ., N. Ireland 1921–6; 1st
Comm. Works 1928–9, 1931; Air Sec. 1931–5; Ld. Privy Seal & Con. Leader in the HofL.
1935; Pres., Northern Counties Area Con. Assoc. 1930–49; Ld.-Lt. Co. Durham 1928–
49; Mayor of Durham 1936–7; styled Viscount Castlereagh 1884–1915, suc. 7th Marquess
of Londonderry 1915, KG 1919.

and he spoke with her. It culminated in his ringing me this morning asking me to 'vet' a letter that he was sending to her. [...] I approved his letter and sent if off by special messenger from the office. With his concurrence I told R. of the episode when we talked on the Norfolk wire in the afternoon. R., rather to my surprise, was in favour of the plan, but insisted that if the N.L.A. were at all implicated Macmillan must have supreme control in equipping the squadron. (I wondered if even R. saw the power that would be in Macmillan's hands – with this private and armed air force ...) I arranged to take tea with R. at 3 to-morrow (Sunday) and to bring Macmillan with me. But the best laid schemes – late in the evening Lady H. rang through to say she wouldn't go forward with the plan because she wouldn't be dragged at the tail of Rothermere and the National League of Airmen. I assured her that that would not be the relationship, but couldn't change her mind. She is going off to her yacht. She told me in deadly confidence where she was going – not as the Press thought to Southampton, but to Yacht Liberty, Post Office, Sandbanks, Dorset. I asked if she were going to watch the mystery experiments, but she would say neither yes nor no. The story is that she will invite Jellico[85] and Beatty[86] and spring on them a surprise demonstration of her young inventor's discovery – but what that is – death ray is suggested – nobody knows. She was charming to me as always.

Sunday 5 May   My present method of keeping this log-book is to enter it when I can from memoranda in my pocket diary. This usually means entering about five days at a time as the week-end affords me an opportunity. I am not getting into it any account of the routine of the days – at the office, with the American Survey, and the like. Neither am I putting into it the dominating fact of the days – that Rothermere and I have been right, and that the Government is now thoroughly alarmed by the menace of Germany with her great modern air fleet. Late last night I met Ward Price in the library at Northcliffe House.

'How did you find Rome?' I asked.

'Very pleasant – I saw Mussolini.'

'And how was *he*?'

'He struck me as being lacking in the old resiliency. I noticed it about them all at Stresa – events are too big for these men. Mussolini feels it and shows it.'

[85] John Rushworth Jellicoe (1859–1938): Royal Navy careerist; Commander of Grand Fleet 1914–16; 1st Sea Lord 1916; cr. Viscount Jellicoe 1918, 1st Earl 1925.

[86] David Beatty (1871–1936): joined Navy 1884; Comm. 1898; Rear-Adm. 1910; Vice-Adm. 1915; Adm. 1919; Adm. of Fleet 1919; 1st Sea Lord 1919–27; cr. 1st Earl of Beatty 1919.

[. . .] At 8–30 this morning R. rang me to say that he thought I might write an article 'Lord Beaverbrook as I know Him' and would I ring up Beaverbrook and tell him so and say that I wanted to see him again soon. After ringing through to Leatherhead I had to leave a message asking Beaverbrook to ring me, which he did about 1 o'clock. He was, as usual, charming – and I said that I wanted to see him to get some new background.

'Any time you like, any time you like.'

'Will you give me some maple syrup at Stornoway House on Tuesday?'

'Yes – at five o'clock . . .' He had been pleased, he said, with my leader suggesting him as the new Minister of Agriculture.

Tuesday 7 May   The event of the day was a visit at 5 o'clock to Stornoway House to call on Beaverbrook. He was working with two secretaries in the garden, looking oddly like an evangelist in a long grey overcoat, a black clerical hat and smoked sun glasses. He hailed me warmly, as he always does, and dismissed his secretaries. He had taken my jocular symbolism seriously and had provided maple syrup for my tea. The ostensible purpose of my call was to procure some new background for an article on him, but he turned the talk – and for an hour impressed upon me that the Associated Newspapers was 'all set' for me, if only I would cultivate the friendship which R. feels for me. R. had been with him that morning. What he conceives as my role is the role he himself played with Bonar Law,[87] a role that a man named Outhwaite[88] (untimely dead) played with R.

'When Outhwaite was alive Rothermere was two brains – just as Bonar was two brains. When Bonar died Churchill said to me, "Max, you're finished. One of the legs has gone from your three-legged stool – you had yourself, Bonar and your newspaper." It wasn't an unjust saying. You must be prepared for an uncomfortable life and you must learn to endure reiteration without minding it. But it's a game worth playing. It's the biggest business opportunity in Britain –'

He began to talk technique. 'Ring him up, go and see him, dine with him, always be ready with the news. When I first ran Bonar I used to be up at six to master the newspapers, even as a young man

[87] Andrew Bonar Law (1858–1923): Con. MP Glasgow Blackfriars 1900–6, Dulwich 1906–10, Bootle 1911–18, Central Glasgow 1918; Unionist leader 1911–21; P.S. BofT. 1902–6; Leader of Opposition 1911–15; Sec. of State Colonies 1915–16; Chanc. of Exchequer 1916–18; Leader of HofC. 1916–21; Ld. Privy Seal 1919–21; PM & 1st Ld. of Treasury 1922–3.

[88] Ernest Outhwaite (1875–1931): Ed. *Leeds Mercury* 1918–20; Dir. Associated Newspapers 1920–31; Rothermere's Ass.

in the House of Commons, after nights of drinking and revelry, I never varied. I was always with him at ten at the latest, priming him. You must do that. Fix your eyes now on the bigger thing, and don't worry about the *Sunday Dispatch*. Back Brittain, because he backed you. You know, Brooks, I would have taken you, but when your name was mentioned I made inquiries and was told that you weren't much good, that you weren't competent. That was wrong. As soon as I met you I knew you were competent. I had no idea that you were the same Brooks that I had corresponded with all those years ago ...'

And so the talk went on. I asked him if the Voltaire bust on his table at Leatherhead was significant.

He said 'Bracken gave it to me. It means nothing. I'm no admirer of Voltaire. My great hero is Knox.[89] There's a bust of him. I have a great collection of portraits of him.'

I said, 'Was that an inherited, religious adoration?'

'No. I liked the man's philosophy – founded on education – education – education.' He walked to the door with me and continued his homily on the steps.

'What you mean is that I should set aside all scruples,' I said 'and play Talleyrand thoroughly.'

'That's just what I do mean – it's a role I've played myself very successfully ...'

And so we parted. I dived into a post office to telephone R., as I had promised. I called. R. was out, but Clark said he would be back any moment, so I waited. When he came (Princess Hohenlohe[90] was with him but he soon dismissed her) he seemed glad to see me. We didn't talk of Beaverbrook but of affairs. As he was having a private telephone call put through I suggested that I was in his way, but he said, 'No, no. I'll give you some dinner if you care to ring up home.' This I did and we went off the Avenue Road in the car. [...] Dinner, as usual, was very simple and good. R. went up to dress for the Prince of Wales'[91] reception and came down to listen to the broadcast for a while.

'... the Prince tonight is holding a reception at St James' Palace and the guests are now assembling' said the announcer.

'Look at you!' cried Judith Wilson, 'the guests assembling and you dozing in your chair ...'

He and I drove off in his car. [...] On the route he suggested that

[89] John Knox (*c.* 1513–72): Scottish Protestant reformer.

[90] Princess Stefanie Hohenlohe-Waldenburg: Hungarian temptress, spy & social beauty. On Rothermere payroll, but caused considerable embarrassment when sued in 1939 for breach of contract.

[91] Edward, Prince of Wales (1894–1972): King Edward VIII 1936; abdicated to marry Wallis Simpson.

we should collaborate on a diary, the diary of two men knowing that war is imminent but watching others who are all unwitting of the catastrophe.[92] I said that it would be better if he let me Boswelise him, but he said, 'Oh, no. You gather impressions, too, and news – let it be both of us.' We discussed the leader page special article for Sunday and, for some reason, he suggested 'If I had £1,000,000.' He was in a very happy and chummy mood.

At St James's he said, 'Come on inside – do a bit of gate crashing – if anybody blames me I shall say "Oh, the fellow's a journalist."'

Thursday 9 May   taxied over to Stratton House. R. and Warden were just leaving for Norfolk. R. showed me Hitler's letter and asked me to superintend the business of having thirty-five photographic copies made for the Cabinet and a fair translation.[93] This sent me back to Northcliffe House and kept me busy for the rest of the afternoon.

Saturday 11 May   At about ten I did a survey of foreign affairs, and had just finished when news came that Charing Cross Bridge was well afire. Britt, short of men, asked me to dash out and organise his news corps – one of them had come in and said there was no story. When I reached the Embankment it was seething with Jubilee crowds. I think I have never seen so many people. I managed, by fighting my way on to a train going West to get to the bridge, but there was no sign of a fire. (The crowd was setting East). A bobby whom I questioned said there had been a blaze. That sent me scurrying and dodging the mob to Hungerford Bridge which I crossed and entered, only to be turned back by another bobby. Him I circumvented and found at last a group of river and land firemen laying on the timbers. It was a strange contrast – the intent quietness of that high dark bridge with its little knot of fire fighters and the flood-lit London beyond packed with returning loyalists and revellers all unaware of the fire near by them. After watching for a while, and looking at the launches darting about the river with loads of sight-seers none of whom recognised the fire-float for what it was, I left the bridge on the South Side, picked up some more information from another bobby, and began to weave my way through the dark streets in search of a telephone box. I found one and sent over a story and then went back to the office via Blackfriars Bridge, being again amazed at mobs of people.

[92] Extracts from the Brooks–Rothermere diary are entered in this edition in italics to distinguish them from Brooks' personal diary.
[93] See appendix A.

Monday 13 May   The great British Public to-day seems to be mightily concerned with the intimate affairs of young Lord Revelstoke,[94] who is being sued for breach of promise by Angela Joyce, whose chief claim to fame is that in 1928 she was chosen as a 'Beauty Queen' to represent this country in an international contest.

Sunday 19 May   R. rang up at 8 a.m. to see if I could dine with him at short notice. I said yes, if he'd give me half an hour to cross the town. At 7 p.m. he rang again and said 'I'm expecting you at eight – don't dress.' So I lifted Bernie O'Neill,[95] who had been with me for a dish of tea, to Hampstead and then went on to Avenue Road. Hertzog[96] was there when I arrived. R. drifted down and the Wilsons, and I thought we were to be just a family party, but General Groves[97] and his charming, French-bred English wife joined us. We had the usual pleasant meal, with champagne instead of the usual Hungarian white wine, and with (for me) the first cherries of the season. We talked war and air development. Groves struck me as being a tedious egotist – a slightly deaf old General, hurt that his early thrust at the Air Ministry didn't result in his becoming a Very Great Man. He has that annoying habit of saying, 'As I said in my book ...' He regards Trenchard[98] as an absolute bonehead. After Groves and Hertzog had gone, it being then about eleven, R. and I sat together in the big room and went over the diary and talked together – I left him about ten to twelve. He was in his best mood. When he introduced me to Groves, Groves complimented me on the Beaverbrook article, and said Beaverbrook himself ought to be pleased.

Wednesday 22 May   I went to-night as Oscar Joseph's guest to the

---

[94] Rupert Baring (1911–94): Royal Armoured Corps (TA); suc. 4th Baron Revelstoke 1934.

[95] Dr 'Uncle' Bernard Price O'Neill: husband of C.B.'s Auntie Bessie. Regular visitor to family home on Sunday nights often bringing boiled sweets for the children. Often referred to as B.P.O'N.

[96] [?] Gen. Hon. James Barry Munnik Hertzog (1866–1942): Boer military commander 1899–1902; Min. of Justice 1910–12; Min. Native Affairs 1924–9; PM 1924–39; Min. of External Affairs 1929–38. Leader Nationalist Party.

[97] Gen. Percy Robert Clifford Groves (1878–1959): served France, Dardanelles, Middle East; Dir. of Flying Ops., Air Min. 1918; British Air Rep., Peace Conference 1919; Dep. Dir. of Intelligence, Air Min. 1939–40; author, *Behind the Smoke Screen* (1934).

[98] Sir Hugh Trenchard (1873–1956): Chief of Air Staff 1919–29; Comm. Metropolitan Police 1931–5; Marshall of RAF; cr. 1st Viscount.

Queen's Hall, where Koussevitzky[99] was conducting. We heard Holst's[100] Fugal Concerto, Vaughan Williams' Tallis Fantasia and the Liszt Faust Symphony. There was one good human minute when Vaughan Williams[101] was discovered by Koussevitzky in the Grand Circle. He came shamefacedly to the rails and clumsily bowed – a tousled grey-haired, heavy man in rough tweeds. The bow was not enough – he was to have an ovation – and eventually he was persuaded to go round to the dais and there take tribute. It was deserved. The Tallis Fantasia was a moving thing. The Liszt was interesting, but no more than that. After the concert Joseph and I went to into the Bolivar, where in the little grill we drank lager and had mushrooms on toast and talked music – and about Ethel Snowden,[102] who had been next to him.

Friday 24 May When my phone went about nine o'clock I thought it might be R. ringing from Paris, where he has gone for a day or two. But it was Admiral Sir Barry Domville.[103] He thought it might be better to talk over his lecture rather than that he should write to me. I suggested that he should lunch with me. He demurred and said he was rather deaf, but eventually said he would with pleasure. I booked a private room at the Savoy, from which we turned out the waiters as soon as food was served – and I had a most interesting hour or so. He has been at practically every peace Conference since the Peace Congress of Paris, and was with Balfour at Washington. He met my objections to his proposed Rosyth base frankly enough. He admitted that a modern bomber could reach it – it is only 500 odd miles from Wilemshaven – but put forward the view that even the one little piece of Northern Ireland that is out of bombing range will shortly be in it. The problem then is to chose the best spot possible. Rosyth would have at least an extra hour's warning and a canal cut from there to the Clyde would enable defences to be concentrated. He allows that the air arm changes the whole face of war. As a personality he was charming. Small, rosy faced, keen eyed, most unassuming – more like a pleasant country rector than an admiral on the active list. I was

[99] Serge Koussevitzky (1874–1951): conductor & double-bass musician; conductor emeritus, Boston Symphony Orchestra 1924–49.
[100] Gustav Theodore Holst (1874–1934): composer & trombonist; Prof. of Composition, Royal College of Music 1919–24, University College Reading 1919–23.
[101] Ralph Vaughan Williams (1872–1958): composer.
[102] Lady Ethel Snowden (1881–1951): Bd. of Governors BBC 1927–33, wife of Philip Snowden, Lab. politician.
[103] Adm. Sir Barry Edward Domville (1878–1971): naval service from 1892; Ass. Sec. CID 1912–14; Dir. of Plans Div., Admiralty 1902–22; Dir. of Naval Intelligence 1927–30. Brooks had written to him previous day about Domville's lecture suggesting a new naval base at Rosyth. Copy also sent to Jellicoe.

amused at the end of the meal when he said, rather wistfully, 'Do you know, I have never before had a meal in a private room at the Savoy – I'm afraid it's rather wasted on me.' He is almost a non-luncher, so I gave him a good sole with sauté potatoes and spinach, strawberries and cream and nothing more. He took a dry Martini and a liqueur brandy with his coffee but would not share my hock. It was really a good meeting.

Saturday 25 May   If I were a proper diarist I would have filled many pages with the Cabinet changes that are discussed everywhere – MacDonald not to go to the Lords, Simon making a fight for the Foreign Office. I suppose I, with my several contacts, particularly with people like R. and with the Lobby men, am as well informed as anyone, but I believe that everything is fluid. Ramsay will give place to Baldwin, and there will be a Tory attempt to thrust Anthony Eden into Simon's chair, but for the rest all is at present in the bargaining stages. Philip Cunliffe-Lister[104] is heavily tipped for the Air Ministry. Simon is persuading Ramsay that both Liberal and Labour men are being jockeyed out of their places by a Tory revolt – and may turn awkward. Baldwin cannot afford a National Government split at this time, and may have to compromise. The tragedy is that any reconstruction means only the same old gang.

Monday 27 May   Last night Stanley Baldwin, addressing a women's meeting at the Albert Hall, confessed that our democratic system of Government is at a tremendous disadvantage in times of international anxiety. A dictatorship can achieve expansion in secrecy; a democracy cannot add a single plane to its forces without discussions and wranglings and the utmost publicity.

Tuesday 28 May   R. and I mounted to the flat. Clark came in to know if R. would see Winston Churchill, if Winston came over.

R.: 'Do you know Winston?'

C.B.: 'Not in any real sense. I've spoken often to him on the telephone, and seen him at crushes.'

A little later, after a few minutes visit from Fuller,[105] Winston came,

[104] Philip Cunliffe-Lister (1884–1972): Con. MP Hendon 1918–35; PS Trade 1920–1; Sec. Overseas Trade 1921–2; Pres. BofT. 1922–4, 1924–9, 1931; Colonial Sec. 1931–5; Sec. for Air 1935–8; Min. Res. W. Africa 1942–4; Min. Civil Aviation 1944–5; Chanc. Duchy of Lancaster 1951–2; Commonwealth Sec. 1952–5; changed surname from Lloyd-Greame 1924, cr. Viscount Swinton 1935, Earl 1955.
[105] Arthur S. Fuller: Dir. of Associated Newspapers & *Daily Mail* & General Trust; Private Sec. to Lord Rothermere.

and stayed about forty minutes. He is ridiculously like his caricatures, full of energy, striding the room with bowed shoulders, gesticulating in little frenzies of rhetoric, relapsing into a kind of brooding silence while a cigarette is drawn for about three puffs before the torrent of speech breaks out again. His feet are noticeably small. I was talking to Fuller when he came but R. called me in, and after introducing us said, 'Tell Mr Churchill about the new Government. You know all these things – you hear everything . . .' So we discussed the proposed Baldwin Cabinet. Winston knew nothing and said that no offices had been fixed. He is intent on a thorough reconstruction, and had come to upbraid R. for advocating only a minor reshuffle. R's view is that after this change about, in a little while there will be a genuine war panic and a big reconstruction, and then Winston will be in an extraordinarily strong position. I mentioned that Ernest Bennet[106] had been canvassed for Cabinet Office. Winston said that when he went out to the Omdurman campaign he travelled in a French boat. There were a few other passengers, but one was a young man representing *The Telegraph*. A year or so ago Winston saw a man sitting on the Treasury Bench who seemed familiar. 'Are you the Bennet who went out with me to Omdurman?' he asked, never having consciously seen him from that day to the encountering day. It was he – a nonentity whose promotion would cause grave revolt among the young Tories. There is strong indignation about the suggested promotion of Malcolm MacDonald[107] – a job of the worst kind. 'This is the hereditary principle introduced into the Cabinet, and by this decayed old Socialist, Ramsay Mac-Donald,' raged Churchill and began to recite Ramsay's sins in the best bitter ranting way of one of Lady Houston's leading articles. He left us about one o'clock.

[. . .] although he seemed fully aware of the domination of the air arm and of Germany's power to make war, his review of possible changes in the Government did not transcend the usual re-shuffle of offices among the old Parliamentary gang. He still hankers after a Ministry of Defence, with himself as Minister. Half his mind is devoted to tactics for fighting the India Bill when it reaches the Peers. At sixty he remains vigorous, dynamic, and passionate in his convictions.

[106] Ernest Bennet (1868–1947): MP Lib. Woodstock, 1906–10, Lab. Cardiff Central, 1929–31, N.Lab. 1931–45, Ass. Post-Master Gen., 1931–5; kt. 1930.
[107] Malcolm John MacDonald (1901–81): Lab. MP Bassetlaw 1929–35 (Nat. Lab. from 1931), Nat. Lab. MP Ross & Cromarty 1936–45; US Dominions 1931–5; Colonial Sec. 1935, 1938–40; Dominions Sec. 1935–8; Min. of Health 1940–1; High Comm. in Canada 1941–6; Gov.-Gen. of Malaya & Singapore 1946–8; Comm.-Gen. in S.E. Asia 1948–55; High Comm. in India 1955–60; Gov., Gov.-Gen., & High Comm. in Kenya 1963–5; Special Representative in Africa 1965–9; s. of Ramsay MacDonald.

Friday 31 May   R., who faithfully rings me every morning between 8 and 9, asked me to look in at his flat at 11 o'clock. He had a number of people coming, so we hadn't long together. When von Ribbentrop[108] comes over for the naval discussions R. wants me to meet him at lunch, so that when R. and I go to Berlin (if we ever go) I shall know him. The rest of the day was the usual busy Friday. R. was lunching with Robert Vansittart[109] and Stanley Baldwin and tonight dined with Winston at Claridges, a dinner of Commoners and Peers to arrange the tactics of fighting the India Bill in the Lords.

[. . .] To minds which see the existing system of 'Democratic' parliamentary Government hastening to its dissolution under the stress of world events, the India Bill, which affronts all the old Imperial spirit of the race at nobody's demand, seems like the last mis-shapen, abortive child of the Mother of Parliaments already entering the madness of her menopause.

Friday 7 June   *Lord Rothermere talked in a private room at the Savoy Hotel with Herr von Ribbentrop, the head of the German Naval Delegation. Herr von Ribbentrop talked with apparent frankness. The naval discussions, he said, were proceeding satisfactorily and he was hopeful of an entirely satisfactory outcome. Germany's policy he declared to be purely pacific. Lord Rothermere suggested that in some quarters it was believed that Germany contemplated an attack on Czechoslovakia, as Prague is a notorious centre of active anti-Germany intrigue and plots. To this von Ribbentrop replied that such a thought had never entered Germany's mind, to the German Government it would be 'inadmissible'. Germany must have her colonies restored – her need of raw materials and expansion made that necessary. She desires a plebiscite in Austria. Against Russia he expressed an undying animosity. 'There can be no amity between Russia and Germany while Russia is ruled by the Soviets.'*

Everybody in Germany, he said, had read Lord Rothermere's speech in the House of Lords.[110] It had caused much misgiving among Lord Rothermere's friends in Germany. To this Lord Rothermere replied that the speech was not directed against Germany. It's one and only purpose had been to awaken the people of Great Britain to the perils of air warfare. No real friendship, said Lord Rothermere, could be possible between a heavily armed nation and a nation relatively unarmed. To this von Ribbentrop responded by saying that nothing would give Germany greater satisfaction than a heavily armed Britain. For Britain, he declared, Germany cherishes nothing but friendliness.

[108] Joachim von Ribbentrop (1893–1946): German Amb. to London 1936–8; German For. Min. 1938–45.

[109] Robert Gilbert Vansittart (1881–1957): entered Dipl. Corps 1902; Ass. Clerk at FO 1914; 1st Sec. 1918; Counsellor 1920; Sec. to Curzon 1920–4; Ass. Under-Sec. & Prin. Private Sec. to For. Sec. 1928–30; PUS at FO 1930–8; Chief Dipl. Adviser 1938–41; kt. 1929, PC 1940, cr. Baron Vansittart 1941.

[110] *Parliamentary Debates: 5th Series: House of Lords* vol. 96 cols. 906–908, 15 May 1935.

He in no way disputed Lord Rothermere's statement in the House of Lords that Germany possesses 10,000 aeroplanes.

He reiterated his protestation that Germany would prefer a well-armed Britain as her neighbour, and spoke of the two countries as natural allies. Germany, he also said, desires no war with France. To his repudiation of the idea of a war on Czechoslovakia he added that that country must realise that it contains many German nationals who must have proper treatment.

In London he had noticed a rapidly growing friendship for Germany, and this was most marked in official circles.

The significant silences of his conversation were France and Austria. For the rest – the words were smooth – the man enigmatical and dangerous. But to his interlocutor the interchange of views had other significances that von Ribbentrop intended to convey. The suggested desire to see a well armed Britain came from an astute student of affairs – who must know – that in their present mood and under their present system of Government the British people literally cannot arm to the strength which circumstances demand. To Lord Rothermere von Ribbentrop's mission emerged as a mission to drive a wedge between Britain and France. Even the naval parties which the German delegation is here to discuss has been freely stamped, as we have noted, by the French as a move to conciliate Britain and wean her from any Anglo-French attachment. This conciliatory approach is not limited – von Ribbentrop spoke approvingly, and hopefully, of an Anglo-German entente. The genuine frankness about the German hostility to Russia conveyed nothing new but re-affirming in a private talk with palpable sincerity which Hitler has publicly declared is itself significant. It follows the recent open attempt of Anthony Eden to cultivate the Soviet's good graces. It implies that sooner or later France must choose between pursuing her security pact ideas with the Eastern race or abandoning it at Germany's expressed or tacit command.

Whit Sunday 9 June After some telephoning, I packed a bag and chartered a taxicab to Heston airport. The driver knowing a short cut bogged us in a rough field, but we extricated ourselves and I met Guy du Bouley only three minutes after the appointed time of eleven thirty. An attendant stowed my bag in Norman Holden's[111] perfect little Moth plane, Guy and I clambered in, and we took off for Norton Priory. To fly thus to Selsey to spend a week-end as the fellow guest of H.G. Wells[112] seemed to me more like a chapter from an early Wells novel than one had a right to expect. There was trouble (quite in the Bealby strain) with Wells luggage. He had gone down to the Isle of Wight, and his blue case had been loaded by mistake on to the wrong air liner

---

[111] Norman Edward Holden (1879–1946): snr. partner Haes & Sons; m. to Marion (d. 1946).
[112] Herbert George Wells (1866–1946): novelist.

and was at the moment in Edinburgh, from where it was to be flown back to Portsmouth, where Guy would later pick it up. It was a wonderfully sunny and smooth morning, and I sat behind the pilot's seat in the glassed cockpit enjoying the panorama of South England – surprisingly uninhabited except where the little black-beetles of motorcar tops crawled through odd townships – and enjoying at 2,000 feet and over 100 miles an hour the illusion of no speed. We came after half an hour to the bit of the coast which holds the Priory – 'there's the house' said Guy over the noise of the engine, and looking left I saw a landing ground, where a few people waited for us, a stretch of gardens and a dream house hard by a minute church. We swooped round full circle over the harbour mud, and made a perfect landing. Norman Holden, Mrs Holden, young David Woodford and a girl of about twenty-four in yellow corduroy trousers and a yellow slip, and not more than a half dozen dogs welcomed us. [...] Lunch was a medley of talk and wine. After lunch Freddie Guest dropped in – having flown his Clem plane from town, for a game of Backgammon. He and his pilot-secretary, Miss Forthsythe, departed, and the others, reinforced now by another guest 'Tolley' – an elderly ex-guards officer of great charm – played golf croquet while I lay with a volume of de Quincey in a swinging lawn divan – and fell fast asleep. At five Guy du Bouley returned from Portsmouth and Shanklin with H.G. Wells. He entered, very like his caricatures, and greeting us all in his curiously high tenor voice, with the intonation of a University Don. We drank deep and then scattered to dress, came down and drank sherry, and dined again in a riot of talk and flowing liquor. The liquor was good, the talk better – Wells defensively refusing to be drawn by Norman Holden.

Monday 10 June   Guy and David Woodford and I left the others gazing, and crossed to the landing ground. We mounted the Moth and Guy flew us off to Portsmouth, which we circled, and then back along the coast. Excepting always a bolting horse, there is nothing in my experience quite so exhilarating as being in a plane flying not more than five yards over the sea, with all the bathers and sand sprawlers and houses seen life size – then one feels speed – Down the coast we went, rose and circled inland to Arundel, the castle and cathedral looking from our height like children's work-boxes, and swooped home again for more liquor and lunch. After lunch I lounged and played with Wanda, still in her yellow trousers – already a divorcee at twenty-four, free of speech and of mind – and slept again until five. In the Abbey of Theleme they don't have tea. They have gin. But I had tea. Dinner, after a round of golf croquet, of which Wells is fond, was an even more flowing feast. Of what verbal indiscretions I was guilty I

dare not think. But it was all very merry. I took two volumes of
Browning off to bed, but they dragged me down again. They had all
become immersed in a crossword that baffled them ...

Tuesday 11 June   This morning everyone was early astir save Wells and
me. From my window I saw Norman and Marion and Guy cross to
the aerodrome at 8–30 and David going off in a car at 8–45. Wells
and I had arranged to breakfast together at 9–15. He was already in
the dining room when I came down. We sat leisurely over our bacon
and eggs and had relays of coffee.

'Do you become bored by your adulators?' I asked him.

'I have no adulators – sometimes a young man is knocked sideways
by my work, as I have been knocked sideways by an author, and he
thinks one had said *everything*. It is difficult. I think the best thing is to
pretend for a while that I have a long white beard and live up to his
expectation.'

[...] The long drive through the sunny morning to Brighton was
even better than the breakfast table talk [...] We talked of methods of
working.

'I write on all kinds of things. I have a good staff, well trained in my
modes. I sometimes jot things down on the edges of newspapers and
they come back to me in nice clean typescript. I only tried typing once.
With one finger. It was a book called *The Undying Fire*.[113] I found that
seeing the words made me discipline my sentences. There is far less
waste of words in that book than in any other I have written. Verbosity
doesn't come from excess of mental energy, but from lack of it – the
energy to discipline ones words.'

(All these are but snippets of a long duologue that would take days
to transcribe. You figure us, two men, the elder and the younger, in a
borrowed Rolls-Royce, talking contentedly in the sun, topic succeeding
topic, sometimes a topic suggested by a village through which they
pass, sometimes a topic deliberately thrown up by one or the other,
sometime a mere exchange of generalities ...) [...] It was during an
afternoon talk on the Monday that he told me that the book into which
he had put most work was *The Work and Happiness...*[114] book, but all
the critics had assumed that it was the most hasty and superficial of his
later works. [...] At the station the aftermath of his missing baggage
troubled him. The aircraft company had sent north a plane for his
bag, but it was too big to be loaded. They had borrowed two smaller

[113] H.G. Wells, *The Undying Fire: A Contemporary Novel* (London: Cassell, 1919).

[114] H.G. Wells, *The Work, Wealth and Happiness of Mankind* (London: Heinemann, 1932).
First published in USA 1931.

bags and into those had repacked his possessions. He was afraid that he might not recognise strange bags at London, so wrote special labels for them. This done we settled down in a First Pullman. He had promised to be my guest at lunch, but protested. (Again, to use his idiom, you figure us, working out our shares of odd expenditure in tipping and ticket buying, and then discussing lunch ...) He decided that a bottle of beaune would be the best drink aboard a train, so that over our burgundy and railway food, and later over cigars the talk went on, exploratory, argumentative, very frank.

Thursday 13 June A sunny day. After a morning's work I strolled into Fetter Lane, found Geraldine House, and had myself announced to Middleton.[115] He asked me to wait in Fuller's room. After a little while (filled by a talk with Parker about N.L.A. finances) R. came in and bore me off to the Board Room. I think the Board was a bit baffled by my advent. They sat like any Board – Cowley,[116] the most human, in the vice-chair, R. in Esmond's place at the head of the table. Szarvasy,[117] the astute Jew, collared me, and sat me down besides him.

R. said, after a jocular introduction, 'Now, Collin Brooks, what would you do with £30,000?'

'It is not a question that anybody can answer unless he knows the spread of your present portfolio and the line of your policy ...'

So Szarvasy and I went over the portfolio, and then I tried to advise, speaking (as it were) through Szarvasy's music. We did manage eventually to make some decisions. Esmond Harmsworth came in late, surprised to find me there, as well he might be, and the talk tailed off into generalities – R. was in his brightest vein, chaffing them like a genial schoolmaster, and making great play of the long-protracted attempts to buy Price Brothers. [...] R. went and we all drifted our different ways – I feeling that I had done nothing but make an aimless fool of myself.

Saturday 22 June A normal hard-working Saturday. London swelters in a heat wave. In such weather a newspaper office is the most damnable of all institutions, with its linos and foundry adding to the heat. Sunday journalism as conducted by illiterates like Brittain is a

---

[115] Edgar Middleton (1894–1939): secretary to *Daily Mail* Trust; author, playwright.

[116] John Cowley (1870–1944): Ass. Cashier *Evening News*; Bd. Member of *Daily Mail* Trust, Vice-Chm. & suc. Rothermere as Chm. of *Daily Mirror* & *Sunday Pictorial*.

[117] Frederick Alexander Szarvasy (d. 1948): dir. *Daily Mail* & General Trust, Chm. British Foreign & Colonial Corp. & other companies.

debasing business. I doubt if there is one man on the staff of any effective power who has any real knowledge of affairs or any depth of culture. The subs' table is probably best equipped, but they are kept in subjection. It would be pleasant if one did not feel the truth of Salisbury's gibe about 'conducted by office boys for office boys'.

Thursday 27 June Lunched solus at the Berkeley off a little smoked salmon, an omelette and hock and seltzer, enjoying quietly the chattering mob of rich people. I was joined at 2–45 by Donegall and Bingham with whom I went to Newman Street to see a private show of a striking American newsreel called 'The March of Time'. This was shown to us by Movitone News, who said that the reel was impracticable in Britain because of the libels in it – the mode of presentation of news in this reel is to take some topical event – the Arms Enquiry, for example, or Nazism – and to dramatise it. Where there are genuine news shots they are used, where not, actors stand in. The effect is a dramatic exposition of event. Compared with the snippets of an English news reel, this American presentation is infinitely better. Someday some enterprising English man will jump to its possibilities, and apply it to home news.

In the evening I took Oscar Joseph to a dinner of the Compatriots Club, in the House of Commons. We took our sherry on the Terrace, which was pleasant. The guest was Huggins,[118] Premier of Southern Rhodesia, and the discussion was very frank. Marshal Hole[119] and Hannon[120] (both of whom were out under Jameson[121]) spoke and another, whose name I did not catch, who had actually held office under Paul Kruger.[122] The feeling between Rhodesia and the Union is much more bitter than the public is allowed to learn. The speeches were interrupted by the Division Bell, and as we sat waiting for the members to troop back a rosy faced man came over to me and said, 'Surely you are Collin Brooks?'

'I am indeed,' I replied.

[118] Godfrey Huggins (1883–1971): PM of S. Rhodesia 1933–53; PM of Central African Fed. 1953–6; cr. 1st Viscount Malvern 1955.

[119] Lt-Col. Hugh Marshall Hole (1865–1941): Rhodesian administrator.

[120] Patrick Joseph Henry Hannon (1874–1963): Con. MP Birmingham Moseley 1921–50; Vice-Pres., Tariff Reform League 1910–14; Gen. Sec., Navy League 1911–18; Dir., British Commonwealth Union, 1918–28; Sec., E.I.A. 1925–50; Pres., Industrial Transport Association 1927–37; kt. 1936.

[121] Leander Starr Jameson (1853–1917): South African statesman; administrator, South Africa Co., Fort Salisbury 1891–5; elected Cape Legislative Assembly 1900; P.M. Cape Colony 1904–8; Pres. BSA Company 1913; cr. Bart. 1911.

[122] Stephen J. Paul Kruger (1825–1904): Pres. Transvaal Republic 1882–1900.

'I knew you from your press photographs. I am Tom Clarke.'[123]

He sat down and had a spot of whiskey with us – and we chaffed each other about Northcliffe and Rothermere. I told him that his book *My Northcliffe Diary* had been part of my bedside reading, which pleased him. I shall never conquer the childish, ingenuous feeling which smites me when some one who in earlier days I regarded as a great man in my trade proves not only human, but friendly. Clarke had come as a guest with Huggins, to whom he afterwards introduced me. Huggins is very deaf – in appearance very like Haden Guest,[124] a man of medium height, with a close cropped moustache, bright eyes, and longish hair scrupulously parted. His eyes, bright; his manner, alert; his voice, low cadenced and undertoned with laughter – not by any means the usual Colonial Politician. He remarked on the success of the Scottish crofter types as a settler. 'Your Englishman wants a rise too soon; your Scottish crofter will work like a crofter and be content to wait for his rise until the farm pays for it.' After the dinner Joseph ran me home in his new car – an adventurous journey, for he seems a new driver ...

Monday 1 July Up at 8–15. Did a cable and sent Miss Stannard[125] off for the day. Spent some time filling in this log book from my pocket diary notes. My post had a letter from Lucy Houston:

'S.Y. Liberty
Sandbanks
Dorset
    30 June 1935
Dear Mr Collin Brooks,
    I have just read your splendid article. It is a masterpiece and I congratulate you most heartily.
    I am going to put it on the back cover of the *Saturday Review* as prominently as possible – with the Union Jack flying in the corner.
Yours sincerely
L.H.'

To this, in pencil, was added 'The heat is overpowering.' The article was 'I am a Right-Wing Conservative' – which I made as frank and outspoken as possible. It contained nothing that wasn't in *The Economics*

[123] Tom Clarke (1884–1957): author & journalist; Managing Ed. *Daily News* 1926, Ed. & Dir. *News Chronicle* 1926–33; author *My Northcliffe Diary* (1931).
[124] Dr Leslie Haden-Guest (1877–1960): Lab. MP Southwark N. 1923–7, Islington N. 1935–50; cr. 1st Baron 1950.
[125] Evelyn Stannard: Brooks' secretary 1933–9. Left to marry in May 1939.

of Human Happiness but a newspaper article is always more provocative than the same thesis elaborated in a book. The *News Summary* today takes excerpts from it and displays them at the top of its second page. Whether the article will have any effect at Conservative H.Q. or on David Margesson, I don't know, but I have an idea that it may attract more attention than any other I have done for the S.D. If Baldwin believes, as he says, that R. is to give him 100 per cent support he will either think that R. is betraying him or that I have got out of hand. R. will rightly say that I am allowed to say what I like under my own name as long as I don't say things in a leading article...

In a conversation with C.B. the official historian of the air force, Captain H. Jones,[126] *said recently that in his sixth volume dealing with Supply he had come to the conclusion that to provide Britain with an adequate airforce would take a least three years – the factory space and buildings, the tools and jigs, the trained personnel would all mean tremendous delay. Jones says that when his manuscript was being 'passed' certain authorities were so struck by his data and conclusions that 100 special copies of that section were printed and circulated to the Cabinet and to others affected.*

Saturday 6 July   I to the office, where I worked until after midnight except for a break for dinner, with Brittain and Emrys-Jones who argued about Sunday newspapers. I told Brittain the other day that by my standards he was an illiterate and so I grade him. This was because he did not know what the Italian risorgiomento was ... and has probably never heard of Cavour.[127] As a technical journalist he is excellent, but as a mind he doesn't exist. To me he is a useful puppet, but that he doesn't even yet fully realise. During the week I had a pleasant letter from Philip Cunliffe Lister, who thinks more highly of Weir[128] as a Government adviser than I would be prepared to think, and one from Huggins, the Southern Rhodesian Premier. I also had a letter from Beaverbrook. Fay of the Incorporated Accountants asked me to persuade Beaverbrook to address his association next Autumn. In his letter of refusal he says 'My speaking days are over – I hope never to step on a platform again.'

---

[126] H.A. Jones, *The War in the Air* (Oxford: Clarendon Press, 1935).

[127] Count Camillo Bensodi Cavour (1810–61): Piedmontese politician & restorer of Italian nationality.

[128] William Douglas Weir (1877–1949): industrialist; Scottish Dir. of Munitions 1915–16; Dir.-Gen. Aircraft Production 1918; Sec. for Air 1918; Dir.-Gen. of Explosives 1939; kt. 1917, cr. Viscount Weir 1938.

Tuesday 9 July   Rea-Price lunched me at the National Liberal Club, on the terrace where the service was terribly bad and the food indifferent. He told me that before Hobson took the City Editorship of *The News Chronicle* they had thought of inviting me to accept the job, but that my tariff views stood in the way. He, Price, had at one time thought Layton had wantonly been treacherous to him but now feels that Walter Layton is merely thoughtless and casual and lacking in imagination.

Friday 12 July   I was called at eight and emerged for breakfast about nine. As nobody else appeared, Edward[129] suggested that I should begin, so I took a meal of bacon and eggs and luscious honey in the dining room [of Stody], looking out over the garden. Soon after, R. asked me to go up stairs and talk. He drew my attention to a review of a new Brontë book by Sylvia Lynd[130] in the *News Chronicle*. Then he said that he had heard that Mussolini had been in conference with his war staff – and suggested that instead of being tentative in my article 'Can Italy Conquer Abyssinia' I might be strong, and plump with my knowledge of mountain warfare for the direct affirmation that of course Italy can conquer Abyssinia. I went downstairs and rewrote the article at the little desk in the lounge. He came down half way through, amused himself until I had finished, and listened to it with approval. He directed a copy and a special letter to be sent to Grandi, suggesting that it might be cabled to Rome, and copies sent to Hoare[131] and Anthony Eden.

Wednesday 24 July   The India Bill passed the Lords to-day. This piece of legislation is a remarkable symptom of British political decadence. Nearly fifty years ago that great Anglo-Indian John Nicholson[132] said (in Newbolt's paraphrase) 'we brook no doubt of our mastery, we rule until we die.' But the British of this generation have devised a weak Constitution for India at the request of no responsible body of opinion, a Constitution which will not satisfy the extremists it is designed to placate, and have forced it upon the Imperial Statute Book without consultation with, or a mandate from, the people. The damage that is done to British potential trade is enormous, but the damage done to British prestige is far worse. If Britain

---

[129] Edward Chinnock, valet to Rothermere at Stody.

[130] Sylvia Lynd (1885–1952): author.

[131] Samuel John Gurney Hoare (1880–1959): Con. MP Chelsea 1910–44; Sec. for Air 1922–4, 1924–9, 1940; India Sec. 1931–5; For. Sec. 1935; 1st Ld. of Admiralty 1936–7; Home Sec. 1937–9; Ld. Privy Seal 1939–40; Amb. in Madrid 1940–4; Con. Party Treasurer 1930–1; suc. 2nd Bart 1915, cr. Viscount Templewood 1944.

[132] John Nicholson (1822–57): soldier, adventurer & administrator.

*is prepared to give away her dominance in response to a few years of riotous agitation
from the natives of India, she is hardly likely to refuse the war-like demands of well
armed and determined European neighbours – so the thinkers of Berlin must reason.*

Thursday 22 August   At 8–15 Rothermere was on the phone from Baden-
Baden, suggesting an alteration in the leader page article. I typed it
after breakfast – on Germany's demand for colonies, which replaces
the lighter holiday article I had written on Tuesday. [...] I reached
home early and devoted the rest of the hottest day of the year to (a)
parts of the *Joseph Review*, (b) and American Survey[133] (c) the Rothermere–Brooks diary and (d) letters. Holmes[134] of the *Investors Chronicle*
wrote today asking me if I could contribute articles for him this Autumn
and Winter. The terms of the letter were so flattering to the little boy
from the Bastille [...]. There is a tremendous intensity today over the
Cabinet meeting on the Italian question. As these things go into the
Survey and into the Rothermere–Brooks diary I need not log them in
this more personal place. It would be odd if Italian and not German
bombers wrought the ruin of London and brought our dominance to
dust. At the moment it is not impossible.

Thursday 29 August   Oswald Mosley's chief of staff[135] has been trying to
secure me to speak in the Fascist campaign to be launched next week
against intervention in Abyssinia. I have fenced the invitation off – and
when Rothermere was appealed to through Morison he, too, assented
to the fence ... Today I was asked to take luncheon with Mosley. I
arrived at 22b Ebury Street at 1–15. In the big room a log fire was
burning and Mosley stood before it. We had not met since the
foundation lunch of the N.L.A. He greeted me warmly and talked of
that day. I said that our difficulty was that we attracted crooks, and
said that this was inevitable, I thought. He cordially agreed and told
me of the trouble he had had in purging the Fascist movement of such
fellows, of how he had abandoned organisation by Clubs and adopted
organisation by ward cadres. 'It is the mastery of the streets which
matters...' Mussolini had said to him when he began the movement
that discipline must be with a light rein at first and only gradually
tightened. He instanced Hitler as one suffering from clever scoundrels,

[133] Covering the topics: survey; Britain and Europe.
[134] George John Holmes (1874–1937): Prop. & Ed. *Investors' Chronicle*; member Hackney
Borough Council 1900–26; Chm. Thames Estuary Building Society.
[135] A. Raven Thomson (d. 1955): ex-communist; joined BUF 1933; Dir. of Policy; Ed.
British Union Quarterly.

which made the night of the knife inevitable. I drank a glass of sherry and he of tomato juice and we were joined by Gordon Campbell (?) – a lean, rather silent man. The luncheon was set on a balcony entered by stairs that might have been designed for Macbeth by Gordon Craig. We talked very freely over lunch. After it Mosley and I were alone again for nearly an hour.

In the long talk I said, 'Let me ask – if it isn't too grossly impertinent. . . .'

M: 'Ask anything you wish.'

C.B.: 'Do you contemplate a coup d'etat?'

M: 'I'll tell you frankly, for I know you won't repeat it – and if you did I'd repudiate it ... no ... one must be legal ... look at Hitler ... he was legal to the point of ridicule "Legality Hitler" ... no ... there will be no coup d'etat, except in strange unforeseen circumstances.'

C.B.: 'Your moment will come about 1938.'

M: 'Yes. We count on that. There will be another economic crisis then. What has amazed me has been our progress despite trade recovery...'

C.B.: 'You may misjudge that. It may be because of it. My experience is that discontent is not evident in bad times, but always in improving times, when the share-out is in question.'

M: 'I believe you're right. You are right.'

I would like to log the talk more fully, but time forbids that. He was flattering about my articles and was rather wrathy with Rothermere not for withdrawing support but for starting the supporting campaign too violently. He said, in passing, that of all the men round Rothermere, Ward Price and I were the only two that mattered. But this was probably flattery for some purpose. On the mastery of the streets he was convincing.

Saturday 31 August   R. phoned from Baden-Baden at about 8–15. During our talk he suggested that I should go to Geneva to-morrow. 'Now you are becoming a great publicist you should absorb all the diplomatic atmosphere you can ...' This opened a very heavy day at the Press, with the mysterious Abyssinian concession to Reckitt the chief news followed by Mussolini's speech to his troops saying they must stay under arms until all talk of sanctions ends.

Monday 2 September   At Geneva [...] I wander about the town for a while, savouring the lake and the mountains and proving that Mon' Blanc can really be seen from Geneva – hired a fiacre and drove to the Headquarters of the League, which is like a school building with some hothouses tacked on to it. One is received courteously by dark garbed officials. I wanted the Press bureau and was directed to it – it is in a pair of back bedrooms fitted as offices. The custodian is a woman of thirty or so, very like a secondary school mistress, polite but not very helpful to the stranger. A ticket for the Council – impossible. The Assembly – impossible. What, then, about the public gallery? I might try – my Consul would have to recommend me ... I departed and took my fiacre to the Consul – but he closes down from 12 to 2, so I returned to the hotel to lunch. Hardly was I seated than a phone message came. It was Challoner James saying he had just heard from London that I was to arrive and could he do anything. I suggested our meeting after Lunch – and at three he came to my room, portly, pleasant and a typical good fellow. [...] He bore me then back to the League. Under his tutelage all was different. My frigid Miss Ward grew less frigid. I could not have a ticket as a weekly paper – but when I said that I was also the seven dailies of Northcliffe Newspapers a way was found. James led me through corridors to *la salle de conversation* – the Lobby. In that corridor stood a bar, and there we anchored ourselves, while men came and greeted us Ibbison James of the *Morning Post*, Bernard More of the *Herald* and *les autres*.

Tuesday 3 September   That evening into the Club came Vernon Bartlett,[136] very brown after a canoe cruise down the Danube. He and Cardozo[137] and James and our two cypher experts[138] and I made sextet, and the wine flowed freely. About midnight somebody suggested a game of 'slosh'. Bartlett insisted upon stripping to the waist for the exertion – revealing as hairy a torso as that of a hairy ainu. I wondered how the staid non-conformist readers of the *News-Chronicle* and the serious listeners to his broadcasts would have regarded the merry, impish fellow. At one-thirty in the morning somebody suggested caviar sandwiches, and four of us taxied over to the Bavaria. The Bavaria at Geneva has a certain historic renown. It is a long, narrow restaurant connecting two streets. It is the rendezvous of journalists. At that hour it was packed with men from the world's ends, mostly drunk. Even Robert Dell,[139] of the *Manchester Guardian*, seemed to be arguing more

[136] Vernon Bartlett (1894–1983): journalist & broadcaster; *Daily Mail* 1915–17, *The Times* 1919–22; 1922; Dir., London office, League of Nations 1922–32; *News Chronicle* 1933–54; Ind. M.P. Bridgwater 1938–50.

[137] Harold Cardozo: journalist; *Daily Mail* staff; reporting Spanish Civil War from Franco side.

[138] Russell and Harvey – from the Foreign Office.

[139] Robert Dell (1865–1940): journalist & author; Paris correspondent, *Manchester Guardian*, subsequently Geneva 1920–1, Berlin 1922–4, Paris 1925–32, Geneva 1932–7.

mistily than usual. The walls are decorated with caricatures and its general atmosphere is something between the Cafe Coupol in Paris, the Cafe Royal in London and a fish-and-chip shop. In the smoky air with the liquor cups passing very freely one set the world to rights, with laughter.

Wednesday 4 September   I lay abed until ten, took cafe on the boulevard, visited *la salle de conversation* – which this morning was very full. Nothing could be done until the meeting of the League Council at 4–30, so after an aperitif or two I wandered back to the Club, where I found the two cypher experts, who drank vermouth with me until about 1–30 when I went off for lunch. The *la salle de conversation* in the afternoon was a veritable mass of men and women, I watching from an alcove. Of a sudden I saw a knot of photographers pressing forward – it was Laval,[140] swarthy, with heavy-lidded cynical eyes and an affable smile. Then we surged down the corridor, I at Laval's elbow, and into the council room.[141] [...] After the meeting I exchanged a few words with Anthony Eden in the *salle de conversation* – he twitting me about writing for *The Daily Mail*. He looks older by twenty years than when he and I talked in the Lobby of the House seven years ago. He puts on glasses now to read, and is losing that slim boyishness of figure. He is automatically charming but lacks impressiveness.

From the Headquarters of the League we went to a reception by Baron Aloisi.[142] It was quite comic in its informality. We entered a little late – were directed to an upper room of the la Paix – and there found a great mob, many standing on chairs, and in the middle of the mob – the Baron, smiling cynically and rattling out replies to questions. He is of those men whose facial skin is tightly drawn over their bones, his bald head and his nasal contour give him just a touch of the hawk, but of a benevolent hawk. I saw him closely both in the Council and at his reception and am still uncertain whether or not he wore a rimless monocle – but his face had all the effect of a rimless monocle in the sparkling left-eye. Somebody thrust on us a pair of huge paper bound books – Italy's case against Geneva – with which and a more colourful pamphlet on Abyssinian slavery we staggered from the room. We went about our work for a while, to write our 'pieces', and foregathered again later, to drink and dine and play crazy 'slosh' and laugh and

[140] Pierre Laval (1883–1945): French PM 1931–2, 1935–6, & For. Min. 1931–2, 1934–5; Headed Vichy Govt., executed for collaborating with Germans.

[141] C.B. describes the scene in article 'My peep at the War League' *Sunday Dispatch*, 8 September 1935.

[142] Baron Pompeo Aloisi (1875–1949): Mussolini's *chef de cabinet* at the For. Min. 1932–6, & Italian delegate to the League of Nations, Geneva 1935–6.

drink again, and watch the antics of Vernon Bartlett, that merriest of imps let lose [*sic*]. It was all very entertaining, but nobody would have thought that we were sane thoughtful men attending the funeral rites of the League of Nations, assisting at the end of an epoch ...

Early this morning Morison rang me from London asking me to ring R. at seven to-night. This I did. R. was in good form and told me that Ward Price was taking a car to Basel tomorrow morning and I too was to journey there. Ward Price, however, had found a train at 7–45. I went to bed at 2–30 cursing the fate that would waken me at 6.

Thursday 5 September   At Basel we took taxi to the Hotel of the Three Kings, which is reputed to be the oldest hotel in the world, the three kings of its name having held carousal there in the year 1000. Rothermere had not arrived, so after parking our kit and telephoning London we took the air. I had lost my hat at Geneva, stolen by some tipsy merrymaker – or lost by one ... but no hat in Basel attracted me. We sat for a while in a terrace cafe over the Rhine and talked. He talks well. He says that Rothermere is far more human than ever Northcliffe was, that Northcliffe was too much of an artist to be comfortable as a companion or a Chief, that he was a poseur. At one we returned to the hotel and sat on its balcony over the opposite side of the Rhine. About twenty minutes after R. came to us, looking very young and vigorous. [...] Our trio lunch was pleasant, although the fumes of last night's liquor gave me no great appetite. Over salmon and white wine and pheasants we talked high politics.

'When are you going back, Ward Price?'

Ward Price said he proposed to take the 3–45 plane. I said that I too ....

'No, no,' said R. 'Don't fly. Stay and keep me company. Go back on the midnight sleeper. My secretary and her mother and sister are coming this afternoon. You stay and keep me company ...' We made it so.

Sunday 22 September   This morning Morison came through on the private telephone to ask me if I had any appointment with Rothermere today. On my saying 'no' he asked if I would dine at 8 o'clock. This I did – it was a meal *en famille*, Rothermere, his two cousins and I. R. told me that the directors had decided that Brittain must go and that he wanted me to edit the *Sunday Dispatch*. I demurred – but he insisted. I said that I was not a trained popular Sunday paper editor, but he said that I had brains and energy enough to do any job. I said the paper was notoriously the grave of journalistic reputations, and he replied, 'Don't forget that these fellows in the business know you have breakfast with me ... If they come in and worry you you say to them, "Get out! I'm doing it as a favour to the business!!"'

'Actually,' said I, 'if you tell me to edit the *Police Gazette* or the *Times* under my contract I must do it or resign, and in any event if you want me to edit the *Dispatch*, I shall edit it.'

For the rest, dinner was a pleasant meal, with any amount of banter that both he and I enjoyed. I left about ten-thirty, he ushering me into the rain. As I rode home in a taxicab I thought I could hardly have been more miserable if he had thrown me out of the business. I was sorry for Brittain, but he has invited disaster.

Tuesday 24 September   Bell had asked me not to tell Brittain of his coup de grace until he had been officially informed. So I did not go to the office until about 11–30. Britt said 'What's it all about?' I thinking he had seen Bell blundered into the whole thing – only to find he was not to see Bell till noon. He took the blow most gallantly, and was out of the place by one o'clock. I lunched with Sir George Sutton at the Carlton. He has always been pleasant to me, and is more than ever so now – has quite taken me into the fold .... He and Bell feel that far from egging R. on to his unpopular policies which lose circulation for the papers I am a restraining influence. George said that apparently I was one of the few men who dared to tell R. what he ought to hear and not merely what he wanted to hear – which amused me. The day was busy – Gayler, my city page assistant away, the deputy news editor on his honeymoon – and the conference held in the afternoon instead of the morning.

Thursday 26 September   Went for lunch to the City Carlton to hear Winston speak. We encountered each other in the urinal and stayed in that unsavoury atmosphere to exchange words. I could not help remembering that it was so that I last talked with 'F.E.'[143] and hoped no ill would befall Winston. His speech was vigorous but his idea of re-arming is a big British Navy. He spoke very straightly at Mussolini, for what that was worth. At the idea of unpursing for a big Navy the cits cheered mightily. Nobody seemed to have heard of air forces.

[143] Frederick Edwin Smith (1872–1930): Con. MP Liverpool Walton 1906–18, Liverpool W. Derby 1918–19; Solicitor-Gen. 1915; Attorney-Gen. 1915–19; Ld. Chanc. 1919–22; India Sec. 1924–8; cr. Baron Birkenhead 1919, Viscount 1921, Earl 1922.

Wednesday 2 October   We had breakfast at nine and R. and I rolled back to town at 9–30 reaching Stratton Street at 1 o'c. I was painfully in arrears with my work (it is no light job being editor, city editor, leader writer and leader-page special writer.) so shot straight back to Northcliffe House. On the journey back we did manage to talk about the paper, and he reiterated that I was to stand no nonsense from anybody and that he wanted me to become a kind of super-editor, delegating all possible detail and gathering round me the brightest minds. [...] in the evening I dined Hoeffding, who is over from Germany and whom I saw for a few minutes last week. He is a Russian who is now on a Nansen Passport as an attache to the U.S. Commercial Attache in Berlin. We dined and wined well at the Cafe Royal and he was very interesting. Hitler will not be overturned, he thinks, and if anything happens to him the most likely thing is for the Army to stage a coup d'etat. Germans now make fun of the high cost of living. Having no free press they live on jokes and ribald songs, but they are behind the Administration.

Friday 4 October   R. rang to ask me to call in about 9–30. I taxied over to Avenue Road and found them all at breakfast, with Szarvasy and Stanley Bell as guests. I had some coffee. After the meal the three of us had a talk in the big room – R. very gloomy about Germany and tongue-lashing Szarvasy for daring to say that Britain could overtake Germany's aircraft production. 'What absolute nonsense; you don't understand the first thing about it; you must be mad ...' After we had talked politics Szarvasy went, and Bell remained. The three of us talked office business, and Bell was then politely dismissed from audience. I stayed on, and joined R. in the car, which took us to Stornoway House.

'Are you coming in? Are you too busy? Come in ...' So in we went. The sight of R. sent the butler reeling back, swing doors were flung open, a vista was disclosed of Beaverbrook dictating to two secretaries, that familiar picture. The secretaries seemed to crumple and disappear. 'Hell, Max – here's Collin Brooks – he's been made an editor since you saw him last ...'

We sat down, they in arm chairs and I sprawled over one end of a settee, and talked politics. They are in queer contrast, these two Press Barons – Rothermere, heavy in build with the face of a bull-dog, Beaverbrook, with a body like that of a benevolent spider, and a large grin. 'Max' is a free talker. He even orates when he expounds a view point. 'I'm just an old gossip monger,' he says at intervals, but his gossip comes from good sources. He says that Neville, Hailsham,[144]

[144] Douglas McGarel Hogg (1872–1950): Con. MP St Marylebone 1922–8; Attorney-

Simon and Runciman[145] are against sanctions, that Baldwin is for the Eden policy but can be weaned....

'You'll find this hard to believe, but it's true – IT'S TRUE – there's been a diplomatic incident over the Suez already. I'll tell you. An Italian ship was going slowly down the Canal – the officials hate the Dago and slow 'em down – and some British Tommies were watching from the bank ...'

R.: 'And they pumped ship on them?'

Max: 'You've heard it?'

R.: 'No, I haven't heard a thing.'

Max: 'Well, an Italian soldier was pumping ship over the side and a Tommie called out, "that's right, make good use of it while you've got it, you won't have it long when you get to Abyssinia ..." And there's been a protest ...'

R.: 'Do you mean that Grandi's visits to Hoare have all been about an Italian soldier's john-thomas!!'

Max: (returning to seriousness) 'I hear that Germany is determined to remain friendly with Britain. She won't be pulled over to Italy. This bluff about the Ambassador spending an hour with Mussolini and the Italian man being accredited a day or two before the Nazi demonstration hasn't impressed our Foreign Office one bit. It's just bluff. Germany won't be aligned between Britain and France. She wants to drive a wedge between Britain and France. And that's her game.'

We talked (or they talked, except when R. said 'What's your view Brooks?' or when I asked a question) about Canadian elections, about the future of Greece, about the coming election. R. told Max about the D.M. ballot which had shown such a vote against remaining in the League.

Max: 'Ah, people you've trained to be Rothermereites – Once when my *Daily Express* was pushing something, I've forgotten what, we got a 90% vote in our favour. The people aren't with you this time. Over Chanack when you pushed Ll.G. in 1922 they *were* with you. This time you haven't a doggone man with you.'

Later in the day R. agreed on the telephone that Max has misjudged the changing temper of the electorate and that he underrates the power of aircraft in modern war, but at the time Max was definite and impressive.

Gen. 1922–4, 1924–8; Ld. Chanc. 1928–9, 1935–8; Sec. for War 1931–5; Ld. Pres. 1938; Con. Leader in the HofL. 1931–5; kt. 1922, cr. Baron Hailsham 1928, Viscount 1929.

[145] Walter Runciman (1870–1949): Lib. MP Oldham 1899–1900, Dewsbury 1902–18, Swansea W. 1924–9, St Ives 1929–37 (Nat. Lib. from 1931); PS Local Govt. Bd. 1905–97; FST 1907–8; Pres. Bd. of Educ. 1908–11; Pres. Bd. of Agric. 1911–14; Pres. BofT. 1914–16, 1931–7; Ld. Pres. 1938–9; Runciman Mission to Sudetenland 1938; cr. Viscount 1937, suc. 2nd Baron Runciman 1937.

Sunday 6 October   Herbert Williams,[146] the M.P., rang me up to congratulate me on my article 'Keep Out of Africa' and to say that a cave of forty back-bench Tories are to wait upon Baldwin on Friday to tell him to 'stop it'. In other words, the party is against Sanctions. He told me I might tell my friends but asked me to publish nothing, in case publicity frightened some of the weaker brethren off the project. He described the Government as a set of bloody fools, and said that in the country people had kept silent so as not to embarrass the leadership but that Baldwin had entirely misjudged the temper of the people, all of whom hated the very idea of being dragged back into a totally unnecessary war. 'They don't mind that young man conducting his mental gymnastics at Geneva, but they won't fight to save his pretty face. . .'. I rang up Beaverbrook and told him that accession of strength to his Isolation campaign. 'I'm surprised it hasn't come earlier,' he said, and passed on to a detailed criticism of today's *Dispatch*, which he said was better than the *Express*. He had only one grouse, about the placing of a panel about election prospects. He thought it should either have been on page one or omitted – but I did not argue this with him, for he was superficially right, but only superficially. On the whole he was very flattering – in fact he was wholly flattering. 'Don't forget to pass on to me any news like the bit you've told me this morning,' he ended. Paul Einzig also rang up to congratulate me on the article. He, being pro-Italian, says that the Italians have lost the war, just as Germany lost the war in 1914. They have been held up for three days by niggers!

Wednesday 9 October   A fairly full day. By 10–00 I was with Sir Charles Craven[147] of Vickers, discussing shipbuilding and steel. He grumbled with free language that the Government should have exercised right of search into private papers for the arms enquiry. 'How would you like letters twenty-three years old to be reeked up again?' he asked. He is a big, clean-shaven man of about fifty, with a trick of searing in an eighteenth century way. British shipbuilding, he says, is now rapidly recovering. Part of the trouble has been yards cutting into each other's kind of trade – battleship building taking orders for tramps, tramp builders taking orders for mud barges – anything to keep the yards at

---

[146] Herbert Geraint Williams (1884–1954): Con. MP Reading 1924–9, Croydon S. 1932–45, Croydon E. 1950–4; PS Trade 1928–9; Chm., London Area Con. Assoc. 1939–48; Dir., E.I.A. 1926–8, 1931–41; kt. 1939, cr. Bart. 1953.

[147] Commander Sir Charles (Worthington) Craven (1884–1944): RN (rtd.); Dep. Chm. & Managing Dir., Vickers; Chm., Shipbuilding Corp; Pres. to British Employers Confederation; Controller-Gen., Min. of Air Production 1941–2; Industrial Adv. to Min. of Production 1943–4; kt. 1934.

work. His plan is to categorise the various firms and ensure them the trade in their own grade.

At Geneva both Austria and Hungary have refused to participate in punitive sanctions. The fire-eater there is Eden, who clamours for immediate and strong action.

Parliament is to be resummoned a week before the expected date and the election will follow in November.

Practically the whole of the Home Fleet is now in the Mediterranean, but no mention of naval movements have been permitted to appear in the British press. Both Europe and America have been well aware of the movement. As the gentlemanly censorship of the British Press cannot have been maintained to keep the foreigner ignorant, the deduction is that the Government cannot trust the morale of its own people. This is bad psychology. The British people are still fools enough to think that British battleships can conquer the world.

Thursday 10 October   Fifty-one out of fifty-four nations represented at Geneva have today pledged themselves to the application of sanctions. Italy has declared that she will meet economic sanctions with discipline and fortitude – and military sanctions with war. The question remains – what is a military sanction? If economic sanctions imply any kind of blockade, that means war.

War news from Abyssinia continues to be fragmentary and unreliable.

There is still a fatuous belief that the war could be ended by merely closing the Suez canal to Italian vessels, thus cutting off the Abyssinian Expeditionary Force. This is solemnly advocated today in the Liberal News Chronicle, *with no indication that such an act would mean war with Italy and the Geneva powers and no mention of Italy's strong Mediterranean forces, which might play havoc with both our fleet and our Eastern Trade.*

Saturday 12 October   There is a very pretty dispute afoot in the Cabinet. It does not, as might be expected, turn on the conduct of foreign affairs, but merely on the date of the election. There is a growing feeling that the earlier the appeal is made the better, but Baldwin refuses to make up his mind – not an unusual thing. Tactically the moment is ripe, the new register is prepared, the Socialist party is divided between Lansbury pacifists and Bevin[148] sanctionists, and the country, while it is far from solid for the Eden policy, is not prepared to embarrass the Government. The Conservatives are likely, on all evidence, to abstain rather than vote against National Government candidates. There is a strong feeling from the Amery viewpoint, that the Abyssinian dispute is not worth the blood of one Birmingham lad. The

---

[148] Supporters of Ernest Bevin (1881–1951): Lab. MP Wandsworth Central 1940–50; Woolwich E. 1950–1; Min. of Lab. 1940–5; For. Sec. 1945–51; Ld. Privy Seal 1951; trade unionist, Gen. Sec. TGWU 1925–40, member TUC Gen. Council 1925–40.

conviction that the League in its present form is a danger spreads rapidly. Bernard Shaw[149] *has entered the lists with strong denunciations of its impotence and against the folly of civilised nations encouraging Abyssinian savagery.*

The European imbroglio has caused a significant frontier clash between Russia and Japan to pass almost without notice. Behind the Italian trouble there looms trouble with Germany and trouble in the Near East, but British newsprints mention neither and the general public still seems incapable of thinking of more than one thing at a time.

Saturday–Sunday 12–13 October   This was undoubtedly one of my unlucky days. At midnight we had produced not a bad paper, but by 2–20 all was changed. THE B.F. WHO HAD DONE THE SPLASH HAD WRITTEN IMPORTS FOR EXPORTS and we had all passed it !!!!!!!!!!! However, by that time nothing could perturb me, for half a dozen things had gone wrong, including a failure to get a picture of London's quadruplets over in time to re-plate. Going home I lost a glove and Emrys and I managed to select a taxi that crawled and grunted and stopped and started until we abandoned it about 3 a.m. at Hyde Park. I was dead tired and slept profoundly, getting up eventually at about noon, although I had had several phone calls between 8 and then. Whether the splash is as bad as I think, I now doubt, but it was annoying, and enough to have all the key men of the paper fired. I would certainly fire myself for such a gaffe. The salvation is that Eden, whose speech was being handled by himself, is confused in dealing with imports and exports from and to Italy under embargo.

Tuesday 15 October   *Laval continues to walk the tightrope in his endeavour to retain both British and Italian friendship. That the choice should so appear to him is a commentary upon the repeated assurances of Baldwin that Britain has no quarrel with Italy. Mussolini may well say, he who is not with us is against us. Whether support of the League be right or wrong, it is patently foolish to blind oneself to the hard fact that no nation can act as the policeman of the League and hope to retain the friendship of the nation assaulted.*

At home labour troubles increase. In Wales the miners have launched a strike and added drama to it by refusing to leave the pits. Such discontent can hardly help the National Government cause at the polls.

Neville Chamberlain pursues his belated campaign for rearmament, saying now what should have been said two years ago. It is incredible that any Administration should seek a vote of confidence on the score that their return is demanded to enable them to repair a long neglect of duty.

[149] George Bernard Shaw (1856–1950); playwright, critic, controversialist.

Friday 18 October   I had arranged to lunch George Steward (of No 10) at the Savoy. At the last minute Stanley Bell asked me to lunch with him, so I switched him into the party and made a trio. George is very contemptuous of Kingsley Wood as a propagandist, says, rightly enough, that the art of propaganda is not to let anyone know it is being done, whereas K.W. began with a great burst of trumpets and thus aroused a mental resistance complex in everybody.

Saturday 19 October   The other interests [to the Abyssinian affair] with which the populace fills its talk at the moment are the normal prepossessions of the English — football dominating the plebs and the death of the Duke of Buccleugh,[150] who's daughter's wedding to the Duke of Gloucester[151] will now be held in private, robbing London of another processional raree show.

With the outset of the election the usual scandals begin to emerge — the First Lord, Sir Bolton Eyres-Monsell, is not to fight his seat because he is shortly to be a party in a divorce case. After a quarter of a century in the Commons trouble with a woman ends his political career as effectively as it ended that of Dilke[152] or Parnell.[153] He will be no great loss, but it is odd that modernism has not yet learnt to distinguish between a man's public and private life. When Cleveland[154] in America was charged with a sexual irregularity and Blaine[155] his opponent was a notorious grafter some wise wag remarked that Cleveland should be kept in public life where was nothing against him, and Blaine returned to private life where his record was spotless ...

Friday 25 October   Took Derek Walker-Smith[156] to lunch at the Savoy

---

[150] John Charles Montague-Douglas-Scott (1864–1935): Con. MP Roxburghshire 1895–1906; suc. 7th Duke of Buccleuch 1914.

[151] Henry Gloucester (1900–74): Brother of George VI. Chief Liaison Officer, BEF 1939–40; Home Forces 1940–1. cr. Duke of Gloucester 1928.

[152] Sir Charles Wentworth Dilke (1843–1911): Lib. MP Chelsea 1868–86, Forest of Dean 1892–1911; PUS, FO 1880–2; Pres. Local Govt. Bd. 1882–5; suc. 2nd Bart. 1869.

[153] Charles Stewart Parnell (1846–91): Irish MP 1875–91; Chm. of Irish Parliamentary Party 1880–91.

[154] Grover Cleveland (1837–1908): US Pres. (Democrat) 1885–9, 1892–7; trustee Princeton University 1901.

[155] James Gillespie Blaine (1830–93): US politician; Speaker, House of Representatives 1861, 1862; sat House of Representatives 1863–76; Senator 1876–81; Sec. of State 1881, 1889–92.

[156] Derek Colclough Walker-Smith (1910–92): Author, *Neville Chamberlain: Man of Peace* (1939); Con. MP Hertford 1945–55, Herts. E. 1955–83; P. S., BofT. 1955–6; Min., BofT. 1957; Min. of Health 1957–60; Mem., European Parliament 1973–9; kt. 1960, cr. Baron Broxbourne 1983.

Grill. He is not fighting a seat, but is to speak for his Father.[157] He was very intent that I should fight as a Tory, and refused to be convinced that my view of the decadence of Parliament really applied to people like him and me. He implied that people of our totem should really now be making an effort instead of waiting for the next wave of change.

Wednesday 23 October   In the Commons debate on the international situation Baldwin made two statements of significance − one was that rearmament is vital and the other that a democratic system of its nature delays the making of necessary preparations. His explanation of the election date − November 14th − was that only now had he made up his mind, which drew the very natural query as to why both the Central Office of his party and the Press were aware of the date some time ago. The episode recalls the old story of the vicar's child who told a visitor that Father had received a call to a better living, and that he was in his study praying for guidance, but mother was upstairs packing. One feature of the debate was very nauseous − the attempt to assume that public opinion is solidly and enthusiastically behind the Government, when it is obvious it is not. If no better symptom were needed the revolt of the 100 back benchers, under Amery and Herbert Williams, would be sufficient indication. Actually while Baldwin talks of the League was the sheet-anchor of his policy, London is plastered with a poster which cries 'Damn the League' − a slogan that has the hearty approval of such diverse elements as the Right-wing Conservatives and the followers of Bernard Shaw.

Saturday 26 October   Tonight the National Government issued its election manifesto for publication in the Sunday press. It was a long, wordy, windy document, more like an address to a local literary society than an election manifesto. It consists for the most part of justifications for past policy, but among the promises for the future are several departures into mock-socialism, including the promise of pensions for blackcoated workers. As these have been available through any good insurance company for a generation it is difficult to see why the State should now intervene with a contributory scheme of its own. The manifesto was actually prepared by the Kingsley Wood publicity department and sent to its three signatories − Baldwin, MacDonald and Simon − to be cut down, but each appears to have added a few qualifications of his own. In consequence the document is guilty of vain repetition and no decisiveness. There is an obvious fear of emphasising too strongly the rearmament need and an obvious desire to catch the Liberal vote by an insistence upon Britain's loyalty to the League, with no courageous suggestion −

---

[157] Jonah Walker-Smith (1874–1964): Con. MP Barrow-in-Furness 1931–45; Controller of Housing and Town Planning, Local Govt. Bd. for Scotland 1910–19; Dir. of Housing, Min. of Health 1919–25; kt. 1925.

which the need demands — that the present League demands either ending or mending.

Tuesday 29 October   At home, the day was notable for a vitriolic attack by Snowden over the broadcast against the Government. Snowden has become quite the most effective demagogue of our time. His stand against his own colleagues in 1931 and his readiness to return to poverty for a principle when he resigned the Exchequer rather than condone tariffs have given him a hold upon the respect and affection of the masses. His talk tonight was wholly without fairness or logic, but was effective. His advice to the electorate is to vote for the Liberals, in order that the National government majority may be weakened. With Snowden and Lloyd-George sapping and bombarding their voters many National Government candidates will find the campaign more deadly than they anticipated. In spite of the proved unpopularity of the League of Nations on all sides, the official propagandists are making support for the truncated thing the main plank of the platform. They forget that many Conservatives never had any faith in the League and others, after the departure of Japan and Germany, realised that it was a perverted and dangerous instrument. The folly of trying to apply economic sanctions with the United States, Japan and Germany outside the ring and many smaller states refusing to participate is growing daily more obvious to the electorate.

Wednesday 30 October   Although there is a spate of speeches, mostly attacks and counter attacks of the 'you're another' kind, there is very little public interest in the election campaign. No foreigner walking the streets of London would guess that the nation's suffrage were being sought. It is very obvious that in 1935 the broadcast has already completely superseded the public meeting. Only a very few personalities can draw together even a moderately well filled hall of electors. There is a growing dissatisfaction among National Government supporters at the official programme on the grounds of its Socialist character — pensions, trading areas and the like. There has been little or nothing said to suggest that Baldwin and his colleagues have any faith left in private enterprise.

It is said, on sound authority, that the Foreign Office officials, led by Vansittart, have protested to the Prime Minister that the dual control at the Foreign Office is unworkable. This means that Eden after the election will probably be moved from his present post and will take the War Office or the Colonies.

Thursday 31 October   The difficulties of sanctions are becoming more and more apparent. In London a secret meeting was held at the Bank [of England] to try to untangle the threads of financial sanctions, and rulings from the Treasury had to be requested. In Wales some 16,000 miners will be permanently out of work owing to the loss of the Italian coal trade. Newfoundland will lose her third best customer for cod – and Britain will have to come to the Colony's support. Japan continues to benefit by our relinquishment of the Italian supply and demand market. In the meantime both France and Italy continue to display a rising temper against Britain, who is regarded as a grasping Imperialistic power endeavouring to embroil the nations for her own benefit and enrichment. The foreigner, as usual, has mistaken a Cabinet of fools for a cabal of knaves.

Thursday 31 October   Macmillan came and ate a chop at the Cock – more strictly tried to eat a bad steak – and we discussed the future of the N.L.A. He has still not moved towards an appeals fund. In the morning, to my delight, R. rang up, back from Canada and full of election wisdom. It was as if a missing focal point had suddenly been restored to my eccentric days.

Friday 1 November   At home the election campaign goes wearily on, with issues muddled and confused and speeches still largely devoted to back-biting and personalities. The municipalities vote today for their local Authorities, but there is no great interest, beyond the natural feeling that the results may be a pointer to the General Election on November 14th.

Sunday 3 November   When I reached home Bernie and Lil and the two girls were just finishing supper. I rang Lucy Houston, who wanted me to enter myself to-morrow (Nomination day) to fight Sam Hoare in Chelsea, promising all the finance I might need. I told her that the moment was not yet, and that I was tied to the papers . . .

Monday 4 November   I had a telephone talk with R. at about 8–30. He suggests writing a letter to the *Daily Mail* drawing attention to the vulnerability of the British fleet in the Mediterranean. I told him of Lucy Houston's urging me to fight Hoare and he agreed that it would be folly. The hatred and derision which he holds for Baldwin was like a fugue subject in our talks yesterday; it recurred and recurred. He regards him as 'that indolent, dangerous old Dud,' and as the greatest political menace Britain has ever had. He dislikes mostly, I fancy, Baldwin's inertness and lack of executive quality.

Yesterday the two present diarists toured a score of London [East-End] constituencies, to test the trust of the many reports that this general election is marked by an abnormal apathy. To the eye there was practically no sign of any election at all. Posters were few, and in small streets, where in previous years the windows would have been ablaze with candidates' cards, in all the constituencies through which we went we found only seven such cards displayed. There was a complete absence of those election 'favours' which were wont to be displayed so profusely in the buttonholes of men and women, by children and domestic pets. The electorate seems utterly comatose.

Tuesday 5 November   Foreign affairs are playing a surprisingly little part in the British general election. After the early brave talk about rearmament, Baldwin and MacDonald are now hedging and talk only of minimum necessary armaments, endeavouring to throw the main electoral emphasis upon trade revival and home reconstruction plans.

Wednesday 6 November   I lunched McWhirter at the Savoy. He was very interesting on the various divisions and groups within the board of Associated Newspapers. He told me that Rothermere now does not control the business, although he behaves as if he did and nobody challenges him. At one time his control came through a holding in *Daily Mirror* shares, which, through the *Daily Mail* Trust, gave him command of the whole group, but these shares he sold. The powerful man seems to be old Cowley of the *Mirror*. What will happen when R. dies is obscure. McWhirter thinks a bargain between Cowley and Esmond Harmsworth. It is all very immoral and like a seven-and-sixpenny novel.

The British public seems at the moment to be far more excited about the marriage of the Duke of Gloucester to Lady Montagu-Douglas-Scott than about the growing dangers of an Italio-British conflict. The stock market remains active and firm. Wall Street is in the early stages of a new boom. Despite the existence of acute apprehension in knowledgeable quarters, there is a complete complacency generally. For the most part the people of this country are still like children playing on the rim of a slumbering, but active, volcano.

Tuesday 12 November   Italy has issued a Note of Protest against the gravity and injustice of the sanctions policy of the League. This note is addressed to the nations individually, not collectively. In older days its despatch would have been the prelude to a complete severance of diplomatic relations and – war. It may still be that.

Wednesday 13 November   This is the eve of the poll. Forecasts of the National Government majority are now generally around 124.

Britain is pressing for a joint reply to the Italian note of protest.

The Government has announced the placing of new orders for several battleships. There is little or no attempt to make the populace air-minded. The spot-light of sentiment is still turned on the Navy, although experts believe that the day of the floating navy is over. Belloc[158] recently weighed up the advantages possessed by Britain and Italy if war came produced an imposing list of British advantages – mainly based upon financial power – and then honestly suggested that they all meant nothing if aircraft have ended the reign of sea power. It is indeed incredible that the one place where the supremacy of the air arm is neither admitted nor emphasised is Whitehall.

Thursday 14 November   Polling day – like a good citizen I took my wife early to the booth. The office kept me busy until about 6–30, when I got away early and came home to eat and dress, then with Lil took a taxi to the Albert Hall, where the *Daily Mail* rally was held. We shared a box with two other people, who were quiet and pleasant. [...] Results came in slowly, the first a batch of National Government triumphs, then some Labour gains, but it was soon obvious that although the Government vote was heavily down its majority must be high. The orchestra and the organ kept the thousands of people singing and happy, but there was no fire in the affair. At 12–30 we were glad to go. At home we listened to a few more results on the broadcast – which kept its service going through the night – but were relatively early a-bed.

Friday 15 November   As results come in, it looks as if the Government will have a majority of about 150 seats. On votes cast this majority under a system of proportional representation would have been about 75.

Two main problems face the Premier – a reconstruction of his Cabinet and a settlement of the coal dispute. In foreign affairs, of course, the problems are unchanged.

Ramsay MacDonald is almost certainly beaten at Seaham and his son at Basset Law. This will mean that the alleged National Government will contain, when the last results are in, only one Labour Cabinet Minister.

[...] R., who had been expecting a majority of not more than 70 for his hated Baldwin, was early on my phone explaining that on P.R. that would have been the majority and that had the *Daily Mail* and *Evening News* at his instigation swung heavily in as propaganda sheets for the decaying Government ... [...] At one o'clock I was talking to George Sutton when Stanley Bell, the managing director, and Fitzhugh,[159] of the *News*, came in. They asked me if I had had any contact with R., and I told 'em yes. They then asked what he thought of the

---

[158] (Joseph) Hilaire (Pierre) Belloc (1871–1953): Lib. MP Salford South 1906–10; poet & historian.

[159] Frank Leonard Fitzhugh (d. 1944): Ed. *Evening News* 1924–44.

election, and I told 'em exactly what he had said of it, which annoyed Fitz in amused sort of way. About 6 o'clock I was in the big editorial room talking to Rhys-Thomas, the circulation manager, when Sutton came up to discuss election results. After a little while he and I walked down the corridor, when he suddenly unbosomed himself.

'I think R. and Ward Price and Morison are a rotten combination for a weekend, something rotten will come out of that, Collin Brooks. I wouldn't put a penny stamp on the judgement of either Ward Price or Morison. They play up to the old man too much. I had to tell Morison this week it was no good his transmitting damn fool instructions that he must know can't be carried out. You know as well as I do, Collin Brooks, that R. doesn't control these papers. He has no right to treat them as a toy. We are a limited company with twenty thousand shareholders. We are under the law, the same responsibilities and the same penalties for directors as any other company ...'

It was a strange, ten-minute-long outburst. He spoke frankly, as if I were already on the Board and decidedly a member of his section of it. Why go into politics, thought I, when you can have the politics of Associated newspapers to amuse you!

Thursday 21 November   Mussolini has granted agricultural leave to 100,000 troops as an anti-sanction measure. Roosevelt has issued an appeal to his countrymen to co-operate with the League in refusing to export oil to Italy. This proposal brings a European war rapidly nearer. Mussolini without oil would be stemmed in Abyssinia. He cannot afford to fail there. He can better afford to strike vigorously in the Mediterranean. Every step of the Genevan diplomacy brings an Italian-German understanding nearer. The situation is graver now than it has been since 1914.

Friday 22 November   The personnel of Baldwin's reconstructed Cabinet was known tonight. Halifax leads the Lords in place of Londonderry, who has been incontinently dropped. The two MacDonalds remain in the Cabinet, but Malcolm takes the Dominions Office from Thomas, who goes to the Colonial Office. Duff Cooper[160] becomes Secretary of State for War. There is enormous annoyance among the Conservatives that Baldwin should spend his time wet-nursing the MacDonalds when he should be active on policy. A proposed addition of a couple of hundred machines to the air force is nibbling at the cherry. The Cabinet is prepared to back the proposed oil sanction if it can be effectively worked. Both Britain and France

---

[160] (Alfred) Duff Cooper (1890–1954): Con. MP Oldham 1924–9, St. George's 1931–45; FS WO 1928–9, 1931–4; FST 1934–5; Sec. for War 1935–7; 1st Ld. of Admiralty 1937–8; MOI 1940–1; Chanc. Duchy of Lancaster 1941–3; British rep. with Free French 1943–4; Amb. in Paris 1944–7; cr. Viscount Norwich 1952.

have sent replies to Italy declaring the sanctions policy to be inevitable.

The situation in France grows more tense. The parties of the Left have condemned Laval for his condemnation of the Fascist Leagues. It is now very evident that France is so torn by faction and so subdued by economic distress that she cannot be regarded as a first class military ally.

Sunday 24 November   Rising early on Sunday morning after reaching home about three a.m. is no fun .... I was relieved as I laggardly dressed to have a call on the telephone from R's valet asking me to come at 10–30 instead of 9–30 as R. was not quite fit. I arrived at 10–30 and found him fit enough. Morison came in to receive instructions about the *Daily Mail* leaders and articles and we discussed policy. (R's invitation yesterday had been supplemented by the remark, 'I want to discuss with *you* the political policy of all my papers .... you are a man of affairs with a wide vision and keen grasp of all contemporary problems ...') In the middle of the talk R. asked me to write a *Daily Mail* article on the Wall Street position. This led us into talk about finance and about fixed trusts. He asked why there was no fixed trust of Americans. I said that there was one available 'Dividend Stocks, Inc.' and added that I had often wished that I were in a position to form an old fashioned management trust to build a portfolio of American stocks. He said he had thought that in 1930, but the market hadn't been ripe. He chaffed Morison for a while, and Morison went. On his departure R. asked if I really thought such a trust were possible .... In ten minutes we had mapped out its lines.

'I say, what about this ... £2,000,000 capital – £1,000,000 issued at par – half a million at call for the original subscribers at par at any time – the other half million to be at call for the promoters at par at any time in five years, in consideration of their paying flotation charges?'

He trotted off to the other room to consult Esmond Harmsworth and returned saying, 'I say – my son says we should clear a million out of it.' Then he bethought him of income tax and surtax and death duties. 'My dear fellow they'll collar 60% of it ...'

I argued that a call might not be subject to assessment, and that the operation would in any event be a casual profit.

'See Needham[161] to-morrow and ask him, do you know Needham? Raymond Needham, K.C., will you do that? Will you ask him? Now what about directors? You and me and three others ...' And so we went on.

---

[161] Raymond Needham (d. 1965): lawyer, called to Bar, Middle Temple 1908, active 1920–40, 1943– ; WO 1915–6; PS, MOI 1917–19; Air Min. 1919; Dir., MOI 1939; Hon. Counsels to Finnish Legation, London 1940; Air Supply Bd. 1940–6; kt. 1957.

Monday 25 November At 5–15 I was on the doorstep of No 3 Temple Gardens, Needham's Chambers. A young barrister was dismissing some other caller. After a moment's parley he admitted me and asked me to wait in the hall, which had several comfortable chairs, a table and a stove. The atmosphere was very different from Dickens – the walls yellowwashed and clean, the electric lighting brilliant. After a while several men emerged from one of the doors and collected their hats and coats. In another moment I was shown into the rooms of Raymond Needham, K.C. His room was an odd triangular shape. It held a comfortable settee, a couple of chairs and a round table. As I entered an elderly, quiet man, with gold rimmed glasses advanced and greeted me as if he and I were old friends, or as if I were a favourite patient. I sat down on the settee and put my problem. The tips of his fingers went together and he reviewed the taxation dangers.

'But, surely,' said I, 'the case of the Tobacco Securities Trust is analogous ...'

'Ah, yes. I argued that case. The Commissioners did not appeal, but you can assume that they will not stand another. No. The call is in the danger zone. It is a right, and right has a value, even if it is a problematical value ...'

[...] By 7–40 I was at Avenue Road, where R. awaited me before the fire. 'What did he say?' was his first question. I told him. 'Ummm – that biffs it – there's another scheme gone ...'

'Hold hard, sir' said I, 'That right will be assessed on the opening quotation. Assume a small premium. By the time the tax is paid you will have a higher premium and can sell a part at a profit to pay tax ....' We talked round it, and were looking at Moddy's service of American stocks when Macmillan was announced.

Tuesday 26 November I reached Avenue Road at ten o'clock and was busy trying to change a note for my taxicab when Stanley Bell and Cranfield[162] arrived. We foregathered in the big room, waiting for R. who was on the telephone.

'How is he?'

'Very serene with me – Macmillan was here with me last night busy talking war – but otherwise he's not very depressed ....'

R. came in and we plunged straight into *Daily Mail* affairs, a business like quartet. Suddenly R. said to them ... 'There's your next colleague on the Board, sitting there, Collin Brooks ...' It was an awkward

---

[162] Arthur L. Cranfield (1892–1957): Ass. Ed. & Ed. of *Daily Mail* 1935–8; Ed. of *Star* 1941–57.

moment. I said nothing and Bell and Cran grunted something which sounded like approval.

The Government's final majority is 247. There was another symptom of the decay of Parliament in the speech of the Speaker before ascending the Chair on the reassembly of the Commons today. He deplored the decay of debate and the growing tendency of members to present set speeches to the House. A House of Commons that is not a debating Chamber obviously has all the disadvantages of a bureaucratic control. The decay of interest in Parliament which he fears has followed a decay of trust in Parliament, but any new system of Government will come too late to arm a nation that has lost all reliance and vigour in a world of distractions.

Friday 29 November   R. asked me to breakfast at 9–15, but himself arrived from a long walk at 9–30. He and I breakfasted alone with Judith Wilson sitting with us. After breakfast we discussed Needham's ruling on R's variation of our trust, which is to replace shares at call by partly paid shares – this we discussed during our walk on Tuesday – and decided to go forward with it after Christmas. On the way to Stratton House he besought me to come and live near to him. In his flat he returned to the attack.

'Here are you, a man with a singularly agile brain – the only one in the business as far as I can see – why not come near to me and we can shuffle our ideas together every morning before the day's work.'

Monday 2 December   After a busy morning at the typewriter I went down for lunch at the Savoy, where Norman Holden had gathered in the Iolanthe Room a queer trio of guests. There was Alexander,[163] head of the Co-operative Society and an ex-First Lord, Victor Cazalet,[164] and mysterious Russian, whose name I did not catch properly. The purpose of the lunch was to discuss some means of getting past the Treasury a *modus operandum* of floating a 20 year Russian Loan with the proviso that outstanding trade debts be paid either in full or by a large token payment. A.V. Alexander let slip that as far as the Co-ops were concerned they had not only been paid such debts but had received payment in advance to December 31st. Their trouble is that having had several millions profitably out with Russia at anything between 6%

---

[163] Albert Victor Alexander (1885–1965): Lab. MP Sheffield Hillsborough 1922–31, 1935–50; PS Trade 1924; 1st Ld. of Admiralty 1929–31, 1940–5, 1945–6; Min. without Portfolio 1946; Min. of Defence 1946–50; Chanc. Duchy of Lancaster 1950–1; Lab. Leader in the HofL. 1955–64; cr. Viscount Alexander of Hillsborough 1950, cr. Earl 1963.

[164] Victor Alexander Cazalet (1896–1943): Con. MP Chippenham 1924–43; PPS to Cunliffe-Lister 1924–7, to J. H. Thomas 1931; Liaison Officer with Polish Forces 1940–3; Killed in air crash off Gibraltar with Gen. Sikorski.

and 7% they are now looking for a mode of investment. We talked the whole matter over – Holden and Cazalet being representative of the bulk of the creditors. The only sound scheme that emerged was to persuade the Treasury to float a loan of its own at 3 to $3\frac{10}{4}$% and to relend to Russia at 7%, the spread to provide a pool for the trade creditors. There is no earthly chance of any loan being approved either by Parliament or the city without the debts being met. The Russian man was of opinion that Russia may soon grow so prosperous that she may have to pay the debts in full and would therefore be ready now to escape with a 25% payment.

Tuesday 3 December   The King's sister, Princess Victoria, died early this morning. This kept the King from the State opening of Parliament. The speech from the Throne was read by the Lord Chancellor. It contained nothing additional to the Government's election programme. A Cabinet yesterday is believed to have endorsed the Hoare-Eden policy and to have approved oil sanctions. If this is true, the Government is inviting war. Oil and coal prohibitions are expected to be enforced by the nineteenth of December, but it is extremely unlikely that this expectation will be fulfilled. Mussolini will show such resistance that the sanctionist powers are likely to be frightened out of their present bluff. In view of the gravity of the European situation it is amazing that the stock market remains so firm and that the general attitude of the public is so cheerful.

In the evening I got away from the office about 8. I had told Lil of R's suggestion and expected her to be other than pleased. She was, in the event, bitterly opposed to our moving to Regents Park. (I have omitted in my haste each day a part of the background, that we have made an offer and paid a deposit on a house in Chiswick Mall.) I saw and sympathised with her point of view, the uprooting of the children and ourselves, but I was intent upon the old adage that a man should live where his bread and butter is made – and R., after all, is the pilot of my fortunes for the moment. When a man flings directorates at my head and makes me his confidant I dislike refusing the first favour he asks that is inconvenient. At the office I told Bell and George Sutton of the request ... Someday I must try and write the savour of office politics more fully – but both George Sutton and Bell seem to regard me as on their side of the battle and Morison and Ward Price as the pernicious pair. On Wednesday I had a long talk with Esmond, and was surprised to find how anti-Ward Price he is and how opposed to his father's policies.

Wednesday 4 December   A morning with R. at Avenue Road – where he lay abed with a sprained tendon. We decided that [Arthur] Fuller would be a good addition to the Board of our proposed big investment trust and within a few minutes Fuller arrived. The three of us had a kind of bedside consultation about many things, F and I getting away about noon. Before Fuller's arrival R. had a telephone talk with Beaverbrook about Sanctions. We decided to ask Beaverbrook to do my leader page special for me next Sunday. 'If we press now, we can kill sanctions and save the country from war,' said R.

The lists opened today for the two great Government loans. £300,000,000 was subscribed within three hours. The list for the issue at 98 of £100,000,000 of 1 per cent Treasury bonds 1939–40 was closed within an hour. The offer at 96.5 of £200,000,000 2.5 percent Funding Loan was open for two more hours. One of the most remarkable things about the present international crisis the steady way in which the British public is investing its surplus money. In addition to these two huge and low rated Government issues there has been a steady stream of new industrial issues, mostly meeting with an excellent response. Industrially Britain is menaced by a coal strike early in the coming year, but nobody seems at all perturbed by it, although any stoppage of coal in the early stages of a rearmament and recovery programme would be fatal.

Thursday 5 December   In the evening I met Holden at the Savage, where we drank sherry with Richard Nevinson,[165] and took him to a dinner of the Compatriots at the House of Commons. Rennell[166] was the speaker, on the international situation. He and Leo Amery were so infantile that I spoke next. Norman Holden said that I expressed diffidence and not diffidence [sic], and challenged the two big-wigs with all humility but was not humble. Actually I was on the verge of rudeness in a polite phrasing, but Morgan[167] (the General, K.C. Morley biographer) who followed me was even hotter. It was preposterous that any man, even Rennell Rodd, should discuss the foreign situation on the assumption that Hitler is a pacifist and that Memel, Prague and the Eastern Mediterranean do not exist. Holden and I returned to the Club and had ale and chicken sandwiches while we left politics for a discussion of rhythm ...

[165] Christopher Richard Wynne Nevinson (1889–1946): artist; s. of Henry Nevinson.

[166] James Rennell Rodd (1858–1941): diplomat 1883–1919; Con. M.P. Marylebone 1928–32; cr. 1st Baron Rennell 1933.

[167] John Hartman Morgan (1876–1955): barrister and journalist: Literary staff *Daily Chronicle* 1901–03; leader writer *Manchester Guardian* 1904–5; army service 1914–19; counsel India Defence League 1933–4; counsel Indian Chamber of Princes 1934–7; Adviser to US War Crimes Commission 1947–9; author *Viscount Morley: An Appreciation* (1924).

Friday 6 December   The N.L.A. conference this morning did not see me, but I managed to scramble along for the lunch, where I was well placed between Marian Holden on my left and a Lady Fulton on my right. There was an amazingly good gathering of delegates. For a show started only ten months ago, the League is virile enough, but most of its supporters (as is inevitable) seem to be cranky mediocrities. Murray Sueter[168] and Simmonds[169] (the Admiral being the chairman and Simmonds the Hon. Sec. of the Parliamentary Air Committee) were the speakers. We got away to our day's work again about 3–15.

Saturday 7 December   At 7–40 a.m. R. rang me from Norfolk to talk about various things. Towards the end of the talk he said, 'Have you arranged to come to Regent's Park, yet?'

'Ah, I must talk about that when you come back ...'

'You fix it and I'll get an extra £400 a year passed for you for expenses ...'

'I'm trying to get out of another contract ...'

'Get out of it: you come to Regents Park and I'll make your fortune for you.'

I feared the effect on Lil, but after a few minutes she came swinging round to my view point and went valiantly off to cancel the other house on the Mall. The rest of the day was the usual long Saturday at the office.

Monday 9 December   Lunched at Cafe Royal A.P. Herbert, Norman Holden and Hindle[170] to discuss the *English Review*. Holden agreed to join the Board, regarding it as something of a lark.

A.P. was in good form and very amusing about his adventures as a Member of Parliament. After his maiden speech Winston Churchill met him in the corridor and said, 'That wasn't a maiden speech – it was a brazen hussy of a speech – a painted tart of a speech...' Herbert to the eye is Jewish, with a queer, Johnsonian habit of twitching his head. His tall figure loses height by a stoop; his voice is well modulated

---

[168] Murray Fraser Sueter (1872–1960): Con. MP Hertford 1921–45; entered Navy 1886; Ass. to Dir. of Naval Ordnance 1903–5; member of Advisory Ctte. on Aeronautics 1908–17; Dir. RNAS 1911–15; Rear-Adm 1920; kt. 1934.

[169] Oliver Edwin Simmonds (1897–1985): aircraft producer & inventor; Con. MP Birmingham Duddeston 1931–45; member exec. Ctte., 1922 Ctte. 1938–45; Chm. Air Transport Ctte., FBI.

[170] Wilfred Hope Hindle (1903–67): journalist, *Yorkshire Post* 1926; *The Times* 1927–33; *Evening Standard* 1934–6; *Morning Post* 1936–7; Ed. *Review of Reviews* 1933–6; diplomat 1938–43; United Nations officer 1947–64.

and he drops his witticisms out with a turn of the mouth and a falling of a semitone. He has no vanity and laughs at himself as well as at the world. Househunting with Lil in Regent's Park all afternoon.

The whole scene of British foreign policy has changed. On Saturday Laval and Hoare talked in Paris. In the morning Mussolini had seen Drummond[171] and the Italian ambassador at Paris has seen Laval. Drummond and Laval were told that Italy would not speak of peace terms under the threat of sanctions. Mussolini himself preluded the meeting of the two ministers in Paris by making a most provocative speech in Rome, one of his most defiant of his recent utterances. The consequence has been the emergence from the Paris talks of a peace plan extremely favourable to Italian arms. This plan the British Cabinet tonight adopted. It means that the policy of provocative sanctions is ended. Baldwin's position has undoubtedly been undermined by the daily reiteration in the Daily Mail of his avowal earlier in the year that you cannot conceive an effective sanction that does not mean war. This constant reiteration has made him seem the most arrant of war mongers while he adhered to sanctions. In light of this swift change of policy the Naval Conference in London has attracted little notice or interest. Japan has rejected the proposal to abolish submarines: she wants parity.

Tuesday 10 December   In the evening Lil and I went to a house warming cocktail party at the home of Michael Joseph.[172] These contemporary cocktail parties never cease to amaze me – rooms packed with the great and the near-great, all jumbled together, drinking short drinks, eating little sausages off pegs and having no time for talk.

Wednesday 11 December   Hobson accuses Rothermere and me of being responsible for changing Baldwin's policy. There is some truth in this. This personal diary has had no room for the drama of the political scene. What little I have preserved of it has gone into the other log book. But R. has steadily reiterated, with deadly effect, Baldwin's attack on sanctions of some months ago ('you cannot conceive an effective sanction that does not mean war') which has made everything Baldwin now says in support of sanctions sound like the utterings of a war monger. When Hoare brought the peace terms out of Paris, the Rothermere newspapers hailed them as the right thing at last – the possible means of saving an unprepared Britain from war. To those who do not grasp the one essential that Britain is unarmed, and is a democracy that cannot arm with speed or mobilise men, this policy is

---

[171] Eric Drummond (1876–1951): Sec. Gen. of League of Nations, 1933–40; Amb. to Rome 1933–9; suc. 16th Earl of Perth 1937.
[172] Michael Joseph: banker; s. of Leopold Joseph.

anathema. Such critics seem to feel that high moral indignation will not only turn a Dictator from his path but will, in some mystic way, disarm him. They will have a rude awakening if Mussolini strikes from the air at our floating fleet in the Mediterranean basin.

Wednesday 12 December   Baldwin now faces a genuine revolt. Many of the younger members of his own supporters feel that by pressing the Peace plan on Abyssinia they are breaking their pledges to their constituents. The terms look as if the aggressor is to receive all and more of the present fruits of his aggression. Seven of these malcontents have placed a motion on the order paper condemning any peace plan that makes large concessions to Italy. As a background to this political tension, the nation is approaching Christmas in a cheery, spending mood. The City does not show any ostensible fear of war, but is concerned at the moment with the untoward effects of a change in America's silver buying policy. Silver speculators and not war lords are the obsession.

Tuesday 17 December   Baldwin allowed it to be known that he will regard the debate on Thursday on the Hoare-Laval proposals as a vote of confidence. He is definitely wavering.

Wednesday 18 December   Late tonight Sir Samuel Hoare resigned his office as Foreign Secretary. It was known to the present diarists some hours before this announcement that Baldwin had turned tail. The position now is that Baldwin having tried by a sanctionist policy to bluff Mussolini into peace, and having won an election on all manner of dangerous pledges to Geneva, has looked into the abyss of European war and recoiled, only to return to the crater in fear of the howls of the disapproving sanctionists behind him. For them there may be the excuse of ignorance, but for Baldwin there is no such excuse. Having heard from Hoare that France cannot aid Britain if oil sanctions lead to war, he is openly dragging Britain to the brink of the greatest catastrophe in her history to preserve intact a House of Commons majority.

Thursday 19 December   The debate in the Commons on the Laval-Hoare peace proposals for Abyssinia was one of the most dramatic, and certainly one of the most significant, in the history of Parliament. Hoare, the government's scapegoat, emerged with the sympathy of everyone. Baldwin, the Prime Minister, emerged with no shadow of reputation left, either within or without the ranks of his own followers. The House was packed. The Prince of Wales sat in the Peers' Gallery over the clock his ear intently cupped in his hand. The diplomatic corps was present in strength. [...] The debate left the prestige of the Government in the mud: it left the country pledged anew to a policy which both Hoare and Laval regard as a policy driving straight to war.

Saturday 21 December   Eden and Baldwin, Eden and Chamberlain,[173] *Chamberlain and Baldwin had talks today. It was believed late today that Austen had been offered the foreign secretaryship and had asked for a few hours to think over the position. Foreign comment seems to support British comment on the recent flurry in policy, and to view Baldwin as a weak man who has emerged discreditably from a nasty episode.*

Sunday 22 December[174]   The day began well by my standing beer and whisky at one a.m. to my *Dispatch* staff at the office, with the last edition hot from the Press. Let us hope it ends as well. By an odd chance I was interrupted at this point by a call from the office – 'Eden appointed foreign secretary'. By such a standard I, as a vulgar careerist, am a rank failure, but it leaves me unworried. It seems a long time ago, although it is only seven years, since he did art notes for me for the *Yorkshire Post*. The appointment fills me with forebodings. I shan't see 'many happy returns of the day' if the Eden policy brings bombs about our heads ...

Monday 30 December   Against this still largely unrealised background of impending disaster, the British people at large are ending the old year in a mood of careless optimism. Trade is better, unemployment is down by a further 49,997 on the month and 217,250 on the year, retail sales are again up by some 7 per cent. The menace of Mussolini is under rated, the menace of Hitler is completely forgotten.

---

[173] (Joseph) Austen Chamberlain (1863–1937): MP Worcs. E. 1892–1914 (LU to 1912, then Con.), Con. MP Birmingham W. 1914–37; Postmaster-Gen. 1902–3; Chanc. of the Exchequer 1903–5, 1919–21; India Sec. 1915–17; Member of War Cabinet 1918–19; Ld. Privy Seal 1921–2; For. Sec. 1924–9; 1st Ld. of Admiralty 1931; Con. Leader 1921–2; KG 1925.
[174] Collin's birthday.

1936

Friday 10 January   George Sutton lunched me at Claridges and we talked office politics and real politics. He seems to have a feud with Stanley Bell, whom he called 'nothing but a superior bookkeeper and a promoted clerk...' Northcliffe House must be unrivalled for feuds and intrigue. George had spent some time at Brighton with Jimmy Thomas. He says that Baldwin is determined to stick out this Parliament, which confirms what Oliver told me. He (Stanley Baldwin) has lost the confidence of *all* his colleagues over the Hoare-Laval peace plan.

Monday 13 January   *The attempt to replace Ramsay MacDonald and his son Malcolm back into Parliament has revealed a serious split in the ranks of the National Government supporters. The refusal of the Unionists in the Ross and Cromarty Division, and their adoption of Randolph Churchill in opposition to young MacDonald, does not in itself mean much, for Unionism is a weak and exotic force in Scotland, but it is symptomatic. A very large body of Conservative opinion throughout the country is outraged by the tenderness which the Conservative leaders display for the MacDonald family, remembering the frankly traitorous conduct of the elder MacDonald during the war. This opinion mistrusts Baldwin as an indolent weakling and construes his love, or fear, towards the MacDonalds as a sign of this weakness. The split is the more significant as its shows itself at a moment when the Cabinet is about to make up its mind finally about the application of oil sanctions to Italy.*

Tuesday 14 January   *Japan is to withdraw from the London Naval Conference. Simultaneously a further coup is expected in North China, where Shansi and Shantung are to be forced from Nanking. The realism of Japan in the East is a parallel to the realism of Germany in the West. It means that the day of Conference diplomacy is over. Security now depends upon national armaments plus such alliances as may be relied upon in times of genuine stress. Britain is herself in a position of unique jeopardy. In the West her only ostensible ally is France, which is again facing a political crisis – a nation that has passed from crisis to crisis as a convulsive child passes from fit to fit. In the East her two allies are America, which is determined to keep out of war, and Holland, whose help is negligible. At the same time, Britain is the one great power whose possessions make her the predestined 'mark' for any predatory state that lusts for land.*

Friday 17 January   Kipling,[1] who was taken ill suddenly in a London hotel, and rushed to hospital, is at the point of death. He has filled my mind all day. I lunched Challoner James (from Geneva) at the Savage, and we talked League politics and scandal, but Kipling obsessed me. In the evening, after a congested day, I wrote a leader page special about him, recalling that which I wrote for the *Yorkshire Post* more than a decade ago, I suppose. At midnight, the office came through on the private wire to say that he was dead. Ten minutes before a Broadcast had issued an unexpected bulletin that the King is ill … It is odd how a man's trade seizes him. My first and dominant emotion was one of readiness for a congested and complicated week-end with the paper.

Saturday–Sunday 18–19 January   At the office by 10–30. A call from Lucy Houston (of whom more later) set me chasing David Woodford, that he may be switched into the campaign at Ross and Cromarty against Malcolm MacDonald, not as a candidate but as a kind of extra-Chief-of-Staff for Randolph. For the rest of the day I was very much the editor. The severe illness of a King means to the likes of us anxiety and care of which the normal citizen has no glimpse. It is necessary to have the ordinary paper running, plus an emergency page 1 to slip on to the machines at the moment of the news, plus many pages which then go onto the machines to make a memorial issue. These have to be cast as time permits. As the day wears on and the ordinary edition time approaches the problems change slightly. After the last normal edition new problems emerge. Decisions have to be taken whether to send out sellers with a re-plated edition on a piece of news, say a bulletin, or whether to wait in case the actual death occurs. If the first, one gains sale but may be 'beaten' on the big news. If the second, one loses sale, and the big news may not come. In the event, I stayed at the office all night, getting to my room for a few hours sleep in a chair about four o'clock in the morning.

Monday 20 January   I forgot to record, in the haste of the days, that one morning Lucy Houston rang me up and asked me to write for her on the *Morning Post*'s alleged 'revelations' behind Baldwin's phrase 'My lips are not yet unsealed' and of how I hastily sent along some 600 words, which she placed in the forefront of her paper, dragging it back from the printer to do so. To my amazement she sent me a warm

---

[1] (Joseph) Rudyard Kipling (1865–1936): author; winner Nobel Prize for Literature 1906; member War Graves Commission; the daily sounding of the 'Last Post' at Memin Gate, Ypres, funded by an endowment from Kipling.

letter of congratulation and a cheque for £25, which gave me a touch of conscience. By some error her secretary sent the letter home to me in her car, and that caused Lucy to worry in case my secretary had read it as she meant it to be 'between you and me, my dear...' Consulting my conscience, I saw no reason why I should not take the cheque, since the words were not signed by me but by Historicus, and why I should not write again if she wishes me to.

Tuesday 21 January   Last night Lilian and I dined Brian Manning[2] and his wife at the Piccadilly Hotel and then went on to see Guilgud in 'Romeo and Juliet'.[3] It was well done. Gielgud was not the Romeo of ones imaginings, but Peggy Ashcroft[4] was a passable Juliet and Edith Evans[5] a nurse upon whom to brood with quiet satisfaction in great artistry. When the curtain had descended upon the carnage in the tomb and the players had taken their curtain calls we waited for the national anthem, but it was not played. The absence of it was eerie. All believed the King was dead ... On the streets paper boys cried their wares. The King was not dead, but in a bulletin timed at 9–25 it was said 'The King's life is drawing peacefully to its close.' We parted saddened [...] It was about ten past twelve when we reached home. The wireless was silent, so we assumed the worst. At about 3–15 I was awakened by a telephone call on the private wire – it was Donegall coming through from New York. Before taking the call I asked for news of the King. He had died just before midnight. When Donegall spoke to me he was first anxious to know if it was true that Edward had refused the throne, such was the rumour believed in 'smart' circles in New York ... At the office we abandoned the usual news conference. There is no news, save that the King is dead.

Wednesday 22 January   At 5–40 I was at Stratton House, to greet R., who has come hurrying back to England because of the King's death. He is more gloomy than ever about the imminence of war. He had travelled with Lord Derby.[6]

[2] Brian O'Donoghue Manning (1891–1964): chartered accountant; Chm. & dir. various companies; JP 1934; Sir John Simon's step-son.

[3] *Romeo and Juliet* by William Shakespeare. Performed at New Theatre from 17 October 1935 to 28 March 1936. Ran for 186 performances. Reviewed *The Times* 18 October 1935, 29 November 1935.

[4] Peggy Ashcroft (b. 1907): actress; cr. DBE 1956.

[5] Edith Evans (b. 1888): actress; cr. DBE 1946.

[6] Edward George Villers Stanley (1856–1948): Con MP Westhoughton 1892–1906; Postmaster-Gen., 1903–5; Sec. for War 1916–18, 1922–4; Amb. in Paris 1918–20; styled Lord Stanley 1893–1908, suc. 17th Earl of Derby 1908.

'People call me a pessimist – but compared with Derby I am an optimist,' he said, 'On the boat I said to him "Why don't you say these things?" but he said that while his two sons are in the Government he has promised to make no pronouncements on public affairs.'

We had tea by the big fire and were going off to dine at Avenue Road, but R. grew suddenly tired and suggested that we came instead the next morning. (One forgets, such is his vigour, that he is nearer seventy than sixty. He had been travelling since early morning.)

Thursday 23 January   At ten o'clock I reached Avenue Road in a crawling taxicab. R. was in bed, not, as I feared, ill, but resting. He had been out on the ice capped streets for a morning walk. Morison was there and we talked high politics and finance in the bedroom, with an interruption when he talked to Vansittart. [...] At lunch we had Sir George Sutton and Fitzhugh as fellow guests. The talk was all of war. Sutton and Fitz went off in Sutton's car, and Morison and I rolled down in the Rolls with R. to the House of Lords, where he was to be with the Peers to receive in Westminster Hall the body of their dead King. Morison sat in front and R. and I behind, and suddenly R. grew perturbed that the trousering he was wearing with his morning coat was not real mourning. We reassured him. 'If it's wrong I'd rather not go. If I don't go, nobody will miss me, they'll think I'm ill or away ...' But he went, and we decanted him at the House, and then decanted ourselves and walked along the embankment to Northcliffe House. The press of people waiting for the procession was terrible about Parliament Square, but once clear of Westminster Bridge our way was clear.

Saturday–Sunday 25–26 January   towards seven thirty I entered a taxicab and drove to Avenue Road for dinner with R.. My fellow guests were Harry Morison, General Fuller,[7] newly back from Abyssinia, General Groves, Macmillan and George Ward-Price. Mrs Wilson and Judith dined with us but were not in the lounge before dinner – and we did not emerge from the dining room, after they left us, until about 1 a.m. when the party dispersed. We must have been an odd assembly. There was R., with his bull-dog face and his downright, Johnsonian manner of speech, little Boney Fuller, like a compact bird, chattering with enormous assurance about the military mismanagement of the Abyssinian campaign, Groves, elderly and pontifical and talking like a man with a soft palate. Fuller almost monopolised the talk, Macmillan for

[7] Gen. John Frederick Charles 'Boney' Fuller (1878–1966): career soldier; served South Africa 1899–1902, European War 1914–18; military historian & theorist.

once did not pour out his amazing stream of air technicalities. [...] I am hoping to get from Cranfield the private memorandum which Fuller wrote, and if I do I will insert it here, but the gist of Fuller's tale was that the Italians in Abyssinia are staggeringly inefficient. After all these months at their chief port they have only one unloading crane, the whole campaign is ridden with graft – de Bono[8] himself, Fuller says, has made a little fortune – and the discipline of the Army is simply nonexistent. 'When we call a parade for six, it is on parade at six; but with them seven o'clock sees the camp just beginning to stir.' He says that their tank drivers and pilots are so inefficient that they move off without even troubling to see if their tanks are filled with petrol. In short, his picture of muddle was so complete that it was incredible. He is convinced that the whole force will be 'bogged' and that the war is lost. This is so different from reports that R. and I have had from other sources that it left us mentally staggered. [...] When we left, Macmillan lifted Fuller and me in his car, and Fuller derided the pessimism of R. and reasserted his own belief that Italy is not really an international menace.

Tuesday 28 January　　Late last night my advertisements department rang up to say that there were two places available in Rootes' window looking on to Piccadilly from where we might see the funeral procession of King George. Until then my feeling had been that of Johnson to Giant's Causeway – worth seeing, but not worth going to see. That feeling changed, so we rose at seven and at eight o'clock took taxicab to Turnham Green station. The platform was packed with people. We had to change trains at Hammersmith – it being then eight o'clock in the morning – and the surging mob had become terrific. The train had perforce to pass many stations and people serried on the platform gazing hopelessly through the windows at people packed like herrings in a tin within the envied train. We could not detrain at Green Park Station, but joined a still greater mob at Piccadilly. By using back streets we came at last, with surprisingly little stress, to Stratton Street, and entered Rootes' by a side door. Once within all was comfort. We were two of a party of perhaps fifty people in a big show room which would hold a hundred and fifty. A buffet of coffee and sandwiches and cakes and cigarettes was there for our comfort. There were deep settees to lounge upon. The great windows were furnished with chairs. But below us in Stratton Street and Piccadilly was the greatest, scrumming,

[8] Emilio de Bono (1866–1944): soldier & Italian fascist; 1928 US Min. of Colonies; Min. of Colonies 1929; led Italian forces in annexation of Abyssinia 1935, dismissed Nov. 1935; 1935 High Comm. for East Africa; executed for part in coup against Mussolini 1944.

pushing, yet good humoured mob that I have ever seen. The jubilee crowds were immense, but these crowds were epic. Little children were lifted on to the backs of the troopers' horses to save them from being squashed underfoot. Women and men fainted and were borne off by ambulance men. At about half past nine Hugh Cecil[9] in full levee dress appeared working his way through the crowd and by some miracle achieved a passage. Not one in five hundred of the people could possibly see the procession except through pieces of mirror held high or mounted on sticks and umbrellas. At about nine fifty the guards lining the route reversed their arms. Shortly after came the advanced escort, at the slow march, but very brave in its uniforms, and kept to step by a band attired like a band of heralds. Then there was a long pause. Then the wailing of Chopin's dead march, and the procession itself. I will not attempt to capture the emotion or even the visual presentation of the next forty minutes. There was the slow marching column of guards, of airmen, of soldiers and sailors, the generals and admirals and marshals, the foreign uniforms – there was the guncarriage hauled by bluejackets with the little, little, pathetically little coffin on top, itself surmounted by Jack and crown and orb, and behind it the young King and his brothers and the great potentates. Then came the coaches with the mourning women inside, very barbaric to sight. After that the procession halted and sagged and grew ragged, and lost nobility. All one felt was pity for the old men marching at so slow a pace through so unfriendly a day on so mournful a mission. The cortege took just an hour and five minutes to pass. Then the mob thinned rapidly, setting into streams west and east. We turned to coffee and cigarettes within the room. And then we too thinned by twos and threes.

Wednesday 29 January   I gave lunch to Patrick Donner[10] at the Savoy Grill. The purpose of the lunch was to see if he would be attracted by the suggestion that he contribute political notes to our newspapers. I have liked him since we first spoke together on some platform. He is by descent a Finn, but he is more furiously patriotic than any politician I have met and has great contempt for politics and politicians. When he first consulted Central Office about a seat in the House they asked

---

[9] Hugh Richard Heathcote Gascoyne-Cecil (1869–1956): Con. MP Greenwich 1895–1906, Oxford Univ. 1910–37; Provost of Eton 1937–44; styled Lord Hugh Cecil 1869–1941; cr. Baron Quickwood 1941.

[10] Patrick William Donner (1904–88): Con MP Islington W. 1931–5, Basingstoke 1935–55; Hon. Sec. India Defence League 1933–5; PPS to Hoare 1939; PPS to O. Stanley 1944; Dir. *National Review* 1933–47; RAFVR 1939; Acting Squadron Leader 1941; Arts panel, Arts Council 1963–66; High Sheriff, Hampshire 1967–8.

him three questions only – not a word of policy – and these were: Will you pay your own expenses, How much will you spend in the constituency, and What Clubs do you belong to? He confirmed Esmond Harmsworth's account of the pressure of ostracism that the Whips' office tries to bring to bear on rebels or suspected rebels or awkward men or men not in 'the gang'. He says that out of the whole house only about forty understood even the elements of foreign affairs. The others think a man who is interested in international politics is 'queer' or has some strange secret motive. We talked with the utmost freedom of the corruption and secret bullying and bribery that makes the Common nauseous. He is only thirty years of age, slim and thin of face, with a quiet very sincere manner. He must work harder than most young men – he was the spear head of the attack on the India Bill, is a coadjutor with Lady Milner[11] on the *National Review*, is secretary to the Imperial Relations Committee in the House, and has now a difficult constituency to look after. He spoke of the snobbery of Parliamentarians. Winterton,[12] who dislikes him, once condescended to dine with him.

'I took him not to my flat but to my father's house. It was amusing to see his bewilderment, that I should have a home with good pictures, that I was obviously cushioned with some wealth. He had imagined me to be some poor adventurer. His manner changed at the first sight of the family butler...'

In the evening I dined again with R., having Ward Price, Morison and Williams (the city editor, most nervous and ingenuous of men) as fellow guests. It was to have been an evening devoted to finance, but war overshadowed all else. Ward Price confirmed Donner. When he was newly down from Cambridge somebody pressed him to enter politics. He talked with the then Chief Whip who asked what special subject he had. Ward Price said that he was a student of foreign politics, whereat the Whip laughed. 'Oh, my dear fellow, that is no use, no use at all. The House isn't interested in foreign affairs. They'd find you a bore...' Incredible!

Tuesday 4 February   Rothermere asked me to go up to Avenue Road at 10–30. When I arrived I found the household agog – there had been a cat burglar at work last night and he had taken about £12,000 of jewels belonging to Mrs and Miss Wilson. R. was up in his room, but the

---

[11] Lady Violet Georgina Milner (née Maxse) (1872–1958): Ed. *National Review* 1929–48.
[12] Edward Turnour (1883–1962): Con. MP Horsham 1904–51; US India 1922–4, 1924–9; Chanc. Duchy of Lancaster 1937–9; Paymaster-Gen. 1939; Father of the House 1945–51; styled Viscount Winterton 1883–1907, suc. 6th Earl of Winterton (Irish Peerage) 1907, cr. Baron Turnour 1952.

Wilsons told me all about it, and I was amused to see a squad of four Yard men traipsing about the garden, exactly like men in a cheap detective novel. Mrs Wilson found it sinister that the burglary had happened on the one night that R. was not in his room at 7. The man had entered R's room, crossed to her room and then rifled the dressing table. A maid had seen him and given the alarm. He had coolly made an exit through R's window, crawling along a ledge to the next house, where Korda[13] the film producer lives, and leapt into the garden – and away. R. was very jocose about it all.

Wednesday 5 February   Lloyd George startled the Commons tonight by advocating the return of the mandated territories to Germany. It is not without interest to watch these professional politicians who refused to talk about any possible war danger gradually being forced to face actualities.

Friday 7 February   Lunched with Pat Donner and managed to find a compromise which attaches him for the time being to the *Daily Mail*. He had recently dined for the first time with Beaverbrook. Why, he did not know. Bracken was there and Aneurin Bevan (whom he found nauseating) and Frederick Lonsdale.[14] After the meal Sylvia had come in and Beaverbrook had embraced her declaring that he had loved her for twenty years.

'You're making Mr Donner embarrassed,' she said.

'I can't have looked embarrassed, for I was thinking of Tanganyika,' said the serious Donner.

He found the whole dinner party purposeless and tedious. All of them were good talkers and some of them reputed wits, and most of them serious politicians, but the talk was as banal as any afternoon tea party in the suburbs. He did not respond to Beaverbrook's charmings at all. As a matter of fact, I was amused by the mere thought of the excellent Donner in such a galley. Beaverbrook has the reputation of being a great lecher. He is said to have prized 'June' Lady Inverclyde, off young Randolph Churchill.

Thursday 13 February   Took David Higham to lunch at the English Review Club, where Amery was the speaker. He spoke after my own heart, against the Franco Soviet pact. Norman Holden and Hindle were at our table, one of them relishing and the other hating Amery's

---

[13] Alexander Korda (1893–1956): film producer and magnate; kt. 1942.
[14] Frederick Lonsdale (1881–1954): dramatic author.

outburst. There is no doubt that there is a very serious split among the Baldwinians. Were I not jotting politics down in the other diary I could fill pages of this one ...

Friday 14 February   The unexpected happened to-day. In a debate launched by Admiral Murray Sueter on a private Bill to create a Ministry of Defence, Sir Austen Chamberlain intervened, and thoroughly castigated his leader, Mr Baldwin. He denounced him for ineptitude in foreign affairs as well as for tardiness in rearming, declared that the thinking machinery of the Government had not been working, and said bluntly that in the present circumstances the Premier was not fitted to be Chairman of the Committee of Imperial Defence. The attack said nothing that has not been said in many places, but it was significant coming from Austen Chamberlain, whose influence in the House is unique and whose character is thoroughly trusted throughout the country. There are many signs that the strange, almost hypnotic, influence which the Baldwin–MacDonald combination has had over the country is waning rapidly.

Thursday 20 February   In the evening I took George Sutton to a dinner of the Compatriot's Club in the House of Commons. He was delighted. Swinton was speaking. He (Swinton) said when he saw me, 'I hope you are writing some more good novels,' and displayed no animosity at my Rothermerian associations. During the discussion Handley Page[15] made a sparkling speech which revealed that all was far from smooth between aircraft makers and the Ministry. Philip Swinton seemed very pleased with himself, but obviously has no idea of what Germany and Italy are doing in the way of aircraft production. I rolled home in George Sutton's Rolls, smoking my third cigar and full of the most ingenuous emotions, pleased that I – the little boy from the Bastille – had taken to a dinner in the House so great a journalistic figure as Sutton and that I had been on terms with the Minister for Air ... It is a mood far from vanity; it implies nothing of misjudgement – it is rather a mood that says, 'I say, Pip, what larks!'

Friday 21 February   Strabolgi,[16] looking older than Commander Kenworthy used to look when we talked in the Lobby, lunched me at the Reform to talk air strategy and the defence of the Pacific ... He says

---

[15] Frederick Handley Page (1885–1962): aircraft designer.

[16] Joseph Montague Kenworthy (1886–1953): Ass. Naval Chief of Staff, Gibraltar 1918; MP Hull Central 1919–31 (Lib. to 1926, then Lab.); Lab. chief whip in the HofL. 1938–42; suc. 10th Baron Strabolgi 1934.

the Labour Party is not Pacifist, that it will vote arms. He also says he would not hesitate to take a job that was not political if he were offered one when re-armament really gets under way. He spoke, I must say, more like a sailor than a politician.

Monday 24 February   Eden made his first speech to the House as Foreign Minister. He showed no realisation of the true state of relative strengths as between a threatening Britain and a threatened Italy. His chief reference to oil sanctions was a remark that they must be judged like any other sanction – the criterion to be whether they will help stop the Abyssinian war. He spoke of the need for Britain to be strong, but did not dilate upon the physical impossibility of making Britain strong in time to cope with an aggressive enemy well armed in the air.

Thursday 27 February   The political quidnuncs are still agitated by the probable person to fill the job of Co-ordinating Minister [of Defence]. In the Lobbies of the House the same old gang of inepts is canvassed – Ramsay MacDonald, Winston Churchill, Swinton, Eustace Percy.[17] MacDonald is regarded by both his colleagues and the country as a man with softening of the brain. His inability to think clearly or to phrase his speeches consistently has caused several painful incidents and the suggestion that he is the forceful, vigorous mind which must drag Britain from her morass of unpreparedness is everywhere regarded as grotesque. Churchill is said to have several disabilities – he is not liked by Baldwin, he is mistrusted in the country as a temperamental war-monger, he is mistrusted by the airmen as a 'blue-water' fanatic too much under the sway of Roger Keyes.[18] Swinton and Percy, nominally younger men, are little better than polite departmentalists.

Monday 2 March   Yesterday was the first broadcast speech of Edward VIII. He spoke well and with great deliberation but there were several open criticisms made of the address. As to its manner – the light voice of the new King came as a shock after the full, fatherly voice of his father; his accent was strangely mixed, partly Cockney, partly Midland and partly American. As to its matter – many people were disappointed that the address contained so little that was affirmative. There was a touching tribute to the dead king, a human appeal to the people to remember that

[17] Eustace Sunderland Campbell Percy (1887–1958): Con. MP Hastings 1921–37; PS Educ. 1923; P.S. Health 1923–4; Pres. Bd. of Educ. 1924–9; Min. without Portfolio 1935–6; styled Lord Eustace after suc. of father as 7th Duke of Northumberland in 1899, cr. Baron Percy of Newcastle 1953.

[18] Adm. Sir Roger Brownlow Keyes (1872–1945): naval officer & politician; hero of Zeebrugge; Con. MP Portsmouth N. 1934–43; C.-in-C. Mediterranean 1925–8, Portsmouth 1929–31; Special Liaison Officer to the King of Belgium 1940; Dir. of Combined Operations 1940–1. cr. Baron Keyes 1943.

the new King is that same man as the Prince of Wales who was able to know them so well, and a quiet pledge to carry on his work after the way of his father — but there was no clarion call, no stimulant to faith and action. These criticisms are reported here as they were heard in conversation and were made from pulpits.

Tuesday 3 March   The Government White Paper on Defence available tonight. It opens with a fatuous repetition of MacDonald's White Paper of last year — that if there is no war there will be peace. It passes into a mealy-mouthed justification of preparedness. The practical steps towards preparedness are merely a bad joke [...] The whole production is a travesty — Parliamentarianism at its worst.

Thursday 5 March   Lunched Strabolgi at the City Carlton. After some talk of politics he divulged a business project and asked me for my advice on it — I shot him by taxi to Hubert Meredith and left him there, but whether to make large sums of money for each other or not I neither know nor care. His project is the marketing of plans and blue prints to Russia for civil aviation. Strabolgi is a re-armer among Labour men. He says that the Labour Party in the Lords has five good debaters only, Snell[19] on his own subject, Arnold[20] and two others, with himself as the bruiser. If Snell displayed more interest in leadership they could make the Lords a marvellous platform, but Snell and the leaders in the lower House do not want to advance the prestige of the second chamber in any way ...

Saturday 7 March   A day of event. In the early hours Germany re-occupied the demilitarised zones of the Rhineland. [...] In the British mind, so far as it showed itself collectively, this peace plan quite overshadowed the breach of the two Treaties, which the march constituted. Within a few hours Britain had become strongly pro-Hitler, with a mood of irritation against France that her damned punctilio might precipitate a war in which Britain is unfitted to participate.

Saturday–Sunday 7–8 March   The usual strenuous weekend, made rather more strenuous by Hitler's coup in the Rhineland. This step was

[19] H. Snell (1865–1944): Lab. MP Woolwich E. 1922–31; Lab. Leader in HofL. 1935–40; cr. 1st Baron Snell 1931.
[20] Sydney Arnold (1878–1945): Lib. MP Holmfirth 1912–18, Penistone 1918–21; PUS Colonies 1924; Paymaster-Gen. 1919–31; cr. 1st Baron Arnold 1931. Took Lab. whip in HofL.

inevitable, and although there was a whiff of cordite in the air, peace was never really at stake to-day.

Friday 13 March   Macmillan lunched me at Rules to talk over the N.L.A. and its lack of funds and its new scheme for training pilots. I thought it odd, in that fane sacred to actors and writers that we should sit there stolidly discussing air war and high politics – but the food was good.

Friday 14 March   London rocks with the latest example of Baldwin's futility – or his cynicism. After weeks of suspense as to who would be the new Co-ordinating Minister of Defence, what strong man, what experienced departmentalist or tough man of business, it is announced that the lot has fallen upon Sir Thomas Inskip, a second-rate Attorney General whose chief claim to fame is that he was a stalwart of the Protestant cause in the prayer-book debates. The best that can be said for him is that Haldane[21] was also a lawyer and the best War Minister we have had. But Inskip is no lawyer of Haldane's calibre. The Locarno powers still confer.

Tuesday 17 March   Met R. at eight o'clock. A car took us to the East End, where we walked for two hours about the Poplar and India dock neighbourhoods. He is scientifically exploring London on foot, and has decided that I should join him. The getting up is unpleasant, but the jaunt once started is pleasant. The savour of mean streets, all very clean to the eye, all filled with hurrying school children, not one other than cleanly adorned, is very different in our time from the savour that has come down through Dickens[22] and Sala[23] and Simms. At about 9–30 we bought two penny buns from a fresh-bread shop and strolled down the Commercial Road furtively eating them – an odd sight had the Press Baron's friends encountered him.

Wednesday 18 March   I reached Stratton House at 1–50. R. was sitting over the lunch table with Madam Ravon, Ravon herself and the married sister. After a little chaff, he and I took car behind the faithful Tanner[24] and set out for Norfolk. It was a perfect day – Spring at its

[21] Richard Burdon Haldane (1856–1928): Ld. Chanc. 1912–15, 1924; W.O. 1914; cr. 1st Viscount 1911.
[22] Charles Dickens (1812–70): novelist & essayist.
[23] George Arthur Henry Fairfield Sala (1828–96): journalist (including *Daily Telegraph*), author, social commentator.
[24] Tanner: Rothermere's chauffeur.

very best. We talked for a while, he slept in snatches while I read Hatchards' second-hand catalogue, talked again, and came at evening to Stody, that friendly house [...] We kept off foreign politics and war a good deal, and talked of books and pictures and the behaviour of men and women. He is a strangely foresighted fellow. He carefully sent to the Cabinet a note of Goering's remark to Ward Price, made in the presence of Hitler, that Germany is making a new plane every half hour – because he desires evidence that these inept dullards were warned, and have no excuse for neglecting British rearmament.

Wednesday 25 March   There is a lull in affairs while Eden prepares for a full-dress debate in the Commons to-morrow. He is now hampered by the knowledge that the National Government back benchers are anti-French in temper. The movement in the Conservative wing to raise the Italian sanctions gains strength.

Sunday 29 March   I rose latish, but about ten Morison came on the private wire from Norfolk to say R. wished to say what a good issue he thought we had produced. A few minutes later R. himself came on, glowing with praise and saying that he had wired Donegall congratulations on his article, and that I was to boost Don as much as I could. For years R. would not admit Donegall's existence. It was necessary that young men should write gossip for the papers, but he for one didn't like them ... Now, after months of steady sapping, Don comes into his own. R. said that he was so impressed with the improvement of the *Dispatch* that he had told Bell that this coming financial year they must allot £100,000 for development and that I was to sit in on the business side with the management.

Tuesday 31 March   The Clubs were startled this evening by the news that Lord Eustace Percy had resigned from the Cabinet. Percy – 'Useless Percy' to the House – was appointed by Baldwin as a Minister without Portfolio to brood over general policy. It was expected, particularly by Eustace Percy, that he would be the Minister for Co-ordination. He denies that his resignation means a squabble on foreign policy and implies that the nation at the opening of a new financial year cannot afford £3000 a year for a Minister of Thought who has no staff with which to enable him to think. His going makes Baldwin's position even more difficult, for now behind him will sit a row of angry discarded colleagues – Churchill, Austen Chamberlain, Samuel Hoare, Percy. These will be bad advertisements for the unity of the National Government. The collapse of the prestige of Baldwin is one of the most remarkable episodes in political history. For years he maintained his position by appearing to the populace as the supremely honest man. His mishandling of the

Hoare–Laval incident burst that bubble for ever. To-day he is despised and distrusted by his own colleagues and has no moral command over his following.

Thursday 2 April   The British government is determined to go forward with the proposed General Staff talks between Britain and France. 'Those whom the Gods would destroy, they first make mad.' Such talks give Germany the old plea of encirclement, the traditional fore-runner of war. A glimpse of the attitude of the British public towards the whole business may be had from a widely applauded 'wise-crack' of a celebrated comedian
    'Mr Ribbentrop is on his way with a new peace plan: nobody knows what is in it; but before he left Berlin France had rejected it . . .'
    It is proposed to hold the Coronation of King Edward VIII in May next year – it may prove to be a furtive ceremony between bombing raids.

Thursday 9 April   on with Lil to Daly's Theatre to see 'St Helena'.[25] Kenneth Kent[26] gave as fine a study of Napoleon, as clever a piece of acting, as I ever wish to see. The play, in which Sheriff had a large hand, is a most faithful chronicle of Longwood, even the dialogue is woven of remembered phrases from the diaries. The play has had an odd history. It was produced at the Old Vic, and was failing when Winston saw it. He was so pleased by it that he wrote a letter to *The Times* newspaper in its praise. It was transferred to Daly's, and there seems to be doing quite well. I told R. that he ought to see it, and about a week ago he went to a matinee and returned equally enthused. He persuaded Winston to write another article in praise of the play, which article appeared in the *Daily Mail* last Wednesday. It is, of course, difficult to judge how an historical chronicle will please those who are not already acquainted with its period and circumstances or captured by its main figure. The classic success, I suppose, was Drinkwater's[27] 'Lincoln' that ran so long at the Lyric at Hammersmith, but that had the war emotion to help it.

[25] *St Helena* by R.C. Sherriff and Jeanne de Casalis. Performed Daly's Theatre from 19 March 1936 to 23 May 1936. Ran for 76 performances. Reviewed *The Sunday Times* 22 March 1936.
    [26] Kenneth Kent (1892–1963); actor, author & dir.
    [27] John Drinkwater (1882–1937): poet & dramatist. Close associations with Birmingham where he was born. Birmingham Repertory Theatre first produced his most famous play *Abraham Lincoln* in 1918. Its first London run was at the Lyric Theatre from 19 February 1919 to 21 February 1920, a total of 467 performances.

Wednesday 22 April   Britain is too busy discussing the Budget to worry about Italy's progress or about the imminence of new demands from Germany. The most frequent topics after the Budget faithfully observed in various circles of society are: the approaching football match between a London and a Sheffield team for the cup; the coming marriage of Lord Derby's granddaughter; the intimacy of the King with two Americans, a Mr and Mrs Simpson; and recent cinematograph films.

Thursday 23 April   Yet another instance of the corruption of democratic government has come to light. It seems that there was some leakage about the increased taxes, and rogues hastily insured on Lloyds, netting large sums. How the leakage came is yet a mystery. The City firmly believes, on no evidence at all, that it was through J.H. Thomas, a Labour Minister always notorious as a stockmarket operator with a son in a broker's office. This rumour may be slander, but it is significant that the people take the veniality of Ministers for granted in such a scandal.

Thursday 7 May   Austen Chamberlain, who was responsible for preventing the Hoare-Laval agreement from ending the Abyssinian war, today told the League of Nations Union that sanctions must now lead to war. He has been very long discovering this elementary political truth.

Thursday 14 May   The mind of the nation is now perfectly centred − not upon international danger − but upon the Budget leakage. Thomas himself gave evidence to-day and protested his absolute innocence. What is doing him far more harm than the original suspicion that he had benefited from some breach of trust is the general realisation of the kind of gambling friends that he cultivates and who cultivate him.

Tuesday 26 May   I spent the morning with R., a long walk before breakfast leading to a hearty hunter's meal. He asked me to come to Stratton House at 6 to talk to Winston. I arrived promptly, but Winston was late. He came at last, very red in the face and chewing rather than smoking a long cigar. He was annoyed with R. for publishing an article implying that bad as Baldwin is he may be as good as any of his rivals. After Winston and R. had enjoyed a slanging match I said,

'But you are merely quarrelling with a metaphor. If Lord Rothermere had said "Let them stew in their own juice" instead of saying "don't swop horses crossing the stream" you would have been content.'

He leapt in his chair, 'You express it admirably . . . .' He alleges that he has no hope of forming a Government or even of entering one, but his ambition still bubbles out. He and I had sudden burst of argument on the old old question of whether aircraft can sink battleships. He does not reason closely, but his images are excellent. 'You can put ten thousand sheep into armour, but they'll still be sheep,' he said once. And again when R. burst out, 'My dear Winston, what is the good of trying to unify twenty three jellyfish,' he replied, 'Well, you might take five of the least jelliferous fish and see what can be done with them...' He went at about 7 o'clock, very red still and angry at the resistant arguments of R. and me.

Friday 29 May I forgot yesterday to record what was a very unusual luncheon party. At about noon I had a call saying R. wished me to join him for lunch at Warwick House, Esmond's town house. I sent home for some seemly dark garb, and Esmond drove me down. He and I had a cocktail and quarrelled about the gold standard until R. came. Ward Price and Morison made up all the party but one – who was Field Marshall Torvey, of Hungary, who had come to present R. with a decoration. The Field Marshall talked of Central European politics. He is in no doubt that Germany means war, and says seven eighths of Austria is Fascist. The little sextet was one of the most informing parties I have ever attended, very intimate and very jolly. R. has given Esmond another El Greco,[28] but I envied more a Romney Pitt[29] and a Hoppner Sheridan.[30]

Friday 5 June *Sir Samuel Hoare has re-entered the Cabinet as First Lord of the Admiralty. This is a distinct blow to the prestige of Eden, and surely heralds the abandonment of the Sanctions policy. Hoare, although he inaugurated that policy, had the wit to see at an early stage that it might lead to war. Thrown from office to gratify Baldwin's fear of the Left-wing electorate, he returns as a symbol that Baldwin himself now realises that the Eden insistence on a British might that no longer exists may bring the Empire to sudden and utter ruin.*

Sunday 7 June went to Bethnall Green for a Fascist rally, which I wrote up for the *Daily Mail*.[31][...] it is lacking the real essence of the matter which is that it was the anti-Jewish references that drew the cheers. These references the *Mail* took out because they thought their Jewish advertisers would be offended. This is the freedom of the Press, and

---

[28] El Greco ('The Greek') pseud. Domenico Theotocopoulos (1541?–1614): artist.

[29] George Romney (1734–1802): artist. His portrait was of William Pitt the Younger (1759–1806), one of Collin's heroes.

[30] John Hoppner (1759–1810): artist. Portrait of Richard Sheridan (1751–1816) statesman and dramatist. Incidentally, Hoppner painted a portrait of William Pitt in 1802.

[31] *Daily Mail*, 8 June 1936, 'Blackshirt Meeting in East End'.

this the power of the Jew. Here in little is the justification of Fascism.

Tuesday 9 June   Took Lord Alness[32] to lunch at the Savoy Grill – a little, soft voiced grey man, with a remarkable fund of Scots stories. He told me one good story of Augustine Birrell[33]. He was sitting on the Treasury Bench between Birrell and Lulu Harcourt[34] when Birrell leaned across him and said 'Who is this terrible person addressing the House?'

Harcourt said, 'It is Cleophas Morton[35] – you must remember him. He stood for a London seat. I went and spoke for him. He was defeated, but now sits for Sutherlandshire.'

Birrell listened to the bore for a few more minutes and then said, with the Birrell twinkle, 'Lulu, I wish you'd spoken for him in Sutherlandshire.'

Among Parliamentarians he spoke most highly of Asquith,[36] whose legal mind, Roman character and great erudition he admired.

Wednesday 10 June   Took Hal Colebatch to the Compatriots as my guest to hear some Australian statesman. It was a sparse gathering as most of the H.O.C. people were away attending a dinner to Neville Chamberlain – an important dinner to signal their preference for him as against Baldwin. The speeches were poor, but Colebatch, as usual, spoke like a statesman. He opened his speech provocatively by saying, 'Really, Mr Chairman, I am sorry I came. I am sorry my friend Collin Brooks came. For we are logical and honest men ...' I suggested to Sommerville,[37] the chairman, that he should invite Shakespeare Morrison to tell the Club what the position really is with regard to the ban on foreign lending.

The flight of the Government from its Sanctions policy is now apparent. To-night the Chancellor of the Exchequer speaking in London talked of a reform of the League. A continuance of the policy of sanctions, he said, would be the very

[32] Robert Munro (1868–1955): Lib. MP Wick Burghs 1910–18, Roxburghshire & Selkirkshire 1918–22; Sec. of State for Scotland 1916–22; cr. 1st Baron Alness 1922.

[33] Augustine Birrell (1850–1933): Lib. MP Fife W. 1889–1900, Bristol N. 1906–18; Pres. Bd. of Educ. 1905–7; Chief Sec. for Ireland 1907–16.

[34] Lewis 'Lulu' Harcourt (1863–1922): Lib. MP Rossendale 1904–16; 1st Comm. of Works 1905–10, 1915–16; Sec. of State, Colonies 1910–15;cr. 1st Viscount 1916.

[35] Alpheus Cleophas Morton (1840–1923): Lib MP Peterborough 1889–95, Sutherlandshire 1906–18; kt. 1918.

[36] Herbert Henry Asquith (1852–1928): Lib. MP Fife E. 1886–1918, Paisley 1920–4; Home Sec. 1892–5; Chanc. of Exchequer 1905–8; PM 1908–16; Lib. Leader 1908–26; cr. Earl of Oxford & Asquith 1925.

[37] Sir A.A. Sommerville (1858–1942): Con. MP Windsor 1922–42.

midsummer of madness. His advocacy was all for regional pacts. This can only mean one of two things – either the Cabinet has agreed to jettison the Eden policy or Chamberlain is flinging a gage in the teeth of Baldwin and Eden. The latter is unlikely – it would not agree with the known psychology of the Chancellor of the Exchequer. It may be assumed that the Sanctions policy is dead. This being so, what is the future of Eden? If he stays in the Cabinet he will be regarded by a vast mass of British sentimentalists as a moral traitor. If he goes, his departure will be a confession that Baldwin is a man utterly without faith, ready to scrap successive Foreign Ministers for opposite reasons as the will or the whim takes him.

Monday 29 June   There has been a political scurry caused by the announcement that the Premier, Baldwin, intends to take a few days rest at Chequers. For some time rumours have been current that his health is failing, and there have long been grumbles at his indolence. That he should absent himself from an important debate like that of today, when Duff Cooper, Minister for War, was taken to task for a speech made in France that gave too Francophile a tone to British policy, was seized upon as a definite symptom that retirement is his immediate plan. While Britain debates the future of its indolent Premier, Goebbels in Germany remarks to a large audience that while the League may be good, air squadrons and army corps are better.

Thursday 2 July   Baldwin to-night made a speech declaring that he has no intention of retiring, that he and he alone must say when he is incapable of sustaining the burden ... He said, also, that he is still hopeful of again being able to discuss the limitations of armaments. It is incredible that the Prime Minister of this nation at this time should be so palpably incapable of gripping the realities of the situation in which he has placed us. At a moment when all that matters is the speedy building of a deterrent air force, he burbles old platitudes about limiting arms – as if Germany and Italy would now be ready for such limitation, could economically endure it, or could be trusted to forgo their avaricious ambitions if they pretended to discuss limitation.

Friday 3 July Walked with R. round Billingsgate fish market at 7–30. He insisted upon buying me a crab. During the walk, as we peered through the rain over the river by a wharf off Upper Thames Street he suddenly said, 'You have had many opportunities now of meeting Esmond. What do you think of him?'

'That's an awkward question. I think he has a first class business brain. I don't think he has your power or your continuity. The business is you and you are the business. Wherever you are, the telephone comes into play. That won't happen, I imagine, with Esmond. And he

will be apt to conciliate the social crowd with whom he consorts.'
'I think you're right. He'll support people like Neville. He's no realist.
Here he is, very rich, but virtually an untravelled man ... Well, you'll
have to keep him straight.'

I was so amazed at this that all I said was, 'He certainly hasn't your
touch with the middle classes. I don't mean the middle classes in the
suburban sense, but in business and finance...'

'My dear fellow, I have no touch with anybody,' he said.

'But you had when you were making the business,' I answered.

'Oh, yes, then I had, a very close touch then.'

*A queer wave of alarm has spread over the country about the Zeppelin 'Hindenburg'
which has flown out of her course over North England and over certain places where
flying is forbidden. There is now a general belief that she is a spy ship of the air.
This is strangely like the scares of 1913, when strange lights were see flying over
London ... German aeroplanes!*

*Wednesday 8 July   To-day the public mind was shocked by the deaths of five
research workers in Woolwich arsenal. They were experimenting with a new and
secret explosive, but this the Press has been forbidden to say.*

Thursday 9 July The day began with Holden and Sadd[38] coming to
Rothermere's place for breakfast to try to disentangle the National
League of Airmen from the coils of ineptitude. R. was in excellent
form, as we sat at breakfast in the garden, and poured out all his
Rothermerisms about the European situation, as eager to talk as a boy
of forty, and as weighty as a sage of ninety. Sadd was impressed by
him, and pleased him by saying that my paragraph in the *Dispatch*
recounting R's prescience about Britain's leaving the gold standard had
been freely discussed at a Board Meeting of the Midland Bank yesterday.
R. promised to write to Reginald McKenna urging him to come and
talk and that he would then tell McKenna it was his duty to summon
a meeting of the most important people in the City to rouse Britain
from her torpor.

'The City has always given a lead — it should not be silent in this
hour of grave peril. McKenna was removed from the Admiralty before
the last war. This is his chance to have it set on the record that he
redeemed himself.' That was the strain of R's talk.

In the evening I was the guest of Gilbert Armitage[39] at the annual

[38] Clarence Thomas Albert Sadd (1883–1962): Vice-Chm. Midland Bank, Chief Exec.
1943–8; kt. 1945.
[39] Gilbert Armitage: lawyer and author; member Whitefriars.

dinner of the Conningsby Club. This club consists of Conservatives from Oxford and Cambridge, a carefully preserved balance. Sam Hoare was to have been the chief guest, but he was commanded to St James's Palace, so Inskip came instead. The members speeches are, apparently, always those Wilde-like flights of impudence and epigram that please the Oxford Union. The first toast was of The Conservative Party coupled with the name of Inskip – and was a brilliant but indecorous attack on both by a young High Tory. Inskip very wisely abandoned his notes and replied in the same vein, witty and wise but not very impressive. Heavy, somnolent, with a broad round face in which are set small, sleepy eyes and an incredibly small mouth, he lumbers rather than moves. The young toast-proposer had ended with a wild peroration about the 'ruins I see around me' from which the Party would arise 'Phoenix-like'. Inskip after the chastisement rose heavily and said very, very slowly, 'Mr Chairman, I rise … Phoenix-like …' and caught the good humour of the diners who a minute before had been widely applauding his attacker. But behind all the fun and chaff it was evident that all these young Tory blades are in revolt against the Party chiefs. Baldwin's name is mud in their mouths. When Bob Boothby[40] responded to the toast of the Guests (which Derek Walker-Smith proposed very brilliantly, and very flatteringly to me) he carried every one with him in a more reasoned critique of the Government's indolence and lack of vision in the face of the European danger.

At home, the British government has suffered a severe set-back by the Derby bye-election. This was the seat held by J.H. Thomas. A 'National' candidate was put into the field, and the help of Conservative Ministers was disdained. Lloyd George entered the campaign and swept the floating Liberal vote to the Labour candidate. The result was a Labour victory by a majority of 2,753 on a large poll. The loss of one seat does not matter to a Government with so large a majority, but the further loss of standing and prestige is serious. It will not, however, affect Baldwin.

Sunday 12 July   I cannot let pass the news yesterday of the Austro-Germanic Pact, which signalises the concord of Hitler and Mussolini, and is, to my mind, the prelude to European war, in which this civilisation may well disappear.

Thursday 16 July   R. left for Sweden last night, and the town seems a bit lonely. A busy day at the office – but home by about 6–30 to dress

[40] Robert John Graham Boothby (1900–86): Con. MP Aberdeenshire E. 1924–58; PPS to W. Churchill 1926–9; P.S. Food 1940–1; cr. Baron Boothby 1958.

and dine – and then to meet Leon M. Lion[41] at the Criterion Theatre. He had asked Lilian to join us. We sat, a happy trio, in a box, to see Lilian Braithwaite[42] in 'The Lady of La Paz'.[43] She was charming as a masterful old lady, refusing to grow old, the queen of a coffee plantation in Costa Rica and the adoring and adored wife of a fourth husband with a family of grandchildren. Her contrasting part of the young grandchild was played by Nova Pilbeam,[44] charming and competent, but as an actress thin and a trifle mechanical. The husband was played by a Frenchman, whose name escapes me, but which I must recover – delightful! After the show Lion took us behind – the first time Lil had ever been behind the scenes – a great adventure for her – to greet Lilian Braithwaite, who was charming in her dressing room as she had been before the footlights. She stood there in her heavy make up, diffident and sweet. We stayed only a few minutes and then on to sup at the Savoy Grill. Lion's other guests were Sybil Thorndike[45] and Lewis Casson.[46] Sybil and he and I began to exchange excited memories of the Manchester Gaiety and Miss Horniman[47] – dropped into an immediate intimacy about books and the theatre. Sybil and I, in short, fell easily into an old friendship, finding book after book and emotional experience after emotional experience that had smitten us identically. We sat over our food and the good Moselle that Lion can choose so well, until about 2–30 and then they came on here, and we sat and walked about the lounge arguing violently about a heap of things, from Irving to Internationalism. Sybil is as eager as a child, full of zest and without a grain of self-consciousness. A very girl in spirit, so that one laughs when she talks of her grandchildren. The excuse for her coming was to collect G.K.C.'s[48] collected introductions to Dickens, which she had read in odd Everyman volumes but not as a volume. It was one of the merriest and happiest quintets that I have ever known, and it broke up reluctantly about half past four. She stood in the garden and raised her hands and cried 'Oh, the smell of Jasmine!' If she hadn't been a grandmother and the greatest actress of her age I could have hugged her, and nearly did ...

---

[41] Leon M. Lion (1879–1947): manager Garrick Theatre; actor, playwright & play producer.

[42] Lilian Braithwaite (1873–1948): actress; cr. DBE 1943.

[43] *The Lady of La Paz* by Edith Ellis ran for 139 performances, from 2 July to 31 October 1936.

[44] Nova Pilbeam: actress playing 'Felicia'.

[45] (Agnes) Sybil Thorndike (1882–1976): actress. CH 1970.

[46] Lewis Casson (1875–1969): actor & dir.; m. to Sybil Thorndike; kt. 1945.

[47] Described in Brooks' *Tavern Talk* (London: James Barrie, 1950), p. 11.

[48] Gilbert Keith Chesterton (1874–1936): novelist & critic; the volume in question was *The Works of Charles Dickens*, with Introduction by G.K. Chesterton (London: Dent, 1906).

Thursday 21 July I have often regretted that this diary cannot find room – or I time – to log the shifting events of the world in which my professional life is lived. The whole fabric would be far more entertaining than a novel – the hours spent reading despatches from, talking about, talking round, happenings in France and Spain, in Germany and Egypt, the hours spent on the technical job of shaping a newspaper, the odd encounters with men and women, famous, notorious, obscure, the moments snatched with my books, the moments snatched with my children – my pleasure in the mere physical things of life, the house and its fitments. So much must be omitted. And everything of that inner thought that is the only real pleasure of keeping a journal – the high moods of faith, the long moods of brooding over the futility of life, the hesitations and the doubts, and the dreams. Let them perish: they would sound jejune and terrible years hence.

Wednesday 22 July To-day I lunched with Lord Alness at his quiet house in Egerton Crescent, Kensington. His wife is away golfing, so after a sherry in the drawing room he and I went down to the dining room together, where a deft maid ministered to us. His cook is enviable. Over his fireplace hangs an excellent portrait of him, by a man named Soclas.[49] I commented upon it, and Alness said, 'It is by a man called Soclas that I discovered in the North. He has a studio now at Brook Green. He painted a picture some years ago of a white girl and a black man ...'

'The Breakdown!' I almost shouted. 'It was withdrawn from the Academy, I often wondered why.'

Alness smiled. 'I'll tell you. It was because Whitehall, the Dominions Office, the Colonial Office, thought it would affront the native races. The artist was so angry that he will accept nothing official. He exhibits at the Academy each year, but he despises it.'

How well I recalled the picture – a nude white girl sitting on the fallen columns and pillars of civilisation listening to and watching a buck-nigger in evening dress, dancing a breakdown as he played to her on the saxophone. It was quite the best commentary on contemporary

[49] Editorial note: the name is unclear. C.B. left a blank space and then in pencil added a name, which is virtually undeciperable. I would like to thank A.W. Potter, research assistant, Royal Academy of Arts, for his help in trying to trace the artist's name. This drew a blank. Potter also disputes C.B.'s version of events, suggesting that the most plausible explanation is that the painting having been accepted by the Selection Committee was then rejected by the Hanging Committee. The Hanging Committee takes an overview of the aesthetics of the complete exhibition, what space is available and what works of art work well with each other. C.B. repeats the story in *Devil's Decade* p. 175, but does not name the artist because most likely he was unable to decipher his diary entry.

civilisation that I remember. After lunch Alness read to me a draft article that he had written for us, in which he recalled that he had known two Cabinet Ministers who had been unhappy despite their successful ambitions . To one Cabinet advancement had come too late: for the other private woe had ruined public success.

'I will tell you who they were. One was Rhondda,[50] and the other Geddes.[51] Rhondda always felt that Lloyd George had really blocked his path. He believed he should have been given Office years before. Geddes was more pitiable. I used to meet him travelling North. I often wondered what took him there. One day he told me. "I am famous and successful, I suppose, but it means nothing, for my poor wife is in a mad-house," he said.'

He spoke, too, of his memories of King George and Queen Mary, and of the days when he was at the Scotch Office and acted as Minister in Attendance.

'The King talked incessantly. When one returned to a Cabinet after an audience, the invariable question was – "well? were you able to get a word in edgeways?" The King often swore. When you talked with him he was very human. But the Queen – one is always aware with the Queen of her majesty. Although she has been known to swear. Louis Greig[52] was once sitting in a darkened room at Balmoral when she came in – it may have been one of the other palaces – and tripped over a line of carpet. She had uttered a very distinct and unmistakable damn before she realised that Louis was there. I'll let you behind the scenes of the *Gazette* – the Court Circular. Once there was a flutter in the dovecotes because I was gazetted as having had audience of His Majesty. What happened was that I was called up to Balmoral to make a quorum of the Privy Council to transact some necessary business. Before it began the King sent for me. He had just heard of my engagement to be married and wanted to know all about it, just how and where we had met, how long the wooing had taken, what were our plans – oh, most human and friendly. That was all that lay behind the baffling audience. The Queen has a good memory. I saw her after a gap of fifteen years. In the old days I had been Liberal Minister in attendance. She shook hands and immediately said, "Ah, what's become

[50] David Alfred Thomas (1856–1918): Lib. MP Merthyr Tyfil 1888–1910, Cardiff 1910; Pres. Local Govt. Bd. 1916–17; Min. Food Control 1917–18; cr. Baron Rhondda 1916, Viscount 1918.

[51] Eric Campbell Geddes (1875–1937): Con. MP Cambridge 1917–22; 1st Ld. of Admiralty 1917–9; Min. without Portfolio 1919; Min. of Transport 1919–21; Chm. FBI 1923–4 & of Dunlop & Imperial Airways. Chm. of Ctte. on National Expenditure 1921; kt. 1916, CBE 1919.

[52] Group-Captain Sir Louis Greig (1880–1953): Scottish rugby union international; ex-RAF; Gentleman Usher to Duke of York.

of your Party?" The best I could think of at the moment was, "M'am, as a Judge, I am not allowed to have a Party." The present king, – Edward VIII as I must learn to think of him, inherits that memory. I was playing golf one day at Walton Heath with George Riddell.[53] As I was hanging up my leather jacket the King, then Prince of Wales, was also changing some kit in the corridor. He looked at me for a moment and then said. "Didn't we meet at Holyrood in the old days?"'

I said, 'He inherits the memory, and the family stubbornness,' to which Alness, his quiet face all troubled said,

'He is a great trouble. When Baldwin and Mrs Baldwin found that man Simpson and his wife[54] invited to the Derby Day dinner they almost walked out. The Queen had been in tears about it. The King, you see, has a theory that if he gives his week to the nation, his week-end is as much his own as that of any private citizen. He'll find that isn't possible. It is a pity ...'

The Spanish civil war causes increasing excitement. News of atrocities perpetrated on nuns and priests by the Communists arouses great anger in Britain, and the falling of shells on to Gibraltar has alarmed the English nationals there. Thirty British men o' war have been moved to Spanish ports, to help to evacuate British subjects, and Italy is also to move ships there. The contagion from Spain has spread to France from where a fresh outbreak of strikes is reported.

Thursday 23 July   I miss R. very much, although every morning he telephones from wherever he may be, Copenhagen, Gothenburg or Stockholm ... [...] During the day I had a talk with Sir George Sutton. I happened to mention King Edward VIII. George picked up a letter from his table.

'He is very difficult. Here is a letter from Horwood[55] saying that he will not carry on. There have been a lot resignations. Louis Greig has resigned. Of course it is right that the King should have men about him of his own age, but his manner is bad. That woman Simpson exercises far too much influence. When King Edward VII took the Kaiser in to see the present King as a baby, the Kaiser stroked his cheek and said, "There lies the last king of England." That is quite true, for King George himself told the story.'

[53] George Riddell (1865–1934): Chm. *News of the World* 1903–34, one-time Chm., Newspaper Proprietors Association. cr. Baron 1920.

[54] Wallis Simpson (1896–1987): American divorcee, subsequently Duchess of Windsor.

[55] Gen. Sir William Thomas Francis Horwood (1868–1943): army 1900– ; WO 1902–10, 1914–15; Chief of Police, London & North East Railway 1911–14; Metropolitan Police Ass. Comm. 1918–20, Comm. 1920–8; part of royal household.

Friday 24 July Lunched the Earl of Cottenham[56] at the Savoy Grill. He is a good fella, about my age, I imagine. His fame as a motor and air ace is world wide, but he carries no side of any kind. [...] Cottenham thinks that some change of leadership must come. The record of Tom Mosley he thinks is too bad. He thinks that anybody in the House of Commons is already tainted – is regarded as part of the Old Gang, but he thinks that a leader might emerge from the Lords. He also feels that an English regenerator need not be a speaker, in the full sense of that word. Demagogy he thinks to be less essential here than it was in Germany or Italy.

Wednesday 29 July   The confidential talks between Baldwin and a deputation of members of both Houses of Parliament ended to-day. Churchill, the moving spirit of the deputation, specifically asked the Premier not to supplement his verbal promise to consider the matters placed before him by a formal reply. His fear was that Baldwin might endeavour by some manoeuvre to shut the mouths of the deputation. If there is not some sign of a speedier and less amateurish progress towards rearmament, the Churchillians in the ranks of the National Government may force a Parliamentary revolt. The difficulty is, of course, that most members of the House of Commons are tied to the Ministry either by hope of advancement or by fear of being forced to fight an expensive election on dissolution. The power of the Whips' office is great – so great that representative Government and democracy are stultified. A private member who refuses to embarrass his leaders may hope for much – minor office, appointments within the Government's gift and the like – that few will carry dissatisfaction to the point of resistance. This is the great justification of Dictatorship in our time.

Sunday 2 August   Took breakfast with R. at Avenue Road. While we were walking round the quiet garden Ward-Price arrived. He produced some albums of photographs of Hungarian estates. R. has decided to buy one. He asked me to arrange if possible for the purchase of 4,000,000 blocked pengoes (about £100,000.) He was most elated with the idea. Turning to Ward Price, Morison and me he cried, 'You know, we know what is going to happen to Britain. You fellows will all have to bolt for it when the economic crisis comes. We'll have this place and live *en prince*. Horses and a swimming pool – we'll live *en prince!*' (This from the tee-totaller, non-smoker.) I left about 11 to catch the noon train to Felpham.

[56] Mark Everard Peyps (1903–43): motor & air ace; suc. 6th Earl Cottenham 1922.

Sunday 11 October It is two months since any entry was made in this diary[57] ... filled by a variety of events that include such items as a quick trip across Canada and into the United States. Immediately after the last entry, while we were still at Felpham, a strange storm shook me. It arose from R's asking if I would give him my Frederick bronze[58] to give to Hitler and Lil's construing that as an affront – although I had refused to toy with the idea, setting what I thought was the jocular condition that not unless he could give me something I treasured more in exchange. (I foolishly told Lil this on the telephone, and the telephone is no medium for nuances.) She told me that for months past she knew that neither she nor the children were first in my life ... And I, amazed, reminded her that before ever joining the *Dispatch* I had suggested that I should abandon staff work and take to writing in good earnest and that only her view that a salary cheque was desirable had sent me into bondage again. To think that my brightsome feeling that at least all the indignity of popular Sunday Journalism was tolerable because it was giving her and the children a good life should have resulted in her discontent struck my mind with a kind of cold horror. But I am tied for a year and a half – then I can get free. Making a great joke of a sacrifice is excellent, if only the sacrifice achieves its purpose. It was grim. Shortly after that R. asked me to go with him to Canada and look into the newsprint situation with him. He gave me deuced short notice. We sailed on the *Empress of Britain* on September 5th.

Monday 12 October *To-day a great body of anti-Fascist demonstrators marched in their turn through the East-end streets, and again there was vigorous disorder, although no Black Shirts were out. Two things are now apparent to the general public that have been visible to close observers for some time. One is that anti-Semitism is a rising force here, as everywhere. The other is that the old Parliamentary parties now fail to catch the loyalty of youth, which in Britain is dividing Right and Left between the more vigorous organisations of militant Communism and militant Fascism. Whether a more virile personnel in the House of Commons would have prevented this is arguable, but it is certain that a misnamed 'National' Government staffed by 'frocks'[59] as lawyer Simon, lawyer Inskip, with the assistance of conventional careerists as Duff Cooper and Eden, has aided the revolt of youth, not checked it.*

---

[57] Gap in entries between 8 August and 11 October owing to trip to Canada and USA.

[58] Bronze statue of Frederick the Great – sculptor unknown.

[59] This term was coined by Sir Henry Wilson to denote the political departmentalists who, to his mind, talked and hindered the fighting services during the later stages of World War One and at the Paris Peace Conferences.

Thursday 22 October   An interesting day. Lunch at the Savoy, where Williams[60] late of Selfridges gave lunch to about ten editors. [...] Most of the table talk was of the Simpson divorce and the growing unpopularity of the King. His infatuation for Wally Simpson has led him to affront the Scots and frighten his Ministers, but he is a firm willed person, like his great-grandmother, and the talk is that he will contract a morganatic marriage when the decree nisi is made. The American press is full of the liaison, but the English press has kept it out, except for Brittain's *Cavalcade* which has a very small circulation. The Queen is said to have overcome her initial prejudice to Mrs Simpson, and to like her because she keeps David off the brandy bottle. When I had lunch with Esmond Harmsworth the other day, he being freshly back from Balmoral, he said that the King cannot stand John Simon and hates to be with him.

In the evening I took the chair at a Whitefriar's dinner in St Paul's Chapter House. Liddel Hart[61] and Henry Nevinson[62] were our two guests. My personal guest was George Sutton. Liddel Hart talked on 'The Real Shape of Things to Come,' and was good, but terribly underrated the menace from the air. Air Commodore Charlton,[63] Harry Jones and a few others, including myself, kept the discussion going well. I thought at one time I might have to call old Henry Nevinson to order. He began his speech delightfully, with reminiscences of his own campaigns, but suddenly broke into a violent attack on Mosley and Fascism. But he is so charming, and so old, that I gave him latitude. He was actually alive during the Crimea war, but not (as he said) old enough to be a war correspondent. Liddel Hart is a strange character to be our first military expert – tall, excessively thin, like a tubercular patient, with rimless glasses that eternally slip on his beak of a nose, and a voice that recalls the junior Common Room rather than the parade ground.

The Air Ministry tonight finds itself in a first class scandal, which – when the news is public tomorrow morning – should rouse tremendous public indignation. Lord Nuffield,[64] the head of the Morris motor company declares that when he offered to make aero engines for the Government he was 'turned down flat'. He denounces

---

[60] Alfred H. Williams: Dir. Selfridge & Co., Selfridge Provincial Stores & other companies.

[61] Basil Liddel Hart (1895–1970): military correspondent *Daily Telegraph* 1925–35, & *The Times* 1935–9; personal adviser to Hore-Belisha, Sec. of State for War, 1937–8; kt. 1966.

[62] Henry Woodd Nevinson (1856–1941): essayist, philanthropist, journalist & war correspondent; Ed. *Daily Chronicle*; war correspondent *Manchester Guardian*.

[63] Air Commodore Lionel Evelyn Oswald Charlton (1879–1958): served South Africa 1899–1902, WAFF 1902–7; European War 1914–17; Air Attaché, Washington Embassy 1919–22; Chief Staff Officer, Iraq Command 1923–4; Rtd. 1928.

[64] William Morris (1877–1963): Chm. Morris Motor Co. 1919–52; OBE 1917, kt. 1934, cr. 1st Viscount Nuffield 1938.

the shadow scheme and charges the Ministry with personal discourtesy. At a time when the nation has tardily insisted upon an adequate air defence this famous manufacturer is virtually told that his aid is not wanted. Nuffield cannot be accused of being a manufacturer on the make, for he has just given away to Oxford over £1,500,000 and is known to have a personal fortune of over £20,000,000. His rise to fortune from an original capital of £5 is one of the favourite examples of self-help in this generation.

Thursday 29 October   Lunched by John Green[65] at the Conservative Club to meet Barnes[66] of the B.B.C., and arranged to give a book talk. The B.B.C. has found that it is useless to try to review new books over the air, as the Press does it first and better, and have recently stopped having one book talker. They have had a change of talkers each week, but Barnes says he thinks that for the sake of continuity the talkers should do half a dozen or so. He asked me to give one, with the prospect of my later doing a further six. I said this would hardly be possible, but I would like to do one for the fun of it. It must be ten years since I did my only broadcast at Leeds.

A number of Cabinet changes were announced to-night, following the death of Godfrey Collins.[67] It was a re-shuffle. Baldwin's original plan had been to strengthen the major Departments with Conservative Ministers, but Simon, as leader of the Coalition Liberals, was too strong for him, with the result that Leslie Hore-Belisha found himself elevated to Cabinet rank without warning. W.S. Morrison, Baldwin's eventual nominee for the Premiership, was also given Cabinet rank. It is preposterous, in most people's view, that in this time of emergency Cabinet offices should be filled on the old stale party lines. The present Cabinet is frankly a balance of old gang politicians and their junior 'good boys' with no regard to competence for the work of rearming the nation. Never in the history of the nation has Parliament and Cabinet Government sunk so low in the public mind. Strong and competent men are excluded from Office, and strong critics, like Nuffield, are bribed into acquiescence. In the meantime, the nation remains vulnerable to its enemies, and Eden, in charge of foreign policy, continues both his strange attachment to Russia and his habit of interfering in all kinds of dangerous matters that neither concern him nor the nation he jeopardises.

The National Government also loses prestige from its inability to deal with the distressed areas. Tomorrow a body of hunger marchers will reach London from Jarrow. 'Hunger marchers' is, of course, a grotesque misnomer. The men are drawing a substantial dole at home and being fed and sheltered on the march – but as a

---

[65] John Green (1909–): BBC 1934–62, Controller Talks Div. 1956–61.
[66] George B. Barnes (1904–60): BBC Head of Talks 1935–48; 1st Head of the Third Programme, later Dir. of TV 1950–6.
[67] Godfrey Pattison Collins (1875–1936): Lib. MP Greenock 1910–36 (Nat. Lib. from 1931); Lib. Chief Whip 1924–6; Scottish Sec. 1932–6; kt. 1919.

symptom their march and the generally sympathetic reception of them is interesting. If there were half a dozen men leading the Socialist Party, men of glamour, the result of the next election would be a foregone conclusion. The strength of the National Government under Baldwin is that to many minds the only alternative is Socialism under Socialists with no competency.

Tuesday 3 November   The King's speech [to Parliament] contained promises of assistance to shipping, unification of coal royalties, a national health campaign and an adjustment of Cabinet Ministers' salaries. It is understood in the Lobbies that a Bill is to be rushed through Parliament forbidding – or controlling – political uniforms. This is the most practical recognition that Mosley has yet had, and it may be that such a measure would be of help to him and his movement. It has long been a deterrent to many people that British Fascism should have had to borrow a foreign name and a foreign uniform. There is a section within Mosley's own circle which wishes to reduce gradually the usage of the title from 'British Union of Fascists' to 'British Union' and to eliminate foreign savour. If the Government forbids uniforms, this transition will be the simpler. Mosley is to put one hundred candidates in the field at the next election.

Monday 9 November   The other day Walter Fish[68] asked me to join him and a few friends for lunch at the Savoy. I arrived to find the Pinafore Room holding about a dozen of us. I sat between General Horwood and Lord Decies[69] with Louis Greig next to Horwood. Very skilfully the talk was manoeuvred to the unfailing topic of the King and Mrs Simpson. Louis Greig is one of the disposed members of the old Household and is more than a little bitter – but his point, when he came to it, was that hitherto the British Press has been too loyal. If something is not done the Monarch will marry Wally Simpson and that will end the Empire, since Canada and New Zealand will not tolerate a twice married middle aged American woman as Queen Consort. He suggested that the only thing which affects the King is his popularity with the public. 'You fellows,' said Louis blithely, 'should begin to frighten him.' He avers – as do others I know – that the King's tender devotion to Queen Mary is merely show to catch the affection of the groundlings. (In this regard George Sutton told me that the Queen said to Ethel Snowdon or somebody near her, 'You know

[68] Walter George Fish (1874–1947): journalist & Ed.; *Daily Mail* from 1904, News Ed. 1906, Ed. 1926–9; Hon. Dir. Coal Mines Dept., BofT. 1914–18; Bd. of Assoc. Newspapers 1919–29.
[69] John Graham Hope de la Poer Beresford, 5th Baron Decies (1866–1944): 7th Hussars 1887–1910; Chief Press Censor, Ireland 1916–19; Dir. Income Taxpayers' Society.

David's awfully naive, wanting to have it in the Court Circular that he telephones me each morning …') We were all very worried and concerned about the affair.

Tuesday 10 November   After lunch I found a message waiting for me, that Sir George Sutton wanted me. I went down. From an arm chair in George's room a figure heaved itself, took the cigar from its mouth, shook me warmly by the hand and said genially, 'Well, Collin, you old bugger, how are you?' It was the Right Honourable J.H. Thomas. Jimmy had been lunching with George and something (said George) had arisen that had nearly broken the friendship of thirty years. It seemed that Jimmy thought there was a conspiracy against him and that nobody would buy his memoirs, declaring that he had been told that neither the *Daily Mail* nor the *Dispatch* would ever consider them, and that this had come from the *Daily Express*.

I said, 'I not only did not know you had finished your memoirs, but if I had known I should have assumed that Bates had a right to them, and I can assure you that the only man who can speak for the *Dispatch* is Collin Brooks.'

He was quite satisfied and for about half an hour talked at large – he had had a few brandies after his lunch. He is much older looking than he was when the Budget enquiry began.

'Collin, I am bitter, very bitter. I said to Baldwin if your great legal men, Tommy Inskip, Simon, and Hailsham didn't know that there was no court of appeal from that tribunal, they were fools: if they did know, they were knaves.'

He says that he would never have given evidence if it had not been for the disclosure of his boy's name. He still says that he told nobody anything about the Budget except to say that there were fools about who still thought they could have armaments without paying for them.

'I gave away no secrets – here am I with all the secrets – what about that bloody time when I had to go to a bloody brothel to buy back the bloody letters before a certain highly placed bugger could get married — I could have told some secrets, Collin, but I didn't and I'm not going to – I've got children and grandchildren and the name of Jimmy Thomas mustn't stink in their nostrils. There was a time when I wanted to make a hole in the bloody water and finish with it all, but not now. I'm not finished – but, by God, they can all go to bloody hell for me. I'm bitter, I tell you, bitter – bloody bitter.'

That is a literal transcript of his talk. He sat there very battered to the eye, his nose shiny and red, his moustache ragged, his eyes watery, like those of a gin drinker, but full of Celtic fire and imagery in his talk between the incessant bloodies and expletives – much more like a

Welsh brokers' man than an ex-Secretary of State ...

Wednesday 11 November   Armistice Day. Edward VIII received a tumultuous reception from the Empire ex-Servicemen at the Albert Hall to-night. His personal popularity is not affected by the gossip and worry of his friendship with Mrs Simpson, which, indeed, occupies the American public more than the British. It is not without interest that among the topics most discussed in press and talk on this day have been the Government Bill to prohibit political uniforms and Mr Baldwin's refusal to receive deputations of hunger marchers from the distressed areas. Malcolm Stewart[70] who was appointed Special Commissioner for the Special Areas and who is resigning after two years has presented his third and final report, making twenty specific recommendations. It is singular how every commentator avoids any suggestion that unemployed men should join the defence forces.

Friday 13 November   Took McWhirter to lunch at the Savoy. He surprised me by saying that within the Board Room there is a suggestion that either I or [Richard] Lewis[71] should edit the *Mail*. He advised me to escape it if possible or to have an editorial board, as otherwise the job is impossible. Fish, he said, was good, but Warden was just a joke. When he, McWhirter, was in charge of the paper and Pulvermacher[72] was editing it, he found P. an impossible fellow, using the prestige of the paper as a means of free tickets and the like. I said that not only had I no desire to edit the *Mail*, but that the likely thing was that I should be out of the organisation altogether for being too strong on some point of policy ...

Monday 16 November   In the evening to see 'Parnell'[73] – which plays havoc with history and glorifies both Parnell and Kitty O'Shea[74] but is none the less good. Wyndham Goldie,[75] who plays Parnell, was very like him, save that the face was a little too full, and Margaret Rawlins[76]

[70] (Percy) Malcolm Stewart (1872–1951): industrialist; Chm., London Brick Co. & other construction businesses; Comm. for the Special Areas (England & Wales) 1934–6; cr. Bart. 1937.
[71] Richard 'Dick' Lewis: journalist; Ass. News Ed. Manchester Office, *Sunday Dispatch*, London staff from Jan. 1934 as News Editor; acting Ass. Ed. 1936.
[72] Oscar Pulvermacher: Night Ed. under Northcliffe & then Ed. *Daily Mail* 1929–30.
[73] *Parnell* by Eslie T. Schauffler. Performed at the New Theatre from 4 November 1936 to 6 February 1937. Ran for 106 performances. Reviewed *The Times* 5 November 1936.
[74] Kitty O'Shea (née Page Wood): mistress of Parnell & wife of Capt. William O' Shea (1840–1905): Irish MP 1880–6.
[75] T. Wyndham Goldie (1897–1957): actor.
[76] Margaret Rawlins (b. 1906): actress.

very like Mrs O'Shea. The chief flaw was the avoidance of any hint that Kitty was still enjoying sexual intercourse with O'Shea and was bearing children to Parnell which O'Shea was made at the time to father. She must have been strongly oversexed, for O'Shea said long before the divorce when they were parted by mutual consent that whenever she came to his flat she insisted on their 'resuming the old relations'. Byam Shaw[77] as O'Shea was excellent.

Wednesday 18 November   In home affairs the visit of the King to the distressed areas of South Wales and his outspoken demand that 'Works brought these men here – something ought to be done to find them work' occupies attention everywhere. There are many signs that the nation approves this vigorous conduct by the Monarch. The suggestion has been made in many quarters for some time past that he could, if he wished, make himself the Dictator of the Empire. Some minds see in the South Wales activity and brusqueness a sign that he may yet dominate the politicians.

Tuesday 24 November   John Simon today addressed the Conservatives of the City Carlton Club. Most of his speech was an apologia for coalitionism, but when he spoke of the need for a strong Britain he was wildly cheered by the assembled taxpayers. It is strange how the English think that applauding a sentiment is equivalent to actually doing something, for it is palpable that rearmament progress is still a farce. Instead of cheering dilatory Cabinet Ministers, they should be scouring them.

25 November 1936   To the Dorchester at noon to hear Winston orate to a large and very mixed gathering in support of a movement for 'The Defence of Peace and Liberty'. Winston now believes that you can only swing the people into line behind rearmament if you can assure them that the League is to be your focal point. He is therefore preaching a well armed Britain as part of a well armed League, which shall apply an international force against any aggressor. I believe that this doctrine is pernicious and shall lather it down on Sunday in the *Dispatch*. How far Winston is sincere is a matter for comment. There is a prima facie case that when Eden's star waned, Winston saw that by a judicious attachment of himself to the League of Nations Union following, through the New Commonwealth League – or whatever is the name of his new following, he might force his way back into Office. [...] After lunch I took a taxicab to Belsize Park for a delightful mission –

[77] Glencairn Alexander Byam Shaw (1904–86): actor & dir.

in 1910 when I first read Fuller's monograph on Rhodes[78] I coveted the bust of Rhodes by Pegram[79] a photograph of which forms the frontispiece. Many many years later when I could afford a small luxury I tried to buy a cast, but the copyright was with the sculptor. I wrote to Pegram, expecting that a plaster cast would be about a pound, but he wrote, very charmingly, and said he only cast in bronze and it would be £50. I said I hadn't £50 and he wrote again and said that if I wished at any time I could come to his studio to see the bust or there was a bigger one very like it in the Guildhall. To the Guildhall I have often been since. A few weeks ago by my advice Lil and Cyril made some few hundred pounds, and I was given an operative share. This led me to buy Lil three silver castors of George II. She declared that she would give me the Rhodes bust, as she suspected me of being about to buy it. So I wrote to Pegram and to-day went up to purchase it. The visit was pathetic. Pegram, very old and crippled, lives with an aged wife and ageing maid in a flat that somehow speaks of poverty – not grinding poverty, but still poverty. I liked them both and felt rather terrible bearing away the bust under my arm, but he was pleased at my faithfulness of attachment to the work. So now the bust stands on my mantle and I have turned my desk round so that I sit facing it, and am as happy as a child with a new toy.

Monday 30 November   The talk tonight is of the destruction by fire last night of the Crystal Palace – that strange symbol of the Victorian assurance of peace and plenty. The fire began at 8 o'clock and more than 60 engines and 500 firemen battled with the blaze unavailingly.

Tuesday 1 December   There are strange rumours that the Cabinet meeting on Friday last, alleged to have been held to discuss Spain, was concerned with a very different purpose. It seems that Baldwin went that night to Fort Belvedere and saw the King, to discuss with him the future of Mrs Simpson. For months past the American press has been full of stories of the liaison and for weeks past it has been said that they are to marry in June. The recent divorce of Ernest Simpson by his wife at Ispwich Assizes added colour to this story. In an Empire with so many devote Catholics and so many puritans, the marriage of the King to a woman with two previous husbands living would be unthinkable.

[78] Sir Thomas Ekins Fuller, *The Rt. Hon. Cecil John Rhodes: A Monograph and Reminisence* (London: Longman, 1910).
[79] Frederick Pegram (1870–1937): sculptor/artist.

Wednesday 2 December In a letter yesterday Belloc said to me that he found the squabble between the King and the politicians laughable and that the King would win. When I rang up the office after we parted at about 1–15 I was told from two sources that the Cabinet had secured a promise from the official opposition that the opposition would not attempt to form a Government if Baldwin had to tender his resignation on the King's refusal to be guided by his Ministers' advice against marrying Mrs Simpson. I decided to go straight to the Commons, where on Wednesdays I have the entree to both lobby and gallery and to lunch in the gallery. There – almost providentially – I was joined by George Steward, of No 10's entourage, who was as discrete [*sic*] as usual but gave me by hypothesis and inference the whole position. The Dominions have protested against the marriage and the outspoken sermon of the Bishop of Bradford[80] followed by frank leaders in the big provincials this morning forced Baldwin's hand. I went into the gallery for a few minutes. Baldwin looked worried and ill. I had been joined by Broadbent, the *Mail* and *Dispatch* lobby man, after lunch, and he and I trooped over to the Lords – but they, in the form of about twenty somnolent gentlemen, were calmly discussing some resolution about the preservation of ancient buildings in Scotland. The Commons lobby was, of course, buzzing with gossip, and as I left Geoffrey Dawson of *The Times* came in, possibly to see Baldwin. I was told in the Lobby that the pistol had already been presented to the king's head and that Baldwin was to see him at 6 for a decision.

Thursday 3 December Lucy Houston and Donegall (to-night) are the only thoroughly pro-King people I have encountered. The city and the lobbies feel that he must abdicate. If it is a choice between the King and the Empire, Britain will be almost solidly against him, even to the point of dethronement and banishing. But he may do anything – as I told George Steward, he may even dismiss Baldwin and send for Mosley, and attempt a fascist coup d'etat. All is very much on the hazard. The situation has had the effect of swamping all other news – the Spanish war, the German menace, the distressed areas have all fallen into the obscure background of the national mind. In preparing the paper for the weekend I have even had to allow for a Royal suicide, for the King is obviously out of the realm of rationality and in the realm of nerve storms. Wally herself is ill, and little wonder. The pity is that such fools as Baldwin should have allowed the situation to

[80] Rt. Rev. Alfred Walker Frank Blunt (1879–1957): Church of England; Fellow Exeter College, Oxford University 1902–7; Ass. & Curate, Carrington, Notts. 1907–11; Vicar St. Werburgh, Derby 1917–31; Rural Dean of Derby 1920–31; Bishop of Bradford 1931–55.

develop this way. The pistol should have been used earlier.

Friday 4 December   Oliver Baldwin told me tonight that the king is determined to abdicate. I had a long talk with Esmond Harmsworth, who devised the via media of the morganatic marriage, which neither Britain nor the Dominions will tolerate – and he gave me some interesting stories of the past few days. The King drinks heavily and does not try to help even his best friends. E.H. declares that Mrs Simpson is not in love with the king and that she hardens him against an abdication. He thinks the line for us to run as a newspaper group is that of 'King's men but not Simpson's men,' which seems sound enough. E.H. says that the King changes his mind, but this does not conform to my other information.

Saturday 5 December   Breakfast with R. who wanted me to write an article 'I support the King'. This I refused to do. We agreed that the King might well send for other advisors, on the precedent of Edward VII and George in 1910 and 1931. The King actually saw Winston last night, but the visit is secret. [...] Esmond rang me up to ask me to lunch with him. In a sudden burst of snow I taxied to Warwick House where we lunched a deux. He repeated much of what he said before. His view is that if Baldwin resigns, Attlee[81] will be sent for, but will refuse to form a Ministry. The King will then send for Sinclair,[82] who will recommend Churchill. Winston will accept – 'he'd take office if only to be Prime Minister for a day,' remarked E.H. not for the first time – and will have the support of the Leyton Liberals. He will face the House, be defeated, and on the division lists will use the Liberal electoral machine to place candidates against the Baldwinites. This, E.H. agreed, would be fatal – tantamount to a silent civil war. In any issue between the King and a democratic Premier, the monarchy would go, even if – as is possible – the king's party won an election.

[81] Clement Richard Attlee (1883–1967): Lab. MP Limehouse 1922–50, Walthamstow W. 1950–5; US War Office 1924; member of Simon Comm. 1928–30; Chanc. Duchy of Lancaster 1930–1; Postmaster-Gen. 1931; Ld. Privy Seal 1940–2; Dominions Sec. 1942–3; Ld. Pres. 1943–5; Dep. P.M. 1942–5; PM 1945–51; Dep. Lab. Leader 1931–5, Leader 1935–55; cr. Earl Attlee 1955.
[82] Archibald Sinclair (1890–1970): Lib. MP Caithness & Sutherland 1922–45; Personal Sec. to Sec. of State for War 1919–21; PS to Sec. of State for Colonies 1921; Chief Whip 1931; Sec. of State for Colonies 1931–2; Leader of Lib. Party 1935–45; Sec. of State for Air 1940–5; kt. 1941, cr. 1st Viscount Thurso 1952.

Sunday 6 December   At the office all day dealing with special editions. Oliver Baldwin assuring me, and E.H. confirming, I was convinced of abdication. Unable to reach E.H. on the phone – and not wanting to compromise him – I talked to R. and decided to let go guardedly the fact that the King had so decided. My issue caused Cranfield to ring up E.H. who panic-ed [*sic*], and he and I had hot words over the telephone. We were hard at work until after nine, when the *Mail* took over.

Thursday 10 December   At about 4 to-day Baldwin made a statement to the House announcing abdication – justifying my special edition on Sunday – but I was tied up at the B.B.C. rehearsing for a time a book talk that I was to give at 6–20. When I reached the office I had a message to say that all programmes were cancelled ... Even in the midst of such political excitement I was interested in my first visit to B.B.C. House. You enter the imposing portico and find yourself in a great oblong hall with an enquiry desk in one corner. There a functionary times your entry in a book and telephones your name. A page takes you to the appropriate floor and you walk down a corridor to a big recess that is a lounge-like waiting room. In my case it was filled by a concert party and a very fat boy with his mother. The concert party told each other what a success their last broadcast had been and the fat boy conned a part. I strolled into an adjoining lavatory – and noticed that the two tuppenny nailbrushes were heavily chained to the wall. In due course, and punctual to the minute – for I had been early – Barnes collected me. We entered a studio, but it was the wrong studio. 'Ah,' said Barnes, 'It is the next one, very appropriately, for this is the King's studio.' The studio itself is a small but adequate room with two easy chairs, an oblong table, over which hangs the microphone, and a contraption like a big gramophone set or cocktail cupboard. This contraption leads into a little confessional box off the studio proper where your attender sits to listen through ear phones and through this contraption he talks to one, rather like a ghostly confessor. After some general talk – for Barnes is the very antithesis of all the B.B.C. caricatures of popular indignation – I began. At the end of the first slip Barnes re-entered to adjust my chair to the microphone and to tell me to avoid being too consonantal – 'You fairly spit out such words as "addict"' he said. Then he retired and I read through the paper, trying, on his advice, to be as histrionic as possible. (When I asked him 'shall I risk being too palpable a reader or being too histrionic?' he said 'As you are not an actor be as histrionic as you can: actors we advise the other way.') When I finished he again emerged and said 'Excellent, very excellent...' and then went over the talk in detail for corrections. There were about four sentences where the style was too literary to flow and I amended them into blatant colloquialisms. There were one or two places where my reading voice dropped. And there were two places where he wanted a double pause. My 'faults' he assured me were far below the average.

He then said, 'Admirals and Generals and people who are accustomed to making short little formal speeches are the worst. They cannot believe that a microphone talk is something very different from an essay or speech. When one tries to persuade them they complain that one is ruining their "style".'

I left, promising to return at 6–15, but, as I have said, the whole thing was cancelled. [...] Baldwin's apparently untutored speech is everywhere commended. He is a veritable Bagstock of a fellow – 'deep, deep and devilish sly, is tough old Joe, sir ...' for having brooded over this inevitable announcement since November 16 he began, Anthony-like, by remarking that he had had no time to prepare a speech, and proceeded to deliver a plain tale of great effective skill. He did more than justice to the King, but lied like a gentleman about the King's behaviour. He gave the impression of the King as a grave and composed man regretfully insisting upon either Mrs Simpson to wife or abdication – whereas the king's friends and Baldwin's friends know that the king on many occasions was 'impossible' as the idiom has it. However, it is all over – and Edward the VIII by tomorrow will be a plain citizen.

Monday 14 December   Lil and I tonight to the first night of Barrie's 'The Boy David',[83] with the Bergner[84] in the title role. This much heralded and twice postponed event was all that it should have been – the world and his wife in the auditorium and as splendid a cast on the stage as London has seen these many years past. I had a couple of words with Clive Brook,[85] the film star, in the corridor, not having exchanged words with him since we were fellow subalterns at Grantham in 1917. He has not changed a whit – but I am grey and bald-pated. The play qua spectacle was magnificent, and Augustus John,[86] sitting just behind me, seemed to gloat over his own work. The acting was excellent,

[83] James Matthew Barrie (1860–1937): playwright. Creator of Peter Pan; cr. 1st Bart 1913. *The Boy David* by J.M. Barrie was performed at His Majesty's Theatre from 14 December 1936 to 30 January 1937. It ran for a total of 55 performances. Reviewed *The Times*, 15 December 1936.

[84] Elisabeth Bergner (1900–86): Austrian actress.

[85] Clive Brook (1887–1974): stage & film star.

[86] Augustus Edwin John (1878–1961): artist; art instructor, University of Liverpool 1901–2; Member RA from 1928.

Godfrey Tearle[87] as Saul seizing a big part in both hands and doing it with all the glow and colour of the early nineteenth century. John Martin Harvey[88] as Samuel perfectly cast, and the others more than adequate. But the Bergner! As a personality she is so appealing that she is devastating. She wasn't David, she was – as doubtless all critics will say to-morrow – merely Peter Pan in a new garb. I discerned dimly what Barrie was after. This Peter-Pan child is not David, who was ruddy of flesh and masculine, but she may well be what was behind that manly exterior. If one forgot all about David of history, and took the play for its own sake, it was a miraculous performance. Little Bergner in one of the vision scenes reciting the lament over the battle field – chaffing Saul as one shepherd to another – afraid of her own prowess – memorable. In one interval I strolled out with George Sutton and we met Walter Fish and his wife. To her I said after an interchange, 'What do you think of this?' meaning, of course, the play. She said, 'I walk about in shame that the world should have seen what a pitiful thing we have bred!' and promptly launched into a denunciation of Edward VIII. After the play, the rain pouring down and taxi cabs being scarce, I took Lil to the Carlton to sup.

Sunday 20 December   To R's for breakfast. He was not pleased with the paper to-day, I suspect because it was a Christmas number with no heavy politics in it. Macmillan came in, hotfoot, from Germany and Italy, where he has been enquiring into the workability of the 'shadow scheme' for aircraft. He was very interesting, and had been over both German and Italian factories. [...] To the flat I went, for some reason convinced that his disapproval of the paper was a symptom, that the Board had been nagging him about me, and that this was a bust-up. But it wasn't. He is contemplating buying *The Morning Post* and wanted to know what I thought, and would I edit it if it was bought – as a strong Right Wing paper.

Monday 21 December   A call to Stratton House at 10, where I found R. almost ready to leave for the South of France, where his wife[89] is a-dying of cancer. We had only a few minutes of friendly talk and then parted.

---

[87] Godfrey Tearle (1884–1953): actor; kt. 1951.
[88] John Martin Harvey (1863–1944); actor & manager; kt. 1921.
[89] Mary Lilian Rothermere (née Share) (d. 1937): estranged wife of 1st viscount, m. 1893.

Sunday 27 December   My old enemy having given me little peace this week or so, I lay abed until lunch, and felt better for it. After lunch I lay down again and slept until Lucy Houston rang me about 4 o'clock.

Monday 28 December   Warner Allen rang me to say that Lucy Houston is now really ill with pleurisy and bronchitis, and consulted me about the cover for the next issue. I told him that she had had a long talk with me yesterday and had said she was very tired, but that I had not thought this more than her usual malaise.

Tuesday 29 December   I opened the *Daily Mail* to find that Lucy Houston is dead. My edition had nothing but the bare fact of the death, but I lunched at the Savage Club with Warner Allen, who told me that she had died very peacefully in her sleep late last night. Apparently there is no will, or if there is a will it is hard to find, and the relatives are already surrounding Byron Cottage like hungry wolves. I shall write of her elsewhere,[90] I shall not write here, only to say how much I shall miss those long telephone talks. *The Saturday Review*, I suppose, will cease to exist, which means an easy £1200 a year out of my pocket.

[90] See *Saturday Review*, 9 January 1937, 'L.H.' by Historious.

1937

Friday 15 January   The official Coronation Programme was issued today. It would be idle to pretend that the change of monarchs has not taken the fire out of the national interest in the Coronation. King George VI and his consort are popular enough in a quiet way, but they do not arose any great enthusiasm. In society itself, the Queen is definitely unpopular. As Duchess of York she was regarded as a rather quiet, uninteresting, highly domesticated person, a little too Scots, if anything. But as Queen she is a little derided as lacking in glamour.

Friday 29 January   Of the 17 men charged in Moscow, 13 are to die.[1] Radek,[2] Sokol'nikoff,[3] Stroiloff[4] and Arnold are sentenced to ten years imprisonment. The behaviour of the prisoners and their 'confessions' has been so strange that all kinds of explanations have been discussed, ranging from torture to hypnotism, from 'truth drugs' to a secret agreement with the prosecution. The chief effect of the trial here has been to startle those minds which have gradually drifted into a tolerance of Bolshevism.

Monday 8 February   I am still unable to shake off the physical and mental malaise that seems to have gripped me since Christmas. I have not even had the satisfaction of suffering from the conventional 'flu which has smitten most people. [...] Yesterday I was to have joined R. in Monte Carlo, but the trip is postponed until next week. He is more than ever gloomy about the imminence of war over the German colonial issue. In this diary I have wilfully excluded contemporary events of great moment: they are recorded in the other log book. That was a mistake. We are all suffering, I fancy, from the heavy apprehension of a new war, and the knowledge that Parliament under its present

[1] Show trial of Trotskyites, 19–29 January 1937, who were accused of plotting to kill Stalin and other leading members of Communist Party: the death sentence was passed on Piatakoff, Muralov, Guslavsky, Serebriakov, Livshitz, Bognslavsky, Knyazev, Rataichak, Norkin, Shestov, Turek, Grashe, Pushin.

[2] Karl Bernhardovich (Sobelsohn) Radek (1885–1939): politician, journalist & leader-writer *Izvestia* until August 1936; member of Central Ctte. of Bolshevik party; leading member of Trotskyist opposition 1923; expelled from party 1927, re-instated 1929; arrested 1936; murdered by Gulag inmate.

[3] Grigorii Iakovlevich (Brilliant) Sokol'nikov (1888–1939): Bolshevik from 1905; People's Commissionar of Finance 1921–6; Amb. to London 1929–32; Arrested 1936, sentenced to ten years; re-arrested, tried & shot.

[4] According to *The Times*, 30 January 1937, given eight years.

control can neither arm and discipline us nor avoid causes for aggression by others.

When Spain is tidied up and is under a Totalitarian Government, then we may expect another strong and aggressive move by Germany, where it is being freely said that Britain has already promised a return of the ex-Colonies. Actually, there is no such decision, and thirty back-bench Members of the House of Commons spoke in favour of a resolution put to a private meeting in favour of opposing any such return. The British public is still under a hazy impression that a return of the mandates would be in some way a carving up of the Empire. Perfidious Albion have trumpeted aloud that she was not fighting the last war for territorial aggrandisement but only to dethrone the Junkers, now blithely assumes that anything taken from Germany is by the Grace of God a part of the British Empire. To see this state of affairs clearly does not imply any 'anti-British' bias or any pro-German bias. It merely means that one has a sense of realities in a world dazed by dreams and illusions.

Monday 15 February   I reached Monte Carlo about 11–30. Tanner and the Professor[5] were waiting for me with the Rolls and I was whizzed out to R's villa. After greetings to him and Geraghty[6] (from Spain) and 'Cammie'[7] and Morison R. and I walked in the garden together. On a balcony, like a grotesque Juliet, came a figure wearing the broadest brimmed hat I have ever seen and waving a cigar to us. 'Come on down – here's your old Friend, Collin Brooks,' shouted R., and the figure came down. It was Winston Churchill. He shook hands, talked volubly for five minutes and then hurried back to a picture he was painting in the olive grove. He and Randolph left just after tea, but we had a merry lunch table, Esmond completing the party. Winston told us of how he nearly ran plump into the arms of the Germans in his last week of the war, and of his adventures on his twentyfirst birthday when he heard his first shot fired in the Cuban war. He was delighted to hear that Inskip's stock is low with the general public. During his after luncheon talk he spoke very highly of Morley,[8] whom he regards as one of the best talkers he has ever heard, and spoke well also of Grey.[9] I gave him Trevelyan's[10] life of Grey (which I finished in the

[5] Rothermere's valet.

[6] Cecil Geraghty: *Daily Mail* foreign correspondent; author of *The Road to Madrid* (London: Hutchinson, 1937), a pro-Nationalist account of the Spanish Civil War.

[7] Ewan 'Cammie' Cameron: manager of Esmond Harmsworth's Mereworth estate.

[8] John Morley (1838–1923): Lib. MP Newcastle-upon-Tyne 1883–95, Montrose Burgh 1896–1908; Chief Sec. for Ireland 1886, 1892–5; Sec. of State for India 1905–10, 1911; Ld. Pres. of Council 1910–14; cr. 1st Viscount.

[9] Edward Grey (1862–1933): Lib. MP Berwick 1885–1916; US FO 1892–5; For. Sec. 1905–16; suc. 3rd Bart. 1882, cr. Viscount Grey of Fallodon 1916.

[10] George Macaulay Trevelyan (1876–1962): Regius Professor of Modern History, Cambridge University 1927–40; author *Grey of Fallodon* (London: Longman, 1937).

train) to read on his way back to London. He was like a boy, and very pleased with his painting. Never was a man who took life with such zest.

Sunday 14 March   It is a couple of weeks since I last wrote in this log-book. From my little diary of engagements they seem to have been the usual crowded weeks. On one day – the 23rd Feb – I took Lil to the United Services Club to lunch with Boney Fuller and his wife. Fuller was about to leave with Yeats Brown[11] and some other man for Spain to see Franco.[12] We talked chiefly of war, a little of occultism, and much of Mosley. Fuller says that Mosley is now intent upon dropping the label of Fascism, and agrees to stress the title 'The British Union'. He, Mosley, still thinks his day will come when the next economic stress affects people. [...] The next day Lil and I went over Holloway Gaol. Mrs Manning arranged it for us and we were shown over the place by the Deputy Governor, a Miss Size. It was here that Wilde spent the fifteen days of his remand and Edith Thompson[13] was hanged. We saw – against all orders – the condemned cell, but could not see the actual drop. A women's prison is more like a monastery than a gaol. There were flowers in the corridor, the cells are decorated with calendars and photographs, the inmates seem less like criminals than members of some quietist institute. The regime provides for a great amount of educational work in their quite long leisure. One prisoner had a three bedded cell – provided for pregnant women who sleep with two companions – from which two beds have been evicted and into which a hand loom had been placed. Others had sewing machines and embroidery frames. Those working in the big rooms – the laundry, the mail-bag room, the kitchens – gave one a queer impression that for the most part they are sub-normal. The library was interesting and the librarian told me that the demand for travel books and biographies almost equalled that for fiction. What impressed me most was the cleanliness of everything. A battleship could not rival the polish of the rails and floors. When I came home everything seemed sooty and dirty, despite the navy cleanliness of Taylor[14] and his wife on our domestic

[11] Francis Yeats Brown (1886–1944): author, incl. *The Bengal Lancer* (1930); Ass. Ed. *Spectator* 1926–8.

[12] General Francisco Franco (1892–1975): Leader of Nationalist revolt in Spain; Dictator from 1939 till death.

[13] Edith Jessie Thompson: hanged in Holloway Prison 9 January 1923 along with lover Frederick Bywaters for the fatal stabbing of her husband 3 October 1922.

[14] Ex-Marine, who along with his wife acted as butler & cook respectively for the Brooks family.

behalf. [...] During the weeks since I came back from Monte Carlo a strange palace revolution has shown itself at the office. It is too trivial an episode to record in detail. R. telephoned me one morning to say that he had sent a letter back by McWhirter and asking me to co-operate with him and Lewis. When Mac presented the letter it was a friendly note saying that he like all of us was worried by the circulation of the *Dispatch* and wanted the three of us to go into the matter thoroughly. On a Wednesday I conferred with the two investigators, who agreed that the root trouble was that we spend in promotion about £300 a week whereas our massed rivals are spending about £20,000. To my amazement George Sutton came back that weekend and said that he had been asked by R. to take the matter in hand – but had not been told of McWhirter's mission. Now, Sutton was deliberately treacherous. He has always been very friendly to me and has always contended that anything like sensationalism would ruin the paper. It was he who had Brittain dismissed for being too sensational and 'sexy'. But having heard R. talk of the success of the *Mirror* with sensationalism and pornography he now held that his view had always been that that was what we needed. The talk was very friendly, over a lunch at Quags, but it angered me. I told Bell, the managing director, that I was not going to be played with in this way – 'buggered about' was the phrase – by old Sutton and that I would probably want to be released from my agreement with the company.

Bell said 'You have to realise that Sutton is a servant – always was a servant – always will be a servant. He was Northcliffe's office-boy and he thinks and acts like an office-boy. Whatever way he thinks the boss is moving he moves. He's treacherous. If you follow his instructions and anything goes wrong he's certain to say that wasn't what he meant.'

I let the thing lie for a day and then decided to send Sutton a letter, thus:

'March 11th 1937
Dear Sir George

I wish to place on record my understanding of our two con-versations this week. On your instructions the *Sunday Dispatch* is to be made more sensational, and at Lord Rothermere's wish, communicated through you, more attention is to be paid to sex.

My chief reason for desiring to have this understanding on record is that it changes considerably a special written instruction as to the shape and conduct of the paper that I had from Lord Rothermere before he left England,
Yours sincerely.'

I consulted Bell unofficially about sending this. He was against it's going, but agreed that I would be perfectly right in sending it. 'Of course, if such a letter came formally before the Board not one of us would dare to assent to it,' he remarked, to which I said, 'Precisely – it looks terribly bad in cold typewriting, doesn't it.' My own decision was to send it, but R. came on the phone to say that he will be back to-morrow (all this was Thursday and Friday – I am typing this on the Sunday) so I held my hand.

Monday 15 March   R. came back today from the South of France. [...] R. was convinced that the anti-British feeling in Italy was again being worked up as a prelude to war. He reaffirmed that he had been told that Hitler was intent upon a new move in Austria. Approaching his sixty ninth year he looks about fifty, and has the energy of forty. He found in Paris a contemporary print of Marie Antoinette[15] which greatly pleased him. It has been hung in the big lounge where he could look at it constantly.

Tuesday 16 March   Lunched with Hobson and Parkinson at the Reform. There was some goodhumoured chaff at my being proposed by anybody but them for membership and at my Tory pride condescending to profane itself in such a way. For the rest we talked mostly of the coming Budget. The Government's borrowing powers have lessened any apprehension that this year's imports will be great.

Wednesday 17 March   As I bathed Lil shouted to me through the closed door that Lady Rothermere had died last night. I discovered that the news reached London a little before dinner.

'How like R. not to mention it. He is like those children in *High Wind in Jamaica* who saw their friend fall to death and never even mentioned his name, less the incident, again,' said I to her.

'I can quite understand it – poor old man,' said she.

'He wouldn't thank you for saying that,' I assured her. They have been parted for nearly a quarter of a century, ever since their two boys were killed in the war, I think, but at the moment of death memories must stir.

---

[15] Josephe Jeanne Marie Antoinette (1755–93): wife of King Louis XVI, m. 1770. Deposed & executed.

[*Editorial Note*: A gap exists in the journal between 29 March and 12 December. Brooks was visiting Canada, travelling via Monte Carlo and New York aboard the Queen Mary which departed 25 April. He went to Canada as Rothermere's representative in the re-structuring of the Abitibi paper and pulp company. Whilst abroad he was taken ill in Canada and hospitalised. Over the course of five weeks and five days in July surgeons at Toronto General Hospital performed five operations. Lil and Rosemary came out at the end of the summer.]

Monday 20 December when we were in Bermuda, and I had already been away nearly half a year from my paper, it was agreed between him [R.] and Esmond Harmsworth and me that I should drop the editorship and become a kind of special correspondent to both papers at a salary of £3,000, relinquishing also the £1,000 a year that since May I had drawn from the Empire Mill. Behind this was R's desire that I should devote myself to two or three books, to rally the Right Wing. During the weeks he and I were in New York together he talked much of his determination to retire from all business ties, ostensibly because he was seventy years of age with a month or two but really because he foresees such a crash coming that the sane man of means keeps as liquid in resources and as free from ties as he can contrive. This new arrangement for me he graced by a gift of £1,000 when we were in New York and 3,000 shares in Abitibi. Later, to compensate me for some loss on my expenses account, he also gave me 1,000 shares in Consolidated Paper, to be sold – and insisted on paying for all the books I bought. These gifts and the general mood that grew between us really gave me a filial feeling towards him, although they were not accepted without protest from me. [...] I am heartily glad to be rid of the editorship of the *Dispatch*. Until one has done the job, it is impossible to realise just what a hodman's business it is – the staff control, the interviewing of innumerable salesmen of articles, the long drag of the week-end, when Friday morning links to Sunday morning with just a break for sleep. If one were running a 'real' paper, and not just a popular sheet, to be sold by sensationalism and idiocy, weekly journalism would be a diversion of tremendous appeal. [...]

Life divided between London and Norfolk, with occasional trips abroad, could be pleasant enough: if R. has his present way he and I will make the Stody estate a famous rendezvous of artists and writers and will re-instate Norfolk in the perspective of Britain to something of its eighteenth century place. We have a grandiose vision of it – but a vision clouded with 'ifs'. The Norfolk plan is that R. shall make the Stody estate the most visually beautiful place in these islands. He has already begun to scatter rhododendra paths and drives with a lavish hand, to add to the fame of the azalea gardens. Within that splendour shall work painters and writers who can not only capture the spirit of rural England, but the very heart of the English tradition. In near-by Norwich we shall seek out Nugent Monck[16] and the Madder Market Theatre and try to add to that cultural miracle good chamber music and ballet. With this shall go forward the attempt to formulate a political policy, and to create Fabian-wise a political party, which shall restore something of Cobbett's[17] vision. It is all dream-like as yet, but it might come to reality with work and a stout heart against disappointments. The danger will be that prigs may invade us. And after Norfolk, or perhaps with Norfolk, shall go forward the same experiment in Bermuda. R. with his great riches believes that for the next decade of his life he should spend, since taxation makes thrift and making of wealth a thankless and harassing job. And it is in this way that he proposes to spend. As I told him, by his gift of the use of The Mount at Edgefield, he does for me what the Bentincks did for Disraeli. If I am not Disraeli, I can at least make a new Collin Brooks. [...] Well, here is the noon hour, and the thick fog which shrouded London has gone with the morning, and I, who have done no line of the Eden book[18], am indicated by what conscience I have left of wilful truancy. There is only one cure – to go up to the lounge and mix myself an aperitif and make a better resolution for the afternoon, or indeed, for all afternoons. I thought when I began what was really a gorgeous holiday with R. in September that it would be hard to learn how to play: I find the difficulty is remembering how to work. If the second half of my roaring forties is to emulate the first for roar, I must bully myself into the old habit, and with a firmer faith embrace my typewriters and all, my dear Copperfield, that pertains thereto ...

Christmas Eve 24 December C.B. to Norman Watson (carbon)
As for my castigation of Eden's foreign policy, I have played truant for three days from it. It stands at about folio thirty three, and must reach folio three hundred or more in the next twenty days. I see no hope in this setting – but we'll see.

---

[16] W. Nugent Monck (1878–1958): founder Norwich Players 1911; Dir. of Maddermarket Theatre 1921–52.
[17] William Cobbett (1763–1835): writer & champion of the poor; unsuccessful parlia. cand. 1821, 1826; MP Oldham 1832–5.
[18] Eventually titled *Can Chamberlain Save Britain?*

1938

Saturday 15 January The intention was that I should nip over to Paris yesterday to meet R., but the journey was called off. He came home to-day through one of the worst storms for years, but when I went round for dinner at 7–45 he was in excellent form. He says that Vansittart, of whom he has seen much, was not promoted but demoted, and that Van and Lady Van are very bitter against Eden. R. had told Winston that the French army is short of ammunition, and the air force are not first class. Winston had been very sceptical, but an ex-French Minister had now confirmed to Churchill R's report.

Thursday 27 January C.B. to Norman Watson (carbon)
My boss is pressing me to forswear my old stand and to take to practical politics ... I say that I shall not touch political life until the crash comes, that life in the galleys of the back benches is not only degrading but will disqualify one from taking hold of events when the real day dawns ... we have compromised to the extent that I am thinking it over, and will discuss it with him in New York or Toronto if I can meet him on his return from South America, to which land he sails from France on Saturday.

Tuesday 31 January C.B. to Rothermere (carbon)
The Eden book is now finished, except for a few pages which I wish to postpone until the last minute before putting it to Press. I now propose to overhaul it again for the purpose of compression and precision. The publishing contract with Dickson[1] is not yet concluded, as we are still arguing about minor terms, but this should be settled one day this week. In its final form the book should make a little over 200 pages, including appendices which will contain parallel speeches from Eden.
My view is that the '1931' book should be a much shorter work, within the compass of Baxter's brochure on the United States position,

[1] Lovat (Horatio Henry) Dickson (1902–87): writer & publisher; Lecturer in English, University of Alberta 1927–9; Assoc. Ed. *Fortnightly Review*; Ed. *Review of Reviews* 1930–4; Man. Dir. Lovat Dickinson Publishing Ltd 1932–8; Dir. Macmillan & Co Publishers 1941–64; Pan Books 1946–64; Reprint Soc. 1939–64.

and marketed at a low price, say 2/6d. I am gathering data for this, and also for the *Canterbury's Archbishop* ...

The broadcast, Press and Cranfield's telegrams will have kept you so abreast of general news that these letters will be stale when you receive them. As I write the most significant item to me is the outburst of Japanese animosity to Britain and the flat warning that unless we mind our own business with extreme circumspection we shall be 'for it'. You know how very much estimates differ of the extent of British awareness of the Eastern danger, but my own observation continues to confirm my view that the great majority of people are well aware of the impossible position into which we have been landed with Japan. Commander Naoki Saito's declaration that war between the two countries is a certainty and that the military development of Italy, Germany and Japan will prevent Britain's sending a strong fleet to the East has jolted the most complacent. I still think the British Government will display what, in a letter, I had better call 'blue circumspection.'
[...]

The city is beginning to discuss, rather glumly, the April Budget. The general impression is that, thanks to Neville's habit of under-estimating and a good first three quarters, Simon may show a surplus on the year 1937–38, and that he will try to keep the picture as rosy as possible for 1938–39, but will have to screw up the Defence Contribution. The real fear is the Budget 1939–40, when, most people now realise, the re-armament bills will have piled up and the Government will have realised that expenditure must be enormous. The minority view (which I share) is that even the coming Budget must increase the Defence Contribution, and will probably tighten the Sur-tax both as to low level and rate.

It grows more and more apparent that civilian defences will have to be taken off the shoulders of local Finance Committees. The inequalities of local budgets, particularly in the North, is such that the local effort will prove unworkable without some kind of aid-plus-compulsion. [...] It still seems to me, although I fear you may not agree, that civilian defences will have to be treated as Public works under a public works loan, probably on the lines of the loans given at low rates to applying municipalities for housing and local improvements. It is quite certain, as you said a week or two ago, that National co-ordination is the first essential.

Monday 21 February If I had any perspective at all in this journal I should have logged first Eden's resignation. That it came yesterday and not a few months hence has wasted all my work on the book – an arraignment so 'savage' that Lovat Dickson says he dare not publish it. That it comes at all is to me a new hope that we may yet escape war with the Totalitarian powers. [...] Before we left Norfolk yesterday, Lady Downe[2] came to lunch. She is standing as a Fascist candidate for that constituency. She says that Mosley gets good meetings everywhere, and is really [trying][3] to eliminate the Fascist savour from his movement, partly by calling it now the British Union, and omitting the 'of Fascists' from the title. She was very anxious that I should have more talk with him. She says that nobody about him has much brain and that he is often misled about the general public feeling. He is extremely anxious to get reports of his meetings into the Press – not support editorially but publicity. She, like so many of us, despairs of the official Conservative Party and quite fervently believes that even energetic and sincere young Tories are sapped by the terrible atmosphere of the Commons.

Thursday 24 February   My post today contained letters from Dr Marie Stopes[4] and Sir Oswald Mosley – as funny a combination as one could wish. My pocket diary reminds me that on Tuesday I lunched with Hobson and Lex at the Reform. Hobson was bitterly furious about Eden's resignation, and his anger, which I had fanned by malicious joking, was fanned further by Ernest Benn,[5] who came to us as we drank sherry in the hall and declared himself better for the events of the week-end. He, as I, was coldly contemptuous of the behaviour of the Commons, who had roared with ribald laughter when Chamberlain had said, very seriously, that Italy had in her mind as strong a case against us as we against her. Lex tried to pour oil on the troubled waters but it was oil on the flames. I try to exclude from this journal my political reactions, which find a place elsewhere, but I ought to record that Eden has had a good public and a good press, although the Labour vote of censure brought Neville back to general popularity with a run. The City is wholeheartedly relieved at Eden's departure. R. cables from the high seas suggesting that far from scrapping my indictment of Eden we change its title and line of approach ... and call it *Mr Eden – Warmonger*. [...] To-day, Thursday, we had a good Fore Club at the Reform. Sadd was host, and in addition to Rodwell[6] and Manning we had Sir John Squire,[7] Stephen King-Hall,[8] Cowley –

[2] Lady Dorothy Downe (d. 1957).

[3] 'trying' was typed out.

[4] Dr Marie Carmichael Stopes (1881–1958): birth-control pioneer.

[5] Ernest Benn (1875–1954): author & publisher; Chm., Benn Brothers 1922–41.

[6] R.V. Rodwell: Leicester-based chartered accountant (Wykes & Co) & company dir.

[7] John Squire (1884–1958): poet & journalist; founder & Ed. *London Mercury* 1924; Ed. *New Statesman*; kt. 1933.

[8] Stephen King-Hall (1893–1966): MP Ormskirk (Nat. Lab until 1942, then Ind.); Dir. of Publicity at Min. of Fuel & Power 1942–3; kt. 1954, cr. Baron King-Hall 1966.

the city man – and Goddard,[9] who was the attorney who flew to the
Windsors and caused scandal by taking his doctor with him, thus
causing the popular press to suspect a pregnancy in Wallis Simpson.
[...] Stephen King-Hall was very different from the man I anticipated.
I had expected a tall, supercilious high-brow Radical. He is small, with
a thin thatch and little sidewhiskers, very clear eyes and a quick incisive
manner of talk. He takes no strong waters. He told us of the inception
of his now famous *News Letter* and of some of the absurd adventures he
had had – as who has not – with newspaper owners. I promised, other
things being equal, to speak for him in his Ormskirk constituency,
where he has just been adopted as National-Labour.

Friday 25 February   I find that I work badly, having no settled job. So
to-day, having promised to inspect some pictures for R., I took Lil
down after lunch to the Redfern Gallery, but the pictures weren't
there. There were, however, some arresting moderns. Lil, not yet
comprehending that people can try to paint states of mind as well as
visions of the eye, was very amusing about them. A quick visit to the
office, to pick up a long and chummy letter from Mitch,[10] led us to see
the event of the Cinema today – Walt Disney's pantomime *Snow White*.
The film will be historic, for it creates a new genre, but historic or not
it is fascinating and charming, a triumph of technical art.

Monday 28 February   I say that I cannot work when I have no routine
job to spur me on to writing – that 'no man but a fool ever wrote
except for money' – and yet I peg along. I have written a new foreword
to the arraignment of Eden and have virtually finished the brochure
on the economic position, which will only make 60 pages. Whether my
coadjutor will approve either, I doubt. But if he doesn't, I'll have to
get John Green to place 'em somehow. [...] The Press has been
unusually 'juicy' for a morbid psychologist lately – the torso murder,
which is an obvious bye-product of homosexuality, the murder of a
pantry boy at Cambridge by another crazed homosexual-necrophilist
of twenty one, and the round-up on Friday or Saturday of six girls and
two men in a disorderly house in London. All were naked, except one
who was dressed as a maid, and the two men and four of the girls
were caught by the detectives all nude on a bed performing 'acts of
gross indecency'. What a world! My own reaction is 'why can't they

[9] Rayner Goddard (1877–1971): lawyer & judge; Ld. Chief Justice 1946–58.

[10] Mitchell 'Mitch' Frederick Hepburn (1896–1953): Canadian Lib. politician; PM
Ontario 1934–42.

leave 'em alone?' I feel as Alice Herbert said about the Savidge case some years ago – we ought to rail off a large part of the Park, label it 'Indecencies', charge a shilling admission and guarantee freedom from interference. I imagine that the worst thing that ever happened to the Western races was the muddling together of religion and morality. Christ was wiser, who saw that it is the mind and not the body which sins.

Tuesday 1 March   Went with Hassall[11] to lunch with a man named Cruikshank at the Conservative. Cruikshank is a retired financier who blames all our present discontents on the German standstill agreements and feels so bitterly about the matter that he is anxious to ventilate the matter by standing at a bye-election ... After two or three hours of financial politics, I crossed to a gallery in Jermyn Street to look at some of Seago's[12] pictures. By a stroke of luck Seago himself came in. He is a tall dark, pipe-smoking, frank and commonsensical person, with no pose and no shyness. I arranged to meet him again after his return from France and my return from Italy.

Thursday 3 March   Lunched alone with Mosley at his place on the embankment. One is received in a large, studio-like room, at one end of which is a dais containing a desk. On a side table stand books and two or three photographs, including a large autographed portrait of Hitler. A pair of foils stand idly against a wall. Mosley, whom I hadn't seen for some time, was, as usual, very frank. He says that Communism is gaining ground in the North and that the Tories are deceived by a new Communist tactic. When Hitler triumphed in Germany, Communism saw that it was folly to divide the Leftist forces and allow Fascism to slip between them. They now work for a Popular Front, contemplate a kind of Kerensky Government, which they will overthrow, and so do not force forward their own candidates. The old Tories thus say – no candidates, no communism. Fascism (which is now called severely The British Union) also gains in the North. He is spending about £23,000 a year on his organisation, a great reduction from a few years ago. The Left draws about £150,000 a year from Russia, as the result of the fruitfulness of Lena goldmines. He said that he considered that my old S.D. articles were the best exposition of Fascism that he had ever seen in the public print, and that I was far

---

[11] Either John Hassall (1868–1948): poster artist, Savage member; or Chris Vernon Hassall (1912–63): poet, biographer & playwright.
[12] Edward Brian Seago (1910–74): landscape artist.

more valuable to the Right outside the movement than in it. He is a little perturbed that nobody will report his meetings. He does not want support, but report. I stayed about two hours, and then left to buy some lira for my Italian trip. After I had arranged things, I had a wire from R. saying that I was not to go to Genoa but to Cap Ferrat.

Thursday 17 March   I left for France on the Friday and spent Saturday at Cap Ferrat and Nice, lounging about the hotel grounds or the old parts of the City. On Sunday at 8 I was at Ville Franche to meet R., whose vessel was very late, not arriving till noon. As the whole coast is full, the Grand Hotel at Cap Farret could not accommodate the whole party, so after motoring to Menton and lunching there, we eventually found ourselves at the Cap Martin Hotel. [...] The week went pleasantly. I redrafted both the Eden book and the Crisis book, and in the intervals walked and talked with R.. [...] The visit was strangely artificial, the sun and colouring and the people all about us making holiday – and Hitler marching into Vienna. R. was very struck by this happening as I had forecast it for March when he and I were in America last Autumn. [...] Incidentally, Lord Cadman[13] was at Cap Martin when we arrived. His slashing report on Civil Aviation had not then been published. He told R. that Swinton wanted to blanket it. It was published last week, and was a terrible expose of muddle and ineptitude. Cadman is a man of no great personality but very rugged and strong. Lord Kemsley was also at Monte Carlo, and is in a panic about the immediate future of newspapers, as he well may be. He told R. that little Beaverbrook, who does not take his money from Fleet Street, will force a pace that will ruin the other proprietors. Newsprint is up 30/- a ton and revenue is already down by 20% and likely to go lower – the outlook grim. R., having withdrawn his interest, and having his own fortune liquid, was cynically amused. He said to me, 'You don't seem to have any sympathy for the Berrybros.' As the Berry Brothers once made me an approach and then jibbed at the amount of money I thought I was worth, I have no particular sympathy for them – or for any other proprietor of newspapers. Before I left for France I had a talk with Esmond Harmsworth, who suggested that Ward Price and I might do the *Daily Mail* leaders. He didn't say a word about cutting my retainer from £3,000 to £1,500, nor did I, but said I was ready to do whatever was needed for as long as I was with the organisation.

[13] John Cadman (1877–1941): businessman & mining engineer; Prof. of Mining & Petroleum Technology, Birmingham University 1908–20; Chm. Anglo-Iranian Co. & Iraq Petroleum Co. 1918; Chm. Cttc. of Enquiry into Civil Aviation 1937–8; Chm. Television Advisory Cttc. 1939; cr. Baron Cadman 1937.

Saturday 19 March   I have just changed my wine merchant, for the excellent and eighteenth century reason that I suspect my butler of drinking too much of my wine and of being in too close concert with the supplier. 'My butler.' How absurd it sounds. He is a little ex-marine with a white scar across his nose, that I imagine came from a bottle fight in a pub in Chatham rather than from an enemy, a lank and depressed wife and an almost witless daughter. Apart from his tendency to indulge too deeply in his own or my liquor he is an excellent servant. [...] R. is still in the South of France, and telephones twice a day. The acute tension in foreign affairs and the oncoming economic collapse that he and I suspect takes much of the zest out of doing. I loll about and waste hours that I would have used advantageously a year or two ago. The *Sunday Dispatch* staff is in a ferment of discontent, because Esmond Harmsworth has appointed a new editor over the head of Lester Wilson,[14] abruptly and without warning as is his custom. One can condemn but not blame him, for he has never had that training in business which gives most men in executive position some sense of commercial honour in these matters. Dick Lewis speaks of the heads of the business as 'the "put not your trust" department,' which is fully justified. R., with all his virtues, is cowardly and untrustworthy in official relations, although his reputation is higher than was that of his brother Northcliffe. Too much wealth, I imagine, will spoil any man, and too much wealth and power in youth must be fatal to honour. 'The cruel things that stir in the childish hearts of kings ...' When Wilson was told of the new appointment he was offered the retention of the assistant editorship. He asked for a day to consider this, and made a quick test of Fleet Street and its possibilities. He found everywhere among the working staffs apprehension and no openings. The advice of people competent to advise was that at this time any job is worth clinging to ... which confirms my own deduction about the coming stress in newspaper life. For my own part, although I am a little restless out of a routine job, I am glad to be out of the professional limelight at this time. The prestige of journalism has fallen almost as low as the prestige of Parliament. There is little honesty of utterance and very little sound judgement on real affairs. It may be a passing phase. Belloc foretold it long ago. For the moment I am prepared to await the effects of my brochure and the book on Eden. I have no heart for fiction writing although I hope the heart will beat again someday. I shall have to find an outlet soon. This semi-lotus-eating life is not good for me. It will soon be four years since my first meeting with R., and during those years I have been sterile, except for *Sunday*

---

[14] Lester B. Wilson: journalist *Sunday Dispatch* 1933– , editor of northern edition 1933– 4, London staff 1934; acting editor during C.B.'s absences in 1935–6; deputy editor 1936– .

Dispatch articles, which I count less than the dust. Generous, humorous, deep thinking – he is still a psychological vampire, and someday there must come a break before I am all absorbed and ruined as poor Morison and the others have been. It is difficult to see how the break will come, for affection for him is a great tie. It may be that affairs will make the break for me. There is already talk of a downfall for Chamberlain and the return of Churchill. I do not give it much credence. It would mean war. If Winston did come into any sort of power I should be inclined to find executive service under him, not as a supporter of his policies but as a supporter of British readiness. Those of us who feel that Parliamentary life is a degrading sham may not have much longer to wait. If affairs do not force a change, then I must gird myself as I did in 1919 and find a new venue.

Thursday 24 March   Took Rodwell to a dinner of the Compatriots' Club in the House of Commons, where Roger Keyes opened a discussion on naval defence. His speech was mainly a rambling reminiscence of the early days of flying and of Murray Sueter's attempt to make the Admiralty air-minded. As a serious contribution to the study of defence it was utterly and entirely childish, and it was amazing that a man of his standing and reputation should have put it forward to such an audience. It was quite obvious that in the mind of Roger Keyes and the other Admirals there that the real questions of naval and air defence matter nothing compared with the burning question of whether or not the pride of the navy will be hurt it if it does not 'own' its own planes, just as the pride of infantry regiments was hurt when machine guns were made into an independent corps, although that independence was the secret of machine gun tactics and strategy. Keyes, with his chinless face and his doddering country-vicar-like mind is a fine example of what R. calls a service patriot.

Sunday 27 March   In the evening [in Monte Carlo] he [R.] and I went down to the Sporting Club, where he entertained Eileena Ackroyd and her two married sisters to dinner. He expressed reluctance to go into the gaming rooms as the Duke and Duchess of Windsor were at a gala at some hotel and would be sure to come over. But we did go in, and had hardly reached the middle table when I clutched R's arm and said, 'Here's the lady...' Leading a little knot of people through the bowing functionaries came a small, tight lipped, dark-haired woman, very regal in her carriage, followed by two nondescripts and then by a miniature of a man with blond hair, a very red face, and the general demeanour of a happy grocer's boy. It was the Duke of Windsor. To my eye he looked tanned and well and far more composed than when I last saw him. There was no fiddling with the tie, his hands were thrust in his trouser pockets. She was the focal point of the little party, not he. Her face has become palpably harder – she is the creature of hard lines altogether, the dark hair parted and smoothed down like the painted hair of a Dutch doll, the line of the mouth, hard, the eyes hard, the severe black dress cut in hard lines. He looked full of contentment, but she looked happy. R. and I escaped and were back in the villa by eleven thirty.

Monday 28 March   The Ackroyds – that is Eileena and her mother and one married sister came to lunch. Eileena said that she had sat near to the Duke of Windsor at the roulette table last night and thought he looked ill. What I took for sun tan she said was a heavy flush, which might be wine, and his face, she said, is puckered into baggy folds. It was an odd example of how two honest eye witnesses can differ.

Wednesday 6 April   I had returned for a dinner party at R's house. The dinner party was pleasant – it was partly to say bon voyage to him and partly to eat a sucking pig from Stody. The guests were Ward Price, Cranfield, Morison and me to meet Cecil Harmsworth, who is the most pleasant of all the Harmsworths. We talked nothing but foreign affairs, although Cecil and I had a few minutes together before dinner talking about his experiences as Under Secretary for Foreign Affairs and a few minutes walking down Avenue Road after dinner talking about Edward Grey and Haldane. He seemed to me to sum up perfectly the difference between Grey and Ll G when said, apropos of Grey's character but little range of mind, 'If I were on the scaffold at a few minutes before eight, or whatever time they hang men, and Edward Grey had promised me to be there at a minute to eight with a reprieve, I should be perfectly composed. But if Lloyd George had promised that, in spite of his much greater assurances and his undoubted sincerity, I should resign myself to death, knowing that he would arrive, if at all, about an hour and a half after my execution.'

Friday 8 April   The proofs of *Britain's Coming Bankruptcy* have been occupying me, and I find that that rogue Alexander Young is threatening to writ Hodge and me for libel[15] concealed in a short paragraph in a list of financial crashes in *The Royal Mail Case*. These things happen, and, thank God, I do not worry about them.

Good Friday–Saturday 15–16 April   The immediate occasion of R's cable was to ask me to take the word Bankruptcy from my new brochure's title ... he had talked with Owen Young, and thought that as I should be widely quoted in America *Britain's Coming Bankruptcy* was too strong a term. 'You have a following ...' he said, which made me think that either his Irish blarney was in strong evidence or that he deceives himself about the power of a booklet to stir anybody these days to any thought at all. Actually I am sunk in a kind of half-happy idleness of mind most unusual in me. It is true that I have finished the little book on finance and re-written both the bankruptcy brochure and the Eden book (which must be again re-written) but there is lacking the old gusto and zest. I may recover tone when August approaches and my income is halved without my being able to half [*sic*] my expenses. Even Alexander Young's writ for libel does not interest me, though it may ruin me. I am mentally comatose.

Wednesday 20 April   I lunched Hobson and Lex at the Reform. Hobman,[16] erstwhile editor of the *Westminster Gazette*, talked with me, and later Professor Robbins[17] ... the tendency of these damned Liberals in the Reform is to bewail any agreement with Mussolini and to wonder why we have not blown his tinpot Empry from the map ... they don't say how or with what ... Having successfully disarmed us they now breathe fire and slaughter. While we were lunching Sir John Simon roamed in, but spoke to no one. Hobson cured the automatic smile which he says Simon switches on for stage effect whenever he enters a room. Simon begins to look older, but he is wonderfully well preserved. He is tanned and walks with a virile step. There is a growing tendency,

[15] When Alexander Young, of Worthington, Lancashire, issued the writ against C.B. it was brought on the grounds that a statement in the *Royal Mail* book indicating his guilt in a fraud case libelled him for failing to point the reasons why his sentence of three years had been reduced to eighteen months. The case was heard by Justice Greaves-Lord and dismissed on the grounds that he could not assess damages for something which did not add to the alleged libel.

[16] Joseph Burton Hobman (1872–1953): Assoc. Ed. *Sheffield Independent* 1898–1912; Ed. *Birmingham Gazette* 1912–21; Ed. *Westminster Gazette*, 1921–8; Ed. Staff, Westminster Press 1928–42; unsuc. Lib. cand. Sheffield Hallam 1928, N. Bradford 1929, N.E. Bethnal Green 1935.

[17] Prof. Lionel Robbins (1898–1972): Prof. of Economics at LSE 1929–61; Member of the Economic Section, Cabinet Office 1941–5.

I find, for people to regret their earlier very harsh judgement on him as Foreign Secretary. [...] After telephoning to Norfolk at seven o'clock I decided to go to the Old Vic to see 'Coriolanus'.[18] [...] It was staged in a rather precious way, and Olivier[19] played Coriolanus rather like a bad tempered high Church curate, writhing and shouting and sobbing, full of surface pathos. To me he ruined the banishment speech by giving a kind of self-pitying value to the line, 'There's a world else-where −' as a man might proposing to seek consolation from nature for some hard fate, not as − I am sure − Coriolanus did, as a man on whom the intention had just dawned of 'letting in the jungle' upon the city which had ungratefully treated and shamed him. Sybil was excellent as Volumnia, looking very like Ellen Terry[20] in her middle years, but not using the famous Thorndike voice quite so conscientiously as usual. As a matter of fact, she acted everybody else off the stage whenever she was on it. The play to our time was most apt. But it is essentially a play from which one carries away whatever emotion one has brought to it. To me it stripped the glamour from democracy, but to Dorothy Sayers[21] it stripped the glamour from war. We agreed, she and I, the comfortable middle-aged pair in the taxicab, that as a play it is marvellously architected and we failed to understand why it is regarded as dull and un-Shakespearean [...] She accuses Laurence Olivier of importing into every part he plays a kind of forced jesting note, a palpable playing for comedy, and of developing that whine which she and I dislike in him. Except in 'Henry V', when he could have used the jesting not to his advantage, she said. I was constrained to say in his defence that it suited his Mercutio [in 'Romeo and Juliet']. In any event, I prefer his acting to that of Gielgud ... but with these as our leading tragedians we compare ill with the past.

Friday 22 April Henry Morgan[22] the accountant having asked me to call on him on a business matter of interest, I played with the idea of being offered a lucrative directorship. At noon George Thompson

[18] *Coriolanus*, produced by Lewis Casson with designs by Bruce Winston. Ran for 35 performances from 19 April to 21 May. Reviewed *The Times* 20 April 1938, p. 8. The reviewer gave a considerably more favourable report of Olivier's performance than Brooks.
[19] Laurence Kerr Olivier (1927–89): actor, dir. 1962–73; kt. 1947, cr. Baron Olivier 1970.
[20] Dame Ellen Alice Terry (1848–1928): actress.
[21] Dorothy Sayers (1893–1957): playwright, novelist & critic.
[22] Henry Morgan (1875–1944): accountant; snr. partner Henry Morgan & Co; Pres. Society of Incorporated Accountants 1929–32; Member, German Debts Ctte. 1935; Member, Enemy Trade Debts Ctte. 1940; Pres., Association British Chambers of Commerce 1942–4.

called to share my taxi to the city. He didn't want to borrow money this time, but to sell me shares in a company. This I was able to avoid, but it was an omen. What Morgan wanted was to interest me in a sulphide paper process ... However, we had a pleasant lunch; after we had eaten he told me of how he headed the revolt against Chamberlain's Defence Contribution tax last April. He said that he found Chamberlain very courteous but very stubborn, and he alleges that his face was saved by the efforts of the Chambers of Commerce who showed him a way out of the first foolish tax. He said, in his narration, one thing that stays in my mind. 'I told him that the Chancellor can ignore industries but cannot ignore industry.'

Wednesday 27 April I taxied over to the city to take tea with Sadd in the Midland Bank. Sadd is still very anxious that I should seize directorships, fearing that I shall be left penniless if R. dies or drops me for any reason. We talked of Germany and freedom and the like. Then to the city office, where Thompson told me that the city calls this 'The office boy's Budget.'[23] But for the most part the thing has been well received.

Monday 4 May I cried off a visit to Norfolk with Rothermere because I wished to get off this morning a score of letters and copies of the brochure on our trade position. After lunch I spent half an hour in Charing Cross Road looking at books and at four o'clock called on Douglas Hacking[24], Chairman of the Conservative Party, at his office in Palace Chambers. He has aged a lot since he was in Yorkshire as an area commandant during the general strike, twelve years ago. 'We've both changed a good deal since then,' he remarked, as we sat recalling the stirring days when he refused to admit the *British Gazette* into his area because we were producing a better *Yorkshire Post*. I went to see him because he had appealed to Esmond Harmsworth to suggest to R. that he should contribute to the Party Funds, which are not too healthy. I had an intimate talk with Hacking about the Party. He says that at recent by-elections Neville Chamberlain has been handicapped because he dare not press too violently his foreign policy.

[23] Sir John Simon's first budget given the previous day. For anaylsis of the budget see B.E.V. Sabine, *British Budgets in War and Peace, 1932–45* (London: Allen and Unwin, 1970).
[24] Douglas Hewitt Hacking (1884–1950): Con. MP Chorley 1918–45; PPS to Sir J. Craig 1920–1, to Sir L. Worthington-Evans 1921–2; Whip 1922–5; US Home Office 1925–7, 1933–34; Sec. Overseas Trade 1927–29; FS WO 1934–5; US Dominions 1935–36; Con. Party Chm. 1936–42; Vice-Chm., Nat. Union 1930–3; Chm., North West Area 1932–4; kt. 1938, cr. Baron Hacking 1945.

'Part of my work is advising the P.M. and I warned him,' said Douglas Hacking, 'that if we seemed even negatively to attack Eden the British instinct of not liking to see a man kicked when he is down would send votes against us. In Ispwich, for instance, Stokes[25] was a Liberal standing as a Labour candidate. He wasn't a Socialist and did not preach Socialism. He got behind him the Liberal vote, and it was almost exactly the amount of the turn-over. When we are able to be more emphatic we can expect to do better. Again it is difficult to attack Bob Cecil's crowd,[26] for if you attack the League of Nations Union people think you are attacking the League of Nations.'

That, I suggested, was a nice comment on democracy! He disapproved, very naturally, of Winston's caperings. Hacking himself is a tall, handsome man with a most friendly and pleasant address, but an obvious Parliamentarian, rather than a great executive. His various Under Secretaryships might have led him higher than the control of the machine: his personality certainly ought to have done so.

Thursday 12 May I am jotting this hurriedly, for I am leaving at two o'clock for Stresa, and Venice and the Asiago. We should have gone on Sunday to Geneva, but R. postponed the trip until Tuesday, and then till Wednesday and now until to-day, when I think we shall be really 'off'. [. . .] Last night I took Lil to see Gielgud's 'Shylock'.[27] I have always been critical of John Gielgud, but at last night he converted me to a warm admirer. His jewish intonation was perfect without exaggeration. He combined a racial dignity with just that admixture of fawning which one supposes any Venetian Jew of that time must have had. He returned to the pre-Kean tradition of the red wig – a sparse grey-sprinkled head of hair – but with nothing of the comic in him. He left, too, the Irving tradition at the end of the Court scene. Veiling his face from the mocking Gratiano, this Shylock almost totters to the door and then breaks into a tumbling, panic run – his feet echoing down a corridor. The pathetic speeches – particularly 'I had it from Leah when I was a bachelor . . . I would not have lost it for a wilderness

[25] Richard Rapier Stokes (1897–1957): Lab. MP Ipswich 1938–57; Min. of Works 1950–1; Ld. Privy Seal 1951; Min. of Materials 1951.

[26] Reference to League of Nations Union led by (Edward Algernon) Robert Gascoyne-Cecil (1864–1958): Con. MP Marylebone E. 1906–10, Hitchin 1911–23; US FO 1915–18 & Min. of Blockade 1916–18; Ld. Privy Seal 1923–4; Chanc. Duchy of Lancaster (with responsibility for League of Nations affairs) 1924–7; Pres., League of Nations Union 1923–45; styled Lord Robert Cecil 1868–1923, cr. Viscount Cecil of Chelwood 1923; awarded Nobel Peace Prize 1937.

[27] *The Merchant of Venice* by William Shakespeare. Performed at the Queen's Theatre from 21 April 1938 to 11 June 1938. Ran for 60 performances. Reviewed *The Times* 22 April 1938.

of monkeys' and the 'I am not well' speech in the Court were perfectly given. The alternations of emotion in the scene with Tubal were achieved without strain and with infinite pathos and anger. My feeling is that it is in the Kean parts that Gielgud is best. Hamlet, Romeo – he is too elocutionary. But Shylock – excellent. His Richard III would be worth seeing. As Portia Peggy Ashcroft did not satisfy either the eye or the mind. 'She plays the part as if it were a masque,' said Lil sapiently. Yet in the Court scene and its little aftermath she was good. The real fault was that her rather pinched, refined personality and technique do not befit the bantering lines of Portia. One felt that she would not have been capable of devising her masquerade, and still less of the ring trick with its jolly bawdy. Leon Quartermaine[28] as Antonio was good. Young Richard Ainley[29] (with much of his father's voice) pleasing to the eye, but uneven in his acting. Glen Byam Shaw as Gratiano was miscast. Gratiano is, surely, a swashbuckling, loud-voice Mercutio-like fellow. Byam Shaw remembered this in his first few lines, but soon forgot it. The setting was now the usual compromise between an apron and a proscenium stage. It was well devised but it gave no savour of Venice. A happy thought was the playing of the Jessica scenes all through and about the dormer window.

R. on Tuesday sent Rosemary another fifty pounds pocket and dress money. I said he must not spoil the girl, so he marked the envelope 'Not for the old folks at home but for yourself,' and sent it by cheque.

My economic pamphlet is out today.[30] Jay[31] in the *Herald* devotes all his city page lead to it, takes it seriously and only disagrees with my remedies. Boothby in the *Mail*[32] attacks it like a politician. He ignores the diagnosis, and slashes at the remedies, saying – like a fool – that we only need a revival in world trade and a revival in America and all will be well with us. The thesis of the book is that even if these come our export industries are falling back – and with this he does not argue, but merely iterates the opposite view without evidence. But, as R. remarked, his attack is a damned good advertisement for the book. I fancy that the bulk of the Press will ignore it, since few dare to support prophesies of doom and fewer still to deny such prophesies when they more than half believe 'em. The best tribute so far is from the Editor

[28] Leon Quartermaine (1876–1967): actor.
[29] Henry Richard Ainley (1879–1945): actor.
[30] *Can 1931 Come Again? An Examination of Britain's Present Financial Position* (London: Eyre & Spottiswoode, 1938).
[31] Douglas Patrick Jay (1907–): journalist at *The Times* 1929–31, *Economist* 1933–7, City Ed. *Herald* 1937–41; Ass. Sec. Min. of Supply 1941–3; Prin. A.S. BofT. 1943–5; Personal Ass. to P.M., 1945–6; Lab. MP Battersea N. 1946–85; Econ. Sec. Treasury 1947–50; FS Treasury 1950–1; Pres. BofT. 1964–7.
[32] *Daily Mail*, 'Can 1931 Come Again?' 12 May 1938.

of *Truth*[33] who says 'Apparently no other publicist possesses the vision or the courage – or the prestige – to perform it' (ie the task of performing a vital service to Britain).

Wednesday 1 June on the Tuesday [17 May in Italy] R. and I set off early one morning, walked to the garages, entered the car and drove for breakfast to Vicenza, and thereafter went to Thiene and up the mountains to Cesuna and Asiago. It was a strange adventure. I had never seen Cesuna by day before, although by night, when the ammunition and ration parties came up I had often seen it. I wandered a while about my old gun positions. But I saw Asiago from the enemy's side looking over towards our old sacrifice emplacements, where I had so many weeks of danger and discomfort and enjoyment, where once I had the Duke of Windsor yards in front of the wire. They have built a glorious castle of a tomb on the plateau to hold and commemorate their dead. I think R. was obsessed by the memory of his two boys, and I by certain others ... [...] And this morning at eleven I attended a Right-wing meeting at Lord Bute's[34] house, with Archibald Ramsay[35] in the chair, and found it futile, so futile that at the end I was moved to speech and rebuke, saying 'This, at least, is certain – that the answer to Communism is not anti-communism, but something positive and aggressive,' and found an unexpected ally in little Mrs Tate,[36] the woman M.P. My brochure *Can 1931 Come Again* is not selling well, but is being much discussed and has brought some interesting letters. I was amused by one commentator who said that my spiritual home was Berchtesgaden.

Thursday 13 June One of the reasons for my return from Scotland[37] was that I could get to work on a new book to be called *Whither Britain?* – this to replace the savage exposure of Eden which was rendered abortive by Eden's resignation. I have managed to do about 11 folios, making a chapter but I have not been in a mood for work. Part of the time has gone in talking to Lilian and my children, and in traipsing Lil about with me while I enquired about itineraries for journeys that R. and I propose to take – the Scandinavias, India, Africa, the Congo, Egypt.

---

[33] Henry Newnham: Ed. *Truth* 1936–40; joined Allied Newspapers Ltd 1940.

[34] John Crichton-Stuart, 4th Marquess of Bute (1881–1947).

[35] Capt. Archibald Henry Maule Ramsay (1894–1955): Con. MP Middlothian & Peebles 1931–45. Involved in various far-right organisations including Nordic League (Convenor) & Right Club (leader). Interned under Regulation 18B from May 1940 to Sept 1944.

[36] Mavis Tate (1893–1947): Con. MP Willesden W. 1931–5, Frome, 1935–45.

[37] Had been staying at Dornoch with Rothermere.

Friday 24 June   Since I have dropped for some months the Rother-Brooks diary of foreign affairs I ought, I suppose, if ever I wish to recapture the tone of this time, to pay some attention to events. But so much of my day is spent discussing international politics that it becomes a weariness to the flesh to set down in typewriting all the alarms that beset us. My own life is coloured by the conviction that Hitler means to polish off Czechoslovakia this year and after to force a way to the Black Sea. The only question is whether or not Britain will be involved during this process. On Wednesday [22nd] I was at a meeting of the Grosvenor Kin. Guy du Boulay said that he learns that Germany discovered during the entry into Austria that her machine did not work as perfectly as had been expected and that this has given her pause. He agrees that Germany must rely on a short war with a sharp decision, but that land forces must play a part. Germany's five year old army, he says, really does lack well trained men in the higher command compared with the fifteen year old army of France.

Thursday 30 June   No walk again this morning. I did a bit of work in the morning and then went to the Great Eastern Hotel for lunch with W.T.C. King.[38] He told me about the changes on the *Economist* and the *Financial News*. Most of it I knew, but I did not know that Walter Layton and Parkinson have been scrapping for about three months on high policy. Apparently Layton's damned Left-wing *News-Chronicle* policy is now to be toned down severely. Maurice Green, it seems, at first refused the city editorship of *The Times*, but took it eventually on condition that he controlled all the trade and economic matter in the paper subject to political direction. He is obviously even now only beginning his career. Bracken remains very awkward and difficult and untrustworthy, but is a little more mellow than in my time. We saw Williams of the *Mail* and B. Joseph. They were both pessimistical about the economic situation, although both chaffed me about *Can 1931 Come Again*.

Friday 1 July   Again no walk, but R. asked me round for breakfast at 8–45. We took it in the garden, he and the Wilsons and I. [...] Morison went and [Arthur] Fuller came, and we walked about the garden. Fuller went, and we walked about the garden. ... Talking of Austrian debts, German loans, the Duncan Sandys incident, the economic situation ... The on dit about Duncan Sandys is that the incident has

[38] Wilfred Thomas Cousins King: financial journalist; *Financial News* from 1935; ed. *Banker* from 1946; author *History of the London Discount Market* (1936), *The Stock Exchange* (1947).

been welcomed in the Party because it means they may get rid of the Jew. (If Hore-Belisha knew this he would be flattered by the echo of Disraelian toryism.) There is no doubt that Belisha has lost face. He virtually lied to Sandys saying that he (Sandys) had been misinformed and then when confronted by the facts took the foolish step of going to the Prime Minister, who, like a rattled man, turned the Attorney General[39] unnecessarily on to the affair. The right way would have been for H-B to have had a quiet talk with Sandys at the start. As it is, the wrath of Parliament has been roused against those who have tried to bully a Member by threats of the Official Secrets Act, and a first class incident, damaging to us abroad, has been wantonly created. How the Germans must laugh at our complete inability to re-arm under such a system!

Monday 8 August – Norfolk When I opened my letters on Wednesday I found a letter from Stanley Bell, managing director of Associated Newspapers, saying that the new arrangement whereby after August they pay me a retainer of £1,500 could not be implemented. I was so angry both by this attempt to break an agreement and by the tone of his letter that I went down to R's flat and told him that I would have to return his retainer of £1,000 and not go to Spitzbergen. He naturally asked why, and I said that I must stay at home and fight the company, showing him the letter. He asked me to leave the matter in his hands, calling Bell a damned fool, and later in the day, having seen Bell rang me up, to tell me the letter had been torn up. That night Bell rang me up, to say there had been nothing unfriendly in his letter and that they had meant to offer me compensation. I let go over the telephone, being very angry. He said that no agreement could go on for ever. 'Go on for ever – the damn thing hasn't yet started,' said I, wrathfully. The truth, of course, is, as George Sutton used to warn me, that Bell wants no rivals near him and is a treacherous little devil. This time he struck the wrong man.

Wednesday 10 August R. asked me to take a letter to Ribbentrop to the German embassy for inclusion in the Diplomatic bag.

---

[39] Donald Bradley Somervell (1889–1960): Con. MP Crewe 1931–45; Solicitor-Gen. 1933–6; Attorney-Gen. 1936–45; Home Sec. 1945; Ld. Justice of Appeal 1946–54; Ld. of Appeal in Ordinary 1954–60; kt. 1933; cr. Baron Somervell 1954.

Thursday 11 August   Noon – a fine, sunny London day. I have just finished *Whither Britain* running it to about 250 pages all told, a fierce diatribe, but not quite as fierce as the original Eden version. I fancy Douglas Jerrold[40] will shy from it, and R. will not altogether like it. In writing the Eden book I kept in constant consultation with R.; this one I have written without any consultation at all. If it goes safely to Press, it will either damn me or make me, for there is no concessions and no compromises in it — a straightforward Jeremiad and damning of Parliament. I have at least a record of consistency, for I was damning Parliament long before R. and I joined forces. [...] to the Comedy to see 'Give Me Yesterday'.[41] Kenneth Kent as an old music professor was excellent, but one somehow felt that he was too much the great character actor consciously character acting. Mary Glynne[42] as the seduced daughter, very lovely and good, with an unexpected touch of Sybil Thorndyke in her voice and technique. Louise Hampton[43] as the maiden aunt, excellent indeed. Here is a genuine actress, restrained, convincing and wholly admirable. Every little touch of 'business' well done, every smile and every frown and one sudden outburst of temper perfectly conceived. Eric Portman[44] as Richard Dahl the selfish young musical genius was also good, acting with a sureness of touch that made one feel that both as the young student and the middle aged disillusioned man he did not over draw a character that might so easily have been spoiled. It seems a long time ago since, as a member of the Baynton Shakespearean Company, he used to come into the Board Room of the *Yorkshire Post* and tell us tales of Baynton's eccentricities. The supporting cast was good, with a youngster, Peter Osborn,[45] playing the son very naturally and freshly, and a still younger youngster with two appearances as a school girl pupil supremely excellent both in manner and make-up. Her name is Bunny Le Marchand.[46] More should be heard of her. But the play – indifferent, turning on psychological behaviour which was not initially convincing and employing too many palpable aids both to atmosphere and character building. It was a second night, and for a hot August night the house was very well filled, with, no doubt, a lot of 'paper' – although the notices were all flattering this morning, and the response may have been genuine.

[40] Douglas Francis Jerrold (1893–1964): author & publisher; civil servant 1918–23; Benn Brothers Publishing 1923–8; Dir. 1929–45; Chm. Eyre & Spottiswoode 1945–59; Ed. *English Review* 1930–6, *New English Review* 1945–50.
[41] *Give Me Yesterday* by E. Percy & R. Denham. Ran from 10 August to 13 August 1938 at Comedy. Total of 5 performances. Reviewed by *The Times* 11 August 1938.
[42] Mary Glynne (1898–1954): actress.
[43] Louis Hampton (1881–1954): actress.
[44] Eric Portman (1903–69): actor.
[45] Peter Osborn: actor; played character of Dick Franz.
[46] Bunny Le Marchand: actress; played character of Betty Robinson.

Friday 12 August   Incidentally, I should have recorded a bit more of my talk with Douglas Jerrold yesterday. When he was asking me about my relations with R., I said, casually, that my chief endeavour was to prevent myself being thrust into bye-elections, and explained, on question, that I believe anybody tarred with the old Parliamentary brush will have no hearing when the crash comes. He took the notion of a crash quite as a matter for granted, and said moodily, 'The best thing will be to be right out of it.' He assented to my thesis that the financial pressure of re-armament may be the end of the system. He agreed that sterling must fall, and *may* fall catastrophically. At the Piccadilly Grill one or two waiters told me that business had never been so bad. One of the attendants, a youth, said that his father had managed a West-end Hotel for thirty five years and had never known it so bad a season, not even in 1931 and 1932. There is now a definite widespread anxiety, quite apart from the war fear. I found most people with whom I talked regretted that the Soviet and Japan have made a truce over the frontier incident; they hoped Russia would bomb Tokio off the map.

Friday 26 August   I sallied forth to visit Douglas Jerrold, to discuss the book, part of the proofs of which I had read on the 'plane from Oslo. The final decision on title is *Can Chamberlain Save Britain?*.[47] It is a better selling title than *Whither Britain* – and may be a good lasting title. After all, if one had Cobbett on *Can Pitt Save Britain?* it would be strangely readable – Not, of course, that I am Cobbett – My arrangement with R. was that I would fly back to join him at Stockholm, but this morning he telephoned to say he wouldn't be there until Tuesday, so I am going back to Norfolk for a couple of days.

Friday 9 September – London   Before I left yesterday to catch a plane R. took me for a stroll and insisted on presenting me with a lovely bowl of Jensen[48] silver. [...] As we walked back from the purchase we talked of Czechoslovakia.

'Hitler must move,' said R.

'He must move,' I agreed, 'because he is the victim of his own momentum.'

'I don't call him the victim – I call him the beneficiary of his own momentum,' said he and smote me between the shoulders.

[47] *Can Chamberlain Save Britain? The Lessons of Munich* (London: Eyre & Spottiswoode, 1938).

[48] Georg Jensen (1866–1935): silversmith and artisan.

Tuesday 13 September   back to the Mount to change into dark clothes and then to dinner with Lil and the two girls at the Lodge with the 'real' Wilsons – very confusing this duplication of names – where Major Spencer and his wife were fellow guests. Spencer has been for some time acting as an observer on an Arctic expedition, and was interesting, although we tended over our port to talk more of the *Daily Mail* and the *Daily Mirror* than of Arctic circles. Actually, of course, the meal degenerated into a wrangle about Hitler. All the world was holding its breath for the Nuremberg speech – old Mrs Wilson is temperamentally anti-Rothermere and anti-Brooks, and there we were, trying to be polite and sedate across a terrible gulf of feeling. The swing of opinion seems to me to be more and more anti-Czech, even if it is not more and more pro-German.

Saturday 17 September   Well, I dunno! Tomorrow I am crossing to Antwerp to rejoin R. I gather he doesn't like the new book much from its page proofs, declares it wants a lot of pulling together, from which I deduce that the reasoned argument bores him. He wants blunt affirmations of dogma. In any event Chamberlain's dramatic stroke in flying to see Hitler has rendered much of the book useless – he has done in advance that for which the book pleads. This political diatribe is destined never to see the light – one version finished and Eden resigns, another version is done and Austria is seized, yet another version done and Neville takes the bit between his teeth ... There is no question that the flight to Germany has not only eased the war fear but has placed Chamberlain himself on a high pinnacle. The apparent friendliness of his reception by Hitler and the welcoming demonstrations by the German crowds have also robbed Hitler's image in the English mind of much of its ogreishness. A few minutes ago Sadd of the Midland Bank rang me up. He has an idea that R. might go later to see Hitler to try to adjust the vexed question of the Standstills and the needed credits. (I say that R. might go, but Sadd, being on the telephone, was very mysterious, and might as easily have meant me!) Oddly enough, when the phone bell rang I had just stamped a letter to Sadd, for I feel more and more that I must avail myself of his suggestions of directorships. My present standing with R. is very precarious. Not that we shall quarrel, but he may tire, and he is not immortal. After my row with Bell, my standing with the newspaper companies is ended. But these things are as the Gods direct. I do not worry.

Monday 26 September   On the Sunday morning [25 Sept.] at 7 a.m. R. and I drove out to the Bois intending to walk for an hour or two, but we walked only for about quarter of an hour. I urged on R. that even though it might seem that Britain and France were too conscious of their lack of own preparation to enter into a war for Czecho-Slovakia, the Czechs would resist, and once war began, none could say where it would end. Also, I reminded him that during the night the Belgian army had returned to quarters, that France was virtually mobilising, that his place and certainly mine was in England. He decided to leave Belgium that day. (He is a funny fellow .... the day before he thought the anti-Hitler States had caved in and decided that he must go to Buda-Pest for the celebrations. He said that Ward Price and I must go with him, and I drafted a message in his name to the Hungarian Press which was duly sent.) Oddly enough, Ward Price appeared at our hotel, hot-foot from Bad Godesberg [...] W.P. said that Hitler had been impressed by Chamberlain but was certain that Germany was over-whelmingly strong in arms and men and would insist upon his own terms. He – Ward Price – had had tea with Hitler in his new home in the mountain. This home is, he says, the most wonderful thing since the hanging gardens of Babylon, but Hitler calls it the tea-house. Von Ribbentrop had told Ward Price that morning, as Chamberlain left the air port, that there would be no war for a week, that Chamberlain had taken back the German ultimatum to Prague which was based on an interesting incident. When the talks were interrupted it was because Chamberlain had demanded assurance that there would be no troop movements during the talks. 'I cannot tie my hands against a possible movement by the Czechs,' said Hitler. Chamberlain had – after the manner of Disraeli at Berlin – ordered his plane and was ready to go home. When he went to say good-bye Hitler agreed that there should be no troop movements provided Chamberlain himself transmitted the German demands to the new Czech premier. This, for the sake of peace, Chamberlain agreed to do. Ward Price said that the new Czech military cabinet did not necessarily mean resistance; it might mean a cabinet whose orders the soldiery would obey if the decision was to retreat from the Sudeten lands. But he agreed with me that the Czechs would almost certainly reject the terms, would fight – and that once the fight began Britain and France would be drawn in, whatever their wish and however relatively unprepared they might be. R. who for years has been prophesying war was busy saying now that Britain would not 'be in it,' but neither Wardy nor I would assent. So the argument was veering as we sped through Malines where the Cathedral held us for a little while, as we crossed the Belgium-Dutch frontier, as we saw both Belgium and Dutch soldiers mining their roads, as we met Morison, who had gone to the Hook by train, and as we sat to dinner on the steamer; and so the argument went, still, as we entered the Rolls at Harwich at six on Sunday morning and sped through sleeping England back to London.

It may be interesting years hence, if there are any years hence for any typed paper in London, to read an assessment of the British mood in this fateful week. Ignorant as most people are of the truth about our lack of arms and the weak state of France, the masses are now determined that the aggressive temper of the Dictators must be checked. They are grateful to Chamberlain for his remarkable efforts to keep the peace. They still feel that for a man of sixty nine to make his first flight on such a peace mission as that to Berchtesgaden was a glorious testimony of his sincerity and love of country. Of the second journey, that to Godesberg, the emotion is more mixed. There is chagrin that a British Premier should thus have waited upon the German leader only to be met with what is tantamount to rebuff. They feel that Britain, France and Russia can overwhelm Germany, because Germany is short of supplies. Many count on a German revolt. (This is the result of ignorance and the lies of the Press and of politicians. There is no evidence that Germany lacks supplies and there is no sign of anything but German unity. Hitler seems to be worshipped like a God, as well he may be by Germans grateful for his great feat in bringing his nation back to dominance in five years of effort and only twenty years after defeat in war.) But even those who realise that Germany is well equipped and will be the most formidable enemy the world has known feel that the time has come to risk everything in the rightful effort to stem a tide of tyranny and arrogance. There is a tremendous sobriety throughout the land, even a subdued fear of what an air war may mean, but there is no lack of resolution. If war must be faced to protect the world from German domination, war will be faced with determination and courage. That is the mood.

To-day Horace Wilson[49] has again flown to Germany with yet another appeal. At seven fifteen this morning R. and I drafted a wire from him to Ribbentrop, asking Ribbentrop to use his influence to have the decisive act of October 1st postponed so that present passions may be allayed and details reconciled. Later in the morning R. told me on the telephone that, with the assent of the Foreign Office, he had sent a telegram to Hitler, speaking as his friend and as a friend to Germany and as one who lost two of his three boys in the last war, asking Hitler to incorporate in to-night's speech some word of assurance to the many millions who feared war. These messages may do no good;

---

[49] Horace John Wilson (1882–1972): Ass. Sec., Min. of Lab. 1919–21, Perm. Sec. 1921–30; Chief Industrial Adviser 1930–9; Perm. Sec., Treasury & Head of Civil Service 1939–42; kt. 1924. Confidant & friend of Neville Chamberlain.

they cannot do harm. It may be that such appeals may give Hitler the occasion he wants to soften his tone. It may be that he does not wish to soften his tone. None can know except Hitler himself. Ward Price says he is full of assurance and a gay confidence, so that war may indeed be inevitable. Roosevelt's cables today to the world, pleading for no use of force, are full of apprehension about the effects of any new war. It may be that the uneasy truce between 1918 and 1938 will end in a new outburst of hostilities which will shatter our civilisation for ever. It may be that we enter a period of German domination. It may be that Germany, miscalculating her own strength, plunges again to defeat. But she is relatively far stronger than she was in 1914 – and better led. It is a bad business. There is one great hope. It is that if Britain emerges, she may at long last adopt a sane standard of life and be herself properly led. The reign of the road house and the cocktail bar and the cheap American cinema and the cheaper slang may be ended. We may return to real values, and the Faith that was once in us.

[...] At breakfast this morning I had the company of Stanley Bell. When he entered he offered me his hand and I, being under R's roof, had perforce to take it. We talked as if we had had no row. Over breakfast Bell gave a characteristic display of treachery. In the office he has been the closest friend of Cranfield, editor of the *Mail*. Cranfield last week was shot out of his job, not for incompetence but because 'they' wanted a change. R. this morning said to Bell, 'I think the change was necessary,' to which Bell, instead of saying a few good words for his friend, cordially agreed. The man is a rat.

Whether and when I shall make another entry in a diary I do not know. Diary and diarist alike may be up in flames before long. And yet my own mood is one of rather pleased anticipation. It is as if the soft, sordid years have gone, and the hard refreshing years are coming back. I do not recall exactly where we were twenty years ago, but we must have been either still on the Asiago plateau or moving down to Piave. Then, I suppose, we were aching for peace to come. Now, with war far more terrible than it was then, it is peace that seems somehow ignoble and unsatisfying. I write this soberly and without pose, recording the mood without excusing it. I suppose many ex-service men must feel it. It may be that Hitler and Hermann Goering feel it. Lil maintains that magnificent composure that she had as a young woman when the last war smote us. She is as calm as a fatalist, putting her trust, I don't doubt, in her God. The outer demeanour of my four children is one of acute interest, some excitement, and no fear. With them it may be lack of imagination.

Friday 30 September   With the quickening of the war danger I packed
the many pages of this journal with other papers in two newly acquired
strong boxes to be taken to the relatively security of Norfolk. Until
Wednesday the pace of alarm grew. Men feverishly dug trenches in the
parks; everybody queued up for gas masks. After we were all fitted, in
that amateurish way that characterises Britain, Lil turned helper and
spent her days helping to fit others. School children began to be
evacuated. Then came, as history will lavishly record, Neville Chamberlain's speech to the re-called House of Commons, culminating in
his announcement that he was to meet Hitler, Mussolini and Daladier[50]
at Munich on Thursday. Immediately everybody became convinced
that it was peace. On the evening of that day I was host at a dinner
of the Fore Club. We met at the Reform. Sadd of the Midland Bank
could not come, but Rodwell who had sent an apology arrived. He
was to have been a guest at some Masonic Installation, but the Master
elect had been called to his unit ... Our guests were Vivian Phillips,[51]
who was once Chief Liberal Whip and Parliamentary Private Secretary
to Asquith, Francis Hirst,[52] ex-editor of the *Economist*, and a man whose
name I forgot who is Deputy Chairman of the Prisoners' Aid Society
among his other offices. There came also that pleasant Scot, John
Senter.[53] By some sort of tacit consent we talked little of the situation.
Vivian Phillips was very interesting about Asquithian politics, which
seemed as remote as the eighteenth century. Asquith, he says, had a
disconcerting habit of tossing to his secretaries documents of importance
and soliciting their opinion, listening to it, and then saying, 'Well I'll
leave it to you ...' One document on the American debt settlement he
so passed to Vivian Phillips with the request that he would draft a
suitable memorandum. This Phillips did, trying to parody the old man's
style. Asquith came back, hovered over the draft with a blue pencil,
made no alteration, and eventually said, 'Excellent. I think we can let
that go.' The next day Spender in the *Westminster Gazette* began an
article by saying 'There is probably no living man other than Mr
Asquith who could have found such right and succinct words for the
embodiment of a view so eminently characteristic of the Liberal leader
....' Thus do even the high-brow journalists make idiots of themselves.
Phillips is very bitter about Ramsay Muir,[54] who in his opinion is *non*

[50] Edouard Daladier (1884–1970): French radical PM 1933, 1934, 1936, 1938–40;
Defence Min. 1938–40; Min. For. Affairs, 1939–40.

[51] (Henry) Vivian Phillips (1870–1955): Lib MP Edinburgh W. 1922–4; PPS to Asquith.

[52] Francis Hirst (1873–1953); Ed. of *Economist* 1907–14; author *The Golden Days* (1948).

[53] John Senter (1905–66): called to Bar, Middle Temple 1928; 1928–35 served with
engineering company, Leicester; in chambers, Valentine Holmes 1935–40; RNVR 1940–
5; Dep. Chm. Northern Assurance Co. 1951–3; member of Fore Club.

[54] (James) Ramsay Bryce Muir (1872–1941): Lib. MP Rochdale 1923–4; Chm. of Nat.
Lib. Fed. 1931–3, Pres. 1933–6; academic & writer.

compos mentis. He said that within a very few weeks of Muir being in the Commons he came to the Chief Whip and wished to resign his seat.

'But why?' said Phillips, 'You've only just taken it.'

Muir, portentously frowning said, 'It is quite clear that this Parliament does not wish to hear my message.'

'Have you a message, and from whom? And how do you know they don't want to hear it. You haven't made your maiden speech yet!'

At this Muir uttered a tirade, complaining that Phillips had wilfully kept him off the Speaker's list. Phillips, very naturally, said 'But you haven't asked me to put you on it. And what is this famous message?'

Muir replied that the Manchester Liberals, of whom he and J.D. Simon, were the leaders, did not see things as Asquith saw them, and had a new evangel. Phillips saw the Speaker and in due time Muir spoke, but no message emerged. At the time of the General Strike Muir again wrote to Phillips cursing Asquith. The same day Asquith said to Philips, 'By the way, there is a letter here which will amuse you,' and tossed over a letter from Muir cursing Phillips. Vivian Phillips wrote to Muir saying he had both letters, to which Muir replied that he was glad to hear it as he now felt that his moral duty had been thoroughly performed. This insight into the mentality of the intellectual Liberals was amusing rather than surprising. [...]

Last night, after a lazy day, I went to the Painters' Hall and was admitted to the Freedom and Livery of the Worshipful Company of Glass Sellers. It was a very simple process. Because of the political situation there was a very attenuated Court. I was introduced to the Master and Wardens by Past-Master Howard and was told by the Clerk that I had been elected and would be required to make two declarations, one as a Liveryman and one as a Freeman. These I read from a kind of roll book. They had a fine ancient savour, pledging me not to conceal any plots, conspiracies or attempts on the majesty of our sovereign lord the King ... and the like obligations. Then I shook hands with the members of the Court and went back to the ante-room. The romantic savour of the business was given by the civic robes of the master and his wardens. There was only a small attendance at the dinner, but it was enjoyable and in the middle of it came an unofficial announcement that the Four at Munich had reached agreement. The whole assembly spontaneously sprang up, crying the name of Chamberlain and toasting him, and singing 'For He's a Jolly Good Fellow.' I wondered how often the same Hall had seen similar scenes, with cries of 'Bolinbroke' or of 'Pitt' or of 'Disraeli.' It was quite moving, even to the blase ones.

Saturday Evening 1 October   About this time last night London was giving to Neville Chamberlain the most frenzied welcome ever given to a statesman – and rightly. Although another Chamberlain once brought back from Locarno a perpetual peace that lasted for only a year or two, Neville has brought back the chance of an Anglo-German accord that may be the beginning of a very long peace. The British have been very frightened, and the relief is unutterable. Watson in a letter discussing affairs says 'personally I am for eating the dirt, as those who refuse to eat the dirt so often bite the dust.' In a long screed to him I went so far as to give him this pragmatic sanction:

> Fire-eating Fuehrer brave in coloured shirt
> Compels white-fronted nations to eat dirt.
> Watson remarks 'Philosophers, I trust
> Would rather eat the dirt than bite the dust,'
> And I agree, more coarsely, for by God
> I'd rather eat the dirt than fight the sod.

It is, of course, a bloodless victory for Hitler and makes him the acknowledged master of Europe. It is absurd to bewail the triumph of force. He relied on force and it did not fail him. We must accept it, with whatever good grace comes from the realisation that for three centuries we relied on force and it did not fail us.

Tuesday 4 October   R. is still at Dornoch, but should be back to London on Monday, after which he and Ward Price and I are to go to Hungary. This afternoon I went down to the Freemasons' Hall for a meeting of the Savage Club Lodge, dining in Lodge afterwards at the Club. A.G. Street[55] was there, last met as my guest under Mitch Hepburn's roof near St. Thomas in Ontario. He and I talked about Canadian politics and English farming, about which he is decidedly gloomy. At dinner I found myself in a nest of musicians – Aylmer Buesst,[56] Julian Clifford,[57] Parry Jones[58] amongst others. Parry Jones was in a bitter mood about what he called the betrayal of Czechoslovakia. After he had foamed at the mouth for some time at our failure to stand up to the Dictators.

I said, gently, 'the trouble with you, you hot blooded Welshman, is that you are sore because you can't fight Hitler,' to which he replied

[55] Arthur George Street (1892–1966): farmer, author & broadcaster.
[56] Aylmer Buesst (1883–1970): conductor & composer, later Intelligence Corps; Ass. Dir. of Music, BBC 1933–6; Prof. of Music, Royal Academy of Music.
[57] Julian Clifford (1877–1921): musician.
[58] Parry (William John) Jones (1891–1963): musician, principal tenor Royal Opera House until 1955.

with great heat, 'I don't want to fight anybody – I am a pacifist.'

This duality is characteristic of the critics of Chamberlain. Never has the world seen a better example of 'Hosanna today: crucify him tomorrow' than in the treatment of Neville Chamberlain. When he returned and war fear passed he was adulated. Now he is reviled. We deserve bombing.

Wednesday 5 October   At 11–30 I called on Sir Douglas Hacking to deliver to him a note from R. and to discuss it ... It was a plea for an immediate General Election. Conservative Central Office has a strange Dickensian savour about it, even to the appearance of a messenger with the words, 'Mr Collin Brooks to see the Chairman, please,' as if the Chairman were Tigg Montague himself. Hacking, as usual, was charming. He has been for many weeks under treatment for ocular trouble, and seemed greyer than when I last saw him. He was very frank. He says that there are 40 Tory malcontents, but that all might not go into the Lobby against Neville tomorrow. His own attempt to 'sound' the constituencies and clubs had resulted in no clear view whether or not the country would swing to Chamberlain or away from him. The real problem, however, was this – it is impossible to re-arm effectively without the good will of the trade unions, and to get that it may be necessary to broaden the basis of the Government. The bitterness engendered by an election would prevent that. Said Hacking, rather wearily, leaning against the mantle shelf in his little room, 'It may seem strange to you, with your Right Wing views that we have to tolerate such a position that we cannot defend the nation against the will of the unions, there it is. It is part of the price we have to pay for this alleged democracy.'

When I suggested that the malcontent Tories could be fought, he argued, very reasonably, that if their local associations adopted them they could only be fought by independents, and that with men like Winston, Duff Cooper and Harold Nicolson[59] that would mean only at best. He said that Baldwin's speech in the Lords would do Neville a lot of good, and shied away from any suggestion that Baldwin was now regarded as a man to be impeached for neglect rather than followed.

'There are thousands of middle class voters whose imaginations he captured long ago and still dominates,' he said. He added that it was hard to apportion blame for unpreparedness.

'If you mean that Neville was Baldwin's first lieutenant during the neglectful years, I agree; but if you mean anything different, I assure

---

[59] Harold Nicolson (1886–1968): diplomatic corps, FO 1909–29; Nat. Lab. MP Leicester W. 1935–45; PS MOI. 1940–1; journalist & author.

you' I said 'that many, many thousands find no difficulty in apportioning blame.'

He then said that no decision about an election would be taken before to-morrow. For his part he thought it would be fatal if the Party seemed to be trying to capitalise Neville's peace making work, but if Labour people forced the issue, then he (Hacking) would welcome it. 'If we are to have an election within the next few months, the sooner the better. I would like it before people have forgotten the gas-masks.'

I asked how Neville was in health.

He reported him well, 'but' he added 'he is an old man, vigorous as he may seem.'

'What about a crown prince?' I asked.

'What Crown Prince?'

'I mean – what about a successor?'

'Ah, there you have one of my worries. I'd like an election while Neville is still here to fight it.' After some more talk, I rose to go, when he said, 'Just before I fell ill, indeed, the last day we met, Rothermere was discussing support of the Fund with me.'   I said that I remembered that only too well, and that I assumed that no cheque had been sent.

Hacking said that R. had even named a possible figure. 'He promised to give us the support of his papers, and that he has loyally done. He seemed fond of Neville ...'

I said. 'If I may talk in perfect confidence, I will say something that probably I ought not to say. I think R. was a little disgusted by the neglect of his brother Cecil. Greenwood,[60] I imagine, had spoken of a baronetcy for Cecil Harmsworth, but just after your talk with R. the Honours List came out without him.'

'But why didn't he mention this to me?'

'How could he? It would have been open to such misconstruction.'

Hacking leaned back and said, 'As a matter of fact Cecil Harmsworth is a very desirable person to be honoured, an ex-Minister and a charming and generous man. But, of course, the two things mustn't be linked. I don't know what Greenwood did as Treasurer, but I as Chairman will not dream of allowing any linking of funds and honours.'

To this I said, 'Naturally. And Lord Rothermere would not link them. I don't link them. R. has never said anything to me about the matter in direct way, but you can quite understand that feeling that his brother has been a little shabbily treated after long and good service, he might well be a little impatient with appeals for his own support of

---

[60] (Thomas) Harmar Greenwood (1870–1948): Lib MP York 1906–10, Sunderland 1910–22, Con. MP Walthamstow E. 1924–9; US Home Office 1919; Sec. Overseas Trade 1919–20; Chief Sec. for Ireland 1920–2; Con. Party Treasurer 1933–8; kt. 1915, cr. Baron Greenwood 1929, Viscount 1937.

an ungrateful Party. I do not know. I am only guessing at this, and I mention it to you because we have always talked in confidence to each other.'

He then asked if he could see R. again.

I said I might promise him that.

'If we are to have an election, we shall need funds with which to fight it, you know,' he said with rather a wry smile.

Reporting this talk to R. – without any mention of the latter of it – I was amused when R. said 'What does he want to see me about?' and I answered, 'I haven't the faintest idea; can it possibly be money?'

Said R. – 'Did you tell him I had lost all mine in industrial shares which were recommended to me by witch doctors like Collin Brooks?' R. then declared that the Party fund was 'broke' and that he was not going to give it any money and that he didn't want to talk to Hacking about it again. To this I said, 'I thought you wouldn't but I think you ought to. . .' and he said 'All right, we'll see him when I come back.' [. . .] At 1 I reached the Reform, where Oscar Hobson, reading the tape, insisted on buying me a sherry, over which we talked until my guest Barnes of the B.B.C. arrived. Oscar is fuming about Chamberlain's surrender and about our unpreparedness. I couldn't resist reminding him of how he used to sneer and rage at my appeals for arms three years ago, which he took good humouredly. Barnes wanted to talk to me about a series of radio talks on the trend newspapers. I told him that if he wanted the truth in such talks they would have to be given by retired functionaries. I suggested Tom Clarke and Bernard Falk or Walter Fish on the editorial side, and Peacock (ex-*Morning Post*) on the managerial side. He wanted me to do one or more of these talks, and I said I would if I were home, and would help all I could in advising him. He was quite ingenuously staggered when I said that a man could control a large newspaper group without owning more than a bare qualification share as long as nobody called his bluff.

'Where is the control of the *Daily Mail*? Somewhere among 300,000 small shareholders, of whom about twenty come to the annual meeting – and of those 20 persons none dreams that the Harmsworths are not the financial controllers . . . .' I said too that the power of the Jewish advertisers would be difficult to discuss on a radio talk.

Thursday 6 October As we capered up to the bar at the Club Oliver Baldwin came along, and after chaffing me about my moustache and Imperial said he was anxious for a long talk. I arranged eventually to join him and some friend for a quick dinner, as he wouldn't join Lil and me. He insisted that Lil should come too, so we went down to the Queens Restaurant in Sloane Square, where he and his secretary, whose name I forgot, and (another) Francis Watson made up the party. Oliver was very angry with Neville, very appreciative of Benes[61] and very annoyed with the Labour Party for not being more united. [...] Oliver says his father, despite the Press photographs, is quite well and hopes he will long stay so as he (Oliver) doesn't relish going to the House of Lords. [...] After my talk with Douglas Hacking yesterday I was interested to find that only 20 of the 40 malcontent Tories abstained from going into the Lobby with Chamberlain. Neville will have no election yet and – to my horror – repeated his pledge not to introduce conscription or any form of compulsory national service in peacetime. (When I urged on Hacking yesterday that one reason for an election was to enable Neville to rid himself of that stupid pledge, Hacking said that it meant only conscription into the Forces, and that National Service would not be covered by it – but Neville today was specific. Little Amery rightly asked whether in view of this pledge we had better not have a change of Government so that a very necessary measure might be taken.)

Monday 10 October   The Scots express was about fortyfive minutes late, and R. emerged looking, I thought, very old and tired. He and I walked from King's Cross to Regents Park, round the Queens Garden and to Avenue Road, talking of last night's speech by Hitler. Hitler's denunciation of Churchill, Duff-Cooper and Eden as potential makers of war on Germany has naturally been construed everywhere as an attempt by Hitler to dictate to the British whom they shall have in their Ministry. It *is* that, of course, and with his amazing superiority in arms and men he can afford to dictate. During the morning, in Stratton House, R. read a letter to me which Ward Price had sent to him from Berlin after a four hour talk with Goering.

Wednesday 12 October   After tea went round to Avenue Road where R. was resting in bed. During the evening he asked me if I would broach the matter of Cecil's barony with Hacking. As I think Cecil Harmsworth has been badly treated and as I had previously told R. that Hamar Greenwood was the wrong person to arrange honours, I said I would do this.

[61] Eduard Benes (1884–1948): Pres. of Czechoslovakia 1935–8, 1945–8; Pres. of the Czechoslovakia Nat. Ctte. in London 1939–45.

Thursday 13 October I took a taxi to Palace Chambers. Hacking saw me at once. I told him that R. hoped he could lunch tomorrow, but as he was going off to his constituency at 1–30 we would have to put if off until next week. I opened up again about Cecil, and said that it was absurd that Ronnie McNeill[62] should have had a Peerage and Cecil Harmsworth not, for Ronnie was nothing more than an Under-Secretary. Hacking said that R's £25,000 suggested contribution must not be mixed up with the question of honours, but that if I would write him a short account of C.H.'s extra-Parliamentary activities since he left the House there was no reason why he shouldn't go on the Premier's list. Hacking said that he was tired of the honours' list.

'Quite a number of men come in here and tell me how pleased they are with the National Government. Then they flatter me by saying I am the best Chairman they remember, at which I smirk. Then they suggest a big contribution, and eventually they remark that their wives are very ambitious. Of course, I have to say "Surely you are not suggesting that we should do anything in return for monetary support!" Then they blush and talk generalities and begin to go, until I say, but what about this contribution, having ready in my desk a form of Covenant ...' He says the blatancy is amazing...

Friday 14 October At three Lil dropped me from a taxi at Cecil Harmsworth's door in Hyde Park Gardens. I was calling to ask him about all his activities. I found him in a big study on the top floor of a tall house, the lift of which refused to work. We spoke for a while of Desmond's verses and pictures, and then of my mission. C.H. said he thought he had been badly treated, and that he had not even been made a Privy Councillor. He spoke very frankly of Curzon and Simon, but was not unfriendly to Ll. George. He said that once when George Curzon was away on one of his many conference trips A.J. Balfour took charge of the Foreign Office.

'He popped his silver head round my door and said "Hallo, my dear fellow, how are you. What a relief – now that the Purple Emperor has flown the F.O. is quite human again." I said that the Marquess was my chief and I couldn't discuss him, and Balfour laughed and said, "Admirable, my dear fellow, but he isn't my chief and I call him the Purple Emperor."'

Simon, he says, is least trusted in his own party – although nobody knows why. He said that the great art of being Under Secretary for

---

[62] Ronnie McNeill (1861–1934): Con. MP Kent St Augustine's 1911–18, Canterbury 1918–27; US FO 1922–4, 1924–5; FST 1925–7; Chanc. Duchy of Lancaster 1927–9; cr. Baron Cushendun 1927.

Foreign Affairs is to keep awkward questions off the paper, and that if you approach the troublesome questioner and tell him where the danger is, there is never any trouble. He says that he has always missed being in the Commons. Had 1922 not been a bad year for him, owing to Northcliffe's illness, he would have stayed there. In the evening I dined at R's, and talked to him in his bedroom from about 6–30 to 10 o'c. It was a very different talk from the talk we had had at breakfast ...

When I arrived for the morning walk he was pacing round the garden, and began immediately to discuss Hungary. At 8–15 I rang up Ward Price and said we were sending a car for him immediately. At about 8–40, while R. and I were eating breakfast, in came Wardy, a trickle of blood on his chin, from a too hasty shave. 'I am sorry to be a bit late, but I stopped to draft something,' he cried, waving two sheets of typescript. R. took them from him and read them. 'Hey! hey! I sound like Napoleon, leaving my bones in my beloved country.' He finished the reading and fluttered the pages over to me.

I read them, stood up, bowed and said, 'Ah! Augustus Caesar, I presume!!' The document was Lord Rothermere's pronunciamento to the people of Hungary, very well done, of course. It lamented at their failure to secure their lost territories now that Germany was being satisfied and was satisfying Poland, lamented that they had not secured foreign support for their claims, said that for 11 years R. had not visited that hard hit country, but, as they knew, had never ceased to work for it, recalling Esmond's triumphal tour of ten years ago and concluded by saying 'Now I am ready to return and lay at the disposal of your Government my counsel and connections ...' It was, in short, a bid for the Regency. We were in the middle of *The Prisoner of Zenda*. I was all in favour of the manifesto being sent, but R. said he would not do it without Hitler's assent. Ward Price offered to go over and see Hitler or to get into touch with somebody, but refused to discuss anything with Ribbentrop, who, he said, was powerless and a mere echo and was supremely jealous of anybody who talked to the Fuhrer.

'If you do go,' he said, 'It will mean a great ordeal, worse than last time, tens of thousands of people and all kinds of deputations. You and Brooks and I will probably be killed, either by the ardours [*sic*] of the episode or by a bullet apiece, but it will be a great memory.'

After talking pros and cons we phoned through to Buda-Pest and talked to O.....sy there – and he ended the adventure abruptly, by telling us that Hungary was now going to wait for the promised Four Power Conference. To my amazement, Wardy now turned very cold on the project.

Saturday 15 October   R's car came for me at 7–15 and he and I walked round his garden in the lovely Autumn sunshine of a perfect morning, talking finance and politics. Ward Price came about 9–30. He is leaving on Tuesday for a whirl round the Middle and Near East. He quite seriously fears he may be killed in Palestine. There was no further talk of Hungary beyond R. and W-P telling me that Winston last night had told them that when Horthy[63] was at Berchtesgaden Hitler had offered him the Hungarian territories by a coup and Horthy had said, 'We are a small nation; what would England say to that?', whereat Hitler flew into a fury, cast down his tea cup to the ground and said he wouldn't be insulted in his own house. However, Horthy was certain that a war was coming and that Britain, France and Russia would defeat Germany, so he refused Hitler's offer – and missed the Berlin boat. Winston, as I prophesied to Hacking ten days ago, has had trouble with his Constituency Committee, which objects to his anti-Chamberlain stand in the debate. [...] Among my other activities in this not uninteresting week has been the final despatch of my anti-Eden book.

Monday 17 October   Early walk with R. – and later to lunch at Avenue Road to meet Michael Harmsworth,[64] who has apparently asked R. to pay half his election expenses as he wants to go into politics. He suggested fighting Sinclair in Caithness, but R. pooh-poohed this, ostensibly because Archibald Sinclair is a great and popular landowner there and a Liberal in a constituency of hereditary Liberals, but really because he thought it would complicate his relations, as the Lord at Dornoch with the Laird in Caithness. ... He suggested that Michael should fight Duff Cooper in St. George, in the belief that the women's vote will go against all anti-Chamberlain war-mongers. I promised to advise and help M.H. He is a husky, blond boy, full of good humour, but very unsophisticated politically. R. told him that he would pay half the election expenses and allow him £1000 a year if he won the seat.

Tuesday 18 October   Breakfasted with R. after a morning walk and then went down to Stratton House to meet Michael Harmsworth, whom I took over to the Berkeley for a midmorning coffee and talk. His young wife was with him, but her we shunted to another room until the talk was over, when she rejoined us. I remembered being twenty-two and having a young wife ... R's great idea was the Michael should canvass all Duff Cooper's committee and thus try to secure nomination by

---

[63] Nicholas Vitéz de Nagbanya Horthy (1868–1957). Regent of Hungary, 1920–44.
[64] Michael Harmsworth (b. 1916).

them, instead of running as an independent, and for that purpose proposed to lend Michael the new Rolls Royce. I promised to get the names of the committee, which after a lot of trouble I did through Dick Lewis, who is without doubt London's most efficient news editor.

Wednesday 19 October   R. was not only glad that Lil should go with me to Buda-Pest but wanted to pay her expenses, which I refused to permit. This afternoon Glorney Bolton[65] and his wife came in for a dish of tea. Glorney brought some galley proofs of his book of memoirs so that I could see what he had said about me. It was pleasant enough. I egged him on to fight Eden in Warwick and he said he would think it over after I had developed the possibilities. [...] Guy du Bouley told me that when our recent Air Force deputation went to France it had the shock of its life. The first factory that was shown to its members had had to call in the strikers for the day; the second was going on strike that evening. The French suggested that Britain should concentrate on making bombers and the French on fighters, but one look at the French fighters was enough for the British.

Thursday 20 October   Glorney Bolton had sent me a letter cleverly written to my specifications of yesterday, offering to fight Eden. I mentioned this tentatively to R., and hope later to leave it with him and get things moving. He today lunches Douglas Hacking and the Cecil Harmsworth peerage hangs in the balance!!!! I am tapping this down at noon, and shall not be able to make any more entries until I get back. For the sake of a record I am entering here a memo. that I drafted for R., so that there can be no mistake about the purpose of my visit to Budapest.[66]

[*Editorial Note*   From 21 October to 15 November Brooks and his wife were visiting Hungary. Maintaining the diary becomes impossible. Rothermere arrived in Budapest 8 November.]

Monday 21 November   My book *Can Chamberlain Save Britain* is being fairly well noticed, but has not aroused the savage retorts from Eden-ites that

---

[65] John Robert Glorney Bolton (1901–nk): author & journalist, *Yorkshire Post* 1923–7; *The Times of India* 1927–30; autobiography, *Two Lives Converge* (London: Blackie & Son, 1938) with wife Sybil Bolton, novelist.

[66] See Appendix C.

I had hoped. I rang R. up when I got back and he asked me to go round to Avenue Road at ten. This I did. He was just back from a high night at the Middle Temple, having been also to the re-opening luncheon at the Press Club, where he sat next to Winston. We drank a bowl of soup and a cup of tea over the fire. He says that Winston is worried at what has happened in France. It was the French who really 'ratted' at Munich. R. and I agreed that what had happened was that the French had realised that Russia would rat. Lord Sankey at the Middle Temple dinner had been very pessimistic, and had said that if Neville went there was nobody who commanded sufficient confidence to replace him. The Jewish pogrom in Germany is arousing great indignation everywhere, but there are some who, despite its brutalities, view it with complete understanding and even sympathy. One old K.C. (said R.) spent most of the evening cursing the Jews and our Government for letting 'em into England in great numbers.

Tuesday 22 November   R. wants me to write a book to be called *Warnings and Predictions* and I am busy wading through his cuttings. I made one of a little party which dined at the Reform to welcome Hoeffding from Berlin. Ormsby, of the *Wall Street Journal*; Ashton Morrison, the stock broker; Logie,[67] of Schroders; Maurice Crowther,[68] of Falks; Oscar Hobson were the party, with little Jock Drummond-Smith coming in late. We sat and talked till after midnight, in the hall, over dinner, in the small committee room and in the hall again – Hoeffding says that the German people were outraged by the pogrom. The resentment was even vocal. But opinion is utterly ineffective and Hitler is very strongly in the saddle. Hermann Goering is popular; Goebbles disliked. Nothing really emerged from the talk, although most of us were fairly know-ledgeable people and many of us had been moving freely about Europe for many months. All agreed that the economic arguments about Germany are futile in an era of Power Politics. Logie, Crowther and Hoeffding all say that Schacht is really out of the picture for a while, but anticipates a recall as the mark gets more troublesome. He is, they say, foolhardy in his outspokenness. Hoeffding says that the worst sufferers are the retailers. As an example of Goering's economics he quoted the episode of cheap rye. Goering was told that neither producers nor sellers could stand any further cuts. The cost, he

[67] G.K. Logie: employee of J. Henry Schroeder & Co, Merchant Bank; formerly head of intelligence dept. Lazard Brothers.
[68] Geoffrey Maurice Crowther (1907–72): reporter & Ed.; joined *Economist* 1932, Ed. 1938–56, Chm. 1957–72; During Second WW served Min. of Supply, MOI, Min. of Production; author *Crowther Report* (1959); Dir. Commercial Union Assurance Co.; kt. 1957.

ascertained, would be about (say) seventy millards of marks. He promptly looked at the profits of other industries – took forty millards from sugar and thirty from brewing. This struck the others as a great economic heresy – but I agreed that it was no different at base from taking those amounts by normal taxation and as the only people who suffered directly were brewers and sugar refiners the people would be quite content.

Monday 28 November   The city to-day was quite dead, because the strike trouble in France and the news of Germany's enlarged army had frightened everybody stiff ... R. having lunched with Winston yesterday says that he – Winston – is now most gloomy, but thinks his Division will support him at the election, which may be postponed again, for reasons not stated.

Tuesday 29 November   As R. is nursing a cold in bed there was no early morning walk, but I went round to breakfast at 8 o'clock, and we began the day with the usual discussion of the news, the course of the markets, the latest political gossip. He gave me the word 'go' on two proposals that he and I have been discussing for some little time, so at about ten I borrowed one of his cars. [...] My first call was in Hatton Garden, at the office of Jerman and Ward, the diamond merchants [...] explained that as advisor to R. I had suggested that as a hedge against sterling, and as an alternative to dollars, he might buy about £50,000 of diamonds. Would they handle such business and what was the procedure. I explained that I was quite ignorant of the diamond trade, which, of course, immediately put them on their guard against a highly sophisticated person. Yes – they could certainly handle such a deal. Many people were doing the same thing. The right thing to do, of course was not to buy new stones. You can't get them at a reasonable price. Good, large second-hand stones were the best buy ... We came at last to the fact that they had for disposal a Royal stone of nearly fifty carats, fortynine-sixtyfour to be exact, a Marquis shaped stone, at present set as a ring. It might be had for £30,000 on a quick sale. It was mentioned only on the understanding that I did not discuss it with Cartiers or any of the big retail jewellers, as one of them had been permitted to show it to a few customers and had been asking £50,000.

'What exactly is a Royal stone?'

'Well, I can't mention the name of the royal owner, but I saw her last week, and the stone comes from the same source as ...'

'Oh, you mean literally a Royal stone. I thought it was a trade classification.'

And then there were three fancy diamonds at present mounted as a kind of belt buckle – three superb yellow diamonds each set in white diamonds – £6,000 for three. The condition of any sale of these or the big stone, in addition to secrecy, must be that the purchaser will not try to re-sell too soon – on a five point fall of sterling, for example.

[... then ...] to Archbishop's House next to the [Westminster] Cathedral. My hurried telephone appointment with the Cardinal's secretary was for 11–45. [...] My graceful, distinguished host ushered me to the easiest of the saddlebag chairs and offered me a cigarette. 'But perhaps you smoke Turkish ...' I didn't smoke Turkish, so that his cork tipped Cravens satisfied us both.

'Lord Rothermere and I were present at the open air Mass at Walsingham when the pilgrimage was held recently. He was very struck by the inestimable moral and social value of the re-creation of such an ancient shrine. He talked to me about doing something for Walsingham, and I suggested that he might give a Bellini[69] that hangs in his house in Scotland. It is a very typical Bellini, the Holy Mother between two Saints, not of great value, perhaps £8,000, perhaps £10,000. His view of his art collection, you may know, is that if he leaves the pictures to the nation they will go into museums and galleries and few will see them, but if they go to Churches they will fulfil the destiny which their painters designed for them, aids to devotion. Before making the offer to Walsingham, however, we wanted to be sure that it would have the approval of the Cardinal Archbishop[70] ...'

So, more or less, I opened the talk. He was delighted, and almost leapt from his chair at the mention of a Bellini – had doubts as to whether the Cardinal was really concerned, as Walsingham was in the diocese of Northampton – was troubled because valuable pictures might so easily be stolen – but returned to his original delight at the thought of a Bellini going to such a fane – Would I wait until he tried to see the Cardinal, who might be praying? I waited. He returned after a few minutes, with the word that the Cardinal regretted that work which engaged him prevented him receiving me at that moment to express in person his gratification and appreciation of R's thought and generosity. Walsingham was not in his diocese, but that of the Bishop of Northampton.[71] Unfortunately, the Bishop of Northampton is not a – a –

[69] Giovanni Bellini (c. 1430–70–71?): artist. The title of the picture is unclear from the journals.

[70] A. Hinsley (1865–1943): Roman Catholic Cleric: Prof. at Ushaw 1893–97; Ass. Priest Keighley 1898; Head, St Bede's Grammar School 1899–1904; Pastor 1904–17; Rector, English College, Rome 1917–28; Apostolic delegate in Africa 1930–4; Canon of the Patriarchal Basilica, St Peter's Rome, 1934–5; Archbishop of Westminster 1935–43 (Cardinal, 1937).

[71] Rt. Rev. Laurence W. Youens (d. 1939): Roman Catholic Priest: Missionary, Egypt 1899–1902; Priest, High Wycombe 1902–6; Rector, Shefford, 1907–33; Bishop of Northampton from 1933.

well, a very artistic person. The picture should therefore be offered to
him through the Very Reverend Monsignor Squirrel, of Norwich, and
should be given, in accordance with Canon Law, on condition that it
must never be alienated from Walsingham. (Otherwise, said my delightful Secretary host, some foolish priest will someday try to sell it and
devote the thousands to building a Church or a school, or some very
utilitarian thing, which will defeat our intentions, for the Cardinal
thoroughly concurs with the view that masterpieces painted for
Churches should return to Churches ...)

Wednesday 30 November   At about seven fifteen this evening I arrived at
the headquarters of the English Speaking Union, where I was to
participate in a discussion on the German colonies with Roden Noel
Buxton,[72] Duncan Sandys, Lord Hailey,[73] a man called Joelson[74] and
Colonel Thwaites.[75] Sir Frederick Whyte[76] was to be in the chair. I
jostled Buxton in the doorway, looking like a flustered Oxford don who
had put on his wife's toupe by error. [...] Thwaites who sat on my left
told me that as Honorary Secretary of the organisation he was tired of
being twitted on being an officer of the Yiddish Speaking Union. 'All the
members who come to these discussion are very "left" and "pinkish",' he
said, and expressed his gratitude to Fate for my presence. I had been
asked, when I accepted the invitation, to be as aggressive as I liked and
to open the discussion after Hailey had spoken for fifteen minutes on
an American hook-up wireless. The affair sounded a little unpromising –
two great rooms full of auditor, many of them dough-faced and stupid
looking women, and a platform on which we sat like so many nigger
minstrels. Partly to give the proceedings an air of informality and partly
to allow microphones to relay the discussion into the second room it
was arranged that we spoke seated. Nobody was permitted to make a
speech, and everyone was encouraged to interrupt and wrangle. Hailey
spoke well and judicially, as befitted a retired proconsul. I opened on
a blunt declaration that Versailles was a piece of fraud and chicanery
and a blot on our national scutcheon and Germany had an ethical
claim to her old territories. This brought Duncan Sandys to my

[72] Edward Noel Buxton (1869–1948): Lib. MP Norfolk N. 1910–18, Lab. MP Norfolk
N. 1922–30; Min. of Agric. 1924, 1929–30; cr. Baron Noel Buxton of Aylsham 1930.
[73] (William) Malcolm Hailey (1872–1969): Member of Viceroy's Executive Council
1932–4; Gov. of United Provinces 1934–9; cr. 1st Baron 1936.
[74] Ferdinand Stephen Joelson (1893–1979): writer on African affairs since 1917; broadcaster & publisher.
[75] Colonel Norman Thwaites (1872–1956): Sec. to Joseph Pulitzer, special intelligence
mission USA, 1916.
[76] Sir Frederick Whyte (1883–1970): Lib. MP 1910–18; Head of American Div. MOI.
1939–40.

metaphorical throat at once. We bandied quotations from Wilson and
the Lloyd George speech of November 11th 1918; and the Jewman,
Joelson – a little, rather suspicious and louring kind of person – entered
the fray with some vigour. From that I shook them off, with the aid of
the chairman, who declared that we had all got into a side issue of
how a Mandate could be relinquished, as indeed we had. I then
launched into the case for the expediency of considering the German
claim, and was again in a struggle with Duncan Sandys, who was
rather handicapped because as the hero of a recent Parliamentary
incident he could not rebut my contention that we were unprepared
for a war with the Axis. I was in excellent form, and used all the
weapons in my dialectical armoury to effect. (This isn't a Gasconade,
but a fair assessment.) We descended at times to mere verbal
slogging.

Duncan Sandys: 'In other words – a policy of funk.' (loud applause)

C.B.: 'Ah, that is a very easy, slick, Parliamentarian's way of trying
to discredit a serious argument. I might retort that your's is a policy of
the swollen head. I wouldn't be so rude.'

At one stage the Jew launched himself into a very rhetorical period
about the ill treatment of natives in German territories before they had
the glories of British rule and the shining hope of self-government.

C.B.: 'Ah, now you are appealing most skilfully to the emotions. You
move me deeply, I am profoundly stirred. You are breaking my heart.
But you quite avoid the argument – which is, are the ex-colonies a
worthy occasion for a destructive and possibly fatal war, and if so are
we and the other democracies prepared for such a war. You talk about
protecting the natives. You might easily talk about protecting the ladies
of this audience from your aggressive method of taking their necklaces,
but it would be quite futile – particularly if I had on my knuckle dusters
and you had none.'

At other times we were supremely and comically statesmanlike.
Buxton came in with a possible compromise – to extend the range of the
Congo Basin Treaties of Bismarck, and permit Germany to administer
territories on an equality. This pleased a lot of people, but there was a
flaw.

'Now, Mister Chairman, I propose to interrupt!' said I, 'Tell us, Mr
Buxton, how you solve this dilemma. If you permit Germany to
administer territories under the Congo Basin Treaties, you destroy the
current argument that she is unfit to administer native territories. If
you destroy that argument, Germany may say to you, "But if we are
to have territories, why not our own territories, which you took from
us by a pre-Armistice fraud".'

This, he admitted, was a point. 'But' he said, 'it would be a basis
for negotiation. Herr Hitler would be told that he must consider Mr

Chamberlain's position, that the British Prime Minister can do nothing unless he carries his people with him, and that the British people are not ready to cede the ex-colonies.'

'To which Herr Hitler might well reply, "Ah, my dear Chamberlain, that is your funeral".' (loud laughter after which . . . .)

Buxton: 'That is hardly the language of diplomacy!'

C.B.: 'No, it is a wilful exaggeration. But it is very like the language recently used by Germany to Benes.'

Buxton did one thing that was significant. He paid a great tribute to Chamberlain and said that many in the Labour Party supported his policy of appeasement. The discussion lasted about two hours before the packed audience was permitted to ask questions or make short speeches. They contributed nothing. [. . .] I was, of course, the unpopular person, the anti-British, pro-German, anti-Jew, anti-native pro-violence devil's advocate. Hailey, who summed up, and did it well, did me justice, and returned to his own opening in which he said that the only valid reasons for returning the colonies were either that their retention would mean a war from which we could not hope to emerge successfully or that their ceding would open the way to a better world understanding – which was, of course, my own case. I rather feared that I had overdone the aggressiveness, but apparently not. At the end an unexpected American matron forced her way against the outgoing stream of people to me and said, taking my hand, 'Mister Brooks, I just have to congratulate you on the way you handled that little bunch. I never saw such readiness or such perfect aplomb!'

Wednesday 14 December At five thirty I attended the installation of officers of the Worshipful Company of Glass Sellers at Painter's Hall. After it was over we all donned fur lined robes and velvet hats, were given nosegays, and processed to Church, where a service was held. From there we returned to dine. The speeches turned largely on Neville's attitude to Germany, and it was noticeable that he had the full support of everyone who spoke and had much applause. I was surprised how little notice was taken of our archaic procession as we moved in our ancient attire through the streets, preceded by the sign of the company and by a processional cross.

Wednesday 21 December Lunched at 1–15 with Gordon-Canning,[77] Raven Thomson and another man – a Parliamentarian – at 21 Connaught Square. Raven Thomson is director of policy for Mosley and had

---

[77] Capt. Robert C. Gordon-Canning: Moselyite; member of The Link; detained under regulation 18B, May 1940.

wanted to meet me because of *Can Chamberlain Save Britain.* We talked very frankly. I told 'em I thought their Cromwell had emerged too soon. I gathered that the movement is short of money. [...] There is tremendous interest in the report that Hudson[78] and Dufferin[79] have revolted against Tom Inskip and Hore-Belisha. Parliamentary revolts won't save us.

[78] Robert Spear Hudson (1886–1957): Con. MP Whitehaven 1924–9, Southport 1931–52; PS Lab. 1931–5; Min. of Pensions 1935–6; PS Health 1936–7; Sec. Overseas Trade 1937–40; Min. of Shipping 1940; Min. of Agric. 1940–5; cr. Viscount Hudson 1952.
[79] Basil Sheridan Hamilton-Temple-Blackwood (1909–45): PPS to Lord Irwin 1932–6; Whip in the HofL. 1936–7; US Colonies 1937–40; killed in action in Burma 25 March 1945; suc. 4th Marquess of Dufferin & Ava 1930.

1939

Sunday 1 January 7–30 pm. After some work and a bite of lunch I took a taxicab for Fleet Street, calling en route at the Press Association Offices, at the Central News and the Exchange Telegraph, to see that Cecil Harmsworth has a good show in tomorrow's Press when his Peerage is announced. At the D.M. office I found Bob Prew[1] by himself and congratulated him on being, even against his will, the acting editor of the *Daily Mail*. While we waited for the honours list he told me the inside story of the 'sackings' of Cranfield and Head and the resignation of Roberts,[2] the Night Editor. It seems that Cranfield was away on holiday. The day before his return Esmond Harmsworth and Bell drafted a careful letter which they sent to Cranfield's flat, telling him to take six months holiday and saying they would announce his health was indifferent. But Cranfield came straight from the aerodrome to the office, to Bell's extreme embarrassment. Esmond was in Scotland and Bell didn't know if the letter had been sent. The next day and the next Cranfield appeared as usual. One night he and Prew arranged to go to their respective flats for dinner, before the proofs came down of the first edition. Prew then had a ring from Cranfield saying that they had both better return together as news had come that Neville was flying to Berchtesgaden the next day. Prew suggested that he would wait outside his own flat till Cranfield picked him up in the office car. He waited and to his surprise the car was driving past him. He attracted the driver's attention and climbed in. Cranfield was huddled in a corner. Prew began to report that by phone he had told them to be ready to open the leader page, had got a leaderwriter waiting, and so on. To all this Cranfield made no response.

'Is anything wrong?' asked Prew.

'Yes' – said Cranfield, 'I've had a letter.'

He then told how by his telephone for some days had been lying a pile of circulars and envelopes and that while turning these idly over as he telephoned to Prew he had lighted upon one from the office. After ringing off he had opened it – and found it contained what was tantamount to his dismissal from the Editorship. There were some days of angry discussion about what payment should be made to him, and

[1] Robert 'Bob' Prew: Ass. & then Ed. *Daily Mail*, 1939–44.
[2] R.E. Roberts (1879–1955); journalist; Literary Ed. *New Statesman* 1930–2; Night Ed. *Daily Mail.*

eventually after signing a document not to write his story of the *Daily Mail* and another renouncing his directorship, they gave him £12,000 in compensation for breach of contract. That left Head, the night editor, Prew and Gordon Beckles,[3] assistant editors, in charge as a kind of triumvirate. Prew demanded that one of them, no matter which, should be prime responsibility – first among equals, but Esmond and Bell would not have this. The news that Cranfield had gone brought several applications for his job from outside the office. One of these attracted Esmond and he arranged with Horniblow[4] of the *Express* to come in at night to make up the paper. The problem then was to get Head out of the way. He was on holiday and was asked to take three months further holiday, but refusing to be made a convenience of in this way, he was eventually 'bought out' with £4,000 in lieu of fulfilment of contract. Then it seemed that Beckles and Horniblow could not work amicably together, so Prew was virtually compelled, largely by appeals to his loyalty, to become acting editor, having told Esmond that he much preferred a quiet life. Prew, who began his journalistic life in 1904, went to Paris for a year and stayed thirteen years, and who is a very solid person with money saved and with a great Fleet Street reputation, did not give a damn for any of 'em – but stayed on. The result has been that the *Mail* has begun to recover circulation. This seems to be a typical episode in Northcliffe House history.

Thursday 12 January   I make slow but steady progress with R's *apologia*.[5] I interrupted myself this morning to give lunch to David Woodford at the Reform. As we sat drinking a second Martini together in the Hall, Oscar Hobson came wandering past and greeted me. I 'collared' him and persuaded him to make our duet a trio, for I was interested to see how the Hot Tory David would react to the Hot Radical Oscar. It was quite a good mixture. Hobson is still very dubious about the stability of the £ and very vehement about Germany. He has taken into his home a young Jewish refugee of 19 and is to take in his younger brother. I refrained from asking if he had ever taken in a couple of young English unemployed... He says that Geoffrey Crowther, of *The Economist*, has just come back from Berlin, and that he confirms the story of Goebbles being beaten-up by some outraged husband. He also says that Hitler has now found himself a German girl-friend. Her name is Braun, she is the usual Teutonic broad hipped, blond type, and she likes swigging beer, but dares not swig when Hitler is present. He

---

[3] Gordon Beckles (1901–54): journalist; staff of *Daily Express* 1928–38; Ass. Ed. *Daily Mail*.
[4] S. Horniblow: journalist, *Daily Mail* staff, Ed. 1944–7.
[5] Viscount Rothermere *Warnings and Predictions* (London: Eyre and Spottiwoode, 1939).

reports further that the regime is split into factions and the people are restive – but here I suspect the wish is father to the thought. David says that he has noticed that important German's who visit old Lord Q⁶ now show a very different front from that shown a few months ago. Then they seemed to be displaying the best qualities of the gentle German, with the implication that all Germans were so; now, he says, they are arrogant and tell Q he should use his influence to gag the British press. Neither Hobson nor Woodford thought that much would come of Chamberlain's visit to Rome.

Monday 16 January   At 11–30 I called on Douglas Hacking at Central Office. He received me as cordially as ever. [...] I asked him if I was right in assuming that R. had promised him £25,000. He said that R. had mentioned that figure, but that he hoped it might be more, I then said,

'Am I right in assuming that you do not like cheques for the Secret Fund? Would you prefer some other form of payment?'

He said, 'Well, this is a straightforward contribution. There has been no connection with anything else. It is a matter for Rothermere or you to decide.' Then, after a pause, 'But suspicious minds might see a connection between the payment and Cecil's barony, so perhaps......'

I suggested bearer bonds, and this he welcomed. Then he said that the premises in which Central Office is housed are old and decrepit.

'They'd have been condemned long ago in any country but this...' He had his eye on new premises but that meant £125,000.

'Do you suggest that R. earmarks his money for that?' I asked.

'Well, frankly, I was thinking that for a specific object like that he might give more. If he'd give £50,000 I could find another donor to go the other half.....'

I said that I'd sound R. about this. I then talked to him about a safe seat for Michael Harmsworth. He told me the problem of raising funds for unwealthy candidates was very difficult. Central Office could do it, but that meant usurping some of the autonomy from local associations. He also said it was hard to subsidise working men candidates.

'You take a man from his job, he may get in, which gives him £600 a year as a Member, and is then defeated. Being a Tory he is a marked man. The Party has no convenient secretaryships, as Labour has. You virtually have to keep him for life...'

I stayed longer than I had intended and had quite a heart-to-heart

---

⁶ Almeric Hugh Paget (1861–1949): Con. MP Cambridge 1910–17; whip 1911–17; Pres. National Union of Con. & Unionist Associations 1928–9, 1940–1; Dir. of several large companies; cr. Baron Queenborough 1918.

talk. He said that Duff Cooper's unpopularity is unbelievable.

'I hope it's shyness but I fear its snobbery,' he said. In St George's Duff addresses a meeting and then walks away without talking to his constituents. When he sat for Oldham they had to ask Lady Diana[7] not to go to the place, as she puts the backs of everybody up ... In the seat he was nursing before they suggested he should fight St. George's the local people almost sent a resolution of thanks for his removal.

Tuesday 17 January   Lunched by Sir George Buchanan at the St. James's Club. (Note for social history: sherry, smoked salmon, cold chicken pie with potato salad, stilton, pint of ale, coffee.) He was thoroughly eulogistic about *Can Chamberlain Save Britain*, thinks Mosley may yet 'pull it off', and is in despair at the Jewish influence over the English press. After lunch when we were sipping our coffee I told him I was hoping to go to Australia and he told me of his tour ten years ago for Stanley Bruce. He said his Report is still worth reading. The Australians, he declares, and declared there, are the laziest people on earth, and will never hold their land against the Japs. If the Germans had Australia, he says, they would make a fine thing of it. As it is the whole prosperity rests on the back of sheep, the country has overborrowed, and it is all precarious. He says that seven million people are selfishly drifting to their own and our destruction. One of his grudges against life at the moment is that his book, exposing the Mesopotamian muddle, has been banned by the Press, he thinks because of some whispering instruction from Downing Street. On the whole, an interesting but pessimistical talk.

Wednesday 18 January   Yesterday morning during his early morning telephone call from Monte Carlo, R. said that he would give Hacking the £25,000 that had been promised and would give another £10,000 if Michael Harmsworth were found a safe seat. About ten minutes later he rang again to say he thought £10,000 too much. He would give £5,000. 'We'll keep the other up our sleeve. *You* may want a knighthood someday, my dear fellow!' (Lil said I'd better get in touch with Hacking quickly before he found himself owing R. money on Cecil's Peerage...) At 12–30 today I saw Hacking. He said there could not be any bargain about a seat for Michael. He would do whatever he could for the boy, and if R. gave another £5,000 he would be grateful, but the two things must not be related. (Here, one observes, the same farce as over the

---

[7] Lady Diana Cooper: wife of Duff Cooper, socialite & beauty, d. of 8th Duke of Rutland.

Peerage, which Hacking, who is a straight fellow, must hate as much as I do or any one else who engages in these things.) He said he would like to talk to R. again, but did not wish to pester him. He said that he had promised R. to put the Rothermere view to the Prime Minister and had spent half an hour with Neville doing this. He had suggested that Neville should invite R. to dine quietly some night. I told him that when it was suggested months ago that R. should meet Neville R. had refused, as such meetings were open to misconstruction. [. . .] managed to do some more work before meeting Oscar Joseph at the Cafe Royal at 8–30. We drank a cocktail there and then crossed in the rain to the Reform for quiet dinner. He was fifteen minutes late, as his taxi had been held up by a Communist demonstration. (Unemployed demonstrations and Irish bombs are adding a spice of excitement to life at the moment. Yesterday a number of unemployed lay down in the middle of Regent Street, one girl 'starving' in art-silk stockings, an odd cast back to my *Economics of Human Happiness*.[8]) Things in the city, he says, are dreadful. Even speculative business begins to dry-up. Joseph is helping at Woburn House advising refugees. He says that he is shocked to find that he grows very 'hard' about them. A perpetual stream of exiles of all classes and kinds is enough, he avers, to dry anybody's first fine emotions of pity for a suffering race. He reminded me that three and a half years ago I warned him that anti-Semitism was rising everywhere and said, 'You were perfectly right, although I didn't then think so, just as you have been right about the German progress.'

Monday 23 January   To-day I lunched Cyril Joad[9] and Frank Whitaker[10] (editor of *John O London's*) at the Savage. Joad wanted advice about some investments. We talked, naturally, about international affairs. He surprised me by saying that he agreed very largely with my views and that as a confirmed Pacifist he was a supporter of Chamberlain. If Labour were returned, he thinks, they would blunder into war. This from one of the intellectual leaders of Labour was interesting.

Wednesday 25 January   For some reason I slept late, wakening, of course, for tea and newspapers at 8 and to speak with R. on the phone about

---

[8] *The Economics of Human Happiness* (London: Routledge, 1933).

[9] Cyril Edwin Mitchinson Joad (1891–1953): civil servant until 1930; then writer, teacher & popular philosopher; later a member of BBC's Brain's Trust along with Brooks.

[10] Frank Whitaker (?1895–1962): Ed. *John O'London's Weekly* 1928–36; Ed. *Country Life* 1940–58.

8–30, but actually lying abed until noon. But before tea time I had finished R's book at about 228 pages, many of them with single spaced typewriting. It will make a volume between 250 and 300 pages in a reasonable type-face [...] R. returns to-morrow. He suggests that he and I go to Norfolk for a week to study the book and amend it where necessary. [...] It is a queer thing, now that the gloom about Britain's desperate fate which I have shared with R. has communicated itself to the City and to many of the provincial towns, I begin to feel it as a personal depression.

Thursday 26 January At 3 I met Michael Harmsworth at the Reform Club to hear of his adventures as a potential Tory candidate. He had seen Hacking for three minutes and been passed on to the Vice-Chairman, Lord Tololer[11] (or whatever the title of old Hennessy now is) who had received him gloomily. There were five hundred people on the waiting list, he was too young, constituencies did not like unmarried candidates ... 'That's all right,' said Michael, 'I'm married.' Not a word was said about his political convictions and eventually he was given a long form to fill in, requiring amongst other things the maiden name of his wife and a list of Peers or Members of Parliament or other influential persons who would support his candidature. The most important question, however, were whether he would pay all his own expenses and how much he would spend on the seat if he won it. He had not been impressed by Conservative headquarters.

Saturday 28 January H. Belloc (British Embassy, Paris) to C.B.
My dear Collin Brooks.
[...] I have been in Spain and had a great many experiences there. Among others I saw the battle in front of Barcelona two days before the town was occupied. The Red Forces crumpled up from loss of organisation. That was always their weakness, because anarchists and socialists do not make for good discipline. Also a very large proportion of their army by that time was disaffected, as the majority of the people even in Barcelona were against them, so that many of the conscripts had no stomach for fighting. [...]
P.S. The Franco people very much want English visitors to come and see their side of things. Hitherto nearly all the English publicity has gone to the other side. They know all about *you* and would be very

[11] George Richard James Hennessy (1877–1953): Con. MP Winchester 1918–31; PPS, Min. of Lab. 1920–2; Jnr. Ld. of Treasury 1922–44; Vice-Chm., Con. Party 1931–41; cr. 1st Bart. 1927, cr. Baron Windlesham, 1937.

pleased if you would come but do not know how to approach you, and I said I would write and suggest it to you. I really think it is worth watching, especially the reconstruction work they are doing on the social side, the forming of guilds and all that.

Sunday 29 January   Breakfast with R.. He agreed that Neville's speech was that of a frightened man, desperately wooing Mussolini. The Cabinet changes much engaged us. I was sceptical of the appointment of Chatfield's[12] being much good. After all, without his badges of rank he is a mild, inoffensive and not very forceful English gentleman with an interest in criminology. The appointment of Dorman Smith[13] pleased me. He is the first Mistery Man[14] to take Cabinet office.

Thursday 2 February   Hitler seemed to coo like a sucking dove – Chamberlain cooed back like a pouter pigeon – tonight they say Mussolini will roar like a lion. The Treasury has revalued its Bank gold holdings. Roosevelt has said that in war the frontiers of the USA are in France – depression gives place to temporary recovery.

Saturday 11 February   I am not to sail on Friday in the *Dominion Monarch*, but am to fly to Durban the following week and join the boat there. This should be an exciting trip. In all my early desires of seeing Africa I had not anticipated a flight from North to South. We spend a night in Khartoum. I am excited as a school boy.

Monday 13 February   had much to look to about the proofs of R's book. He had gutted a good deal of it and in a panic about its seeming too pro-Nazi had scrapped two chapters and added a purely patriotic ending. He has also taken out several passages about the opposition he encountered in the early days of his rearmament campaign which is a

[12] (Alfred) Ernle Montacute Chatfield (1873–1967): entered Navy 1886, Rear-Adm. 1920, Vice-Adm. 1930, Adm. 1935; 4th Sea Ld. 1919–20; 3rd Sea Ld. 1925–8; C. in C. Atlantic 1929–31, Mediterranean 1931–2; 1st Sea Ld. 1933–38; Min. for Co-ordination of Defence 1938–40; kt. 1918, cr. Baron Chatfield 1937.

[13] Reginald Hugh Dorman Smith (1899–1977): Con. M.P. Petersfield 1935–41; Min. of Agric. 1939–40; Gov., Burma 1941–6; kt. 1937.

[14] The Mistery was a 'masonic' splinter group. C.B. was a member of both the Grosvenor Kin (which met at Claridges) and the St James Kin. The Mistery's ideal was to recover some of the lost values of older England, and to nuture men of all classes who might be fitted to, or worthy of, leadership.

pity. It is now less a human document and more a broad sheet, less a statesman like survey of what national organisation *must* mean and more a mere fanfare of trumpets. But it is *his* book.

Tuesday 14 February   Breakfast with R. and Michael Harmsworth. At one o'clock back to Avenue Road where Douglas Jerrod came to lunch. He and R. and I had a very frank talk about Germany, with Morison as a silent fourth. D.J. thinks that I over-rate the destructive power of aircraft. He says that what differentiates Franco from any other Dictator is that he is a Christian and a solider. He thinks that Franco is less tied to the Axis than I suppose.

Wednesday 15 February   I had hardly been in the house ten minutes when Miss Stannard came up to say that Lord Londonderry was on the phone. I thought it a mistake, as I don't really know Londonderry except as a political host. But he it was. He was abed with 'flu and had telephoned to congratulate me on the Chamberlain book, which he had just finished. He said that the explanation of Hitler's off-hand treatment of Halifax at the time of the first visit was the folly of Halifax. Londonderry had pestered the Government to make some kind of visit to Hitler but had not been able to stir them. Even Chamberlain, he said, does not yet appreciate what Germany means, and certainly did not then. Much less Baldwin. When Halifax was invited to Munich sports he asked Londonderry if that might be an excuse for a talk with Hitler. Then – instead of making a first-class occasion of it – Halifax went with a single valet, whom he lost on the train, and apparently presented himself to Hitler as a rather vague person who wanted to talk generalities. Had the visit been properly arranged, the reception would have been different, and the course of policy altered. When I thanked him for telephoning he said that he considered I had done a great public service and that he and I were among the few who really were trying to present the real Europe to Britain. He asked if I could go up and have a talk with him. I explained that for two days I would be unable to do so, but that I could manage it next week. He then said he was leaving on Friday, so we arranged that I should phone him on Friday morning to say if I could dash up for half an hour to see him. After a jolly lunch at the Bolivar Grill, where I entertained Lil and Vivian and Edward – these two very thrilled by their surroundings which included an imitation old English brick fire-place and a smattering of BBC stars – I picked up from R. about £11,000 worth of bearer bonds and took them on to Douglas Hacking at his flat in Chelsea. Hacking, just up from a bad bout of 'flu, received the news that only

£11,000 and not the full £25,000 which had been promised was in the packet without a murmur, and said he would be grateful for the balance when R. cared to send it. R's reasons for not delivering the whole amount was that his income tax advisers thought it well not to pass out of his accounts income to the value of about £2,000 as the authorities would be curious as to where it had gone. Hacking, I fancy, was as little impressed by this explanation as I, but only said,

'I confess I don't quite follow his reasoning, but it isn't for me to dispute a man's method of making so large a donation.'

He said, 'What kind of receipt do you think he would like?'

'He wants no receipt to pass,' I answered.

'No. I can't agree to that.'

'Well, he certainly thinks you are honest, and he knows I am,' I assured him.

'What I shall do is this. The money will be banked in my name and that of — as joint trustees of the Fund. I shall tell him to get duplicate receipts from the bank, and send one to you. That will remove any possible suspicion that I may be a crook or that you may be ....'

On that we agreed. He was anxious to canvas [sic] my views about Europe, and my views about R's views. He was frankly pessimistical in a general way, but thinks Hitler will not make war. The Government will hold off an election as long as possible.

'The difficulty isn't the country, its the House. But the House is better than it was. It's becoming more unified.'

He thinks Neville Chamberlain could command a large majority at any time. He says that the apparent splits in the Labour opposition must not be taken seriously.

'I always feel that as Chairman of the Party I can only be influenced by our own programme and performance, and never by any supposed weakness in the others.'

I said, 'You mean that you must always fight on a positive thing, never on a negative,' to which he assented.

He was very critical of Chatfield's appointment as Minister of Coordination.

'I knew Chatfield years ago, when he was Fifth Sea Lord. He seemed to have a great reputation even then for drive. But in recent years he has grown very deaf, his mind has contracted. He is a nice, gentlemanly fellow, but no more than that. He suffers from being too gentlemanly.'

Of Dorman Smith he said, 'Well, I don't quite know how he will go over in the House. It was a strange appointment. It was tantamount to saying to the Farmers Union, "We can't handle the nation's agriculture, you come in and do it for us".'

I said that as evidence of Neville's readiness to step outside the coteries of the front bench the appointments had done good, to which, again, he agreed.

Thursday 16 February Round early to Avenue Road with page proofs of R's book. He lay abed and went through 'em while I at a side table advised and altered and tried to eat breakfast. He wanted a new shorter chapter on Munich, which I did during the morning. In the evening I went back at six and stayed for dinner. He is like a schoolboy with a new toy – an aquarium of little tropical fish that stands in the hall. These are something of a vogue and are very gay and delightful. During the day Hacking's co-trustee rang me to thank me for handing over the £11,000 and said he would send on the bank receipt. When I told R. this he said that no doubt Hacking and this noble Peer were afraid that they might be accused of being like old Lord Farquhar,[15] who robbed and muddled away not only Party funds but the trust funds of the Connaughts, who was reputed to be a millionaire when he was entirely insolvent.

Friday 17 February Last night R. and I did what he said would be his final corrections on *Warnings and Predictions* but at seven this morning he rang up and asked me to come round to him early. When I arrived he was up. De Valera[16] had made a speech about Irish neutrality, or its impossibility, and this affected R's book enormously. I gutted a chapter and arranged to write in another 'boosting Neville'.

Saturday 18 February: Norfolk Later: I finished the amendments to R's book and after lunch 'employed' Lil and Vivian to read it through for slips, errors and the like. Bond came with the car at six to say that the post left Holt early on Saturday. However, we pegged on, and at seven I was able to take the revised proofs to Holt and register them to Bungay. Just as I was parcelling them up another wire came from R. saying 'Urgent – keep out all reference my remarks submarines on crossing Atlantic.' The idea of Rothermere as a man of sudden decided dogmatic views is quite wrong. He is cautious to the last degree of nervousness. He wavers and havers. When this book first took complete

---

[15] Earl of Farquhar (1844–1923): Lib. Unionist MP Marylebone W. 1895–8; Con. Party Treasurer 1911–23; Ld. Steward 1915–22; cr. 1st Earl 1922.

[16] Eamon de Valera (1882–1975): Sinn Fein MP Clare E. 1917–21; member of Dail for Co. Clare 1921–59, Pres. of Dail 1919–22; Pres. Sinn Fein 1917–26; Pres. Fianna Fail 1926–59; Min. for External Affairs 1932–48; Taoiseach 1937–48, 1951–4, 1957–9; Pres. of the Republic of Ireland 1959–73.

shape it was about 300 pages of stern warnings and constructive advice: now it is about 200 pages many of which are the veriest patriotic 'blah' written in to prevent any attacks or 'come backs' by political opponents.

Monday 20 February This time next week, I suppose, I shall be approaching Khartoum. Whether the world goes up in flames in March or not, this voyage will have to be a turning point for me. I shall have to tackle R. about the future. The difficulty is to see a way of breaking loose from him without hurt to him. If I don't break loose, there is going to be no 'me' left. And, if he died suddenly, I should be left high and dry with my brood to support, having been out of the way of any recognised profession for two or three years I could make a few hundreds a year and Lil has a few hundreds a year, so we shouldn't starve. [...] Talking of the world going up in flames – the fear of a move in March has spread to Roosevelt. Should it happen I foresee a dramatic flight back from wherever I may be. The family has orders to bolt for cover to this remote spot. They should be alright. But I don't want to be thousands of miles from them, nor do I want to be thousands of miles from whatever unit would employ me. I would rather go under commanding a barrage of sixteen Vickers guns than be interned in some damned Pacific Port 'for the duration.' [...]

[Rothermere] had a touch of gastric flu and stayed abed [...] His touch of flu is awkward. I had arranged for him to give tea to Hacking on Thursday so that he could hand over the balance of the £25,000 that was the secret price of Cecil's peerage. He had to cry off and is to see Hacking to-morrow morning. If he isn't better both that and the conspiratorial dinner party will have to be cancelled – which will be a nuisance. I still cannot conceive why he didn't pay the whole sum over at once, when I took along the first £11,000, for neither Hacking nor I believe in his income tax fears. While we were away Cecil made his maiden speech in the Lords and actually achieved a small *Punch* caricature. R. says the Peerage has entirely rejuvenated him. 'I was very keen about his Peerage; I somehow felt I owed it to our mother ...' said R. As Cecil was disgracefully treated by Ll.George after being an admirable and devoted Junior Minister, I was myself pleased – but what a commentary on democracy that the thing was done as it was done, by my intervening after Greenwood had failed, and then really only by my recalling the precedent of Ronny McNeill to reinforce the payment to the Party Fund. Shameful.

[*Editorial Note*: On 24 February Brooks departed from Southampton by air for South Africa. The air route took him via Rome, Khartoum and Durban. The flight, by flying boat, was not without incident and included a forced landing at Port Elizabeth when the engines failed. In Cape Town he joined the Rothermere party, including the Ackroyds, Morison and Arthur Fuller. The return journey, via Maderia, was by sea aboard the *Windsor Castle* reaching Southampton in time for the Easter Weekend. A few days later on 15 April Brooks and Rothermere left Southampton, via Portugal, en route for Spain. They returned after three weeks. No diary was kept during these trips but an account is made during two long retrospective entries.]

Monday 22 May   Breakfast with R. at Avenue Road after a walk round the garden for an hour. He wanted me to lunch on the lawn, as it was a perfect Summer day, but I told him I must lunch at the Savoy to arrange things for his dinner tonight, so Dilly and I lunched in the Grill. The dinner was, I think, a towering success. The guests were: Lord Sankey, Lord Harmsworth, Charles Bruce-Gardner,[17] Douglas Hacking, Gerald Russell[18] (the solicitor), Anthony Harmsworth,[19] Professor Lindemann[20] (the inventor of the balloon barrage), Sir Mayson Beeton,[21] and myself, if I can be called a guest. After the waiters went the talk was very free. Bruce-Gardner told us of the improvements he had been able to make in the production of aircraft. He told me, personally, that he had just had a week in France with the French manufacturers. They had been very bad, but were now better. His view is that our curve of preparation is rising so swiftly that if there is no war before September, the Axis will not risk it. I told him that Hobson had told me that after Albania Catterns,[22] Deputy Governor of the Bank, had said that the odds were nine to one *on*. He says he never sees Catterns, his only touch is with the Governor and Henry Clay. Of Clay he spoke very highly. Sankey and Harmsworth – the Lord – became embattled about democracy and I delightedly cut in. Sankey having spoken of democracy as 'this rather troublesome system'

[17] Charles Bruce-Gardner (1887–1960): Controller of Lab. Allocation & Supply at Min. of Aircraft Prod. 1943–4; Chief Exec. for Ind. Reconstruction at BofT. 1944–5; kt. 1938, cr. 1st Bart. 1945.

[18] One of Rothermere's solicitors.

[19] Anthony (Perceval) Harmsworth (1907–68): barrister.

[20] Professor Frederick Lindemann (1886–1957): experimental pilot; Dir. of Physical Lab., RAF Farnborough 1914; Prof. of Experimental Philosophy, Oxford 1919–56; Personal Ass. to Churchill 1939–42; Paymaster Gen. 1942–5, 1951–3; cr. Baron Cherwell 1941, cr. Viscount 1941.

[21] Sir Mayson Beeton (d. 1947): Special Visiting Comm., West Indies for *Daily Mail* 1896; Pres., Anglo-Newfoundland Development Co. 1903–13; Administrator, Newfoundland Forestry Corps 1915–18; s. of Mrs Beeton, cookery writer.

[22] B.G. Catterns (1886–1969): Dep. Gov. of Bank of England 1936–45.

incautiously said, 'I believe in democracy, although it is no use in an emergency' which drew from me the challenge,

'Can you defend that! You believe in a system that is no good in an emergency!'

After some sparring he said 'Well what do *you* want?'

I said 'A Totalitarian England – with all its hard standards and clean ideals instead of muddle and mess and graft of our own system ...' and orated.

Lindemann, who says he is an Alsatian, but looks like a costive German Jew, sneered 'With Concentration camps complete?' – and that I dealt with.

Hacking said, 'Are you speaking of this as an ideal or as practical politics?'

To which I replied 'Both – both –' and went on with my oration.
... Actually, Sankey, despite his position as Labour ex-Lord Chancellor, patently despairs of democracy. He is for peace at any price. Hacking was very discreet. (R. this morning handed over the balance of the £25,000, which was the real price for Cecil's peerage, for which Hacking seemed very grateful). After the dinner ended, at about midnight, Russell, Bruce-Gardner, Anthony and R. and I were chatting in the corridor. Anthony told us a good story.

After the event Mussolini went to Hitler and cried, 'That's alright, Chief, I've taken Albania.'

Whereat Hitler roared, 'You bloody fool – I said "Take Rumania".'

In Rome the goose-step is called the Pas de Roma. The mot is, 'We have given up the Pass de Brenner for – the Pas de Roma.' It was very interesting that with the exception of Lindeman, there was no real opponent of some form of Right Wing reform of our own system. Lindeman oddly enough says that the night bomber cannot be beaten.

'You might get down three per cent, or even five per cent. If you could get down ten per cent they would not come.'

I said 'Why not?'

With great pity he said, 'Because in ten trips all their planes would have gone.'

To which I responded, 'That isn't so. If 10 per cent of a raiding party is outed, one has not lost ten per cent of one's forces...'

At which he blinked his pigmented circles of eyes for a moment and then conceded the point. B-G says that British types are now infinitely superior to anything the Germans have. In the corridor talk he also said that Hitler had not only missed his chance in September but that he was now intimidated.

Whereat R., in his solid way, said 'Bruce-Gardner, I don't agree. I'll tell you where your reasoning is unsound; since September we have had Prague, Albania and Memel-land.'

It was a good point, which B-G admitted.

Whit Sunday 28 May   Went over to the Lodge for luncheon, to meet Lady Downe. [. . .] Lady D and I exchanged reminiscences of Yorkshire fifteen years ago, when she declared that I had egged her on (sic) to Fascism because even then I was impatient with the official Conservative Party. [. . .] As we rose Lady D pleaded with R. for five minutes alone, to which he said, 'Certainly, come into the long room and talk to Collin Brooks and me,' which she gladly did. Her desire was to request in the *Mail* a column as a kind of open forum, with the idea of giving Mosley some publicity. She grew angry that a meeting of many thousands in the Free Trade Hall at Manchester could be entirely ignored by the national press. R. assured her that his retirement from newspapers was real, and she then said

'Why don't you start another Sunday paper and put this man in charge of it; look at the people who used to follow his weekly articles. More people are ready for your politics than you imagine. . . .'

We told her that a new paper to-day meant millions of capital – which isn't quite true – but she kept hammering on. She also said that she wanted R. to have Mosley down and give him some advice.

'Is he susceptible to advice?' I asked.

R. said, 'He wasn't. At the beginning of his campaign I gave him jolly good advice, and he wouldn't listen. I supported him very strongly, but I found he was on wrong lines. You know, I fear he isn't the adroit leader that Hitler or Mussolini is . . .'

However, at the end of a long talk it was agreed that Mosley should come down to Stody some night and that Lady D and I should be the other guests and the whole thing would be talked over.

Monday 12 June   Had Philip Farrer[23] to lunch at the Reform. He was glowing about *Can Chamberlain Save Britain?* and said that he and Chaplin[24] had sent dozens of copies to important people, including 'royalty'. He says that 'Buck House'[25] is very Right Wing and ardently pro-Neville. Lord Chaplin he avers is eager to meet me as he wants to get some kind of cohesion among the Right Wing people. I told him that tonight I would be dining with C and would fix a meeting between

[23] Philip Tonstall Farrer (1887–1966): served European war 1914–19; ADC British Military Mission, Albania 1919–20; Priv. Sec., Ld. Pres. of Council 1922–4, to Ld. Privy Seal & Leader of HofL. 1924–9, to 4th Marquess of Salisbury 1929–39.

[24] Eric Chaplin (1877–1949): suc. 2nd Viscount 1923.

[25] Meaning the King and his immediate entourage. The phrase is a play on words referring to Buckingham Palace.

the three of us. We agreed that David Woodford should have a seat found for him with some hope of winning it. At 6–30 I was at the BBC for a time rehearsal for my book talk at 7–30. I had twelve minutes on recent books and a man named George had five minutes on the 16th Century. He turned out to be a meek and inoffensive little man, like an elementary school master. After I had done my talk, I bolted precipitately for the Savoy. There I found Anthony Harmsworth already arrived. We drank sherry together until – in this order – the party assembled. First, our host Rothermere. Then Cecil (Lord) Harmsworth, Tom Mosley, Lord Chaplin, Shrimpton, the solicitor, Lord Philimore,[26] Oscar Hobson and Ernest Benn. Mosley sat on R's right, I next to him and Hobson next to me. Chaplin was on R's left, but before dinner I had a chance to talk with him. The dinner was good, the talk moderate. Mosley was very quiet, but towards midnight Cecil Harmsworth drew him out about how a national leader is found. Mosley was marvellous – very quiet, very expository, very modest, and very impressive.

Wednesday 15 June   Dined with Chaplin at the Carlton annex, with George Drummond[27] as the third member of the trio, as Philip Farrer couldn't come. Discussed the Right Wing situation thoroughly and the possibility of a newspaper.

Monday 19 June   Pegged away over the week-end at R's book, but not much progress. Had lunch with Philip Farrer at the Marlborough Club to-day. He is intent that he and I should be the Head-quarter brains of the Right Wing movement and should between us co-ordinate all the scattered efforts. He thinks Mosley would fall into line with this. Suggests that I run down to spend the night with Queenborough with him and should meet privately Lord Clive[28] and one or two other people who have been 'enthused' by *Can Chamberlain Save Britain?* To all this I agreed. Incidentally, I told him privately that it was a scandal that the Marlborough having banned *The Mirror* as a red and pornographic rag should house as a member the man responsible for it. That Cecil King[29] was responsible for it surprised him.

Later over tea at Avenue Road I said to R., 'How serious were you

[26] Lord Philimore (1879–1947): co-founder of the Imperial Policy Group, suc. 2nd Baron.
[27] George Drummond (1883–1963): banker; Chm. of Drummond's branch, Royal Bank of Scotland; High Sheriff of Northampton 1927; Member House of Keys 1946–51.
[28] Mervyn Horation Herbert Clive (1904–43): RAF Squadron Leader; suc. Bart. 1929.
[29] Cecil Harmsworth King (1901–87): journalist, Ed. & Dir.; Chm. of *Mirror Group*; Dir., Reuters 1953–9; Dir. Bank of England 1965–8.

when you said you'd take steps to have Cecil King's position drawn to the attention of the Marlborough?'

He heard of my action, and said (characteristically) 'You haven't told me anything about it ...' but during the afternoon returned with palpable glee to the topic. He says that Cecil Harmsworth, who is King's godfather and from whom he takes his name, said at a family dinner table that it would rejoice him to see King sent to jail for a year.

Friday 23 June   During my talk with R. this morning I told him that his proposed book *must* look like an attack on British *morale* and he has dropped it – to my great relief.

Tuesday 4 July   Borrowed R's car and went down at 10 to greet Tibor Eckhardt,[30] who is over for a day or two. He and I had lunch on the lawn with R. He says that Germany has 35,000 planes and 100,000 trained pilots. In September, he thinks, Germany had only about a fortnight's full supply of materials and munitions, but now has over six months' supply. He does not believe that Germany could win another war. He has seen Chatfield, Burgin[31] and others during his visit, but did not disclose why. I promised to arrange a meeting for him with Winston.

Wednesday 23 August   While we were in Monte Carlo R. fulfilled his intention of giving £50,000 to the Treasury for national defence. When he first told me of this in Paris he said if he gave this sum, following a recent £10,000, he could leave the country without people doubting his patriotism. He then said, a few days later, that as he pays 14/6 in the £ income tax and a huge amount in death duties he really wasn't giving anything. On the way back, in Paris, he was talking to Esmond on the telephone and told him that the £50,000 was really the money that Vivian and Vere, his two boys killed in the war, had left him, which he had kept for some suitable purpose. It was interesting to see his mental processes on these conflicting explanations. Actually I believe that the boys' money was actually used to found the two Harmsworth

---

[30] H.G. Tibor Eckhardt: Hungarian politican. On first meeting him in Budapest, Brooks noted that 'he is to Hungary exactly what Winston [Churchill] is to us, a man of great brilliance whose judgement is not trusted, a man who has somehow missed his real chance now and belied his promise'. Journal 23 October 1938.

[31] Leslie Burgin (1887–1945): MP Luton 1929–45 (Lib. until 1931 thereafter Nat. Lib.); P.S. BofT. 1932–7; Min. of Transport 1937–9; Min. of Supply 1939–40.

scholarships in their names, years ago. It is hardly likely that he would wait over twenty years for some suitable purpose. He probably feared Esmond's reaction to so large a sum being given away …

Thursday 24 August   Everybody is agreed that war is unthinkable – that ridiculous word – but the gulf between the British and the Hitlerian viewpoints is so wide that it really seems all but unavoidable. If it passes – the engines of destruction may become so many and so terrible that there will be no war for generations. […] Vivian last night arguing with me about solipsism turned idly to the topic of possible dictatorships here caused by war, saying that if the war lasted four years Neville would doubtless be dead before the end of it. We discussed a Mosley coup d'etat.

'In that event', said I, 'Tom Mosley will either make me Governor of the Central Bank or hang me for not displaying his colours in the early days of the struggle.'

Said Vivian, quite seriously, 'I don't think he'd hang *you*!' She then generously allotted me the joint job of Chancellor of the Exchequer and Minister of Propaganda … To irritate her vigorous anti-semitism I suggested that the most likely war dictator would be Hore-Belisha. She moaned and groaned and agreed, on the score that he had shown great energy and ability and as a Jew had reason for determination to fight Hitler to the last ounce of effort and perish rather than admit defeat. Incidentally, W-P told me yesterday that Sam Hoare talking to a group of editors said that the Russo-Germanic pact had really infuriated Italy and Japan, but begged them not to stress this, as English satisfaction would probably re-unite them.

Friday 25 August   News today seems more promising. Roosevelt has sent to Hitler and the President of Poland a plea for peaceful modes of settling their problems. This follows his message yesterday to the King of Italy. The Spaniards have taken umbrage at the Russo-German pact and are to be neutral. Japan angry and perturbed is reconsidering her policy towards Europe. In Britain, preparations go forward against the start of war … For me, I lie abed keeping my leg still.[32]

Friday 1 September, Norfolk   This, probably is THE date in the history of my times, and not as we supposed August 4th 1914. Because of the news that Germany this morning bombed Polish towns and the

---

[32] Suffering from a thrombosis – ordered to lay up for 3–4 weeks.

knowledge that before nightfall we, too, would be at war I have done nothing all day. I foolishly stayed awake until three am reading the new life of Edward Clarke,[33] so that today I have browsed on this and that, played cribbage with Austen, listened to news broadcasts – and waited. It is now 8–30 pm. I have yet to hear Chamberlain's speech, but the first sentences which were broadcast at about 6–30 were firm enough. My only real worry is for Rosemary, who may have to face terrors in London. Yesterday R. wired 'what do I owe you?' and I replied 'the only honest answer is nothing' and later elaborated it by letter. The danger has always been that I should become a paid lackey, as poor Harry Morison has become, and that I must avoid. When the new war is over – if I survive – I shall have to set about earning my living in a new job. By that time, it will be a different England, a different world. [...] I begin this bedfast with a swollen leg, damning the lighting rules which make us cover windows with thick curtains and so convert a lamp lit room into a furnace.

Sunday 3 September   So September 3rd and not September 1st becomes the great day in British history. Lying here in the remote country I felt with Arthur Greenwood that the delay was inexplicable – that 'planes should have been over Berlin the moment our protege was attacked. (W-P on the phone this morning said to me that Gort[34] desired that but Anderson[35] wanted as much time as possible to complete his evacuations and prepare his civil defences, and that Halifax was feared that France would 'rat' on the excuse of the Italian offer.) Last night there was the devil's own thunderstorm. A flash of lightening wakened me about five a.m. The type of flashes and peals was such that I thought it was a naval engagement off the coast. When the rain came, I was reassured and went off to sleep, leaving the storm to thunder itself out. There was no real news on the 8 a.m. broadcast, but at 10 – or 10–30 – we heard of the two hour ultimatum. The address of the Premier at 11–15 was simple and moving, his speech to the House equally so. Winston indulged in a piece of Churchillian rhetoric, with the ambiguous phrase 'while our hands are active, our consciences are at rest.' The news later of a war cabinet was not unexpected but it is

---

[33] Derek Walker-Smith and Edward Clarke, *The Life of Edward Clarke* (London: Butterworth, 1939).

[34] Gen. J.S.S.P.V. Gort (1886–1946): career soldier; C-in-C, BFF 1939–40; Chief IGS 1937–9; Gov. & C-in-C Gibraltar 1941–2, Malta 1942–4; High Comm. & C-in-C Palestine & Transjordan 1944–5; suc. 6th Viscount, later Field Marshal.

[35] Sir John Anderson (1882–1958): Ind. MP Scottish Universities 1938–50; civil servant 1905–32; Gov. of Bengal 1932–7; Ld. Privy Seal 1938–9; Home Sec. 1939–40; Chanc. of Exchequer 1943–5; cr. Viscount Waverley 1952.

horribly old – Hankey, Churchill and Chatfield were in their prime at the outbreak of the last war, and Neville is over 70. The King's broadcast was well heard, but was too palpably read. His hesitation of speech was not very marked.

Monday 4 September   I forgot yesterday to jot down a phone talk with Ward Price, who said that an expeditionary force is going over – or is over – and that 20 correspondents are allotted to it. This is three times as many as for the last show. He is to go for the D.M., and the *Evening News* is also to have a man. He said that France almost 'ratted' when the Italian offer of a conference came in. Gamelin[36] said a good thing.

'If the Italians come in against us, we shall need 5 divisions to defeat them; if they are neutral, we shall need ten divisions to watch 'em; if they come in with us, we shall need 15 divisions to reinforce 'em.'

Fleet Street, he says, is calm. This time most of the younger men are in khaki and the Press Club is like an estaminet behind the lines, with everybody getting very tight.

Tuesday 5 September   In Wales a woman has been fined £25 for refusing to billet children. The people here – have something of the grasping nature of the peasant – largely look on the evacuation as a means of making a bit out of the wretched children, who made Lilian weep last night, so pathetic had they been. Stripped of propaganda 'guff' ones fellow countrymen do not stand out as glorious or generous creatures in villages. Townspeople are, I am sure, more gracious, and the West Coast has a better type of citizen than the East.

Saturday 9 September   Ward Price telephoned me this morning and came in for a late cup of tea this afternoon. He says that the Ministry of Information is one glorious muddle. Esmond Harmsworth is Chairman of the Newspaper section. He is a decorative but useless person. He has as his deputy Tom Clarke, a good fellow, who has been out of practical journalism and at the head of a diploma course for a decade or so. The Ministry cannot be made to understand that a newspaper has a time for going to Press. In consequence news is given to the BBC for the 9 o'clock broadcast which misses the provincial editions of the London papers. Lord Perth summoned the editors – snatching them away from urgent business, for they are harassed by 8 page papers in

---

[36] Gen. Maurice Gamelin (1872–1958): French C-in-C until 20 May 1940.

lieu of the normal 20's – kept them waiting half an hour and then gave them an elementary lecture:

'I – ah – know nothing about newspapers. But I believe that you have an institution called – ah, ah – the headline ah, ah, ah! Well, don't make the headlines too sensational. And don't – ah – invent any news . . .' and so on, to the great anger, disgust and horror of his highly skilled and mature auditors.

In addition to its other follies, the Ministry of Information refuses to give foreign correspondents information as to its telephone number! One Spanish correspondent, serving forty nations that read Spanish, not only complains that he can't get information, but must write his stuff in either French or English, which he does badly, which is then retranslated at the other end back into Spanish, so that it isn't *his* stuff at all. Meanwhile, Germany is said to be feeding neutral correspondents with all the information they want and that Germany desires them to have. London, says W.P., is pathetic. Bond Street with its jewellers shops emptied of jewels and the boards to the windows makes him feel that it will never re-open as Bond Street, that this is indeed the end of an epoch.

He said, sadly, 'By the end of this war we'll have the bloody Proletariat in command, Greenwood as Premier, and nobody allowed to have more than ten quid a week.'

I assured him that I thought that was certain, and that it would be a different system entirely, and probably a better one. He glumly agreed. R. has kept me busy. First he would hold his book indefinitely. Then he would have 25 copies bound. Then 1500 copies and publish at the end of the war in two months time!!! Then he would add two pages of postscripts on a patriotic note – which I wrote, read to him on the phone, and shot off to the printers – and then, to make things amusing, the *T.L.Supplement* yesterday actually reviewed it, from a copy Cave had lent 'em. This caused R. great perturbation. Three times he rang from Dornoch and was three times cut off. At length he wired. He has sent a window-dressing telegram to Winston, pleading with him to bomb, torpedo or capture the Bremen, but on the phone this morning he was positively exultant about the alleged German seizure of Poland, which he said was 'the quickest thing on record.' He is still englamoured by Hitler, and cannot believe that a nation which has not employed R. or Esmond in its counsels can possibly be any good or be in any way prepared. His insistence that South Africa would not come in has been proved false; his declarations that evacuation would be a fiasco, falsified; his sneers at the Air Force, falsified. It is a pity that one who has been so right on most things should be so wrong about his own people.

Monday 25 September Yesterday I had a relatively busy day for a convalescent. Philip Farrer came down to see me for an hour, and brought a young man of High Tory principles, but a charming manner, with him. P.F. is anxious to get Neville with a Right Wing view of the dangers of a major war … the prospect of the collapse of civilisation … of a revolt to the Left. I warned him that the mood of the masses now was to end Hitler and risk chaos. […] When R. rang up from Dornoch to canvass my views on the news I told him of P.F.'s visit and project, and he was at once on fire to write a letter to Neville in the same strain. Would I draft it and read it over the phone to him 'in the morning.' This morning however, he said he'd think about it later – to my great relief, for I think anything of that kind in writing might damn a man for ever. Britain is in no mood for peace until Hitler has been dealt with, and whatever high motives may be behind a peace move it would be misunderstood, as Lansdowne's[37] was in the last war. I will insert the draft in this diary later, when he has made up his mind whether or not it is to be sent.[38]

Friday 6 October today there has been the shadow of Hitler's speech. R. rang me from Dornoch, saying he thought it would have a good reception here. I said it would put British backs up – that it was a repetition of 'my last territorial claim' and was too damned unctuous. He said

'Ah, but we're a very unctuous people,' to which I answered,

'That makes it worse. We are allowed to say that God is on our side, but the other fellow mustn't.'

Sunday 15 October R. arrived. He was close muffled in a white muffler and swathed in a heavy coat. He looks less robustious than normally, but was in good form. He had had what breakfast he now took, he said, but thought he'd drink half a cup of tea. So we each drank two cups of tea and talked about the war. He still ranks Germany and Hitler high. He thinks Hitler and Stalin[39] may have a world plan of conquest, that Stalin, a Caucasian, may have been pumped full of

[37] Reference to the letter written in 1916 suggesting the need for a negotiated peace. The author was Henry Charles Keith Petty-Fitzmaurice Lansdowne (1845–1927): Under-Sec. for War 1972–4; Under-Sec. for India 1880; Gov.-Gen. Canada 1883–8; Viceroy of India 1888–94; Sec. of War 1895–1900; For. Sec. 1900–5; Min. without Portfolio 1915–16. suc. 5th Marquess 1866.

[38] See Appendix D for 'draft'.

[39] Joseph Stalin (1879–1953): Gen. Sec. of the Central Ctte. of the Soviet Communist Party 1919–53; Chm. of the Council of People's Commissars 1941–6.

South-Eastern ambition – with India as the final objective – and that Hitler has egged on the round-up of the Baltic countries.

'Hitler knows that when the great breach comes in, say, five years, Germany can count on the Scandinavians, the Russianised Poles, and probably Britain. He knows that the Russian Army won't stand against German troops...'

All this I assented to as a feasible theory, but said, 'This is war. Strange things happen in war. As late as 1918 people told me Britain had lost the last war. But Britain is the most tenacious of all nations. It is true that we may emerge from victory or defeat a Bolshevised country, but it isn't true that we are foredoomed to defeat. Let us have a first class show on the Western Front, and then we shall have a basis for judgement...'

To this he assented, and added, 'The U Boat campaign has failed. That is one of the things that hasn't "come off." I admit that.'

On the whole, however, he believes that Britain is 'finished'. I remarked that she had been 'finished' so often, and lent him the life of Nicholson.

'You'll find there just how brutal and cruel and hard a Briton can be in times of stress. We may throw up five million John Nicholsons when we need them. In any event, it will be better to be skinned dead than to be skinned alive.'

After which patriotic outburst we diverged to other topics.

Tuesday 17 October   R. was in good form. During our drive he discussed the project of his – that means us – writing another book about his attempt to re-arm Britain and said I ought to publish another book shortly. I kept mum about the autobiog. which probably nobody will publish.

Wednesday 8 November   The news today has livened up a little. Last night Queen Wilhelminia[40] and King Leopold[41] issued an offer to mediate; Halifax, preaching like a thick-voiced High-Church curate, restated Britain's war aims on the radio. The general response to the mediation offer seems to be that if Germany wants peace she can have it – by kicking out the Hitlerite thugs.

[40] Queen Wilhelminia (1880–1962): Queen of the Netherlands 1898–1948; suc. Father 1890 with Queen Emma acting as Regent.
[41] King Leopold III (b. 1901) Belgian King 1934–51, exiled following German invasion May 1940 but not allowed to return to throne after the war; abdicated in favour of son.

Tuesday 14 November   I arrived punctually at the Carlton Club Annexe, and was ahead of my host. Robert Kindersley[42] is about six feet one, looks twenty years younger than his 69 years, and was very 'matey' from the beginning of the encounter. We discussed the state of trade and agreed that the 'gap' is the only thing that matters. He says he would have introduced rationing of all foods immediately because of foreign exchange, and thinks Shakespeare Morrison should have stressed that attitude even as Minister of Food. He thinks Morrison has had rather a raw deal, being called a failure at the Ministry of Agriculture and at the Food Ministry when really he has had impossible tasks. I said I liked him, but having heard him stand at the Treasury table and discuss finance like a fourth form boy in an idiot school, I had not now much opinion of his ability. K then said that he really wanted to thank me for my pamphlet,[43] which had been slightly amended, but only slightly, and would be going into 8,000,000 homesteads. [...] After luncheon over my coffee – for he took none and said that after smoking for forty-seven years a heart trouble had caused him to give it up – we talked personalities and finance again, until he said that what he really wanted to meet me for, 'and I'll be quite frank', was to say that with the oncoming loans his department might expand a lot, and he would feel happier if he knew he could approach me to take a position with him for the duration of the war. 'Remuneration on your scale may be difficult, but these things can always be got over.' I told him what I had already told Buckie Taylor,[44] and he said he quite saw that I wanted to do something more national than advising a millionaire. He then said he would write when the expansion took place, and I said that if there was a definite end to the suggestion would he write also. He said yes. We strolled to Pall Mall together and parted amicably.

Tuesday 21 November   I refused lunch with R., but went round for a cocktail at noon. He told me he has to leave for S. Africa on Saturday, to fight an income tax case, and is leaving me to write the book and publish it without further reference to him – an odd mark of confidence.

---

[42] Robert Molesworth Kindersley (1871–1954): company dir.; merchant banker; Pres., National Savings Ctte. 1920–46; Dir., Bank of England 1914–46; Senior Rep., Dawes Ctte. 1922; member Bankers' Ctte. on German Finance 1921–5; cr. Baron 1941.

[43] The subject of the pamphlet was thrift and it was prepared for the National Savings Committee.

[44] W. Buchanan-Taylor: acting publicity director for Twentieth Century-Fox Films until 1940; early 1900s involved with Lyons; Hon. Publicity Adviser, National Savings Ctte. from 1940; post-war publicist for Bertram Mills circus.

Thursday 23 November   I was to lunch David Woodford. R. suggested that I might take him to Avenue Road, if two other guests could be shuffled off, but it ended in David drinking a sherry there and then coming with me to le Jardin des Gourmets, where I did him and myself well. He was full of news. Eric Olyer[45] is acting as kind of ADC to Munster,[46] who gave up minor office to act as Gort's ADC. Gort is very sound on 'Mistery' principles. We are to have access to the GHQ 'bag' that comes and goes with a 'Greyhound'. Leslie Hore-Belisha is terribly unpopular. On his visit to the front which has just ended he arrived arrayed like a Bond Street bum-boy, even wearing spats. They took him through all the mud they could find and tired him out. At the Chateau there were two privies, one upstairs which was civilised with running water and one outside which was primitive. They concealed from His Majesty's Secretary of State the existence of the civilised one, so that he excreted in extreme discomfort. While there he repeated some remark that Winston, he said, had made in a Cabinet .... 'he said you were established here in austere security, an austerity which doesn't suit the younger members of the Staff' ... which annoyed somebody coming from this pushing Jew-boy. It was taken up with Neville Chamberlain, who denied that Winston had ever made such a remark. It is said that several 'higher-ups' waited on Gort and said that H-B had got rid of the people who had to go, but had done it in a particularly dirty way.

'It was a swine's job and he did it like a swine, but now his use is finished ...'

Gort almost wept over them, saying, 'I know exactly what you feel, and I feel it, too, but he "made" me – and what can I do?'

Sunday 3 December, Norfolk   I wish I had time to log here the machinations of the Princess [Hohenlohe] and the full reasons for the urgent haste of this new book – begun one Monday and sent to press in seventeen days – In going over his files I found one letter which might be awkward if she published her photostats. It is Ribbentrop, denying that he, R., ever intrigued with the Crown Prince [of Hungary] for a restoration, and saying 'You know I have always been a fervent admirer of the Fuhrer ...' In war, the populace gets angry with fervent admirers of the arch-villain.

[45] Capt. Eric U. O'Brian Olyer: Royal Regiment of Artillery. Appointed Personal Assistant to General Gort, 4 September 1939.

[46] Geoffrey William Hugh FitzClarence 'Boy' Munster (1906–75): Ld.-in-Waiting 1932–8; Paymaster-Gen. 1938–9; PUS for War 1939; ADC & Priv. Sec. to Gen. Gort 1939–40; PUS for India & Burma 1943–4; suc. 5th Earl 1928.

Saturday 9 December, London   On Tuesday I managed to see Gerald Russell[47] at 11, and to discuss the future movements of the Princess, and then to go to an urgent appointment to see Robert Kindersley. He was charming, and said that he could, he thought, persuade the Treasury to pay me £1,250 a year if I would come to him for that.[48] I said I would if he would allow me a reservation – that I must look into my affairs first and I must get R's formal as well as his tacit assent. I wired R. who said 'of course you must accept' but asked me to serve for no pay, allowing him to make up the amount.

Thursday 28 December   What am I to say about the National Savings Committee. On the Wednesday after my return from the North, Kindersley launched me by lunching thirty-two editors at the Savoy, which was jolly, for I met old friends. But inside the organisation I find a war between Buchanan-Taylor and Leslie,[49] the two honorary advisers, plus their satellites and the permanent officials. The officials are very 'civil service' – they go in awe of the Treasury – they think first of why not to do things. The incomers are 'peppy' and crude and forceful. I, waiting for a Fleet Street office, considered the battle, and stood aside, except when Bucky Taylor asked me to straighten out one tangle and insisted on two nights on cracking a bottle of champagne at some theatrical hostelry near the Hippodrome. Kindersley seems a grand fellow – very earnest, very efficient, very over-worked. On the whole, the life suits me. To-day we have been interviewing applicants for jobs in my new office, where I hope to begin work properly next week. It is amazing the poor quality of applicants, even with wartime unemployment. [. . .] R's affairs have kept me fairly busy. A strange side-light was supplied by a letter from Paul Einzig this morning. Here it is:
[. . .]

You may or may not be amused to learn that I had a hand in hastening the departure of Princess Hohenlohe from these shores. I heard some time ago towards the end of December that the Home Office was considering her deportation but was reluctant to take a decision for fear of suggestions that they did it in order

[47] R's solicitor/lawyer.
[48] His position was Honorary Press (Editorial) Director of National Saving Ctte.
[49] Samuel Clement Leslie (1898–1980): lecturer in philosophy 1922–5; Publicity manager, Gas Light and Coke Co. 1936–40; Hon. Publicity Adviser, Nat. Savings Ctte. 1939–40; Home Office 1940–5; Dir., Council of Industrial Design 1945–7; Head of Information Div., Treasury 1959; member Northern Ireland Development Council 1955–65.

to please your lord and master. I persuaded George Strauss,[50] therefore, who as you know is an extreme Left Wing Socialist and cannot be suspected of wanting to please Lord Rothermere, to put down a question. Several others had tried it before but had not passed the Clerk of the House. I managed to word the question in a way in which it had to be accepted. Quite a number of people tried to persuade Strauss to withdraw his question. One of the arguments with which they sought to soften his heart was that Princess Hohenlohe's son was put down for British diplomatic service and his mother's deportation would wreck his career. Strange as it may sound, in spite of this unanswerable argument Strauss persisted, and the Home Office jumped at the opportunity to drop a gentle hint leading to the voluntary departure of Princess Hohenlohe.

Gerald Russell's detectives picked the Lady up in New York when she landed from the Dutch boat, but as they want $75 a day we are taking the shadows off her, and merely having a weekly report as to her whereabouts. So far the reviews of R's *My Fight to Rearm Britain* have been good. Everybody now seems to realise that the nation owes him a true debt both for the rearmament campaign and the attempts to keep Germany and Britain in some kind of accord. To-day there arrived from Port Said a long memo from him – posted on the 16th – retelling his policy with regard to Hitler, and covered by a letter asking me to keep it by me 'in any case it will be useful for my memoirs', by which I think he means his biography by Boswell-Brooks.

[50] George Russell Strauss (1901–93): Lab. MP Lambeth N. 1929–31, 1934–50; Lambeth Vauxhall 1950–79; Jnr. Min. 1945–7; Min. of Supply 1947–51, cr. Baron. 1979.

1940

Sunday 7 January   This threatens to become a weekly log-book, instead of a daily diary. [...] Last Sunday Gordon[1] of the *Sunday Express* was to have published an article by Kindersley, which he returned to us with the plea that if Kindersley said people were not to spend money on luxuries, the advertisers would be angry. He suggested K should amend the article accordingly. After some trouble we managed a compromise, and the amended version was published to-day. Gordon's letter contained this heart wail: 'I don't want to do anything that is going to hamper my advertising. After all, that is our life line and thank God it has been better than we anticipated.' In other words, let the nation lose the war, let inflation with all its miseries come upon us, but for the love of God don't let us offend some fat Jew who wants to sell quite unnecessary goods through our advertising columns. We deserve defeat. [...] I gave a sherry to D[avid]W[oodford] on Wednesday evening. He had lunched with Eric Olyer, who had been acting as a kind of extra ADC to the King in France. The King is still imbued with a kind of family Liberalism, but is palpably turning towards the Right. When Chamberlain was in France he and Gort and the High-Ups had some frank talks. He told bluntly some home truths about Hore-Belisha .... with the result that yesterday there was announced the 'resignation' of the Minister of War. The popular Press, of course, has made a song and dance about the democratic Minister being sacrificed to the Brass Hats, but there is no doubt, from what one knows that the Jew is better out than in, and so I think most people think. [...] Reviews of R's book continue appreciative. P.F. still feels that with R and Q both of our type of political thought we ought to strive towards a new Daily, which the Argus Press, through the good offices of Burton-Baldry and Ned Foster, would produce for us at a cut rate. I am not so certain that this is either desirable or practicable as long as we are at war, but it certainly seems the right line of development when peace comes. Although – before peace comes there will be many changes, that may affect us all dramatically.

---

[1] John Rutherford Gordon (1890–1974): Ed. *Sunday Express* 1928–34; Dir. of Beaverbrook Paper 1931–69; Trustee of Beaverbrook Foundation.

Sunday 21 January For a fortnight I have been trying to make some kind of entry in the Log book – but to no avail. Even now, I am sitting at a type-writer with a snuffly nose, a hot head, burning eyes ... after three days abed. The first real event worth chronicling was the Mansion House speech of Neville a week last Tuesday. He spoke indifferently well. I am told the reception over the broadcast was better than in the Hall, but those in the Hall were enlivened by the fusing of a lamp in a batten just over his head, which set fire to a beam. For a moment or two it looked ugly ... but Neville, conscious of his duty to the microphone, spoke on, while agitated officials on the floor waved the blazing batten down and others in the balcony waved it up. Up it went at last, and was put out without a fuss. [...] There was great hope that N would say something of the sacking of Hore-Belisha, but he did not. The town is agog with rumours. The Jews say H-B has gone before a wave of anti-Jewish prejudice. The Right-wing say that he has 'sold' contracts to his racial friends. The truth, I believe, is that he grew bumptious and cocky with office, and became just an impossible person with whom to work. [...] The Hore-Belisha debate went off very calmly. The Press almost without exception tried to make a martyr of H-B and to down Neville, but they over-did it. The public reacted. It was generally realised that a Prime Minster had a right to chose his own colleagues.

Sunday 11 February Three weeks gap this time [...] My pocket engagement book is a good remembrancer of one or two things ...

Friday Feb. 2nd 1940. Lunched Arthur Mann at the Waldorf. He had aged, but was still virile and much the same in manner. His attitude to me seemed to have changed. He was flattering. Once he said, grumbling about Neville, 'He is incapable of recognising new men, like Beveridge[2] or Keynes or yourself ...' If it hadn't been A.H.M. I should have laughed. His story of how Chamberlain snubbed him was amusing. He entered Neville's room, and to break the ice said, "I'm afraid, Mr Prime Minister, you don't regard me as a friendly critic..." Neville said, with palpable annoyance and contempt, "Oh, I'm much too busy to read the provincial newspapers."

At one point Arthur said, "With great respect, Mr Prime Minister, I must say I think your policy invites aggression ..."

Then, to his – but not my – amazement, Neville looked at the

[2] William Beveridge (1879–1963): 2nd S. & P.S. Min. of Food 1919; Dir. LSE 1919–37; author of Beveridge Report (1942) on social insurance.

clock and said, "I'm afraid I have an appointment at 11–15, and it is now 11–14."

[...] Kindersley finds the way to Neville is always blocked, and others tell me that Horace Wilson is the difficulty. Mann's view, he having known Neville since his early Birmingham days, is that Neville is essentially a man of narrow mind, impervious to new ideas, and very jealous of other men's talent. This confirms H.G. Well's view that Neville's mediocrity compels him always to appoint mediocrities, and, for choice, familiar mediocrities. On the broad political field there is little new. The Hore-Belisha scandal has faded to nothingness. [...] In my new capacity I have wrangled myself back on the lobby list. Meeting Einzig at the Keynes dinner I heard from him that he spends most of his time in the Lobby, so I promised to look in soon. On Friday I managed half an hour there, and was warmly welcomed in the little tea bar by Nixon, of the *Birmingham Post*, Holdsworth, of the Y.P., the *Daily Post* man, whose name I always forget, and Hurlyhea[3] (if that is his horrid name) the Honorary Secretary of the Lobby Group. I was also greeted warmly by Turnbull, who must now be almost the father of the Lobby. It was odd to be back there, after twelve years' absence. The House seemed more than ever shoddy to me. My prejudices go deep I find ...

Thursday 14 March   C.B. to Norman Watson (carbon)
After I had been laid aside, I wrote to old Kindersley suggesting that I should resign the National Savings job, and make room for a fitter man. I fancy he won't hear of it – which is a pity. Like all Civil Service work, it is a disappointment. The idea of a running stream of pamphlets, of innumerable articles by celebrities poured into the eager columns of the Press, was a folly. It boils down to endless committees, of great fears about 'what the Treasury will say', what questions will be asked in the House, of guarded jealousies, of routine items for the trade journals ... of time wasting ... Had I been a highly paid official, as I nearly became, I should have felt in honour bound to resign a couple of months ago.

Sunday 17 March   Clark telephoned me on Friday that R would reach London that evening. After some thought and talk with Lil, I decided to go up and greet him. I waited in the hall [of the Savoy] for R. As he came through the swing doors I was shocked to see how old and

[3] Gerald Hurleagh: Hon. Secretary, Lobby group; PA for Lobby group 1941.

tired and 'shrunk' he looked. He seemed glad to see me. To my 'how are you? are you better?' he said, 'I nearly petered out – but don't tell the doctor.' Dr Liston was hard on his heels.

Friday 12 April   No diary writing for many days, during which the Germans have invaded Denmark and Norway. [. . .] Yesterday, waiting for the Lobby to fill after Winston's speech, I sat in the little room given to Lobby journalists and jotted down in pen and ink a few momentary impressions. [. . .]

> 11 April 1940 It is just after 4 o'clock. Churchill is in the Chamber upstairs making his statement on the Norweigan naval battle. The lobbies and tea rooms are deserted. From the minor lobby one catches a glimpse of a House packed to its capacity, with Members wedged at the bar like spectators at the public games. As I drove to the House the streets were lined with people. My taxicab halted to let past a car filled with naval 'brass hats', detectives and a smiling Winston. It sped so swiftly that the mob had no time for cheers, although recognition ran through the ranks as a wind passes through corn. [. . .] The little old lady who serves tea in the Lobby bar said,
> 'There's something about a naval action that stirs the blood as nothing can do on land or in the air; although perhaps it isn't so to the younger generation!'
> But I think it is so. With news that the Fleet was engaged there was a palpable stiffening of morale. Everywhere, in the streets and in office lifts, there was a new satisfaction in this strange war.

[. . .] I ought to add a line or two to my House of Commons notes. After the speech, Members and journalists alike thought Winston's speech disappointing but Broadbent of the *Mail* said it had an undertone of confidence. A little later Winston left the Chamber and crossed the Lobby. He is a great showman. He stood in the porchway talking to Admiral Keyes, while he took snuff with the attendant. (There has always been a convention of snuff taking with the attendant and his predecessors.) He then moved slowly across the Lobby, looking bent and tired, and like a man who was getting no sleep – but smiling . . .

Thursday 18 April   Incidentally, John Bingham, now in Military Intelligence and seeking out traitors, looked me up yesterday and enlisted me as a listening post. It was rather like a cheap detective novel.

Sunday 28 April The Press and, presumably, the people are now beginning to realise that the war in Norway is not to be the gallant picnic they first thought it, when Narvik rivalled a Nelson exploit in mens minds. The Black Week in South Africa, the retreat from Mons, and further back the muddle of the Crimea and Corunna – all goes according to plan, the British plan of starting a war ill equipped, badly led and thoughtlessly envisaged. Let us hope it will end as the others ended, in victory snatched from the jaws of defeat. On St George's day Winston failed to appear to address the St George's Society luncheon and a chain of Empire radio listeners. Duff Cooper deputised for him. 'A giant's robes upon a dwarfish thief ...' There was something nauseating in the spectacle of that small, pimp-like, dapper Parliamentarian abusing Bismarck like a fish-wife. After the luncheon I smoked a cigarette with Q, who is still intent upon getting R and others to form a Trust to transform the Society into a more definite political instrument. [. . .] On Budget Day I haunted the Lobby, having arranged to meet Kindersley when the speech was over. I had a chat with Walter Layton, growing more mellow as the years pass, and as usual very 'chummy' to me in private however horrific in print. Kindersley gave me three examples this week of his innate ineptitude. The first was a paragraph which I wanted him to give to the Press immediately after the Budget. This was of about three short sentences. He and Kingham[4] and I wrestled with it all that morning, and he and I for half an hour that evening. The next day Jobson of the Ministry of Information wanted 500 words from him following Simon's Broadcast speech. I spoke to Kindersley over the phone, and he thought he couldn't do it, as these things must be done well and so should take time. Refraining from reminding him that the 1500 words of *Times* leader on the Budget had been managed somehow, I overcame his reluctance, and wrote the 500 words, They were for use in obscure provincial papers. In the evening he and I and Theodore Chambers[5] sat over them for a couple of hours, and K said he would like to sleep on them. The next day he phoned 500 words to his typist with the request that Kingham should vet them, so Kingham and Jones and I sat over them again for about an hour. Thus, 500 commonplace words, which a leader writer would have knocked off well in twenty minutes or so, occupied one highly trained leader writer, one Director of the Bank of England, one company chairman, two highly paid civil servants some five hours of time!! It is incredible. On a Broadcast talk of seven minutes he also took three days of preparation. It is no wonder Keynes doubts the

---

[4] Robert Dixon Kingham (1883–1966): secretary Nat. Savings Ctte. 1937–46; kt. 1945.
[5] Theodore Chambers (1871–1957): Sec. & Controller National Saving Ctte. 1916–19, Vice-Chm. 1919–43; Vice-Pres. 1943.

efficacy of the voluntary savings system. I note this in passing as an excellent example of how Britain tries to win a war against highly organised, skilled and speedy antagonists. If Kindersley is like this with us, the thousands of other Kindersleys who abound must be like that in the other services. I had breakfast with R on Wednesday and an early cup of tea at 9–30 on Thursday. He says that whereas the Germans are fighting in Norway in white equipment and snow shoes, our poor wretches haven't a snowshoe between 'em. Winston, he repeats, is rattled and drinking more heavily even than usual. There is, he declares, a move to 'get out' Ironside,[6] Newall[7] and Pound[8] as being no good. This I hear also from other sources. I had lunch with King, of the *Financial News*, on Friday. He says that the City thinks the Budget bad, and full of the potentialities of inflation. On the other hand, he says that the younger generation of whom he is one are now convinced of the rightness of the war, whereas two years ago they would have been pacifist.

Tuesday 30 April   Had an aperitif with Peter Kemp[9] before lunch. We met at the Warldorf, and in the quietude of the Palm Court he told me of how he and five other officers set off in a submarine with Bren guns and ammunition to slink into Norway and make their way to a Norwegian force ... but were torpedoed a few hours out.

'I was sleeping in the Diesel room ... a magnetic torpedo burst some yards ahead and another some yards astern ... we were able to limp back ... the Norwegian force has been scuppered but we prepared an alternative plan ... they sent for us to the War Office and gave us seven days leave that none of us wanted ...'

Thursday 2 May   In the evening, having failed to contact Oliver Baldwin for dinner, I took Vivian and Rosemary to see Gielgud in 'Lear'.[10]

---

[6] Field Marshal Edmund Ironside (1880–1959): career soldier; Chief of the Imperial Gen. Staff 1939–40; C-in-C Home Forces 1940; cr. 1st Baron 1941.

[7] Cyril Newall (1886–1963): Marshal of the RAF, Chief of Air Staff 1937–40; cr. 1st Baron Newall 1946.

[8] Sir Dudley Pound (1877–1943): Adm. of the Fleet; C-in-C Mediterranean 1936–9; Chief of Naval Staff 1939–43.

[9] Peter Mant MacIntyre Kemp (b. 1915): journalist and soldier; Cambridge University graduate; 1936 *Sunday Dispatch* war correspondent, Spanish Civil War; joined Nationalists Spanish Foreign Legion; 1939–46 Commando with Special Operations Executive, including missions to Norway, Albania, Poland, Far East; as foreign correspondent expelled from Hungary 1956 during uprising; author several autobiographical book including *Mine Were of Trouble* (Cassell, 1957) which was dedicated to C.B.

[10] *King Lear* by William Shakespeare. Performed at Old Vic Theatre from 15 April 1940 to 25 May 1940. It ran for 38 performances. Reviewed *The Times* 16 April 1940.

None of us had seen 'Lear' played before. The Old Vic was full. We could only get standing room in the Pit for ninepence, and stood it out. To me it was like going back twenty five years. To them it was an experience to see a play in physical discomfort. Gielgud was excellent. Jessica Tandy was terrible. The others were more than good. Lewis Casson as Kent was especially good, his excellent voice and technique almost acting the rest off stage. I had not realised how macabre is the scene in the hovel. Robert Harris[11] as Edgar was a magnificent Tom-a-Bedlam, and Stephen Haggard[12] as the Fool better than the critics had led me to suppose, though he 'read' the role as a simpleton, and not as a whimsical wiseacre. Gielgud managed in the early scenes to suggest a great breadth of shoulder and a roaring majesty, which his natural physique and mannerisms did not promise. In the mad scenes he was reminiscent of his own Shylock, but always impressive and convincing. If his voice lacks a certain rotundity, he uses it well. Not again shall I believe that Lear is unplayable. The whole episode was a true Old Vic adventure, for we ate sandwiches in an inn hard by the theatre before the play, and had to scrum through the black-out to Waterloo station for a hackney coach after it.

Friday 3 May   Under all talk runs the threnody for Norway. What fools we British are at the beginning of any war, is the kind of reflection on most people's lips, with a snarl at Chamberlain. Poor Chamberlain has had more of 'Hosanna to-day; crucify him to-morrow' than anybody since Christ I should imagine – not that he is a particularly Christ-like person.

Wednesday 8 May   Yesterday's debate on Norway was fierce. Labour is not to press a vote of confidence.

Thursday 9 May   Labour pressed a vote of confidence. The speeches so far have been venomous against Chamberlain, with Lloyd-George particularly vitriolic. This is he who refused to aid our rearmament campaign in 1935–37 and told R that 'the case for British rearmament has not yet been made out.' Chamberlain's small majority amounts to a defeat.

---

[11] Robert Louis Anstruther Harris (1900–95): actor.
[12] Stephen Haggard (1911–43): actor.

Friday 10 May This morning Belgium and Holland were invaded by Germany. Much coming and going and speculation here whether Neville will reform his Cabinet or resign outright.

Saturday 11 May On the midnight broadcast last night I learned that Neville has resigned and Winston invited to form a Ministry. We missed Neville's own statement on the 9 o'clock news.

Sunday 19 May I had a pleasant enough letter from Bracken during the week and an even pleasanter one from Beaverbrook yesterday, but no sign of my being lifted out of National Savings and its irritations [...] The Sunday press very little perturbed by the force and extent of the German advance, which may be a display of admirable nerves or merely lack of imagination.

Tuesday 21 May At 7–30 a.m. R rang up to ask me to go round to Avenue Road as soon as I could. Damn all men who ring at 7–30 a.m. thought I and dressed. I found him very highly strung, and worrying whether I could get myself released from National Savings to sail for New York on Saturday. He is going, apparently, as Beaverbrook's ally to speed up aeroplanes. He pathetically said he could do nothing without me. [...] At 10 a.m. I saw Kingham who was aghast that I should want to go on the verge of National Savings Week, but quickly said,

'A man's own shop! We all think our little Department the most important. Of course you must go. But it's a matter for Sir Robert .....'

I saw Sir Robert and sprang my bombshell. I think he was glad of the chance to be rid of me, but was flatteringly kind, and insisted on my trying to find a predecessor [sic]. Gave lunch to Lil at the Piccadilly, and after bought some clothes and 'a coat to be torpedoed in ...'

Thursday 23 May Great excitement in Great Smith Street – the British Fascists being rounded up by the police. Later in the day came the news that Captain Ramsay had been arrested which puzzled me. I took tea with him once and found him the conventional anti-Jew fanatic, tracing all our woes back to the *Protocols of Zion*, which most people, even anti-Semites, believe to be forged. A rather crazy man, was my summing-up of him. Arthur Bryant gave me lunch at the Oxford and Cambridge Club, and we discussed reconstruction. Funny!

I had imagined him a grey-haired, elderly scholar – he is slim and youngish, round-headed with deep-set intelligent eyes. He avers that he mastered economics only within the past few years, under the urging of Drummond-Wolff.[13] We talked reconstruction on the lines of my 'England' article and his book *English Saga*.[14]

Sunday 4 August We left Liverpool on May 25th, and I sailed from New York on July 15th, reaching home, in London, on July 25th. Between those dates no diary was possible. But I want to note as briefly as possible the salient facts of the 'mission'. After a few days at sea R gradually let me know that what had really happened was that he was at Tours and heard of Beaverbrook's appointment, he had wired him congratulations and had said 'I am going to America almost immediately: can I be of use to you there,' and the Beaver had wired back saying that he might be of use in America. Morison then told me that he believed that Beaver had consulted Esmond Harmsworth and that the whole thing was 'fixed' so that R should have a good excuse for being out of Britain. (It is possible that they, like R himself, feared that his friendship with Hitler and his known defeatist attitude might bring him under arrest.) So the Mission was not really a mission at all. I was angry at having been taking from War Savings and the BBC on false pretences.

Wednesday 7 August Yesterday when I was with old Lord Q, his secretary came in about 12–45 as he was about to depart for luncheon and reminded him that he had promised a letter to *The British News Letter*. I said, 'I'll dash that off for you, if you'll lend me a typewriter,' which I did, the whole job taking about fifteen minutes. This morning I had a letter from Jarrott[15] saying that he and Q had thought the letter too good to waste on the *News Letter*, and that Q had rung Geoffrey Dawson and it was to go to *The Times*[16] ... When I recalled how Kindersley took about two weeks to draft a letter for *The Times* I was slightly amused.

---

[13] Henry Drummond-Wolff (1899–1982): promoter of the Commonwealth; Vice-Chm. of Empire Economic League 1949, Pres. 1952.

[14] Arthur Bryant, *English Saga 1840–1940* (Collins, 1940).

[15] Lt.-Col. Charles Jarrott: Gen. Sec. The Royal Society of St George.

[16] *The Times*, 'The Time of Waiting', Queenborough to editor, 8 August 1940, p. 5. The subject concerned the risks of waiting for the German invasion, including the risk of national disunity. Called for the MOI to reinforce the message that every job, no matter how mundane, was vital.

Friday 16 August   trotted over to the BBC. I found Sir Richard Macon-achie[17] waiting for me in his room, and very genial. We listened to the news together ('British Somaliland – bad show!') after which he conducted me to my studio, where I delivered another Northcountryman talk. We met again at the end of the talk and he took me down for a whisky and soda, over which we talked about celebrities and their broadcasting habits, and later our estimate of various politicians. We agreed on a low estimate of Duff Cooper, who is really an unpopular little 'squirt.'

Thursday 29 August   I meant to get up early and polish off the BBC script, but it was 11 a.m. before I dragged myself out of bed, having had six and a half hours sleep despite Hitler's bombers. Barnes in amending the draft script had done it by marginal suggestion and comment. Two amused me. 'Weak – you sound like Duff' 'Weak – you are talking like a Cabinet Minister.' I don't know if Duff Cooper and his esteemed colleagues realise that they are regarded by the BBC professional staff as the world's worst broadcasters. The devils will try to make speeches into the microphone, and only Winston can pull it off.

Wednesday 4 September   Incidentally, Q told me yesterday that he had a quiet lunch with Lady Salisbury on Monday or Tuesday, and she told him that Winston is dead against any idea of reprisals. This is probably because of America, for the whole of British opinion now seems hot for retaliation. One of the things that has set people aflame is the German habit of filling full of lead pilots bailing out of their machines. I was saying to Jarrott that I feel this is justified, since the job of the Bosche is to kill pilots not to let 'em live to fight another day, but that we should make it clear that we, too, can be ruthless in the same way. The real cleavage of this war seems to show in the very obvious fact that the two Governments are not prepared to discuss details for reducing 'total war' to anything less terrible. Otherwise it would be easy enough, through the Vatican, to make a pact that prisoners shall be treated with equal consideration on both sides, and that a pilot bailing out shall be treated as a quasi-prisoner. The snag, really, is that any such arrangement would tempt pilots to bail out rather than fight on, if their morale is at all weak – as the German air morale seems to

[17] Richard (Roy) Maconachie (1885–1962): Controller (Home Div.) BBC 1941–5; British Min. to Afghanistan 1930–5.

be. The papers today report the death yesterday of Bob Horne.[18] This meteor of the last war barely commands more than a couple of paragraphs. His great error was refusing to join Baldwin as Minister of Labour, and refusing on a point of punctilio. He died thereby a richer man, but the British, generally, did not think much of that refusal at such a time. His career was spectacular – the parson's son who became a don in philosophy, led the Scots Bar, did wonderful administrative war work, became Chancellor of the Exchequer, all at an early age and with great speed – but the man was shoddy. He was the very archetype of the story-telling Scots Commercial Traveller to be found in my youth in too many Commercial Rooms.

Friday 6 September I went to bed about 12–30 after the news. The explosions became louder and nearer, so I woke Rosemary and she and I slept beneath the stairs. At about 5–45 I woke, very cricked in the back, and went back to bed, thinking the all clear must have gone, but it went ten minutes after. There was another warning at about 9 a.m. this morning, but I slept blissfully till nearly noon. It is now about 1 p.m. and yet another warning has just gone. This last week the town seems to have decided that life shall go on despite warnings and that things shall not stop until the stuff begins to drop, which is eminently sensible. It means, amongst other things, that taxi-cabs ply, which is a great boon to a man who owns no car and dislikes unnecessary walking.

Thursday 12 September went to see my opticians. Just as I rejoined them [the family] off went the warning. We took shelter in a huge basement of some stores, the name of which I have forgotten. It was an interesting experience. True, I fell asleep on a packing case, but a girl selling sweets woke me, so that I heard all the shop girls chattering like the starlings at Charing Cross. Most of them were needing sleep, many lived in the heavily bombed areas – but they knitted, and manicured themselves, or did other jobs, and laughed and joked and swopped experiences as if the war were a great lark. The all-clear went after an hour or so.

Tuesday 17 September Last night was a furious one. Bombs all round the place, even whistling past the windows. I went to bed – *we* went to

[18] Robert Stevenson Horne (1871–1940): Con. MP Glasgow Hillhead 1918–37; Min. of Lab. 1919–20; Pres. BofT. 1920–1; Chanc. of Exchequer 1921–2; kt. 1918, cr. Viscount Horne of Slamannan 1937.

bed, the young uns in the basement – about 11 pm. I slept through it all, wakening once when Lilian touched my arm because a bomb shook the house. (Fearing that I might have to dig somebody out, or something, I slept half clothed under an eiderdown .) [...] At the Polish Embassy, I found J.B. Priestley[19] as the first guest to arrive. He had had a lucky escape last night. Staying at the Langham, he was 'sent for' by Marjorie Wace[20] to do an American broadcast, and went over to the BBC. While he was broadcasting his wing of the Langham caught a bomb. All his stuff has gone West. The First Secretary came in a few minutes afterwards. His flat had also caught a bomb, and he was wearing one of the Ambassador's[21] suits of clothes. General Sikorski[22] and the Prime Minister came next. Bevin, who, said Eden, 'was listening entranced to what Winston intends to say this afternoon' came last. We were a merry and select party. The General took, not the head, but middle of the table, with Anthony Eden on his right, flanking the Ambassador, at the real head of the table. I sat on the Ambassador's right, with the Prime Minister on my right, and Bevin next to him [...] The talk was general, although Bevin and I rather rudely talked over the Premier's knee about the Macmillan Committee[23] and Winston's folly in 1925 in countenancing deflation. Bevin agreed that Ernest Harvey was the best of the Bank of England group. [...] Bevin made a great impression on our Polish hosts. He looks amusingly nowadays like Mark Hambourg – a chubby man with long locks and kind eyes peering through glasses – but he talks the right stuff. He is more of the Right than many of the Right itself, although he doesn't know it. He says that 'We' – meaning Labour – won the General Strike because 'We' made the City aware of us. 'I told that to Montagu Norman,' he said with relish. He made Eden seem feminine and petty. Eden has gone romantically grey as to the thick hair, but is still brown as to the barbered moustache.

Saturday 5 October   Hitler and Mussolini have met on the Brenner, to discuss the failure to subjugate Britain, to discuss plans for the long war, to discuss the African campaign ... nobody knows. The morale has never been higher, for it is now vindictive. The Cabinet changes,

[19] John Boynton Priestley (1894–1984): novelist, playwright & essayist.

[20] Marjorie H. Wace (d. 1944): BBC; Ass. Adult Education Dept. early 1930s; Empire Talks Organiser 1936–8; Talks Organiser 1938– .

[21] Count Edward Raczynski (1891–1993): Polish Amb. to London 1934–45; Polish Pres. in exile 1979–86.

[22] Gen. W. Sikorski (1881–1943): Polish PM 1922–3; Min. of Military Affairs 1923–5; C-in-C Polish Army 1939–43; PM of the Govt. in exile 1940–3; killed in air crash off Gibraltar, along with Victor Cazalet MP

[23] Macmillan Committee on Finance and Industry 1929–30.

with the exit of Chamberlain, have not caused as much discussion as I expected. The most significant aspect of the reshuffle would seem to be the steady advancement of Bevin and the return of Cranborne.[24] My American 'message' has been fairly widely quoted and well received. To-day Q's follow-up (also mine) goes out. In the present spate of words, these things have probably little effect, but they may help to clear the general mind. They go automatically to all Members of both Houses.

Tuesday 8 October   Last night I did the second of the Taking Stock Talks. We were a funny quartet. Wickham Steed,[25] elderly and very distinguished, like a white bearded Spanish grandee; Kenneth Pickthorn,[26] small and pointed of face, angry and aggressive; Robert Byron,[27] fat and flabby of both mind and body and incredibly precious, like a second-hand Wilde. After rehearsal for time, Steed and Pickthorn crossed to the partly shattered Langham with me for a Sherry. Pickthorn was furious – but furious! – with Churchill about the reconstruction of the Ministry. He was particularly 'down' on Herbert Morrison, whom he regards as a kind of inept traitor, since it was he who would not rearm or even permit cadet corps in schools, and on Ellen Wilkinson,[28] of whom he recalls that she said on the night of the Norway Debate that the Womens Auxiliary could hold the Western Front. He said one good thing, in his Rabelaisian way.

'Poor old Neville. He was a good fellow. He simply didn't know that there are shits in the world. He didn't believe they exist. Now, Winston knows that shits exist – *and likes 'em!*' (In case gutter slang ever changes – a shit is the lowest form of human being conceivable to a normally honest and decent person.)

Pickthorn, who is the son of a master mariner, is less like a Don than any Don I have ever met, and less like a Member of Parliament

---

[24] Robert Arthur James Gascoyne-Cecil (1893–1972): Con. MP Dorset S. 1929–41; US FO 1935–8; Paymaster-Gen. 1940; Dominions Sec. 1940–2, 1943–5; Ld. Privy Seal 1942–3, 1951–2; Commonwealth Sec. 1952; Ld. Pres. 1952–7; Con. Leader in HofL. 1942–57; styled Viscount Cranborne 1903–47; summoned to HofL. as Baron Cecil of Essendon 1941; suc. 5th Marquess of Salisbury 1947.

[25] (Henry) Wickham Steed (1871–1956): Ed. of *The Times*, 1919–22, thereafter Ed., lecturer & broadcaster. Rothermere's private secretary in late 1920s.

[26] Kenneth William Murray Pickthorn (1892–1975): Con. MP Cambridge Univ. 1935–50, Carlton 1950–66; PS Educ. 1951–4; Fellow of Corpus Christi, Cambridge 1914–75; kt. 1959.

[27] Robert Byron (1905–41): travel writer, art critic & historian.

[28] Ellen Cicely Wilkinson (1891–1947): Lab. MP Middlesborough E. 1924–31, Jarrow 1935–47.

than any Member I have ever met. He is most like an angry little boy annoyed with the prefects.

Tuesday 15 October There was a medley of fireman opposite the Carlton – which, as I approached it, I found was completely shattered. The Reform still stood. But when I mounted the steps, there was chaos within, and the old custodian [. . .] was in mufti. He shook a sad head. 'Nothing doing, sir,' he said. A big incendiary and a blasting out of the windows was their damage. It had caught The Travellers next door. I turned the corner to the Savage. That still stood. But there, again, was chaos, and in the inner hall sat poor old Tom Clare,[29] his hands beswathed with cotton-wool, his face and head bound in bandaging. Two fellow members were with him, and he was sipping a brandy and looking very shaken. [. . .] It was a queer characteristic thing – having lost two Clubs I arranged to run a monthly account with the Carlton, as I usually do with the Savoy. But when I met Q at 3–30, to talk over St George's affairs, he said 'You can use the Royal Thames Yacht Club – we've just told the Carlton so.'

I said, 'I was never a member of the Carlton: it's members always make me feel a rabid radical.'

'Then' said he, 'You simply must join the Royal Thames *now.*'

He proceeded to give me a card bidding the Club to treat me with open hospitality until I am elected. At the moment when historic London clubdom is disappearing in smoke and flame, I join another Club – this makes the fifth, not counting dining and lunching clubs – and on the monetary standards of which are far in excess of my ragged means.

Tuesday 22 October joined Sadd at the Athenaeum at 1–30. Sir Joseph Ball[30] was a few minutes late. We had a simple kind of meal, they off roast pheasant and I off cold roast beef, followed by cheese. Joseph and I drank a good claret; Sadd with great self-denial had water, as he wisely won't drink until evening. He left us to our cigars and coffee. J.B. then opened up – and it amounted to an invitation to me to consider editing *Truth.* I said, 'I'll be perfectly frank with you . . .' and told him of my attempt to buy the thing for George Sutton. We

---

[29] Tom Clare: author, *The Nine Club* (London: Hutchinson, 1929).

[30] (George) Joseph Ball (1885–1961): worked for MI5 1919–27; Dir. of Publicity, CCO 1927–30; Dir. of CRD 1930–39; Dep. Chm. of Nat. Publicity Bureau 1934–9; Dep. Chm., Security Executive 1940–42; Acting Chm. of CRD 1943–5; kt. 1936. Brooks considered him to be 'one of the too-many Grey Cardinals of official Conservatism'.

discussed terms on which I would be agreeable to take it over.

He said, 'Would you want a financial interest?'

I said 'I'm a journalist, not a capitalist. If I can do it without putting up any money, that is what I'd prefer; if not, I'll consider a proposition.'

He said Newnham had taken a small salary. I said I'd take a small salary but I'd have to be free to write or broadcast as I pleased in addition to running the paper.

I said, 'I'd naturally want a major say in both ordinary and business policy.'

He said 'You mean you'd want to be a director as well as editor. We'd certainly welcome that ...'

We left the matter half vague, and it may come to nothing.

Said I to conclude, 'You are quite sure you know what you'd get with me – a Right Wing Tory policy hammered hard,' and he said, 'That is exactly what we'd like.' He told me some of the background history of *Truth* and its well-hidden proprietorship, and we discussed figures, etc.

Tuesday 29 October   I rang up Joe Ball from the BBC. He said that things had moved since he spoke to me, and that subject to final accord from L, the editorship of *Truth* was at my disposal. Newnham was leaving them in perfect amity, and would write for me if I wished. He had taken £900 a year and had even cut that by £200 when finances became difficult, but Joe Ball had suggested to L that I should have £1,000, if that was agreeable. I said it would be subject to my original proviso that I was to be free to write elsewhere and to broadcast. He said I would know who 'L' was, and I said I could guess – and my guess is Cunliffe-Lister, but it may be Londonderry.

Wednesday 30 October   at the Carlton Grill at noon, where I met Lil, J.B. came in. I ordered another place to be set for him. Lilian tactfully 'hopped it' after a few minutes. The mysterious L is neither Cunliffe-Lister nor Londonderry, but Lord Luke of Pavenham,[31] the Bovril King. J.B. repeated that it was 98 to 1 on Luke wanting me to take over – said Luke was grateful to him for finding a man who could do both sides of the job, the general and the financial – said Luke knew me by reputation very well – and so on. We talked of other matters – of Stanley Baldwin's sloth and deterioration – of Neville, from whom J.B. had that morning had a letter in very virile holograph – and of

---

[31] George Lawson Johnstone (1873–1943): Chm. of Directors of *Truth*. Chm. Business Ctte. of Nat. Publicity Bureau which bought *Truth* 1936; cr. 1st Baron Luke of Pavenham.

Reith,[32] whom J.B. dislikes, as most people do. Reith, incidentally, was two tables away from us, his new title shining about his head like a halo.

Thursday 31 October   At noon I rang up J.B. from the BBC, where I was collecting a typescript, and he said Lord Luke had a busy and tangled day, but would be glad if I could go straight up to see him, and if not he would be taking a late lunch at the City Carlton. I went straight along to the Bovril building in Old Street. Lord Luke was peculiarly pleasant. He began by showing me the walls and windows of his room that were blown in by a recent bomb, and then sat me at a big table-desk and said how delighted he had been to hear that I was available. I asked him if Sir Joseph had told him the circumstances ... He said no, so I told him. He said, 'I hope that doesn't mean when R returns you'll disappear ... a paper needs continuity ...' I reassured him and we talked of the potentialities of *Truth*. He revealed, almost casually, that Newnham was anxious that Kemsley should buy the paper, but that Joe Ball had raised a fund to guarantee any slight loss and was eager to keep it independent. Luke said he would stand the capital racket for the same purpose. He was very keen that the paper should be vigorous in defending small share-holders and debenture holders from being rooked by the big institutions ... We did not talk figures or detail. He said he'd rather that he told Newnham than that I told him. (I had gathered from Joe Ball that Newnham already knew ...) I said, 'Well, do I assume that you think that I am the right person for the paper ...' and he glowed and said he had throughout assumed that, and had only asked me to call to make my acquaintance etc etc. [...] And so I am, I suppose, editor-designate of *Truth*! Whether I can bring it back to the great days when Labby[33] was its chief, I wonder. It will be an interesting experiment. Bib[34] said, 'What are you going to do with your new toy, now you've got it?' My chief emotion was one of speculation as to what my father would have thought had I ever forecast the day would come when I should run *Truth*, a paper for which he had a great regard.

---

[32] John Reith (1889–1971): Dir.-Gen. BBC; Chm. of BOAC 1938–40; MOI 1940; Min. of Transport 1940; Min. of Works 1940–2; kt. 1927, cr. 1st Baron Reith 1940.

[33] Henry Dupré 'Labby' Labouchere (1831–1912): Lib. MP Windsor 1866, Middlesex 1867, Northampton 1880–1906; diplomatic service 1854–64; editor *Truth*.

[34] Bib was the pet-name for Vivian Brooks.

Saturday 9 November   Ward Price told me yesterday that Neville Chamberlain is 'finished' and the morning papers confirm it. It was only last week since J.B. showed me a letter from Neville written over four sheets in quite virile handwriting, as I may have noted at the time. Well, there is no need to moralise about Neville Chamberlain. When Lil first met him, and heard him make a short speech – at some little luncheon – she was convulsed by his likeness to Groucho Marx, the film comedian. He was an arch mediocrity, vain, limited and earnest. Had he not been completely hypnotised by Horace Wilson, the world might have gone better. Beaverbrook, incidentally, said yesterday that he would serve under Bevin if anything happened to Winston, which I thought was significant. I think his opinion of Herbert Morrison is not high. There seems a general view that Morrison has not increased his reputation. In the days when R and I walked around the East End, at the time of the Hackney Marshes scheme – when he came unexpectedly and lunched with us at the Ritz – I did not think him as able as his legend would have the mob suppose, although I did think him sincere and honest and as competent as the next man. There is a growing feeling, first openly voiced by Newnham, that Winston must shortly stage some kind of action with success if he is to survive.

Sunday 10 November   Yesterday I met Newnham. He came hurrying into the American Bar of the Carlton about 1–30, and came straight over to me, knowing me by the press photograph that once used to adorn town. He – with whom I have had so many interchanges by letter and telephone but none in person – proved to be a big man, with a strong clean-shaven face, with deepset, very intelligent eyes behind shell rimmed glasses. His rather deep voice was as reverberant as it sounds on the telephone. We were 'on terms' immediately. He is, I gather by inference, about forty-three and owes his Balliol career and his later progress entirely to a kind of Samuel Smiles self-help. Esteeming me, as he has done in print, for my technical knowledge and political views, he was excessively frank. I stood the aperitifs, and he the lunch, which was of oysters, cold pie, cheese, burgundy etc, and we talked freely. He bade me beware of Joe Ball, who, he says, is essentially an ignorant person and inclined to plant the first dagger.

'If all goes well he'll say you followed instructions; if anything goes ill he'll shake his head and say, "Ah, yes! Collin Brooks! A disappointment."'

He also told me to bind down both Luke and Ball, to trust to no gentleman's agreement. He regards himself as having been somewhat shabbily treated by both Ball and Luke, who made promises of support which they didn't carry out. He expressed himself as glad that I was taking over, and said he would do whatever he could to help me. In other conversation, over china tea at 3–30, when lunched ended, he said

'I have always said frankly that I am pro-British first but next pro-German. Our gang of grafters is worse than any Germany has. The time may come when people like me – and perhaps you – ought to go to gaol for the privilege of speaking their minds.' He said that the attempt of M.I.5 to put him behind bars began with a memorandum he sent to Churchill, saying that to beat Germany we must be more totalitarian than Germany, and as that is what we are fighting to avoid, the war is nonsense. I told him of the enquiries made by B[ingham] of me about him. I said that I thought at first they were after me, because of *Can Chamberlain Save Britain*, but I then realised they were after him.

He said, 'They were after us both – and any other anti-semite, anti-flummery man with any guts in expressing his own views.'

I promised to take over from him on Monday at 11 a.m. When I said, 'How long do you want the change keeping secret?' he said, 'My dear fellow, from this moment you are editor of *Truth*, and you can tell anybody who is interested . . . . .'

Our talk was full of that odd freemasonry that grows in Fleet Street, and his attitude to me was that of a master of the craft talking to an elder master.

Friday 15 November Entered *Truth* office as editor at 10–30. It was odd to be sitting behind Labby's own desk in Labby's unaltered, dingy, stained-glass windowed room. Everybody very nice and helpful. Lunched at the Danish Club, as the guest of Anderson, and helped to 'make a Club' for King Haakon[35] and Prince Olav,[36] who were lunching there privately. The King is balder then when I talked with him in Oslo, but no fatter. But Olav is fatter and is no longer a young Prince Charming. In the afternoon went back to the office, to wrestle with my new problems. Nobody who has not edited a paper can ever realise how much of editorship is pure 'housekeeping.'

Wednesday 20 November Met Joe Ball at 12–30 and again at 3. He wants us to lay off Winston, and to be kindly to Kingsley Wood. Eden he agrees can be slated.

[35] King Haakon VII (1872–1957): King of Norway 1905–57; exiled during German occupation.
[36] Prince Olav (1903–91): King of Norway from 1957; exiled from Norway 1940–5; Olympic yachtsman.

Sunday 8 December   It is over a fortnight since I made an entry in this diary. R is dead. I was in the tangle of *Truth* – tangle because the printers' works is hampered by bombing effects and because the staff is small – and the general distractions of life in war time, when on Tuesday 26th Ward Price telephoned to tell me the end had come, having on Monday warned me that R's condition was serious. I do not propose to try here to record the many and conflicting emotions which were aroused in me by the news. The chief of them was grief and self-pity. Grief that R should have died in Bermuda virtually alone, and self-pity that I no longer have the resort to his good humour, his sagacity, his kindness that has been mine for over five years. Forgotten now are the moments of anger in New York that I once recorded, and forgotten too the impatience that I sometimes felt with him. I remember only his great heart and his loneliness, and his affection for me and mine for him.

APPENDIX A
BERLIN, 3 MAY 1935 ADOLF HITLER TO LORD ROTHERMERE

[English translation organised for Lord Rothermere by C.B.]

Dear Lord Rothermere,

May I sincerely thank you for the letter which you were kind enough to send me through Princess von Hohenlohe.

The knowledge that I have found in you, Lord Rothermere, a sincere friend of an Anglo-German understanding, is for me the more happy and significant, inasmuch as it concerns a task for which I stood unswervingly long before my public political activity and before my Chancellorship. The correctness of this idea cannot better be proved than by the course of the World War, by its sacrifices and by its results.

I believe that a methodical, scientific examination of the European history of the last 300 years will show that 9/10ths of the blood-sacrifices of the battlefields has been shed entirely in vain. That is to say, in vain measured by the natural interests of the participating nations.

I make no exception in the case of Germany. On the contrary, our people have in the course of these 300 years, lost at least 20 to 25 million souls, probably even more, from wars which have been essentially profitless to the nation if one measures the success not in terms of a questionable fame but in those of practical profit. Europe has sometimes senselessly squandered her strength. The only nation that has understood how to keep clear of these events, at least for long periods, and to derive advantage therefrom, is England. Thanks to the shrewdness of the English people and many of their governments, England has built up with a fraction of such sacrifices the greatest empire in history. I do not believe that a cool survey of the English participation in the World War will show the same favourable results for the strengthening of the British Empire as might undoubtedly have been attained by other action, involving an immeasurable smaller stake. Germany has lost everything by this war with its great Germanic neighbour. England has, I venture to state, at least gained nothing but has probably helped in the creation of world conditions which are not in the interests of the British Empire. I do not say this in order to deliver judgement on the question of war guilt. I can hardly believe that any responsible statesman with any knowledge of the magnitude and consequences of this event, would have wished the war, as, in fact, no party entered upon it with conscious intention; but through careless fallacy and unfortunate pre-possessions, coupled with inadequate knowledge of European interests, drifted into it.

For 500 years the two Germanic peoples have lived close together without having become involved in any serious military difference. England opened a great part of the world to the white race. An immortal and never-ceasing service! Germany was a coloniser in Europe, whose aggregate culture and, also, economic activities for the welfare and greatness of this old Continent are difficult to estimate. This $4\frac{1}{2}$ years war swept away the pick of the manhood of both nations; severely hit Germany's influence in Europe; and by no means strengthened, if it did not actually weaken, England's importance in the world. Worst of all, however, there was left behind a legacy of prejudice and passion, which affronts appropriate soil to all those who aim at the sabotaging of the consolidation of Europe and to those who are inwardly hostile to the strengthening of white supremacy in the world. I believe that clever German statesmanship, and a no less calm British, in the years from 1900 to 1914 would have found ways and means not only to assure peace to the two Germanic peoples but also to bring them high advantages. The picture that the world today offers is at any rate, from the point of view of both peoples, less satisfactory than it might otherwise have been. Bolshevism tears away a mighty slice of European-Asiatic breathing-space (Lebensraum) from the structure of what is, in our conception, the only possible international world economy. The safety of the British Empire, which is to the interest of the whole White race, is weakened rather then strengthened by the lining up of, in part, new international power factors. The tendencies to a declaration of independence by former colonial territories have increased as much as the efforts by an unnatural, because artificial, industrialisation of certain raw-material producing districts to destroy the natural balance evolved in the course of centuries between areas of production and areas of consumption. When, at last, will reason step in and tear the White race away from a development which otherwise inevitably must spell its doom?

I believe, my dear Lord Rothermere, that if the initiative is not taken by England and Germany one can bury all hope for the future or, at least, for such time as man can foresee. Certainly, one cannot look at this problem with the eyes of the everyday politician, whose horizon is all too frequently bounded by petty interests. I myself have in any case endeavoured to seek no compromise but to regard principle as the essential and deciding factor. For fifteen years I have been scorned and ridiculed and represented as a visionary by the petty politician, who possessed no understanding of this fundamental handling of the problem. However, I was right, and these small antagonists saw that their conceptions were wrong and that mine were right. Success could at last no longer be denied by them. This experience of the last 15 years, however, gives me hope that in the next 15 or 20 years work, likewise dictated by basic right and steadfast principle, will be crowned with success, and help that natural interests to triumph and bring to silence the carpers and grumblers. For, as already stated, Lord Rothermere, if today I stand for an Anglo-German understanding, this does not date from yesterday or the day before. During the last 15 years I have spoken in Germany at least 4000 to 5000 times before small, large, and immense mass audiences. There does not, however, exist a single speech of mine, nor a single line ever written by me, in which I have expressed myself, contrary to this opinion, against an Anglo-German understanding. On the contrary, I have during all this time fought for it by word and in writing. Before the war, I had this conception of the necessity of the collaboration of the Germanic peoples against the rest of the wakening world, and was profoundly unhappy when the events of 1914 led to Anglo-German hostilities. I never saw in this war anything but a desperate, Niebelung-like war of annihilation, rising to frenzy, between the Germanic peoples. Since the War, as an active politician, I have preached unswervingly the necessity of both nations burying the hatchet forever. Anyhow, I am convinced that such an understanding can only take place between honourable nations. I hold that there is no possibility of concluding agreements with a people without honour, and I regard such agreements as entirely worthless. I have derived from Fate the heavy task of giving back again to a great people and state by every means its natural honour. I see in this one of the most essential preparations for a real and lasting understanding, and I beg you, Lord Rothermere, never to regard my work from any other point of view.

You are right. The feelings and views of parliamentary demagogues are liable to rapid and unexpected changes. The world may, however, for what I care, reproach me with what it will. One reproach they certainly cannot level at me: that I have been vacillating in my views and unreliable in my work. If an unknown man with such weakness set out to win over a nation in 15 years he would meet with no success. Herein resides perhaps the faith – exaggerated, as many believe – in my own personality. I believe, my dear Lord Rothermere, that in the end of my unchanging standpoint, undeviating staunchness and my unalterable determination to render a historically great contribution to the restoration of a good and enduring understanding between both great Germanic peoples, will be crowned with success. And, believe me, Lord Rothermere, that this is the most decisive contribution to the pacification of the world. All the so-called mutual-assistance pacts which are being hatched today will subserve discord rather than peace. An Anglo-German understanding would form in Europe a force for peace and reason of 120 million people of the highest type. The historically unique colonial ability and sea-power of England would be united to one of the greatest soldier-races of the world. Were this understanding extended by the joining-up of the American nation, then it would, indeed, be hard to see who in the world could disturb peace without wilfully and consciously neglecting the interests of the White race. There is in German a fine saying: that the Gods love and bless him who seems to demand the impossible.

I want to believe in this Divinity!

I have just read Viscount Snowden's manuscript, brought to me by Princess Hohenlohe, entitled 'Europe Heading for War'.

While I understand the difficulty of holding such language, I am strengthened in my conviction that insight and truth in the end, and also today, find their courageous exponents.

In about 10 days time I shall give a big and comprehensive exposition of my standpoint and that of the German Government on the political problems which at present occupy us all. I believe dear Lord Rothermere, that you would be hailed by those Englishmen whom you have invited to express their views in *The Daily Mail*.

To yourself, my dear Lord Rothermere, I would express once more my most cordial thanks for the great help which you have afforded to an endeavour which, in the event of its realisation, some day will be regarded as one of the happiest developments which the peoples through their governments could attain.

With sincere friendship,

Yours,

(signed) Af. Hitler.

APPENDIX B
20 DECEMBER 1935 ADOLF HITLER TO LORD ROTHERMERE

[Original English translation]

Dear Lord Rothermere

You were good enough to communicate to me a letter in which you expressed the desire to be informed of my views on some of the burning questions of the day. Owing to great pressure of work which has steadily increased towards the end of the year I have been quite unable, in spite of every goodwill, to reply at once to your letter. In replying to you now I ask you, dear Lord Rothermere, not to make any public use of my reply because it contains opinions which I would otherwise express in a different wording or probably not express at all. This letter contains only opinions and I have not the slightest doubt that they are entirely unsuited to influence public opinion or to make it change its own views in a world and at a time in which public opinion is not always identical with the innermost insight and wisdom.

You ask me, my dear Lord Rothermere, whether in my opinion oil sanctions against Italy will put an end to the Italo-Abyssinian war.

It is impossible to reply to this question apodictically. But I would like to seize this opportunity to explain to you, as fully as is possible in a short letter, my views on the principles underlying this problem.

1. Governments very often err as regards the percentage of raw materials which a nation requires for military purposes. The percentage is very low compared with the total requirements of a population. The civil activities of life require in general more than 95 per cent of all necessary raw materials. I admit that in the case of oil this percentage may not be quite exact in a war. However, a restriction placed on the non-military users will certainly enable an army for a long time to covers its own requirements.

2. Sanctions naturally lead to restrictions and in consequence certain tensions. Weak systems of government may perhaps be defeated by such tensions. But a strong regime will hardly be exposed to that danger. It is even possible that a powerful regime will on the contrary receive fresh and increased strength, as a consequence of such tensions. At any rate time and perseverance play a decisive part on both sides.

3. Sanctions are not only a burden upon those against whom they are

directed but also upon the Powers applying sanctions. And here again time and perservence have a decisive influence.

4. In the Great War Germany was not defeated by the sanctions but exclusively by the internal process of revolutionising. If I had been in Bethman-Hollweg's place in 1919 as Chancellor of the German Reich no revolution would ever have occurred. The collapse in 1918 would have been avoided. I presume that the Great War would ultimately have reached its end without victors or vanquished. I know, dear Lord Rothermere, that you as an Englishman will have a different opinion but I am merely explaining my own conviction. To-day an oil sanction against Germany would be of no avail as our own fuel-production and our own oil-fields can produce an annual quantity several times as much as we needed in 1914/18 during the Great War.

I do no know the conditions in Japan. For it is obvious that the question of existing stocks is also in all these cases of decisive importance.

5. In my opinion the decisive factor is only a question of systems of government and thus of personalities. Who governs in the sanctionised countries and who governs in Italy? I would like to say here that the man who is to-day Italy's leader will be one of the rarest and most important personalities of world history whatever may happen. Much that may appear bad in English eyes in this man finds its simple explanation in the different mentality of the two nations. And a great man will almost always be the most characteristic representatives of the innermost character of their nation.

In making these sober statements I ask you, dear Lord Rothermere, not to forget that I as a German cannot take any real interest in this conflict. You know that we are the nation concerned which a more than stupid treaty said that it did not belong to the 'progressive' nations which had a right to administer colonial territories. In addition I can say that from the human point of view there is much that attracts us to the English, while on the other hand, from the political point of view, we have a good deal in common with present-day Italy. Obviously the German nation will not to-day be able to give noisy expression to its enthusiasm for a nation which not only a year ago referred in its press to Germany very unfavourably not to say rudely. On the other hand we cannot forget that years before that Italy and Signor Mussolini in particular have given us many proofs of a reasonable and often more than decent sympathy with our fate. We cannot be ungrateful. There are people in Europe who believe that we have every reason as Germans to welcome this conflict. They say that it provides for us the best opportunity to re-arm. My dear Lord Rothermere these people know neither me nor the Germany of to-day. Since the outbreak of this conflict I have not taken a single step which was not planned long before and which I would not have taken otherwise. The decision to restore the German position was taken, initiated and carried through at a time when nobody could have the slightest inkling of this sad conflict. There is nobody in Germany with any political insight who welcomes this conflict except perhaps some enemies of the State who may cherish the hope that it might constitute an international example which could one day also be applied to Germany. But these elements must not be confused with the German people. The only thing which fills us with certain satisfaction, I must admit, is the revelation of the true value of all so-called collective agreements. For here we are concerned with two collective agreements which have ultimately both failed: the Covenant of the League of Nations and Stresa Alliance, and it is the only pleasure we have in this matter to know that we are outside the agreements and that we have no longer anything to do with the League of Nations.

For believe me, dear Lord Rothermere, the problem is not whether this and that sanction will to-day bring down Italy on her knees, the real problem is whether one is in a position to remove the causes underlying the tensions from which the world suffers at present. For a hundred million years this earth has been moving around the sun and during this long period it has always been filled with the struggle of living beings for nourishment and later for dwellings and clothing, etc. It is certain that beings whom we can call men have existed on it for many millions of years. Innumerable influences produced constant changes in the distribution of property. Just as in each nation the economic structure is constantly changing, changes occur outside the national limits. Climatic changes, discoveries of raw materials, more or less strong increases of the nations on the one hand, while other nations become sterile, continually produce tensions which urgently require solutions. And now in a certain year after millions of years in which the earth has moved around, an American professor proclaims the formation of a league of partly heterogeneous nations with completely opposed interests with a view to excluding any future change in this world. That means from the year 1919 our Christian era or say from the 997 millions 365 thousands revolution around the sun, the whole earthly development must come to a standstill. Only one thing was forgotten: this League can perhaps prevent the *adjustment* of the tensions, but it can by no means prevent the tensions themselves from arising. The only consequence will be that while formerly the tensions arising out of the national laws of development were currently adjusted, at least partially, the safety valve is now abolished, which means that the tensions must accumulate. If that, however, is the ultimate result of the so-called 'collective policy' the end can only be disaster of the first magnitude.

I deeply regret Sir Samuel Hoare's resignation because I feel that a great big British patriot and an excellent man has fallen victim to public opinion and that he was one of the first who seemed to have recognised this weakness in the League of Nations' system. For it is clear that the League of Nations is not governed to-day by the influence of wisdom but by the influence of the street, that is to-day by the so-called public opinion which as history shows hardly ever has Reason as its godmother. I would be very glad, dear Lord Rothermere, if beyond all present misgivings people in England were ready to study the problems from a point of view of the underlying principles and perhaps to discuss them in a small committee. I think that the English can do this better than the other nations because they are broad-minded and realistic to a greater extent than other peoples. I believe that our Anglo-German naval agreement was a striking proof of this. You will understand, however, dear Lord Rothermere, that these problems more than others are wholly unsuited to be handled in front of the masses, but that ultimately they can only be discussed on a small and select group. If you come again to Germany I would be very glad if you would see me and if I could discuss these problems with you or other Englishmen.

Whatever may happen I want to assure you at the conclusion of this letter that I firmly believe that a time will come in which England and Germany will be the solid pillars in a worried and unstable world.

You ask me, dear Lord Rothermere, whether I do not think that the moment has now come to put forward the German colonial wishes. May I ask you, dear Lord Rothermere, not to raise this point now because looking forward to closer collaboration with Great Britain I do not want to give the impression as if I wanted to avail myself of the present situation of your Government and its many difficulties and of the British Empire to exercise a certain pressure.

In conclusion I send you, dear Lord Rothermere, my best wishes for Christmas and for a happy new year.

Yours truly,

(signed) Af. Hitler.

APPENDIX C
19 OCTOBER 1938 MEMORANDUM FROM COLLIN BROOKS TO LORD ROTHERMERE

Visit to Hungary

My understanding of your instructions regarding my visit to Hungary is as follows:

1. I am to proceed to Hungary via the Hook of Holland on the evening of Thursday, October 20th.

2. The specific object of my visit is to arrange an investment in real estate of the £40,000 (approx.) now standing to your credit in the Hungarian National Bank, with such other sum as, after consultation between us, you may think desirable.

3. My first duty will be to investigate the exact taxation position, i.e., the avoidance of double income tax, etc.

4. I am to re-examine the proposition originally investigated by Ward Price as to whether the particular estate would best suit your purpose in comparison with other possibilities. In considering this I am to be influenced by the possibility of a strong reduction in the purchase price on the one hand, and the adaptability to your use of the 18th Century Chateau on the other.

5. I am to make use of whatever assistance Hordosy can render, and am to liaison with H.E. Tiber Eckhardt.

6. In examining the possibilities of such an investment, I am to examine whatever properties suggest themselves, and am not to rule out the possibility of land within Budapest itself.

7. In addition to this specific mission I am to assess to the best of my ability the political situation and trends in Hungary and report to you discreetly, bearing in mind the potential possibility of your own visit to Budapest.

8. I am to maintain the ostensible purpose of my visit, and to exercise the greatest caution with regard to local politics.

[*Editorial Note*: From C.B.'s mainly retrospective account of the visit in his journal, it is clear that point 7 was the principal purpose of his visit. No mention is made of the purchase of an estate for Rothermere, but C.B., and later Ward Price, were clearly involved in engineering Rothermere's visit, against the wishes of Imredy and Admiral Horthy, the regent, in October 1938 to participate in the nation's celebrations at the return of a substantial element of Slovakia. As one of the defeated nations at the end of First World War, Hungary had lost territory by the Treaty of Trianon to Czechoslovakia in the north, Rumania in the east, and Yugoslavia in the south. Rothermere had been championing the cause of the lost Hungarian territories since Princess Stefanie Hohenlohe-Waldenburg had persuaded him of the virtues of the case in the mid-1920s. The opposition to his visiting undoubtedly arose from a fear that he might seek to use the occasion to make a bid for the throne: an idea first proposed by Hungarian supporters in 1928.]

APPENDIX D
24 SEPTEMBER 1939 LORD ROTHERMERE (GHOSTED BY C.B.) TO NEVILLE CHAMBERLAIN

[Draft and never sent]

Dear Prime Minister,

In light of Signor Mussolini's speech, may I put to you a conviction which is held not only by me but by others of competent judgement whose views have been communicated to me.

As you know, I have been for many years a close student of European affairs with special professional and personal facilities for acquiring information on both politics and economics. What I wish to convey to you is based on the knowledge thus acquired and not merely on some mere emotional wish.

The partition of Poland is now a historical fact. Lacking material aid from her allies, Poland has had to submit to superior force. The moral purpose of Britain and France in striving to resist such aggression was admirable: but moral purpose alone could not save Poland from disaster.

If the major clash of armies and air forces now begins, Western civilisation in Europe must be imperilled, if not, as President Roosevelt seemed to foreshadow, doomed. Should the Democracies be victorious in such a war, they must emerge exhausted. Britain will be immediately faced with menace from Japan in the Far East.

Whether victorious or not, Britain will emerge from such a conflict with her social and economic fabric destroyed. That may well mean a revolution of the Left in these islands, which might be more deadly than the war itself. Without our complex economic system, skilfully managed, the flow of exports and invisible exports cannot be sufficiently maintained to provide necessaries even for the diminished population which might survive protracted war. The years of terrorism by land, sea and air would be succeeded by an era of famine equally horrible.

And for what? Not a reconstructed Poland, for that is now a palpable impossibility.

Such a total sacrifice of the British civilisation would be seen by historians as one made to justify a hasty and – as the events of the last three weeks have proved – an unwise pledge to Poland which could not be made good. In other words, Britain and all that Britain means would perish for no material good, but as the price of saving Britain's political honour.

The question, therefore, is – can Britain without loss of honour avoid so horrible a sacrifice? Does the intervention of Signor Mussolini afford a means whereby a major conflict can still be averted and Europe assured that the aggression of the Reich shall never be repeated?

Any settlement now, it must be admitted, will mean that Britain has again lost "face", but even a victorious major war may mean that she will then have lost not only prestige that sank without inability to help Poland to avoid extinction, but her very means of survival. After an orgy of slaughter and destruction she, with the other combatants, will have fallen to the social and economic depths of Russia under the terrorists or Hungary under Bella Khun.

No one is more jealous and zealous for the national honour than I, and I put this point of view not from defeatism but from realism.

If the Italian approach has to be rejected, let it at least be rejected only after the full consequences of a prolonged major war have been weighed against the fact that no victory now can leave us in a position to restore Poland or to say that we successfully opposed aggression in Europe.

Believe me, my dear Prime Minister,
Yours sincerely
ROTHERMERE

[Added as a minuted postscript in C.B.'s hand.]
'Letter not sent after further consideration of the national mood and temper.'

APPENDIX E
THE PUBLICATIONS OF COLLIN BROOKS
[VARIOUSLY AS WILLIAM COLLIN BROOKS,
COLLIN BROOKS AND BARNABY BROOK]

Non-Fiction

Account Paid pp. 288 (London: Hutchinson, 1930)

Can 1931 Come Again? An Examination of Britain's present Financial Position pp. ix + 84 (London: Eyre and Spottiswoode, 1938)

Can Chamberlain Save Britain? The Lesson of Munich pp. xii + 247 (London: Eyre and Spottiswoode, 1938)

Company Finance pp. ix + 104 (London: P.S. King and Son, 1939)

A Concise Dictionary of Finance pp. vii + 406 (London: Pitman, 1934)

Devils Decade: Portraits of the Nineteen-Thirties pp. 208 (London: MacDonald, 1948)

The Economics of Human Happiness pp. xiii + 311 (London: Routledge, 1933)

An Educational Adventure: A History of the Woolwich Polytechnic pp. xii + 153 (London: Woolwich Polytechnic, 1955)

The First Hundred Million: A History of the Woolwich Equitable Building Society pp. 208 (London: Woolwich Building Society, 1947)

The History of Johnson and Phillips pp. xi + 211 (London: Johnson and Phillips, 1950)

How the Stock Market Really Works pp. x + 150 (London: Pitman, 1930)

More Tavern Talk pp. viii + 127 (London: Barrie, 1952)

Profits from Short-Term Investment and How to Make Them pp. ix + 114 (London: Pitman, 1935, 2nd edn. 1935)

The Royal Mail Case: Rex v. Lord Kylsant, and Another editor pp. xlii + 276 (London: William Hodge, 1932)

Something in the City pp. 266 (London: Country Life, 1931)

Tavern Talk pp. 197 (London: Barrie, 1950)

The Theory and Practice of Finance pp. xiv + 411 (London: Pitman, 1928, 3rd edn. 1930)

This Tariff Question pp. 271 (London: Arnold, 1931)

Fiction

Poetry
Echos and Evasions pp. ix + 162 (London: Lovat Dickson, 1934)
Poems pp. 226 (London: David Nutt, 1914)

Novels
The Body-Snatchers pp. 282 (London: Hutchinson, 1927)
The Catspaws pp. 288 (London: Hutchinson, 1929)
Found Dead pp. 256 (London: Hutchinson, 1930)
Frame-Up pp. 287 (London: Hutchinson, 1935)
The Ghost-Hunters pp. 284 (London: Hutchinson, 1928)
Mad-Doctor Merciful pp. 288 (London: Hutchinson, 1932)
Mr Daddy-Detective pp. 288 (London: Hutchinson, 1933)
Mr X pp. 283 (London: Hutchinson, 1927)
Seven Hells pp. 286 (London: Hutchinson, 1929)
The Swimming Frog pp. 240 (London: Hutchinson, 1951)
They Ride Again pp. 332 (London: Mathews and Marrot, 1934)
Three Yards of Cord pp. 284 (London: Hutchinson, 1931)

As Barnaby Brook
Gay Go Up pp. 380 (London: Gerald Howe, 1933)
Harriet Walk pp. 240 (London: MacDonald, 1947)
The Jug pp. 320 (London: MacDonald, 1946)
Mock Turtle pp. 316 (London: Humphrey Toulmin, 1931)
Prosperity Street pp. 363 (London: Richards and Toulmin, 1929)
Wife to John pp. 333 (London: Gerald Howe, 1928)
Young Mrs Rawley pp. 271 (London: MacDonald, 1949)

INDEX